# Unsettling Empathy

# Peace and Security in the 21st Century

Series Editor: Charles Hauss, US government liaison

Until recently, security was defined mostly in geopolitical terms with the assumption that it could only be achieved through at least the threat of military force. Today, however, people from as different backgrounds as planners in the Pentagon and veteran peace activists think in terms of human or global security, where no one is secure unless everyone is secure in all areas of their lives. This means that it is impossible nowadays to separate issues of war and peace, the environment, sustainability, identity, global health, and the like.

The books in this series aim to make sense of this changing world of peace and security by investigating security issues and peace efforts that involve cooperation at several levels. By looking at how security and peace interrelate at various stages of conflict, the series explores new ideas for a fast-changing world and seeks to redefine and rethink what peace and security mean in the first decades of the new century.

Multidisciplinary in approach and authorship, the books cover a variety of topics, focusing on the overarching theme that students, scholars, practitioners, and policymakers have to find new models and theories to account for, diagnose, and respond to the difficulties of a more complex world. Authors are established scholars and practitioners in their fields of expertise.

In addition, it is hoped that the series will contribute to bringing together authors and readers in concrete, applied projects, and thus help create, under the sponsorship of Alliance for Peacebuilding (AfP), a community of practice.

The series is sponsored by the Alliance for Peacebuilding, http://www.allianceforpeacebuilding.org.

# Unsettling Empathy

*Working with Groups in Conflict*

Björn Krondorfer

**ROWMAN &**
**LITTLEFIELD**
INTERNATIONAL

*London • New York*

Published by Rowman & Littlefield International, Ltd.
6 Tinworth Street, London SE11 5AL, United Kingdom
www.rowmaninternational.com

Rowman & Littlefield International, Ltd. is an affiliate of
Rowman & Littlefield
4501 Forbes Boulevard, Suite 200, Lanham, Maryland 20706, USA
With additional offices in Boulder, New York, Toronto (Canada), and London (UK)
www.rowman.com

Support for this publication was provided by the Martin-Springer Institute, Northern
Arizona University

**British Library Cataloguing in Publication Information**
A catalogue record for this book is available from the British Library

ISBN: HB 978-1-78661-581-7
ISBN: PB 978-1-78661-582-4

**Library of Congress Cataloging-in-Publication Data Is Available**

Library of Congress Control Number: 2020931533

ISBN: 978-1-78661-581-7 (cloth)
ISBN: 978-1-78661-582-4 (pbk.)
ISBN: 978-1-78661-583-1 (electronic)

# Contents

# Acknowledgments

Though the bulk of this book was written during my 2019 spring sabbatical, *Unsettling Empathy* has been in the making for a long time. I have published smaller pieces on reconciliatory processes and unsettling empathy over the years, but I always found it daunting to write a more comprehensive account of my work with groups in conflict. People familiar with or curious about my work kept asking about such a book because they wanted to learn more about how trust-building intergroup processes unfold in conflict settings. They wanted to understand the dynamics that make or break a process in which people explore adversarial relations due to past and present injuries and injustices. I hope that *Unsettling Empathy* meets their expectations.

Twenty-five years ago I published my first monograph, *Remembrance and Reconciliation: Encounters Between Young Jews and Germans* (1995). In that book I tried to make sense of how the Holocaust affected relationships between non-Jewish Germans and Jewish Americans born after 1945. I reported on various encounters between these two groups, relying on examples from the then-available literature as well as on my own experience as active participant and facilitator. I situated and contextualized these encounters within the intellectual and public debates of the 1980s and 1990s on *Vergangenheitsbewältigung* (coming to terms with the past). The book emphasized the vital role of memory in dialogue and reconciliation settings. Without fully acknowledging the past, I argued, trust would be impossible to establish, thus thwarting the restoring of relationships between the Jewish community and German society.

I still consider the acknowledgment of an unjust and traumatic past essential for reconciliatory processes, but I have since realized that memories can be as much a stumbling block as a building block when working with groups in conflict. Memories tied to large-group identifications, iterated in national narratives, embraced as chosen cultural traumas, and recounted in personal storytelling have the power to fixate our gaze on the past in such a way that we are no longer capable of imagining a different future. Since the 1995 publication, I have arrived at a more nuanced and complex understanding of the (psycho)social and (psycho)political dynamics that obstruct or advance our efforts of seeking alternative pathways in protracted conflicts.

In this light, *Unsettling Empathy* can be seen as a companion volume to *Remembrance and Reconciliation*. Each book has been written in a different moment in time. *Remembrance and Reconciliation* was completed in the optimistic spirit and enlightened certitude of the 1990s when coming to terms with the past coincided with real signs of political progress: the fall of the Berlin Wall, glasnost, and the expansion of liberal democracies. *Unsettling Empathy* has come into being during a period of increasing cultural pessimism, where we are witnessing the spread of populism and the rise of illiberal democracies that hark back to nationalist and ethnocentric narratives of the past. Because of this changed landscape, *Unsettling Empathy*, I believe, is more important today than it would have been twenty-five years ago.

I could not have completed this book without the inspiration, encouragement, and support from many people and organizations over the years. First and foremost, I want to thank those who have collaborated with me as cofacilitators, friends, or in facilitator-mentor teams. Among them, in alphabetical order, are Sybol Anderson, Karen Baldner, Marco de Carvalho, Avner Dinur, Wafa Ebenberi, Michal Hochberg, Elke Horn, Tara Kohn, Antwan Saca Saleh, and Michael Sternberg. For lively conversation, wise guidance, caring support, and warm hospitality, my thanks go to Mehnaz Afridi, Alexander Alvarez, Elizabeth Anthony, Sami Awad, Andreas Beier, Sharon Benheim, Julia Chaitin, Melissa Cohen, Lisa Green Cudek, Jackie Feldman, Janice Friebaum, Moti Gigi, Dorota Glowacka, Pumla Gobodo-Madikizela, Amos Goldberg, Beata Hammerich, Doa Hassouneh, Andrea Leute, Albrecht Mahr, Brigitta Mahr, Hanns Maul, Naomi Morrison, Samson Munn, Sondra Perl, Johannes Pfäfflin, Peter Pogany-Wnendt, Gerburg Rohde-Dahl, Shifra Sagy, Srdjan Sremac, Erda Siebert, Zilka Siljak, Joram Tarusaria, Jacob Tor, and Wilhelm Verwoerd. There are numerous other people who have helped me to understand complexity when I could not see or appreciate differences. Even though they will remain unnamed here, their love, labor, and patience are not forgotten.

Special gratitude goes also to the following organizations with which my work has intersected: Bridge of Understanding; Center for Reconciliation Studies at the Friedrich-Schiller University in Jena, Germany; Friendship Across Borders; the Martin-Springer Center for Conflict Studcies at Ben-Gurion University of the Negev; the Olga Lengyel Institute for Holocaust Studies and Human Rights in New York City; Stephen Weinstein Holocaust Symposium in Wroxton, United Kingdom; and the Study Group on Intergenerational Consequences of the Holocaust, Germany. Special thanks also to the Ministry of Foreign Affairs of the Republic of Armenia and Tigran Mkrtchyan for their invitation to Yerevan for the 2018 Global Forum Against the Crime of Genocide, where I was able to present my work on unsettling empathy.

Two fellowships were particularly helpful in advancing my research on this book. In December 2016 and June 2017, I received a research fellowship through CLUE+ at the Vrije Universiteit Amsterdam, The

Netherlands; and in March 2019, I received a one-month residential fellowship at the Santa Fe Art Institute's program "Truth and Reconciliation" in Santa Fe, New Mexico. Without the sabbatical granted by the College of Arts and Letters and the support of the Martin-Springer Institute, both at Northern Arizona University, this book would have taken much longer to complete.

On a personal note, I would like to mention my daughters, Zadekia and Tabitha, who demonstrate their care and curiosity about the world in their own brave ways. At the completion of this writing, one is guiding travelers through Alaska, Patagonia, and along the Danube and has (solo) biked across Cuba, Hawaii, Thailand, Vietnam, and Laos; my other daughter spent several weeks in refugee camps in Uganda and Germany while completing her bachelor's degree in anthropology and international relations and is now availing herself of opportunities to work in the international arena.

In this book I have integrated some previously published materials in thoroughly revised, rearranged, and expanded form. These publications include "Introduction" and "Interpersonal Reconciliation with Groups in Conflict," in *Reconciliation in Global Context*, edited by Björn Krondorfer (SUNY, 2018); "Unsettling Empathy: Intercultural Dialogue in the Aftermath of Historical and Cultural Trauma," in *Breaking Intergenerational Cycles of Repetition*, edited by Pumla Gobodo-Madikizela (Barbara Budrich Publishers, 2016); "From Pulp to Palimpsest: Witnessing and Re-Imagining through the Arts," in *Different Horrors, Same Hell: Gender and the Holocaust*, edited by Myrna Goldenberg and Amy H. Shapiro (University of Washington Press, 2013); and "Reconciliation: A Commitment to Unsettling Empathy," in *The Holocaust and Nostra Aetate: Toward a Greater Understanding*, edited by Carol Rittner (Seton Hill University, 2017).

# Introduction

## *Working with Groups in Conflict*

As human beings inhabiting this planet, we have responsibilities toward each other and toward the earth we share. But as we are inescapably pushed with our backs into the future, facing the rubble of history piled on top of earlier rubbles, our ability to respond responsibly is diminishing. More often than not, we are reacting, not responding. More often than not, we are defending, not embracing. We become closed off, not welcoming. We retreat into fear and lose trust in those with whom we live in proximity. We yearn for safety and end up imprisoning ourselves in enclaves of sameness, which divide the world into those we believe to be friendly and those we deem dangerous. And the rubble of history seems to prove us right, for we all claim our own particular pile, and we imagine ourselves, each in our enclave, to be reasonably secure.

But we are not. In a double sense. Neither are we sheltered in our enclaves of sameness nor are we bound to the dictates of history that abdicate our responsibility to be responsive to the other. This book is about responsibility: what it takes to become responsible toward each other, how we might approach such a task, and why embracing a relational vision of a practice of care releases us from the restraints of our enclaves of sameness. To adopt a caring responsibility toward each other, we need to become unsettled by empathy.

Walter Benjamin's Angel of History, to whom I am alluding above, is steeped in a melancholic view of progress.[1] In Benjamin's image, the Angel of History is blown by a storm from Paradise toward the future, with his face not looking forward but backward, gazing at a single catastrophe of an ever-growing pile of rubble, a storm so strong that the angel cannot close his wings or pause for a moment to repair "what has been smashed." "This storm," Benjamin concludes, "we call progress."[2] Indeed, we are currently living in a moment of history when the relative safety promised by progress in the form of liberal democracies—albeit a safety ensured on the backs of impoverished, tormented, displaced, and colonized peoples—has become fragile and endangered, so much so that we might fall into a melancholic state of helplessness. What we have assumed to be stable, lasting, and secure is threatening to fall apart. Like the Angel of History, who cannot close his wings, we might feel rather helpless as the storm blows our way.

We are not, however, the Angel of History who, from a metahistorical perspective, can afford such melancholia. The German Jewish philosopher Walter Benjamin writes: "Where we [humans] see the appearance of a chain of events, *he* [the Angel of History] sees one single catastrophe, which unceasingly piles rubble on top of rubble."[3] To behold all the agonies of the past as "one single catastrophe" is the sole privilege of the Angel of History. It is not ours to claim. Benjamin knew this in the bone-chilling manner of someone faced with only bad choices. Threatened with deportation at the Spanish border when escaping Nazism in 1940, he committed suicide rather than be returned to Germany. When humans adopt the angel's metahistorical view, it smacks of philosophical fatalism and moral aloofness, for we would willingly refuse to distinguish between culpable wrongdoing and the all-too-real experience of human suffering. We would abdicate our responsibility toward justice. As opposed to the Angle of History, humans are confronted with specific events that have produced "rubble on top of rubble," and these events demand a response from us.

Not only are we not the singular Angel of History, we are also not angels in general. The storm that is blowing from paradise is not paradise itself but rather a reminder of our loss of innocence. As the storm grows stronger and we seek shelter in our enclaves of sameness, we tend to believe in the innocence of our own communities while perceiving ourselves as under attack by malevolent outsiders.[4] Not being angels ourselves implies that we must acknowledge the loss of innocence also in our midst, for it is this awareness that calls us into responsibility toward each other.

Being humans, not angels, has its advantages. In Benjamin's image, the Angel of History "would like to linger for a moment,[5] to awaken the dead and to piece together what has been smashed"; but he cannot linger because the storm pushes him relentlessly forward, with his gaze fixed on the debris he cannot do anything about. As humans, however, we can: we can linger or ignore; we can remember the dead or be haunted by them; we can inflict wounds or repair harm. We have choices. We can imagine. We can relate. We can care.

Even when we are apprehensive about the future because of the debris of the past, we need to make choices. Doing so, we embrace our human agency. When conflicts feed resentments and hostilities, we need to be cognizant of levels of culpability, complicity, and victimization and to acknowledge acts of resilience and survival. We need to assess the politics of memory and moral emotions, probe personal motivations, and open ourselves up to sincere self-questioning.

When groups in conflict engage in reconciliatory processes, they are taking on a responsibility toward just relations, tasked with developing relationships of trust even when justice is not yet attained. Investing in a relational practice of empathy, we keep an eye on the past while directing our gaze toward future generations. When acknowledging past traumatic events, we must do so without retraumatizing new generations: our children and children's children deserve not to be overdetermined by communally enshrined memories.

## UNSETTLING EMPATHY

The particular practice of care that feeds and inspires this book is my facilitation of workshops and interactive seminars with groups that find themselves in conflict, past and present. This book does not look at efforts of reconciliation, peace-building, and conflict resolution through an analysis of theory, legal frameworks, truth commissions, or human rights organizations. Nor does it do so through a critical study of history, literary texts, or memorial sites. Rather, this book's approach is that of thick description and judicious reflection on materials drawn from my facilitation work that I have called elsewhere reconciliatory processes, intergroup reconciliation, intercultural encounters, or intercultural memory work.[6] I will share observations about these processes, at times in descriptive detail, to illustrate the painstaking labors and deliberations necessary for working with groups in conflict. While attentive to context and the relevant literature, I will unfold and elucidate the bearing of these materials on helping us to understand the dynamics of conflict, which are often enmeshed in historical traumata and passed on collectively through narratives and memories. The purpose of these deliberations is to improve candid interpersonal and intergroup communication,[7] reduce communal mistrust, mend broken relations, and seek commitments for mutual support in the face of past and current conflict. On one level, these are modest goals, and they do not easily translate into grander political solutions; on another level, when these processes thrive, they demonstrate the best of the human spirit and validate a visionary ethics of interrelatedness.

Empathy plays a vital role in these processes. Empathy is a complex and complicated phenomenon that is not without its critics, who occasionally alert us to its dark side.[8] Hence, empathy needs a qualifier to distinguish it from related phenomena, such as pity, compassion, sympathy, benign paternalism, idealized identification, or voyeuristic appropriation. The word "unsettling" is just this crucial ingredient without which I would hesitate to bring empathy into our conversation when seeking pathways to mitigate current conflicts and to lessen the brunt of historical trauma.

"Unsettling empathy" is a marvelously ambiguous phrase, for it can be read in two ways. If "unsettling" is read as a verb in the form of a gerund, then we are about to "unsettle" empathy—that is, we set out to dismantle, dislodge, or invalidate empathy as a moral good. But if we read "unsettling" as an adjective, it qualifies the noun "empathy." In this case, empathy unsettles us. I am mainly interested in the latter. We need, of course, to keep in mind the caution expressed in the first case—that is, reading "unsettling" as a gerund—for this provides a critical antidote to the ease with which pity and compassion can be appropriated for self-interested purposes. However, in this book I pursue the second meaning, wherein empathy unsettles us. This dimension—or, better, dynamic—of empathy has the force to unsettle our complacencies. It unsettles our unquestioned assumptions of how the world is supposed to operate according to our own political imaginations and psychoemotional comforts. It unsettles our taken-for-granted views of ourselves and our neighbors and questions our embeddedness in national and sacred histories. Unsettling empathy can pull us out of self-absorption and self-centeredness. Such "unsettling" might occur for the duration of only a few moments, but it is a disruption of significant transformative potential that moves us toward an other-directed care.

## FACILITATION

Concretely, what are the places and occasions from which I draw observations and thoughts on unsettling empathy? My experiences with facilitating and guiding groups in conflict go back to the 1980s, and over the last four decades this practice has informed—and, vice versa, was informed by—my corresponding scholarly and academic activities.

My first extensive intercultural encounter (more as participant than facilitator) happened in the early 1980s in a performance group with American Jewish and non-Jewish German dancers and actors. Together with a Jewish friend, I cofounded The Jewish-German Dance Theatre, where we confronted communal, cultural, and personal memories of the Holocaust and turned these explorations into a full-length performance. For almost four years, we toured in the United States and Germany, presenting our performance in diverse locations such as Jewish communities on the U.S. East Coast, small towns throughout Germany, historically fraught places like Nuremberg, and urban centers like Berlin and New York.[9] In June 1989, a few months before the fall of the wall that separated Germany for twenty-eight years as a result of the Holocaust and the ensuing Cold War, our group crossed the heavily guarded border into East Berlin as guests of the East German Jewish community. It was one of our last performances.

After The Jewish-German Dance Theatre disbanded, I started organizing and leading four-week-long educational Holocaust programs for Jewish American and non-Jewish German students, first through the Philadelphia Interfaith Council on the Holocaust and later through St. Mary's College of Maryland, where I was teaching at the time. Between 1989 and

2005, these summer programs invited university students to explore their relationships to history and to each other as third generation after the Holocaust.[10] The students lived and traveled together for one month in the United States, Germany, and Poland. Exposed to survivors and witnesses, academics and activists, as well as sites of atrocities and memorials, the students were continuously immersed in a dynamic process of making sense of their relationships as a post-Holocaust generation. At times, they were deeply distressed when realizing seemingly unbridgeable differences due to their national, religious, political, and family identifications. In the last program in 2005, we also included Polish participants.

Due to my academic study of religion and culture, I have also been actively involved in the Bibliodrama movement. This movement started in Germany and is now practiced throughout Europe, in parts of Asia, and in North America. Bibliodrama is the facilitated dramatic encounter with biblical narratives by people wishing to explore creatively the richness of the biblical traditions.[11] Not to be confused with Bible drama, in which a text is reenacted faithfully according to a particular belief or exegetical tradition, Bibliodrama encourages participants to allow the meaning of a text to unfold interactively through psychodramatic approaches and embodied enactments. I facilitated such workshops within and outside of established networks in the United States, Germany, Finland, Switzerland, and South Korea, and later expanded it to experimentations in "hagiodrama" and "sutradrama."[12] They sharpened my attentiveness to the deep-rooted cultural strata that shape a person's grasp of reality, both positively (as a guide through life's precariousness and anguish) and negatively (as entrenched investments into particular, often exclusionary, views of the world).

Those experiences set the stage for my work with groups in conflict. In 2002, for example, I facilitated a Jewish-Christian interfaith seminar in Weimar and Buchenwald for Protestant and Catholic clergy from Germany and rabbis and Jewish religious leaders from the Chicago area. For three days the group explored personal stories of grief and remorse and became sensitized to the emotional impact of religious variances. In the end, the group agreed to hold a shared prayer service at the remnants of a barrack in the former concentration camp of Buchenwald. Other short-term workshops followed that focused on Jewish-German relations and, generally, on the legacy of family history at various locations for different constituencies. They included, in Germany, workshops on memory and identity for a professional association of psychotherapists and psychoanalysts of Jewish and German descent.[13] In 2005, I led an interactive seminar on intergenerational issues for the Australian Jewish community in Melbourne. In 2015, at a symposium in Vienna for descendants of Austrian accomplices and perpetrators and descendants of Viennese Jewish survivors, I led a workshop called "Unsettling Empathy and Triangulation." In New York, I offered several interactive workshops for American educators from around the nation, in which we explored how our proximity and distance to the Holocaust affects our teaching.[14] For many years I collaborated with a Jewish German artist residing in Bloomington, Indiana, to make sense of our divergent European family histories through the medium of visual arts, particularly by creating original lithographs, prints, artist books, and installations.[15]

Expanding the circle of conflict zones, together with an African American colleague (with philosophical training on identity construction and antiracism), I embarked on experimenting with racial reconciliation retreats for American college students. Sharing the same living quarters over the span of multiple days, we helped groups of diverse students bring into articulation the tensions they felt over ethnic, religious, cultural, and economic differences.

Since 2009, through the auspices of an organization in Germany,[16] I have facilitated numerous trilateral, intergenerational workshops and mentor-training programs for Israelis, Palestinians, and Germans. Depending on the political situation, we met at locations in Jerusalem, the West Bank, Germany, or Greece. Finally, to name a last example, under my current directorship of the Martin-Springer Institute (founded by a Polish-born Jewish Holocaust survivor and her husband),[17] and in collaboration with partners at Ben-Gurion University of the Negev, we started to lead interactive seminars in southern Israel and northern Arizona. Mindful of the impact of systemic power asymmetries on intergroup relations, ethnically diverse groups of Israelis and Americans probed the fraught and fragile relations between majority society and minority communities (specifically Bedouins and Native Americans).

## HESITATIONS

Writing about and reflecting on actual group processes with real people comes with a number of complications and worries, and they have delayed the writing of this book for quite some time. Group processes—as they unfold over several hours, days, or, in some cases, weeks[18]—are so dense, complex, and multifaceted that not even the most detailed description would do justice to them, let alone to the inner processes that each individual participant undergoes. Any attempt at such detailed description would overwhelm readers and ultimately exhaust them. Hence, the scenes and episodes described in this book are chosen for their exemplary value, illustrating specific dynamics I deem crucial when working with groups in conflict.

Although each group needs to be understood within its specific historical, sociopolitical, cultural, and local embeddedness, the ways I have worked with these dynamics are relevant and applicable to bridge-building efforts and mediation in other conflict zones. My hope then is that, beyond the particulars of my examples, a wide range of people can bene- fit from the insights presented in this book. I expect that practitioners, scholars, community leaders, peacemakers, interfaith activists, NGO rep- resentatives, grassroots initiatives, and governmental commissions are able to adopt them with the necessary adjustments for specific settings. I further hope that any reader—whether practitioner, scholar, engaged citi- zen, or activist—will be productively challenged and inspired by the po- tential of unsettling empathy.

Another complication is the degree to which the public is permitted to peek into processes that are, in principle, confidential and protected from the gaze of nonparticipating, external observers. This also extends to pro- tecting the privacy of individuals. As a general rule, groups under my facilitation agree at the beginning of a meeting to certain rules of confi- dentiality. For example, we give ourselves permission to talk about what we experienced and learned in these processes—since part of our inten- tion is to bring fresh insights and inspiration back to our communities— but to talk about it in such a way that no individual can be identified or singled out.[19] This is particularly important when individuals are at risk of being ostracized by their family or community if it became known that they were meeting with their "enemy" (such as in Palestinian-Israeli groups). In the rare instance that outsiders—like photographers, journal- ists, filmmakers, or other guests—are allowed to join the group, they do so in circumscribed settings during which more volatile processes are put on hold.[20] Given these parameters, I have changed (with a few excep- tions) all names of the participants and modified a few identifiers. In some cases, I introduce characters that are composite figures in order to highlight a particular dynamic. These composite figures are not inven- tions but pull together sentiments that were expressed by several people on similar occasions.

A third complication has to do with my choice of reporting on these processes. Enriched by, filtered through, and indebted to insights from the relevant literature on topics addressed in this study, the materials for this book are based on my notes and observations.[21] Though I employ vocabulary and discuss concepts gleaned from different disciplines, I do not always practice fidelity to how specific terms are used by other schol- ars. Rather, I adopt these terms for my own purpose and mine them for their explanatory potential.[22] The interpretations I suggest and the con- clusions I draw are inevitably mine and as such are open to criticism. Although I occasionally insert the words and thoughts of participants that were shared in follow-up correspondence, I do not claim to represent comprehensively those individuals' experiences, feelings, insights, ambi- guities, and skepticism.[23] What I will do is to suggest interpretive pos- sibilities without always exploring the full complexity inherent in these processes.

My motivation to facilitate processes with groups in conflict is not driven by an ambition to prove scientifically the validity of this work through collecting and evaluating qualitative and quantitative data; nor is it driven by a desire to authenticate the effectiveness of a particular method. My occasional infidelity to discipline-specific term definitions is echoed in a certain unorthodoxy of my facilitation practice. Just as I am indebted to critical insights gleaned from scholarly sources, I borrow and modify techniques of various therapeutic and creative practices. Without them, I could not have written this book, let alone facilitate groups. Yet, at the center of my work with groups in conflict are neither theories nor techniques but the people who have had the courage to step outside their comfort zones and who have chosen to seek pathways out of acrimonious relationships, communal grievances, and seemingly insurmountable walls of mistrust.

When I presented my thoughts on empathy as a crucial component of conflict resolution at a genocide prevention forum in Yerevan, Armenia, the attending historian Omer Bartov responded with skepticism.[24] Though intrigued by the term "unsettling empathy," he shared in a brief follow-up conversation that his graduate students do not find such terminology "analytically useful." Bartov is right, of course. Unsettling empathy is not an analytical category in the sense of helping us to understand historical processes. Rather it is a dynamic that plays out in present social relations burdened by the past and emboldened to envision a better future. In this sense, unsettling empathy has affinity to an ethical vision, yet with real practical implications, something that cannot be enforced but can transpire.

Given the centrality I ascribe to the specific dynamics that evolve in each group process, it might come as no surprise that my workshops and interactive seminars do not follow a cookie-cutter model. There is no step-by-step method that each group needs to pass through. An ability to improvise is an essential part of the skill set of a good facilitator. Though there is careful advance planning, I am always ready to stop, adjust, and change any preset ideas. For a facilitator, this requires fine-tuned attentiveness to the mood of a group, improvisational skills, and eliminating ego attachment to preconceived notions about content and process. It also requires an ability to balance a group's need for protection with occasional direct interventions. "Holding" a group while keeping it responsible for its own conduct, goals, and aspirations is another essential element for effective facilitation.

## STRUCTURE

Because there is no theory to be defended and no step-by-step method to be introduced, there is no ready-made order by which this book proceeds. Instead we may want to think of this writing as a layering of concepts, examples, and meaning, which gives this book a motion of circularity more than linearity. Such circularity, I hope, is not experienced as repetitiveness but an intensification of the materials presented.

The layering consists of three levels that have different explanatory and heuristic value. I will call these layers, respectively, "frames," "dynamics," and "approaches."

"Frames" establish a broader context for explaining the materials and observations of this work. These frames command, organize, and focus the materials on which this writing relies, and they do so within established transdisciplinary fields. The frames most helpful for my work are "reconciliation," "memory," "trauma," and "empathy," and they are presented in the first part.

In the second part I explore the various dynamics and approaches that unfold and characterize my work with groups in conflict. "Dynamics," here, refer to my observations of how conflicts surface and are expressed when working with people in adversarial relations. Dynamics are the kind of psychosocial, psychopolitical, and emotional forces we need to pay attention to when guiding people away from acting out and toward working through. These dynamics include, for example, the sway of large-group identifications and master narratives, the emergence of moral emotions, the courage to become vulnerable, attachments to collective history, the acting out of transgenerational obligations, or the ability to develop trust and relational empathy. Though this book focuses on how these dynamics positively affect groups in conflict, it will also introduce moments of disappointment and frustration. As these dynamics evolve in intergroup encounters, they can operate as stumbling blocks or building blocks.

"Approaches," the third layer, are defined as the practical means by which the dynamics of a conflict can be articulated or made visible in particular intergroup encounters. Every facilitation relies on a set of techniques and exercises that have proven useful to a facilitator depending on his or her expertise and training. What we do in my workshops and seminars does not neatly line up with a standard method, which is why I prefer calling the practical components "approaches" rather than tools, techniques, or exercises. When I guide groups in conflict, these approaches are never devoid of content (as the terms "tool" or "technique" might suggest) but constitute an integral part of the process. Put differently, "dynamics" and "approaches" are inseparably tied to each other as they evolve together. What a particular approach can do is to vocalize, visualize, intensify, or mediate certain dynamics that either thwart or encourage the trust-building that is necessary for working through past and current agonies. Approaches introduced in this book include, among others, living sculptures, timelines, loaded words, witnessing circles, triangulation, memory objects, amplification, and the arts.

To assist the reader—and also provide a guide for the practitioner—I have included a glossary at the end of this book. The glossary contains those terms that I deem particularly helpful for my work. They include conceptual terms related to *frames*, analytical terms related to *dynamics*, and practical terms pertaining to *approaches*. When a glossary term appears in a substantial way for the first time in the text, it is marked with an *asterisk.

Reading this book, I hope, will inspire people to join those walking on a path of unsettling empathy for the sake of future generations.

## NOTES

1. On melancholy in Benjamin's thought on history, see Raymond Barglow, "The Angel of History" (1999).

2. This passage of Walter Benjamin's 1940 essay, "Theses on the Philosophy of History," was first published in English in the collection *Illuminations* (1969; edited by Hannah Arendt and translated by Harry Zohn). Many translations, with small variations, are now circulating. Below is the full passage as translated by Dennis Redmond: "There is a painting by Klee called Angelus Novus. An angel is depicted there who looks as though he were about to distance himself from something which he is staring at. His eyes are opened wide, his mouth stands open and his wings are outstretched. The Angel of History must look just so. His face is turned towards the past. Where we see the appearance of a chain of events, he sees one single catastrophe, which unceasingly piles rubble on top of rubble and hurls it before his feet. He would like to pause for a moment so fair [*verweilen*: a reference to Goethe's Faust], to awaken the dead and to piece together what has been smashed. But a storm is blowing from Paradise, it has caught itself up in his wings and is so strong that the Angel can no longer close them. The storm drives him irresistibly into the future, to which his back is turned, while the rubble-heap before him grows sky-high. That which we call progress, is this storm." www.marxists.org/reference/archive/benjamin/1940/history.htm (accessed January 9, 2019).

3. Emphasis in original.

4. Similar to my wording of "enclaves of sameness," Daniel Bar-Tal and Dikla Antebi speak of the "siege mentality" of communities that have established a sense of collective and competitive victimhood. Such a mentality contributes to a lack of empathizing with the suffering of others ("Siege Mentality in Israel" 1992).

5. Most translations use the phrase "to stay" here for the German word *verweilen*. Dennis Redmond (see note 2) translates it as "to pause for a moment so fair." I chose "to linger" as an alternative.

6. See Krondorfer, *Reconciliation in Global Context* (2018); ibid. "Unsettling Empathy: Intercultural Dialogue in the Aftermath of Historical and Cultural Trauma" (2016); "Interkulturelle Erinnerungsarbeit als offener Prozess" (2013a); "Interkulturelle Begegnungsprogramme zum Holocaust" (2010); and *Remembrance and Reconciliation* (1995). Psychologist and scholar-practitioner Herbert C. Kelman, who has worked in the field of conflict resolution since the 1970s (especially in the Israeli-Palestinian context), describes the kind of "problem-solving workshops" he and a team of social scientists have offered as "microprocesses" in a "private space in which politically involved and often politically influential . . . members of conflicting communities can interact in a nonbinding, confidential way." Kelman conceives of these workshops as providing "opportunities to penetrate each other's perspectives; to explore both sides' needs, fears, priorities, and constraints; and to engage in joint thinking about solutions" ("The Role of National Identity in Conflict Resolution" 2001, 198). There is overlap between Kelman's and my approach in terms of essential components, such as

safe spaces, confidentiality, exploring of perspectives, and attention to needs and fears. But there are also differences. My approach is broader and less focused on solution outcomes. It is not limited to conflict resolution settings for politically influential members. Rather than "thinking about solutions," as Kelman puts it, my facilitation encourages participants to explore and imagine alternatives to current stalemates.

7. Though often used synonymously, there is a difference between "intergroup" and "interpersonal" interactions and dialogue. Whereas "intergroup" refers to individual members of one group interacting with individual members of another group, "interpersonal" refers to interactive contact on the basis of personal relationships. As Miles Hewstone and Rupert Brown put it, both terms relate to "actions of individuals" (rather than social or institutional bodies), though "in one case [interpersonal] they are the actions of individuals *qua* individuals, while in the other [intergroup] they are the actions of individuals *qua* group members" ("Contact Is Not Enough" 1986b, 14; emphasis in original). See also Miles Hewstone and Ed Cairns, "Social Psychology and Intergroup Conflict" (2001); Rupert Brown and John Turner, "Interpersonal and Intergroup Behavior" (1981); and Henri Tajfel and John Turner, "An Integrative Theory of Intergroup Conflict" (1979). When working with groups in conflict, we are clearly talking about "intergroup" dialogue and interactions.

8. For the dark side of empathy, see Chapter 4 in this book.

9. Television appearances and coverage include CBS's "Sunday Morning with Charles Kurault" (November 13, 1988), Westdeutscher Rundfunk (WDR3), Südwestfunk (SWF3), and Hessischer Rundfunk (HR3). For two essayistic pieces, see Esther Röhr, "Steine sind wie Zeit: Das Jewish German Dance Theater" (*Religion Heute* 3/4 1989), and Lisa Green, "Jewish German Dance: Jenseits der Sprachlosigkeit" (*tanz aktuell: Zeitung für Tanz und Theater* 4/VI June 1989). A sample of newspaper reviews includes *The Jewish Times* (May 1, 1986), *The Jewish Exponent* (February 27, 1987), *Frankfurter Rundschau* (October 29, 1988; November 12, 1988), *Berliner Volksblatt* (November 3, 1988), *taz Berlin* (November 11, 1988), *Nürnberger Zeitung* (November 15, 1988), *Allgemeine Jüdische Wochenzeitung* (December 12, 1988), *The Pittsburgh Press* (March 30, 1989), *The Philadelphia Inquirer* (April 2, 1989), *Greenwich Time* (May 3, 1989), *Wiesbadener Tagesblatt* (June 16, 1989), *Frankfurter Allgemeine Zeitung* (June 20, 1989), *Offenbach Post* (June 20, 1989), and *taz* (July 17, 1989).

10. These programs are described in more detail in my book *Remembrance and Reconciliation* (1995).

11. The Bibliodrama movement is not limited to one particular method but open to a great variety of approaches, depending on the expertise and creativity of the facilitator. See Krondorfer, *Body and Bible: Interpreting and Experiencing Biblical Narratives* (1992; translated into Korean in 2008). Among the many publications, see Hildrun Keßler, *Bibliodrama und Leiblichkeit* (1996); Gerhard Marcel Martin, *Sachbuch Bibliodrama* (1995); and Peter Pitzele, *Scripture Windows* (1998).

12. *Hagiodrama* is the creative encounter with stories from the history of Christianity unfolding in group processes; *sutradrama* is the creative encounter with texts and vignettes from the Buddhist scriptural traditions unfolding in group processes. See Krondorfer, "Werkstattbericht: Bibliodrama und Sutradrama" (2008b).

13. The association is called The Study Group on Intergenerational Consequences of the Holocaust, formerly PAKH. According to their website, it was "founded in 1995 by Jewish and non-Jewish German members, most of them psychotherapists. It is open to all persons who are interested in a better understanding of conflicts in the context of politically and individually motivated violence." http://pakh.de/EN/index.html (accessed January 11, 2019). The group's publications include Liliane Opher-Cohn et al., *Das Ende der Sprachlosigkeit* (1998), and Beata Hammerich et al., "A Reflection on the Dialogue Process Between Second Generation Descendants of Perpetrators and of Holocaust Survivors in Germany" (2009).

14. The Olga Lengyel Institute for Holocaust Studies and Human Rights (https://www.toli.us/).

15. The artist is Karen Baldner; see Krondorfer, "From Pulp to Palimpsest: Witnessing and Re-Imagining through the Arts" (2013b). Since 2004, our work has been exhibited in solo and group shows in numerous venues. See also Baldner's website, http://karenbaldner.com/the-jewishgerman-dialogue-project.html. Our collaboration is described in more detail in Chapter 10.

16. The organization is *Friendship Across Borders* (FAB). Founded in 2003, FAB is, according to its website, "a non-governmental peace-organization, in which Germans, Palestinians and Israelis work together. Our principle activity is to train young adults in mutual understanding, respect and acceptance through their own personal transformation, so that they become 'Peace-Carriers' in their societies. In the framework of trilateral dialogues, FAB promotes peace between Palestinians and Israelis and contributes to reconciliation between Germans and Jews." http://www.fab-friendship-acrossborders.net/en/ (accessed January 11, 2019).

17. Located at the campus of Northern Arizona University, the Martin-Springer Institute was founded and endowed by Ralph and Doris Martin in 2000. Doris Martin (née Szpringer) was born in Bedzin, Poland, and survived the Holocaust. The institute attends to the experiences of the Holocaust in order to relate them to today's concerns, crises, and conflicts. With educational and public programs that promote the values of moral courage, empathy, reconciliation, and justice, it fosters dialogue on local, national, and international levels. See http://nau.edu/martin-springer and Facebook.com/MSIatNAU.

18. The workshops and interactive seminars I offer can last from a few hours to several days, and in some cases, weeks. The ideal group size for such intergroup, intercultural, and sometimes intergenerational encounters is twelve to eighteen participants, but I have worked with fewer people and with groups of forty and more participants.

19. The rule of not being able to identify individuals applies to the readers of this book. It does not apply in the same way to people who participated in particular programs since they might remember specific scenarios and people I am describing in these chapters.

20. Individual participants can, of course, choose to speak publicly or to the media as long as this does not happen during the sessions themselves. See, for example, the video link to interviews with Palestinian and Israeli participants of the Eighth International Seminar "Touching Borders," a workshop I conducted in 2015: www.fab-friendshipacrossborders.net/en/ (accessed June 4, 2019).

21. Since I am engaging various fields of inquiry, which are themselves dependent on transdisciplinary scholarship (such as trauma studies, memory studies, reconciliation studies, peace and conflict resolution studies, and studies in empathy), I have consulted a wide range of disciplines, including history, sociology, social psychology, philosophy, international relations, literary studies, art history, religious studies, psychoanalysis, political science, anthropology, humanities, and gender studies.

22. My footnotes will provide the reader with the necessary sources and references; they also indicate discrepancies in the usage of particular terms and concepts.

23. When I am quoting from personal correspondence shared with me—often via email—I have occasionally made editorial corrections concerning grammar, spelling, syntax, and length.

24. The 2018 Third Global Forum Against the Crimes of Genocide was organized by the Ministry of Foreign Affairs of the Republic of Armenia. Invited participants included a select group of international scholars, representatives of the UN and European Human Rights commissions, directors of memorial museums, and NGO practitioners.

# 1

# Frames

# ONE

## Reconciliation

### *Setting the Stage*

Representing himself in 2012 at the International Criminal Tribunal for the former Yugoslavia (ICTY) in The Hague, Netherlands, the then-sixty-seven-year-old former Bosnian Serb leader Radovan Karadžić denied all charges of war crimes and genocide against him. He also questioned whether thousands of Bosnian Muslim men had been massacred in Srebrenica under the Bosnian Serb commander Ratko Mladic, and he furthermore credited himself for doing everything "in his power to reduce the war." He told the court that he was "not an autocrat" and "not aggressive." "On the contrary," he said, "I am a mild man, a tolerant man with great capacity to understand others."[1]

If we contrast Karadžić's claim of innocence and his self-avowed compassionate nature with the violent ethnic cleansing committed throughout former Yugoslavia, the cynicism displayed by this former perpetrator could not be more appalling. Paul Mojzes, a scholar of religious studies, summarizes the strategically pursued cleansing operations in former Yugoslavia in these words:

> Paramilitary units of one ethnic group would take over a town and first kill those members of their own ethnicity who were known as proponents of pluralistic integration . . . [T]hey would then start killing the most prominent citizens of the other ethnicities . . . [and put them] into concentration camps where the most fearsome tortures were common. These included genocidal rape (of women and men), beatings, electric shock, sexual mutilation, forcing inmates to eat each other's body parts or excrements, and so forth.[2]

Karadžić is, of course, no exception but the rule when it comes to the self-exculpation of perpetrators in post-conflict societies. Karadžić, however,

3

did not get away with his self-aggrandizing claim of innocence. After years of hiding under the false identity of a new-age healer—earlier in his life, he had been a psychiatrist and a poet—he was arrested in July 2008 and handed over to stand trial at the ICTY. In March 2016, he was sentenced to forty years in prison for war crimes, crimes against humanity, and genocide.

Given the audaciousness with which perpetrators deny wrongdoing, and given their unwillingness to acknowledge the harm inflicted and their refusal to recognize the trauma left in the wake of their criminal actions, any reference to reconciliation and empathy might come across as rather callous. Would these terms not play into the hands of former perpetrators and accomplices who, like Karadžić, want to bury and distort the past? Should we not, instead, put all our efforts into verifying acts of atrocity factually and forensically, followed by legal prosecution of the responsible parties? Does the invocation of a concept like reconciliation undermine the legitimacy of victim voices? And does not the seemingly soft moral category of empathy compare unfavorably to the harsh reality of injustice and traumatic injury? If trauma is the result of a severe disruption and destruction of the integrity of an individual or a community, is any talk of empathy nothing but a "sentimental political discourse [which] domesticates the traumatic impact of suffering"?[3] Radovan Karadžić, we have to remember, asserted in his own defense at the ICTY that he was a "tolerant man with a great capacity to understand others." Indeed, one would expect a certain gift of compassion from a poet and psychiatrist— Karadžić's prewar professions. Hence the cynicism of his defense is even more biting. If an unrepentant perpetrator like Karadžić can claim for himself "empathetic understanding"[4]—regardless of whether it is done disingenuously for the sake of self-exculpation—of what value is empathy in a post-atrocity situation?[5]

Although I will argue that "unsettling empathy" is beneficial to communities shattered by conflicts and a traumatic past in order to live together in the present, I am raising these grim questions at the onset of this book because I am not immune to the sense of frustration and indignation they express. As someone born in Germany, I have experienced these feelings in my reckoning with the legacy and aftermath of the Holocaust. As a neighbor in different regions of the United States, I have experienced them with people who unabashedly embrace injustices in the name of patriotic pride. As a global citizen, I am experiencing them in light of a hardening political landscape. Since 9/11, we have witnessed in the name of democracy the legitimization of torture and, in the name of freedom, *1984*-style surveillance of all citizens.[6] We are also witnessing a steady rise of autocratic, demagogic, and populist leaders who are intent on weakening and destroying democratic governance—and such intentions go hand in hand with an illiberal disregard for the law and a suspension of human rights. Whether we look, at the time of this writing, at Jarosław

Kaczyński's ruling Law and Justice Party in Poland, the right-wing auto-crat Viktor Orbán in Hungary, the election of the violent populist Rodrigo Duterte in the Philippines, the nationalist turn of Benjamin Netanyahu's government in Israel, Vladimir Putin in Russia, Donald Trump in Washington, Recep Tayyip Erdoğan in Turkey, Abdel Fattah el-Sisi in Egypt, Jair Bolsonaro in Brazil, the military rulers in Myanmar and North Korea, and a host of failing nation-states and strongmen in other countries, the global political situation is deeply worrisome. It seems to dwarf any of the grassroots efforts that seek reconciliatory alternatives to restore trust and build peace.

When we open the newspaper, watch and listen to the news, or follow social media, we are inundated with reports on old and fresh conflict zones around the world. They overwhelm us and, perhaps, render us helpless—pushing us into the melancholic view of history that Walter Benjamin's Angel of History evokes, the angel who is unable to move or flap his wings, trapped as he is in a storm he can do nothing about. And yet, less apparent in political rhetoric and public awareness are the many attempts at bringing together conflicting and warring parties through various large- and small-scale reconciliatory efforts. We need to remind ourselves that questions of how to redress wrongdoings are as enduring as the observation that human history has been marred by violent conflict. Active individuals, grassroots initiatives, nongovernmental organizations, and national and international bodies of law are working continuously toward some form of rapprochement (a neutral and underdetermined term) and *trust-building (a value-laden term) between adversaries.[7]

Given the cynical appropriation of compassion at the hands of men like Karadžić, it behooves us not to jump too quickly into a vindication of, or advocacy for, compassion and empathy. Rather, we first need to set a larger stage. One such stage is to approach efforts of repairing damaged, harmed, and adversarial communities through the frame of reconciliation.

## RECONCILIATION AS A CONCEPT

Reconciliation is both an idea and a practice that seeks individual and collective repair in situations where seemingly irreparable harm has left people in broken relationships characterized by fear, mistrust, and anger. While proponents of forms of reconciliation differ in their understanding of the term, the questions in post-conflict situations remain the same: Can enmity be replaced by amity? Can the seemingly unforgivable be transformed into peaceful coexistence? Is reconciliation desirable? Is it possible? What intellectual resources and practical experiences do different communities provide to stitch together a ripped and stained social fabric?

In the broad terms of social repair, the concept of reconciliation shifts the focus away from how to prevent atrocities from occurring and whether to intervene militarily and politically in the midst of a conflict in order to address what needs to be done when a conflict has occurred. Rather than being primarily a means of *prevention* or *intervention*, reconciliation can be seen as the labor of *postvention*. Postvention refers to efforts of bringing together communities and societies ripped apart by violent conflict, of establishing conditions for coexistence, of social healing, and of overcoming fear and mistrust on collective and individual levels. Insofar as postvention efforts can contribute to preventing recurring cycles of violence, the lines between pre-conflict and post-conflict cannot be clearly drawn.

The term "reconciliation," with its religious connotations, is employed today in international debates about transitional and restorative justice.[8] It did not enter into the philosophical vocabulary until late in the twentieth century, though the Western philosophical and political traditions have addressed related concepts, such as right conduct, virtue ethics, forgiveness, tolerance, and rapprochement. Arguments have been put forth that query the assumption that reconciliation is a moral good in and of itself. For example, one trajectory—with such proponents as Sonali Chakravarti, Thomas Brudholm, and Margaret Walker—is to value anger as an appropriate response to injury and injustice.[9] In this view, retribution, anger, and resentment—rather than reconciliation and forgiveness—are seen as ethically appropriate and politically effective ways to ensure moral and social repair.

In the aftermath of the Holocaust, the international community and civic initiatives have called for greater accountability for crimes and awareness of the legacy of traumatic memories.[10] Although retributive justice based on the idea of punishment is a strong international mechanism to seek legal redress, reconciliation is based on a different way of thinking about the needs of communities in which people have experienced massive violence. The concept of reconciliation can be approached religiously as an issue of healing, mercy, and atonement; psychologically as an issue of social affect within interpersonal relations and intersubjectivity; philosophically as an issue of resentment and forgivability; judicially as an issue of restorative justice and rehabilitation; and politically as an issue of coexistence and interdependence. In the last decades, the political dimension of reconciliation has become more prominent because of the work of various national truth commissions.[11] Given that reconciliation has entered the vocabulary in international and interstate relations, we can ask whether reconciliation should become a tool in the power of the state, or, to the contrary, whether it should be put into the hands of individual agents. We can also ask whether deeds of radical evil fall outside the sphere of reconciliation because they are unforgivable, or, alternatively, whether it is precisely in the shadows of mass violence that we need to advance a transformative vision of personal and political reconciliation, as South African archbishop Desmond Tutu has argued.[12]

Reconciliation is polysemic: it cannot be contained in or reduced to a single meaning. This becomes apparent when we become aware of the multiple ways through which it can be understood and approached. When we claim it, what dimensions do we foreground: the personal or political? social or intrapsychic? institutional or attitudinal? relational or structural? interpersonal or communal? Reconciliation has been implemented as bottom-up practices by grassroots initiatives and top-down policies by governmental agencies.[13] Some venues focus on individual transformation in therapeutic or semitherapeutic settings, others on nation building; some see in reconciliation a rich topic for philosophical inquiry, others a legal path toward restorative justice.[14] But despite such diversity, most studies of reconciliation center on key terms such as "trust," "forgiveness," "truth," "justice," "trauma," "empathy," "societal healing," "rehabilitation," "coexistence," "conflict management," and "transformation." Some of these terms are value laden, pointing to a moral good; others are praxis oriented, directing us to social policies and legal mechanisms.

Reconciliation might be difficult to implement, but it is one promising possibility to counteract the damage done to communities that have been literally and symbolically disfigured by widespread injustices and violence-induced harm.[15] I like to think of reconciliation not as a static concept but as an active dynamic that combines and circles around the key terms mentioned above, propelling former adversaries into newly defined relationships. I therefore suggest we speak of *reconciliatory processes to indicate the open-endedness of the work that needs to be done. Rather than being prescriptive of a particular goal, reconciliation is a commitment to a specific posture of thinking and acting.[16] In this sense, reconciliation might be best understood as a core phenomenon of human interaction that is future oriented, constructive, and empathetic. It transcends the limitations of self-interested action by moving toward an other-directed care. And insofar as former victims and enemies remain neighbors in post-conflict societies, either literally (like in former Yugoslavia or post-genocide Rwanda) or more remotely through globalized cultural, political, and economic networks, we need to find pathways of living together in a troubled world.[17]

## RECONCILIATION AS A PRACTICE

Because reconciliation is multifaceted and polysemic, it lends itself to becoming a screen onto which we project our hopes and quasi-messianic expectations or, in contrast, our misgivings and political suspicions. Self-help literature and therapeutic models may praise the curative power of reconciliation (often indistinguishably blending forgiveness with self-forgiveness), speculating that observations from the fields of intrapsychic and personal distress can be applied to large-group conflicts. In contrast, in societies still recovering from major violent upheavals, the term "reconciliation" might come across as a cynical attempt at forgiving, forgetting, and delaying justice indefinitely. We can see such mistrust playing out in post-conflict Bosnia and Herzegovina, where the European Union tried to mandate reconciliation policies; post-apartheid South Africa, where critics have lamented the failure of the Truth and Reconciliation Commission to implement lasting systemic changes; or in Palestine and Israel, where some accuse peace builders of being hopefully naïve while others reject reconciliation as a feel-good Band-Aid covering up the unjust realities of occupation.[18]

Reconciliation, in other words, invites a kind of projective identification, a screen onto which we project what we fear or desire.[19] Hence, when people or communities in conflict respond to my employment of the word "reconciliation," I have little idea of why they either praise or reject it. For this reason, I almost never use "reconciliation" in the titles of my workshops and intercultural encounters. I rarely mention it in brochures or invitations, although I use the term regularly in my writings and presentations. This is not false advertisement. The point of working with groups in conflict is not to argue philosophically for or against the validity of an abstract notion but to utilize reconciliation as a way to analyze dynamics as they emerge and express themselves in guided group processes. The framework of "social reconciliation," as I will describe further below, is one lens through which we can understand such processes. Other frameworks also assist in reading and interpreting these processes, and I will introduce in this book three additional frames: memory, trauma, and empathy. These explanatory frames do not define the actual facilitation practice; what they do accomplish, however, is directing our attention to diverse elements that need our analysis and understanding.

When facilitating groups, I provide spaces safe enough for people to be held in their turmoil and anguish and—and this is vital—to encourage them to take risks. *Vulnerability and *risk-taking—not defensiveness and empty speech[20]—are important ingredients to get people to reestablish some level of trust. Participants are welcomed and appreciated as individuals, but they also come as members of social groups who share an antagonistic past or are still in the midst of conflict. Keeping the personal and social dimensions in balance is another important ingredient. In conflictual situations, we need to pay attention to both individual choices and *large-group identification. The latter is, in general, much stronger than well-meaning individual intentions. Large-group identifications get amplified in heterogeneous settings because of feelings of obligation and loyalty to one's in-group.

Another essential component of my facilitation work is to switch between verbal and nonverbal sessions, allowing creativity and physical embodiment to do their magic. Such nonverbal elements, often imbued with an improvisational quality, take people out of their comfort zones and lower their habitual guards. They allow the subliminal to speak through bodily gestures and move into fresh patterns of thought beyond the circumscribed boundaries of one's community.

## YOU ARE WHAT YOU EAT

A brief example illustrates the seemingly odd ways in which tensions over social identities can come to the fore in mixed-group settings. In this particular case, American Jewish and non-Jewish German university students examined and discussed the history and legacy of the Holocaust and World War II during a four-week summer program. As briefly mentioned in the introduction to this book, between 1989 and 2005 I organized and facilitated several of these programs designed for the so-called third generation—that is, students whose grandparents lived through the 1930s and 1940s.[21] During one month of traveling together and sharing living quarters, the Jewish- and German-identified students learned how to discuss with sincerity and integrity their culturally different perspectives on the impact of history on their lives.

The incident I want to recount—it took place in the late 1990s—has to do with loyalty conflicts and felt obligations to one's community of belonging. In mixed groups that set themselves the task of making sense of past and present injuries, some participants will inevitably arrive at internal conflicts about loyalty to their own community. Getting too close to understanding the other side, they feel that they are betraying the memories of or bonds to their own families, religious traditions, cultural and linguistic customs, or ethnic and national communities. This can be experienced *directly* among actors in ongoing conflict zones or *vicariously* among descendants in a post-conflict society. People can identify with a past trauma or societal guilt even if they did not experience those things themselves, like descendants of victimized communities and descendants of former perpetrator societies, or *secondary witnesses.[22] *Vicarious identification, then, refers to people strongly identifying emotionally and mentally with communal or societal events that they themselves were not part of. What is important to note here is that vicarious identifications are not artificial constructs but come with their own intense and complicated emotional burdens.[23] For example, unresolved issues in one generation can be delegated to the next generation, either subconsciously in families or deliberately through cultural products (such as memorial museums, films, and literature). In this case, vicarious identification is the result of delegated emotional burdens, and those delegated burdens can become vicarious obligations. When people identify with the past not directly their own, and when this identification gets challenged—as in the case of encountering the other in reconciliatory processes—they might feel obliged not only to defend their large-group identity but, as occasionally occurs, verbally attack the other group. A *generational delegation thus turns into a present obligation that is acted out in front of (or against) the other rather than worked through.[24]

The example I have in mind from the third-generation Jewish/German program demonstrates how vicarious *acts of obligation can be activated in intercultural encounters due to subliminal delegations of unfinished tasks. As a matter of fact, the example I have in mind is so trivial that I hesitate to mention it here for fear of mocking the gravity of inherited burdens. Yet it illustrates well how the emotionally fraught and intricate links between delegation and obligation can be acted out, thereby disrupting the very dialogical process to which one has committed. In this particular case, midway through the one-month student program, the group had gathered for dinner at a German guesthouse, having just arrived in Berlin from the United States. It was a typical German evening meal consisting of bread and assorted cold slices of cheeses and meats. Unexpectedly, Dafne, a Jewish female student, got up from the dinner table, grabbed a slice of meat, dangled it from her fingers, and loudly proclaimed: "Look! Who would want to eat this shit?" She then threw the slice across the room.

There was some initial laughter, then embarrassed puzzlement and silence. Her act was impulsive. This otherwise thoughtful and sensitive young woman was later unable to explain what had driven her to do it. Yet, the act was so startling and callous that it could not be ignored. It suggested an aggressiveness stemming from an unresolved inner tension at being in Germany, the land of murderers, together with her German peers studying the Holocaust. If we were to take seriously the anthropological insight that food is elemental to culture, then declaring the slice of meat "shit" and flinging it across the room conveys an unselfconscious, yet unmistaken, message about Germans: "You are what you eat."

Dafne's gesture went deeper than violating reciprocal rules of hospitality. On a basic level, hospitality begins with sharing a meal and opening one's home. Such a gesture of welcoming always risks misunderstandings, discomforts, and sometimes confrontation.[25] Instinctively, this young woman went for the guts.[26] It seems plausible—though I am careful of not pushing my interpretation too far—that a generationally delegated mistrust was given vent through an impulsive acting out. It almost seemed as if this dismissive act against German culture—and implicitly against her German peers with whom she had bonded over the last two weeks—was demanded of her, like a subliminal obligation, at a moment of great internal challenge to her Jewish identity.[27] Although none of the German students spoke up at the moment when this incident occurred,

Dafne's outburst activated defensive reactions, such as subsequent comments on the "snobbishness" of American (read "Jewish") students. In
reconciliatory processes, such incidences do not go unnoticed. Because
they happen, they need to be addressed—equally in a face-saving manner for the protagonist and in a productive way for the whole group.

Dafne's impulsive reaction is one of many examples of what can
transpire when people dare to move into the borderland of empathic
engagement that threatens social identities and family loyalties. I remember how unsettled I was when I first met Holocaust survivors upon arri-
val in the United States as a graduate student in the early 1980s. Trying to
tell my parents back in Germany about these encounters was equally
unsettling. My parents did not grasp the significance these meetings had
for me. Nevertheless, my parents defended themselves against accusations they felt emanating from my relations with Jewish people. My parents, belonging to the so-called Hitler Youth generation, were raised as
children and teenagers during the Nazi regime. They were drawn into
the war's last two years. When my mother and father were age sixteen
and eighteen, respectively, the war ended. After 1948, my parents became
solid West German democrats. Among several unresolved emotions typical for the Hitler Youth generation, one message became increasingly
clear: due to their young age at the time, they were innocent. I strongly
felt the pull to abide by and maintain the myth of my parents' youthful
innocence. I did not, however, remain loyal to this obligation, which, in
turn, affected my relationship with them. Over the years, my attitude
toward my parents went through multiple stages: first rebellious, then
sheepish (as if betraying their trust), then half hopeful about being able to
convert them to my views, then frustrated when more spirited times of
open-mindedness closed down with age. Growing up I had soaked up
stories of *Flucht und Vertreibung* (flight and expulsion)[28] and messages of
German suffering, but as an adult I also rebuffed the unspoken delegated
obligation to show loyalty to the version of postwar German history as
told by my parents' generation. I eventually sensed how threatened my
parents must have felt by my choice to immerse myself in understanding
the legacy of the Holocaust and to bond with the Jewish community.
Over time, I developed more kindhearted listening skills regarding their
hardships and learned to live better with the differences between us.

Generationally transmitted delegations of unresolved emotions are
accompanied by implicit and explicit obligations, the degree of which
differs from family to family. If left to themselves, such delegations become impediments to intercultural encounters because they can quickly
activate large-group defensiveness. What reconciliatory processes can
achieve is to open up possibilities of overcoming such defensiveness,
even though they do not promise any quick fix to repair historical trauma.

## POLITICAL AND SOCIAL RECONCILIATION

Implicit in what I have presented so far is that my facilitation work falls into the area of *social reconciliation, as distinct from *political* reconciliation. Valerie Rosoux, who teaches international negotiation and conflict transformation in Belgium, distinguishes between three approaches to reconciliation as part of peace-building processes: "structural, social-psychological and spiritual." Whereas the first (structural) focuses on fixing political, economic, cultural, and security problems in order to establish cooperation and coexistence between the affected parties, the latter two prioritize the improvement of relationships between parties. According to Rosoux, the social-psychological approach emphasizes "cognitive and emotional aspects" in order to affect attitudinal and motivational changes, whereas the spiritual approach emphasizes "collective healing and forgiveness." The social-psychological approach aims at "forging a *new* relationship," the spiritual approach at "*restoring* a broken relationship." [29]

Rosoux's suggestion to differentiate between "restoring" relationships and "forging new" relationships may not be fully persuasive, but her point of distinguishing between structural and relational approaches is important. Whereas a structural approach tries to change societal structures (legal, economic, institutional, etc.), the relational approach to reconciliation occurs when, according to social psychologists Ananthi Al Ramiah and Miles Hewstone, "members of previously hostile groups come to mutual acceptance" and "experience a changed orientation toward one another." [30]

Somewhat paralleling Rosoux's distinction between the structural and social-psychological approaches, I suggest we differentiate *political* reconciliation from *social* reconciliation. *Political reconciliation* has the purpose of "moving beyond collective forms of enmity." [31] It prioritizes issues of structural interdependence (economic, sociopolitical, security) over interpersonal relationships and is usually negotiated by officially authorized bodies, like truth commissions. *Social reconciliation*, on the other hand, seeks to overcome "alienation between and within communities." [32] It prioritizes human relationships (psychological, emotional, cognitive, reparative) over structural concerns and is usually practiced on grassroots and communal levels, like intergroup dialogues and intercultural encounters. These two kinds of reconciliation differ in their emphasis and prioritization of two basic elements that are operative in the practice of reconciliation: knowledge and acknowledgment. Discussing briefly this difference below, I will also introduce the elements of truth-telling and storytelling.

Let us begin with *knowledge*. Knowledge is necessary in order to establish a factual basis regarding the acts of wrongdoing that precede the need for affected parties to reconcile. Establishing a knowledge base is necessary for political reconciliation. Although facts in the aftermath of violent conflicts will remain contested within a politicized context, an attempt must always be made by domestic or international bodies to arrive at some judgment on past wrongdoings. By collecting testimonies and scouring archives, various national truth commissions over the last decades have sought to establish some truth, even if such commissions may decide to abstain from recommending particular legal options, like retribution, restoration, reparations, or amnesty.[33]

In social reconciliation, however, the verification of factual knowledge is less urgent. In these settings, knowledge is transmitted through a different mode of communication, often through storytelling, in which the truth of personal memory is more vital than forensic evidence or what can be reasonably verified through historical research. As Michael Rothberg puts it in his work on multidirectional memory, "The truths of memory are often in tension with the truths of history." Memory truths, he states, "produce insight about individual and collective processes of meaning-making."[34]

Operating in a different mode of claiming truth-based knowledge, both political and social reconciliation nevertheless need forms and forums of credible and genuine communication in order to create a base in which knowledge becomes verifiable and accepted. Otherwise, the knowledge that is gained will fail to motivate political transitions or social change. The difference between political and social reconciliation is that the former gives credibility to truth-telling, ruled by legal or quasi legal frameworks, while the latter puts its trust into storytelling, ruled by what is perceived as personal sincerity and integrity. In political reconciliation, truth-telling is seen as a valuable tool to repair some of the rifts between social macro-units, often in the service of advancing national unity.[35] Social reconciliation, on the other hand, relies on storytelling to build up trust between people in order to forge human and communal bonds on meso and micro levels.

Truth-telling and storytelling operate according to different principles. They follow what we might call different reconciliation modes. In the case of truth-telling in national truth commissions, the prevailing mode could be described as social verification and public drama. Truth-telling in these cases can be backed up with archival and forensic evidence, be incentivized with legal promises of amnesty, and may lead to public apologies.[36] The resulting proceedings and reports are eventually debated, assessed, and criticized by numerous national and international players (media, politicians, judges, interest groups, journalists, scholars, clergy, etc.). It is no exaggeration to state that every official truth commission has received its share of public criticism.[37]

In distinction to truth-telling in political reconciliation, the prevailing mode in social reconciliation is *storytelling that relies on personal honesty and interpersonal trustworthiness. Storytelling in settings like intergroup dialogue or intercultural encounters is backed up by the integrity of the personal narrative.[38] Many of these groups opt for some degree of confidentiality about what transpires in their meetings. The incentive for participants is emotional release, seeking trust, being listened to, and human connectedness.

## FEEL LIKE A CLOWN

The distinction I am drawing between different understandings of truth in the social and political mode of reconciliation has a direct bearing on facilitating grassroots reconciliatory processes for a simple reason: when people decide to join a group that includes members of a social group with whom they are in conflict, their initial motivation to join is frequently guided by a desire to set history straight or to explain to their opponents the factual truth of the political situation. The underlying assumption is that the other side has had no prior opportunity to hear the real truth; if they only heard it from "me," then "they" (the other side) would change their attitudes and beliefs. Needless to say, people on both sides arrive with the presumption that the other group's lack of information must be rectified by a truthful account of facts. What ends up happening is that any ensuing conversation becomes more of an assertion of one's position rather than a bridge-building effort. I often get the impression that people come to these meetings because they see them as an opportunity to "educate" the other side. But what happens is mostly this: what starts as a well-meaning lesson taught in polite terms eventually takes on a sharper pitch, increasing in intensity as those lessons fall on deaf ears or are contested.

Group processes in the mode of social reconciliation aim at changing patterns of communication away from habitual and defensive postures of lecturing and toward a *shared language. What a group slowly develops, according to Dan Bar-On and Fatma Kassem's observation of Jewish-German and Palestinian-Israeli groups, is an emotional bond through a common "conceptual language that differ[s] from the separate languages that characterize the communities" of those present.[39] Reconciliatory processes are not history lessons. Any attempt to teach the other side one's own historical truth is destined to reenter into the very cycle of conflict that one seeks to escape.

Every group process needs to begin somewhere, and some space must be given for the exchange of what each group considers factual truth or historical evidence. In my observation, politicized and didactic exchanges are a form of gendered communication that is readily employed by men. This is, of course, not to say that I have not seen women engaging in it as well. Yet, this kind of one-upmanship is more familiar to men. They seem to be comfortable with it and hence are more reluctant than women to switch to a discourse that focuses less on what is presented as factual truth and more on the emotional truth of what is shared.

I remember numerous situations like this—for example, the highly alert Jewish Israeli man who jumped at any negative utterance about Zionism by Palestinian participants and then proceeded to explain to them the many historical and intellectual facets of Zionist history, its European roots, its utopian beginnings, and its different schools of thought—none of which, this Israeli emphasized, could possibly justify reducing Zionism to a colonial ideology of occupation.[40] His corrective statements were, for the most part, politely ignored by the group. At stake in this particular Palestinian-Israeli encounter was not the correct writing of the history of Zionism but mistrust among the participants.

I recall, to name another example, a German social worker in his mid-thirties whose whole being resisted the "emotional" turn that a group had taken, in this case a trilateral meeting of Germans, Israelis, and Palestinians. This man considered sessions that dealt with identity and emotions highly dangerous. "I am working with radicalized youth in Germany," he explained, "with young men who use Islam or nationalism for their identities and to act out violently. In my work," he argued, "I need to fight against identity, against the power of identification. We need to teach facts, because these young men know only distorted things about religion and history." He had come to this workshop, he said, to learn methods for multicultural and anti-extremism training, not to engage in interpersonal explorations of large-group identification. Midway through this four-day workshop, the social worker admitted, visibly shaken, "I am upset and confused"—and I was briefly concerned that he would leave the group. But to his credit, he did not. And then something clicked. When the seminar ended, he said that he wished it would continue for a little longer. A few days after the seminar, this social worker wrote in a group email: "I am the third day back at work [in Germany] and I am really more on autopilot. Still unsettled. Just too many things that won't let me concentrate. I try to figure out what happened to me in those four days. . . . Feel like a clown. Stumbling, switching from this to that without any logic. . . . Still the encounters with all of you run through my mind. It almost feels like I was numb to inspiration before."

I also recall a situation when a young Palestinian man kept insisting that the 1917 Balfour Declaration[41] was the beginning of Israel's occupation policy, a point to which he returned incessantly, goading some historians in the group and draining the energy of others. One participant remembered the tediousness of this session in a report shared with me soon after the workshop:

> In the evening session everybody criticized the previous session. Some mutual anger and frustration came to the surface: between the Germans themselves (rather academic) and between the Israelis and the

Palestinians (about the roots of Zionism, the role of victims, the use of nonviolent resistance, empowerment, taking responsibility . . . ). [I asked] what the Palestinians expect from us at meetings such as these, and if there is anything that we "pro-peace" Zionist Israelis can do to gain some more trust. Though the tone was respectful, it became clear once more that an enormous gap existed between the various needs and perspectives and that each side has to learn an awful lot about the other. There was no lack of fake history in the room. For example, several of the Palestinians kept mentioning the Balfour Declaration as if it was the starting point of Zionism, which of course is far from the truth, as is the claim that the Jews today do to the Palestinians what was done to them by the Germans, or the allegation that Palestinians/Arabs/Muslims are today's Nazis.

I am mentioning these three examples to point to the initial resistance of participants (mostly men) when they encounter a process that asks them to leave behind political rhetoric or professional and academic expectations and, instead, to open themselves up to a more unsettling experience. It would be a waste of time, not a wise investment, to use reconciliatory processes in the social mode as a fact- and truth-finding mission. It would not work if the hoped-for outcome is transforming contested relations. In this sense, social reconciliation really operates in a different mode than political reconciliation, with the latter's task to establish knowledge through history or national truth commissions that can stand the test of time or the legal test in courts. In social reconciliation, in contrast, what is important is not so much an agreement on factually established truths but the probing of the emotional investments that certain truths hold for people. What clinical psychologist Sue Grand stated about storytelling in abusive situations can apply to reconciliatory process. "Stories," she writes, "are told to register a truth that cannot be found in the simple telling of facts."[42] Rather than asking whether something is true in an evidentiary sense, we can ask why it is so important to tell. What is at stake in the telling? What is at stake in the insistence of telling? Instead of figuring out, as in the examples above, how to interpret Zionism or the Balfour Declaration correctly, we can take note of the emotionality with which a position is presented. We can try to give such emotional investment a name; we can express it visually (say, through a physical gesture) in order to understand the sway it has for a person; or we can take note of the moment when a particularly loaded word is yet again thrown back at the group and ask why this is done. Rekindling a debate about some historical truth can be a distraction when a process becomes scary—when, for example, an emergent flame of soul-searching renders people vulnerable. The German social worker might have been right: emotions are dangerous. But not for the reasons he had objected to them initially. Emerging emotions in trust-building processes are perceived as a danger not because they manipulate us into adopting false identities and fabricated truths but because they are unsettling.

For facilitators, it is especially important not to enter into the fray of political maneuvering over factual truth-finding when working with groups in conflict. No matter how tempting it is to jump in and correct flawed or misguided information, the moment facilitators intervene in this way, they will lose the trust of the group. Why? Because they have switched from the role of facilitator to teacher and because they are no longer perceived as impartial—no matter what their intent. Instead, the task of facilitators is to help a group to get out of a routinized discourse and to leave behind a desire to correct the respective other side with unsolicited "accurate" information. A good facilitator aims at replacing the comforts of a rehearsed argument with the discomforts of new forms of communication.

I am, of course, not arguing that knowledge is unimportant. After all, I pursue scholarship and teach at a university. We are capable of assessing knowledge, evaluating the credibility of sources, and analyzing the content of an argument—and we have the responsibility to do so. What I am suggesting is that those ways of learning have limited usefulness in inter-group reconciliatory processes. Facilitators ought to do their homework *before* a process starts (read books, consult sources, learn about context, etc.); participants, if all goes well, get inspired to inform themselves more thoroughly *after* a workshop.

Why do I insist on this issue? Because in social reconciliation, it is not *knowledge* but *acknowledgment* that really matters.

## ACKNOWLEDGMENT: AKEEM'S STORY

Scholars and practitioners of restorative and transitional justice have repeatedly pointed out that injured parties want their suffering to be acknowledged. "The woundedness of those who have suffered," writes Daniel Philpott, a political scientist and expert in peace and reconciliation studies, "includes a lack of recognition by the surrounding community." Many victimized communities want public recognition from official bodies for the injustices and harms they have endured. Whereas knowledge alone is limited to gathering evidence and factual information, *acknowledgment is a moral activity. "Official acknowledgment can be powerful," writes Priscilla Hayner of the International Center for Transitional Justice, "precisely because official denial has been so pervasive" at the time when wrongs occurred. Public acknowledgment is partisan insofar as it gives voice and agency back to people who have been harmed and victimized. In this sense, acknowledgment is a crucial step toward moral repair, which, according to philosopher Margaret Walker, "is the process of moving from the situation of loss and damage to a situation where some degree of stability in moral relations is restored."[43]

Within the mode of social reconciliation (as distinct from political reconciliation), there are no official or governmental bodies that recognize buried truths, acknowledge the suffering of communities, and issue public apologies. Yet, wanting to be acknowledged is a central motivation, albeit often veiled, that brings people together in grassroots-level reconciliatory processes. This longing won't be admitted openly—at least not in the early stages of a process—because it might come across as weakness. To ask for acknowledgment directly, even in the safe space of facilitated encounters, renders a person vulnerable. There is the fear of being perceived as needy and self-pitying or of making oneself dependent on the mercy of others. Asking for acknowledgment might actually disempower the person in the presence of his or her (perceived) adversary. Or, in any case, this is what people fear because distrust prevents them from stepping outside their comfort zones and taking risks.

I would like to introduce Akeem. Akeem is a tall, strong Palestinian man who, when you first meet him, leaves you with the impression that he would not fear anything. I met him as part of a workshop for peace activists from Israel and Palestine. Akeem is involved in a number of peace initiatives on the Palestinian side and also with Israelis and Palestinians trying to build bridges across stark differences, including Israeli settlers and their Palestinian neighbors in West Bank territory.

In the workshop that Akeem attended, a group of eighteen people (ranging in age from midtwenties to midfifties) wanted to find out why communication in the peace movement frequently breaks down and how this negatively affects people's commitment and reliability. There was no other agenda. We called the workshop "The Unspoken in the Movement." Rather than assuming to know what the "unspoken" might be, the first sessions were spent honing in on those topics that seemed most pertinent to this particular group. Letting a group define and name their concerns—by way of fairly simple and time-efficient steps[44]—sends a strong signal to the group: you, as a group, have agency and, hence, responsibility toward your own journey of exploration. I also let groups know early on that our workshop is meant for those in attendance and not for discussing people and issues not present. It is an opportunity for and about *this* constellation of people in *this* room and about what *we* (in this group) allow to happen when opening up to each other, as if we were ourselves the texts that we want to read and understand. "Think of it," I tell them, "as a conversation you cannot have in any other circumstance. What do you want to learn here, from and with the people who are present now?"

In the Palestinian-Israeli workshop "The Unspoken in the Movement," the peace activists eventually identified two topics deemed urgent: gender relations and the question of friendship. The story that relates to Akeem has to do with gender relations. But before we get to the heart of this story, some background information is necessary.

A concern over gender issues had been in the room even before the group decided to focus on it. During an earlier *open forum—a term that refers to an unstructured, nonthematic talking session—tensions surfaced, and several women expressed their anger about a male-dominated discussion. It was not a constructive session in itself—as a matter of fact, an Israeli participant took me aside afterward and, in tears, voiced her frustration about the unacknowledged male dominance. It was a session that functioned more like a reality check on the "unspoken," which women, and in this case also a queer man, have experienced at peace movement gatherings elsewhere.

After a coffee break, we split the participants into a men's and a women's group, with each of them tasked to create a *living sculpture (a technique about which more will be said later in this book). Their assignment was to come up with a sculpture made from their own bodies that expressed their perspective on gender relations in the peace movement. Together, the Israeli and Palestinian women created a close-knit circle, with their backs touching each other and their faces looking outward, conveying a combative and supportive posture, with traces of a defensive "circle-the-wagons" mentality. The men's sculpture, in contrast, was more loosely organized, with none of the Israeli and Palestinian men touching each other. Akeem and another Palestinian man faced each other, standing perhaps nine feet apart, thus constituting a kind of axis that accentuated Akeem's physically imposing presence. But otherwise, the men's sculpture had no discernible center or *gestalt*;[45] it felt lifeless, with little energy radiating from it.

What I always do with living sculptures is to lead the group through a guided discernment, often starting with those outside the sculpture sharing simple observations and eventually zooming in on a particular mood or gesture that the sculpture expresses. I asked the women about their impressions of the men's sculpture as they were circling around it. Their comments expressed confusion, skepticism, and judgment. "What the heck are you guys doing?" one woman asked. Another wondered: "Where is the life in your sculpture?" Understandably, the men did not take lightly the judgmental feedback they received. They felt somewhat belittled and not taken seriously, so much so that two men voiced their discontentment with this "silly exercise."

Earlier in the morning, Akeem, who assumed a somewhat pivotal position in this otherwise loosely structured men's sculpture, had drawn the ire (and restrained ridicule) of the women. When the topic of gender had been raised in the morning session, Akeem expounded his views of male-female relationships. Men and women, he stated, are equal, and women need protection. He would never impose himself on women, he insisted, but would always signal to women that he can be counted on for their safety. Simple gestures, like eye contact, he explained, would send those signals.

Akeem presented these views with great sincerity—and also with adamant intensity. His sincerity, no doubt, came from a place of wanting to convey that women need not be afraid of him as a man and that he could be relied on if things got rough, say, in a nonviolent public action. His view on gender relations could be described as benign paternalism, but this is not a term the group employed. Women participants responded first with some snickers, then arguments, and eventually irate head shaking when Akeem kept defending his views in an increasingly circular fashion, taking up much time and space. As a matter of fact, the way he talked resembled the kind of educational lecturing that, as I mentioned above, is detrimental to trust-building processes.

Akeem's earlier position in the group is important to know in order to appreciate what happened next. After the women's adverse reaction to the men's sculpture—"What the heck are you guys doing?"—I asked for women volunteers to stand behind the different male figures in the sculpture. Choose the one, I suggested, who intrigues you most. Adopt and imitate, as best as you can, the poses they have assumed. I then asked each woman what she felt in the man's place. Everyone, in their own words, felt the same thing: heaviness and self-questioning. Akeem, who stood straight and mighty across from another Palestinian man, held his hands folded in front of his upper chest, almost like in prayer. His fingers nearly reached his face, with space left between his hands so that they did not touch. A Palestinian woman—the oldest woman in the group—adopted Akeem's posture. She shared with the group what intrigued her about Akeem's pose. "I want to find out what these hands tell us," she said. "What are they about? Why are they apart?"

Listening to the women imagining and verbalizing different parts of the men's sculpture changed the mood in the room. It seemed that everyone was now ready to listen to each other attentively. A few of the men responded to what they had heard the women saying, and they felt somewhat understood. When it was Akeem's turn, he unexpectedly began speaking about his mother.

His mother, he said, had been a lifelong Palestinian activist, and she paid a price for it. She was frequently arrested and imprisoned. As a boy around the age of ten, Akeem saw little of her. Because his mother was either in jail or participating in the political struggle, she was rarely home. And yet, his mother taught him respect. It is this respect, Akeem said, that he wants to convey when signaling to women through small gestures that they can trust him and that he will protect them. Akeem explained that his hands in front of his upper chest, slightly apart, symbolized the space that defines man-woman relationships. His hands "signal" (a term Akeem used repeatedly) that women can feel safe around him.

Akeem was utterly serious as he proceeded to connect his mother's absence—which he described with both sadness and pride—to his general views on gender. But the moment he talked about sending "signals" to women (as he had done earlier in the morning session), he lost the group's attention. Some people started laughing, which, in turn, bewildered Akeem, possibly making him feel publicly humiliated and threatening his dignity.[46] We were at risk of losing the precious mood we had been building up over the last hour. As facilitator, I stepped in to refocus our attention. Turning to Akeem, I asked whether he would be open to some feedback. He nodded. I made him aware of what was happening. While he held our complete attention when telling us about his mother in a soft and vulnerable voice, he lost our attention the moment he returned to lecturing us about gender. I suggested that he might want to go back to his mother's story.

And he did. Akeem recounted how her absence affected him in his childhood, how much he admired her strength, and how much he loved her but also felt abandoned by her. Without her presence, he said, he had to shoulder too many responsibilities at a young age. "When I came home from school," he said, "I could smell the food from the kitchens of our neighboring houses. But not from my home. Those smells, I remember them. I wished they would have come from my mother's kitchen, but they didn't."

"Akeem," I said, "can you return to your pose in the sculpture, with your half-open hands in front of your chest?" He did. Standing in front of him, I waved with my hands through the air as if pushing imaginary smells of cooking through the space between his hands toward his nose. "You can smell it, but you can't have it," I said. He nodded, with an utterly distraught expression. I asked whether he could return to his story and tell us what it was like for him, back then. He couldn't. Akeem froze.

There are a number of options to choose from when a person freezes in a situation like this. When a person is overwhelmed—perhaps by painful memories, perhaps by conflicting emotions—a kind of mental and emotional paralysis sets in. One of the techniques that can help in these moments is *amplification or doubling. It can help a person to reconnect to his or her feelings. When I asked for assistance, Salem, also a Palestinian man, volunteered. Salem was placed behind Akeem, touching and supporting Akeem's shoulders. I counseled Salem to close his eyes, connect to Akeem, and when ready to give words ("amplify") to what Akeem might feel but couldn't articulate. After a few moments of silence, Salem spoke softly: "I miss my mom. I wish she could be with me. I wish she would cook meals for me. I am proud of her, but I did not always understand her choices."

Silence. When Salem's amplifying voice stopped, no one talked. Akeem remained standing stiff, still frozen, with his hands in front of his chest. We all remained silent for quite some time. No words were spoken, but the room was filled with resonances of loss, pain, and regrets.

Akeem eventually relaxed his hands and sat down. After the group offered him some gentle feedback, he found his voice again. "I am amazed," he said. "Salem gave words to exactly what I felt." And then he shared one more story. Years later, after his mother had been released from prison and grown older, Akeem's brother died. When this happened, his mother gave up her political struggle. She never got over her son's death, and she passed away within two years. She stopped connecting to the world and stopped connecting to Akeem, her other son. "I begged her," Akeem said, "to notice me by sending signals to her. I wanted her to recognize me, but my signals remained unanswered."


## TRUST

The sense of loss and sadness emanating from Akeem's story can be easily grasped. Surprising, perhaps, might be the way this story unfolded in the context of Palestinian-Israeli peace activists, a group that had started in the morning with a rather acrimonious debate about gender but moved toward an adult man recalling an early childhood experience. This wasn't the end of the group's debate about gender dynamics (it accompanied us through the remaining days), but it shifted the group's understanding of how to deal with the "unspoken" and to rethink habitual communication patterns. We could have easily remained on the level of wrangling over the right attitudes toward women, staking out our positions on benign paternalism versus feminism or dissecting colonial traces that surfaced in assumptions about Arab masculinity uttered by a few Israeli women. These are, no doubt, important topics—but for a different setting, because they would not have brought this group of peace activists any closer.

What this example demonstrates is the limit of verbal exchanges in reconciliatory settings when they are delivered in the form of an "I-know-it-better" lecturing mode. It is not that the content of such verbal exchanges is invalid; rather, it is that it is incomplete. It does not allow us to understand where people come from and what pains and disappointments might drive them. Could we have anticipated that Akeem's oft-repeated word "signal," which maddened the group in the beginning, would take us to a place of confounding loss? Within the realm of political gender discourse, Akeem's use of "signaling" seemed profoundly untrue in the sense of echoing an unreconstructed masculinist view on gender relations; but it sounded profoundly true when it came to the tragic neglect that a Palestinian boy experienced when growing up—which, of course, had everything to do with the political situation in the West Bank.[47] In reconciliatory processes, the choice, in other words, is not between "political" and "individualistic" but to develop sensitivity for the motives and motivations that propel or block people who live in and through protracted conflicts.

A reader might object at this point that it was simply a lucky coincidence that, after a long detour, the word "signal" moved us from an unproductive debate over gender to a sorrow-filled childhood memory. Others might suspect that I, as a facilitator, must have had some prior knowledge about Akeem that helped me to gently steer him in this direction. Such skepticism is understandable, but I did not know anything about Akeem's background. If Akeem's story had been the only time that a serendipitous intensification occurred in a reconciliatory process, I would not write about it. But these moments happen, and they happen regularly. When a group witnesses them, it feels like magic. Yet, it has nothing to do with miracles. On the contrary, those moments of intensity and clarity evolve because we pay close attention to intergroup dynamics as they unfold when working with groups in conflict.

I need to make another disclaimer. Akeem's story does not demonstrate that there is a causal connection between his view on gender and his childhood experiences. I am not retelling his story to claim that his mother is the source of his views on gender. This would be a shortsighted claim and bad analysis. I simply do not know enough about Akeem to attempt any psychological interpretation. What this example shows, however, is that we need to pay attention to the emotional baggage that can be hidden in simple words or gestures. The seemingly innocuous word "signal," which was richly textured for Akeem, became, at first, a lightning rod for the group and, later, an entryway into the vulnerable regions of memory that were both deeply personal and acutely political.

Most importantly, Akeem's story demonstrates the need for acknowledgment. On the level of "knowledge," perhaps someone in the group could have persuaded Akeem over time to change or moderate his understanding of gender relations. Perhaps. But what would we have gained? Following an unplanned, circuitous route, we picked up messages that led us to childhood memories. At any time Akeem could have refused to walk down this path. At key moments, however, he must have felt safe enough to continue walking. In the end he received a little of what he craved—acknowledgment. The recognition he could not get from his mother because of choices she made in tough political circumstances he finally received in a small dose from the group. Feeling rejected and scorned earlier in the morning, when he had exposed his views on gender to the group, he was later held and acknowledged when telling us of the delicious smells emanating from kitchens he could not enter as a boy.

When entering reconciliatory processes framed in relational and psychosocial terms, we do not aim for structural change on a grander scale. Such change is important, of course, but it is not the only way of thinking about reconciliation. When scholars of reconciliation speak of restoring "right relations"[48] or of "coming together again, in restored relationship, after a rift from actual or perceived wrongdoing,"[49] it rings true for social reconciliation efforts. Akeem allowed himself to explore in front of the other (in his case, Israelis and women) a primary relationship that unraveled in an unjust situation. He was enabled to do so because we provided enough safety to develop a modicum of trust. Reconciliation, on a fundamental level, is just that, an overcoming of "distrust and animosity"[50] and a "building or rebuilding of trust . . . in the wake of tension and alienation."[51] It is a deep commitment to the flourishing of "the conditions of human relationship"[52] within a conception of justice after trust in human relationships has been gravely violated or destroyed.

## NOTES

1. Quoted from Marlise Simons, "Former Bosnian Leader Begins His Defense at Genocide Trial," *New York Times* (October 17, 2012). http://www.nytimes.com/2012/10/17/world/europe/radovan-karadzic-former-bosnian-leader-begins-his-genocide-defense.html.

2. Paul Mojzes, "The Genocidal Twentieth Century in the Balkans" (2009, 168). He asserts, correctly, that these acts of brutality were not limited to ethnic cleansing perpetrated by Serbian forces but were also practiced by Croat and Bosnian Muslim (para)military units.

3. Stef Craps, *Postcolonial Witnessing* (2013, 125).

4. Jean Harvey, "Moral Solidarity and Empathetic Understanding" (2007).

5. A few of the accused perpetrators at the ICTY expressed remorse, while others steadfastly expressed pride in their actions or rationalized them. See Saira Mohamed, "Of Monsters and Men: Perpetrator Trauma and Mass Atrocity" (2015, esp. 1178–1190), where she cites examples from the ICTY and the South African Truth and Reconciliation Commission.

6. A reference to George Orwell's (1948) dystopian novel *1984*, where citizens become victims of omnipresent government surveillance.

7. On the importance of trust and trust-building in reconciliation and conflict-mediation efforts, see the contributions to Ilai Alon and Daniel Bar-Tal's edited volume, *The Role of Trust in Conflict Resolution* (2016); Roderick Kramer and Peter Carnevale, "Trust and Intergroup Negotiations" (2001); Amal Jamal, "Trust, Ethics, and Intentionality in Conflict Transformation and Reconciliation" (2016); Herbert C. Kelman, "Building Trust among Enemies: The Central Challenge for International Conflict Resolution" (2005); and Trudy Govier and Wilhelm Verwoerd, "Trust and the Problem of National Reconciliation" (2002a). For a broader view on trust and distrust, see Russell Hardin, *Trust and Trustworthiness* (2002).

8. For connection to religion, see, for example, Desmond Tutu, *No Future without Forgiveness* (1999), and Daniel Philpott's section on "religion and reconciliation," in *Just and Unjust Peace* (2012, 97–167). Also Herbert C. Kelman, "Reconciliation from a Social-Psychological Perspective" (2008, 15). Specifically on theology, see Stephen Pope, "The Role of Forgiveness in Reconciliation and Restorative Justice: A Christian Theological Perspective" (2014), and Ralf Wüstenberg's theological analysis of South Africa and Germany's transitions to democracy (*The Political Dimension of Reconciliation* 2009). For international relations, see, for example, Renée Jeffrey, *Confronting Evil in International Relations* (2008), therein specifically Daniel Philpott, "Reconciliation: An Ethic for Responding to Evil in Global Politics" (2008).

9. Sonali Chakravarti, *Singing the Rage* (2014); Thomas Brudholm, *Resentment's Virtue* (2008); Margaret Walker, *Moral Repair* (2006). Also Ian Hall, "Avenging Evil" (2018).

10. See, for example, Daniel Philpott, *The Politics of Past Evil* (2006); Ervin Staub, "Reconciliation after Genocide" (2006); Krondorfer, "Beyond Uniqueness: The Holocaust and Transitional Justice" (2012).

11. Priscilla Hayner, *Unspeakable Truths* (2002); John De Gruchy, *Reconciliation: Restoring Justice* (2002); Helena Cobban, *Amnesty after Atrocity?* (2007); Robert Rotberg and Dennis Thompson, *Truth v. Justice: The Morality of Truth Commissions* (2000).

12. The question of forgiving the unforgivable has been framed by people like Hannah Arendt, *The Human Condition* (1989); Jacques Derrida, "To Forgive: The Unforgivable and the Imprescriptible" (2001); and Vladimir Jankélévitch, *Forgiveness* (2005). See also Trudy Govier's chapter on "Forgiveness and Reconciliation," in *Forgiveness and Revenge* (2002); Yehudith Auerbach, "The Role of Forgiveness in Reconciliation" (2004); and Hent de Vries and Nils Schott's edited volume *Love and Forgiveness for a More Just World* (2015). For an application of forgiveness to a particular conflict, see the edited volume by Graham Spencer, *Forgiving and Remembering in Northern Ireland: Approaches to Conflict Resolution* (2011). On political and personal transformation, see Desmond Tutu, *No Future without Forgiveness* (1999), and Martha Minow, *Between Vengeance and Forgiveness* (1998).

13. "Hand in hand with macrolevel interventions must be the development for grassroots programs that facilitate interpersonal interactions," write Jodi Halpern and Harvey Weinstein in "Rehumanizing the Other" (2004, 582). Halpern and Weinstein focus particularly on interviews and case studies from Croatia and Bosnia and Herzegovina. For differences between macro- and microlevels, compare Wilhelm Verwoerd and Alistair Little's grassroots work with combat veterans in Northern Ireland and South Africa ("Beyond a Dilemma of Apology" 2018) with Heleen Touquet and Ana Milošević's macrolevel critique of reconciliation imposed by the European Union on former Yugoslavia ("When Reconciliation Becomes the R-Word" 2018). For other case studies in countries like Zimbabwe, Rwanda, Ghana, or Cambodia, see Mohammed Abu-Nimer, *Reconciliation, Justice, and Coexistence* (2001a), and Krondorfer, *Reconciliation in Global Context* (2018). Among the many examples of grassroots efforts, I like to mention the little-known history hike about the Armenian genocide, described by Eugene Sensenig-Dabbous, "The Musa Dagh History Hike" (2016).

14. See the following select literature: on individual healing transformation, see Marshall Rosenberg, *Getting Past the Pain between Us: Healing and Reconciliation without Compromise* (2005), and Peter Levine, *Trauma and Memory: A Practical Guide for Understanding and Working with Traumatic Memory* (2015); on nation-building, Ruti Teitel, "Transitional Justice Genealogy" (2003), and Janet Keeping, "National Reconciliation in Russia" (2003); on philosophical inquiry, Trudy Govier, *Forgiveness and Revenge* (2002); on restorative justice, Elizabeth Kiss, "Moral Ambition within and beyond Political Constraint: Reflections on Restorative Justice" (2000), and Tom Keating, "What Can Others Do? Foreign Governments and the Politics of Peacebuilding" (2003).

15. See, for example, the seven conditions that Armin Wildfeuer deems necessary for a process of reconciliation during or after a conflict—a process that is "interminably fragile" and yet a "condition for justice" ("Justice and Reconciliation" 2011, 123, 129).

16. For thinking about reconciliation as a process rather than an end goal, see Herbert Kelman, "Reconciliation from a Social-Psychological Perspective" (2008).

17. For former Yugoslavia, see, for example, Dinka Corkalo et al., "Neighbors Again? Intercommunal Relations after Ethnic Cleansing" (2004); for Rwanda, Jean Hatzfeld, *The Antelope's Strategy: Living in Rwanda after the Genocide* (2009). In the context of South Africa, Pumla Gobodo-Madikizela writes in *A Human Being Died That Night* that the question of how to "transform human relationships" in societies "marked by violent conflict" is of utmost urgency when victims and perpetrators

continue "to live as neighbors" with each other (2004, 15); for a similar argument, see Saira Mohamed, *Of Monsters and Men* (2015, 1165).

18. On Bosnia and Herzegovina, see Heleen Touquet and Ana Milošević, "When Reconciliation Becomes the R-Word" (2018); on South Africa, see Antje Krog, *Country of My Skull: Guilt, Sorrow, and the Limits of Forgiveness in the New South Africa* (1998); Richard Wilson, *The Politics of Truth and Reconciliation in South Africa: Legitimizing the Post-Apartheid State* (2001); and Sonali Chakravarti's chapter "Confronting Anger: Where the South African TRC Fell Short" in *Singing the Rage* (2014, 57–78); on Palestine-Israel, see the literature referenced in Chapter 5.

19. The term "projective identification" is usually not applied to a concept (like reconciliation) but to human interaction. It was introduced by psychoanalyst Melanie Klein to describe how the unwelcome, bad parts of the self are unconsciously forced onto another person. Klein's analysis focused on mother-child relations, though she also intimated its larger usefulness for humanity. See Melanie Klein, *Love, Guilt, and Reparation and Other Works, 1921–1945* (1975); see also Orna Ophir, "Looking Evil in the Eye/I" (2015), and Albert Mason, "Beyond Right and Wrong" (2015). The intensity of projective identification differs from simple forms of projection in that the former develops mechanisms by which the other person will be coerced into believing the falseness of the assumptions made about him or her.

20. "Empty speech" can be described as a way of filling a conversational space with words divorced from their affective content. It could be a defense against the emergence of difficult emotions. Gabriele Schwab, who grew up in Germany in the immediate aftermath of World War II, remembers how her parents' stories left her confused as a child, "as if the words themselves were emptied of the very feelings [they] invoked." The "false emotional ring" that accompanies abstract and detached empty speech, Schwab states, is a symptom of "haunted language" (*Haunting Legacies* 2010, 43, 54).

21. See Krondorfer, *Remembrance and Reconciliation* (1995). In later writings, I have suggested the replacement of the broad term "third generation"—especially for postwar German generations—with a more differentiated model of "generational cohorts" ("Nationalsozialismus und Holocaust" 2006).

22. The term "secondary witness" has been primarily used in the literature to discuss the effects of Holocaust memory on those born after the Holocaust. See Dominick LaCapra, *History and Memory* (1998, 40–42, 135–136). For a detailed discussion of "witnessing," see Chapter 10.

23. For a positive assessment of vicarious identifications, especially related to guilt and responsibility inherited in perpetrator societies, see Arne Johan Vetlesen, *Evil and Human Agency* (2005); for a more critical view, especially as regards "vicarious experience" and "surrogated victimage," see Dominick LaCapra, *Writing History, Writing Trauma* (2001, 40–41). See also Froma Zeitlin, "The Vicarious Witness" (1998). Vicarious identification is further explored in Chapter 4.

24. In *Writing History, Writing Trauma* (2001), La Capra distinguishes between "acting out," where "tenses implode . . . as if one were back in the past reliving" and "working through" as an "articulatory practice" where one "distinguishes between past and present" (21–22).

25. See Catherine Cornille, "Interreligious Hospitality and Its Limits" (2001). "Food is a blessing, one that bears social responsibility," writes Frank Clooney about hospitality in the Hindu tradition ("Food, the Guest and the *Taittiriya Upanishad*" 2001, 140).

26. On the issue of disgust as a political emotion in cross-cultural encounters, see Sara Ahmed, *The Cultural Politics of Emotion*, especially the chapter on "The Performativity of Disgust" (2004, 82–100). "The fear of contamination," Ahmed writes, "that provokes the nausea of disgust reaction hence makes food the very 'stuff' of disgust" (83).

27. To avoid any misunderstanding: it is unlikely that the Jewish family told this young woman to act impolitely and rudely toward Germans. Yet, it is quite conceiv-

able that messages of mistrust and subdued anger were verbally or nonverbally transmitted in the family.

28. My father was born in 1927 in the Sudetenland, the part of the Czech Republic that had a strong German population. In the summer of 1946, he and his mother were expelled by the postwar Czech government. He made a new home for himself in West Germany, a region under the control of the American Allied forces. My mother, born in 1928, grew up in Königsberg in East Prussia, today Kaliningrad in Russia. In January 1945, at age seventeen, she fled by herself from the advancing Soviet army and had to make her way across war-torn Europe to a region in West Germany, where she met my father.

29. Valerie Rosoux, "Reconciliation as a Peace-Building Process" (2008, 544–545; emphasis in original). "Social reconciliation" in the context of conflict resolution overlaps with social-psychological approaches; see the work of Herbert C. Kelman, "Reconciliation as Identity Change: Social-Psychological Perspective" (2004), and "Reconciliation from a Social-Psychological Perspective" (2008).

30. Ananthi Al Ramiah and Miles Hewstone, "Intergroup Contact as a Tool of Reducing, Resolving, and Preventing Conflict" (2013, 535).

31. Stephen Pope, "The Role of Forgiveness in Reconciliation and Restorative Justice" (2014, 179).

32. Pope, "The Role of Forgiveness" (2014, 179). Also John De Gruchy, *Reconciliation* (2002, 26–27); John Paul Lederach, *Building Peace: Sustainable Reconciliation in Divided Societies* (1997), and ibid., *The Moral Imagination: The Art and Soul of Building Peace* (2005).

33. Helena Cobban, *Amnesty after Atrocity* (2007); Priscilla Hayner, *Unspeakable Truths* (2002); Robert Rotberg and Dennis Thompson, *Truth v. Justice* (2000).

34. Michael Rothberg, *Multidirectional Memory* (2009, 14). Rothberg is a professor of English and comparative literature and holds the Samuel Goetz Chair in Holocaust Studies at the University of California.

35. Generally speaking, around the time of the collapse of the Soviet Union in the 1980s, which was "a period of accelerated democratization and political fragmentation," transitional justice shifted from international trials of retributive justice to forums of political reconciliation and restorative justice "associated with nation-building" (Ruti Teitel, "Transitional Justice Genealogy" 2003, 71). Theologian Ralf Wüstenberg, who echoes this perspective in his comparative analysis of post-apartheid South Africa and post-1989 Germany, writes: "To overcome the division of the past, political decision making prioritized nation-building" (*Die Politische Dimension der Versöhnung* 2003, 139; also *The Political Dimension of Reconciliation* 2009). For a positive ethical assessment of political reconciliation, see Daniel Philpott, *Just and Unjust Peace: An Ethic of Political Reconciliation* (2012).

36. See Nicholas Tavuchis, *Mea Culpa* (1991); Trudy Govier and Wilhelm Verwoerd, "The Promise and Pitfalls of Apology" (2002b); and Raymond Cohen, "Apology and Reconciliation in International Relations" (2004).

37. To name but one exemplary case: the widely praised South African Truth and Reconciliation Commission has also come under intense scrutiny for its alleged focus on forgiveness, amnesty, and incomplete truth-finding. See note 18 above. For a response to such criticism, see Wilhelm Verwoerd, "Toward a Response to Criticism of the South African Truth and Reconciliation Commission" (2003).

38. Julia Chaitin, *Peace-Building in Israel and Palestine* (2011, 55–75); Dan Bar-On, *Bridging the Gap* (2002); and Bar-On and Fatma Kassem, "Storytelling as a Way to Work Through Intractable Conflicts" (2004).

39. Bar-On and Kassem, "Storytelling" (2004, 292).

40. Those who have observed or participated in Israeli-Palestinian conversations— whether public or semiprivate—can attest to the recurring battles over the correct understanding of Zionism. Bashir Bashir and Amos Goldberg summarize it thus: "The vast majority of Israeli Jews generally perceive the Holocaust as a catastrophe that justifies their Zionist position favouring a Jewish nation-state on the land of Israel/

Palestine. . . . The majority of Palestinians, for their part, perceive Zionism as a European colonial movement that emerged as one of the many responses to the 'Jewish problem,' itself a European problem exacerbated by the Holocaust. . . . Confronting Zionism is regarded by many Palestinians as a legitimate, even necessary and justifiable form of anticolonial resistance" ("Deliberating the Holocaust and the Nakba" 2014, 81). No attempt will be made here to list select titles from the immense literature on Zionism. Instead, I direct the reader to Robert Eisen's *The Peace and Violence of Judaism: From the Bible to Modern Zionism* (2011); in his extensive chapter on Zionism, Eisen presents two different views to further the discussion: first, Zionism as a movement and ideology that "spawned aggressive violence by Jews" (145), especially against its Arab neighbors but also Gentiles in general; second, as a less violent movement and ideology that was more defined by modern nationalism than religious roots in Judaism. Since Eisen himself has participated in Jewish-Arab dialogue groups, this chapter might be helpful.

41. In 1917, the British government, after it gained control in World War I over Palestine (formerly part of the Ottoman Empire), issued the Balfour Declaration in which it announced its support for the establishment of a "national home for the Jewish people" in Palestine. The incident I am recalling here happened at a workshop in the summer of 2017. The young man's persistence was probably spurred by the hundredth anniversary of the Balfour Declaration, which was festively commemorated in Israel that summer but recalled with distress among Palestinians.

42. Sue Grand, *The Reproduction of Evil* (2000, 41).

43. Daniel Philpott, "Reconciliation" (2008, 128–131); Priscilla Hayner, *Unspeakable Truths* (2002, 27); Margaret Walker, *Moral Repair* (2006, 6). See also Trudy Govier, "What Is Acknowledgement and Why Is It Important?" (2003).

44. For a description of these steps, see "topic selection" in Chapter 2 and the glossary.

45. I used "gestalt" here in a more general sense of referring to a unified whole or an organized configuration that is more than just a summation of its different components.

46. Human dignity is important in general but has special value for men in Islam. In an article on the clash of emotions in Middle East politics, Khaleed Fattah and K. M. Fierke write: "If negative emotions and betrayal relate to loss of value, a loss of trust, and loss of agency, then it follows logically that the desired end is to restore that which has been lost, that is, dignity" ("A Clash of Emotions: The Politics of Humiliation and Political Violence in the Middle East" 2009, 85). The root of the word *karamah* (dignity) is derived in Islam from *karam* (generosity), which determines a person's worthiness and hence is highly charged with emotions. According to Mohammad Hashim Kamali, dignity is also related to compassion: if the oppressed are not acknowledged, dignity is absent (*The Dignity of Man: An Islamic Perspective* 2002, 77).

47. For the experiences of Palestinian women in the political context of contested Israeli-Palestinian history, see, for example, Rosemary Sayigh, "Women's Nakba Stories: Between Being and Knowing" (2007), and Isabelle Humphries and Laleh Khalili, "Gender and Nakba Memory" (2007).

48. Jennifer Llewellyn and Daniel Philpott, "Restorative Justice and Reconciliation" (2014b, 23).

49. Trudy Govier, *Forgiveness and Revenge* (2002, 141).

50. Krondorfer, *Remembrance and Reconciliation* (1995, 71).

51. Trudy Govier and Wilhelm Verwoerd, "Trust and the Problem of National Reconciliation" (2002a, 185).

52. Llewellyn and Philpott, "Restorative Justice and Reconciliation" (2014b, 22).

# TWO

## Memory

*Making Choices*

As in the case of reconciliation studies, the field of memory studies has exploded since the mid-twentieth century, with groundbreaking works on national, cultural, and collective memory,[1] followed by a host of additional concepts proposed in scholarly publications, such as "communicative memory," "absent memory," "mediated memory," "traumatic memory," "prosthetic memory," "nostalgic memory," "belated memory," "postmemory," "second-generation memory," or "multidirectional memories."[2] In this chapter, memory—like reconciliation in the previous chapter—will serve as a frame that helps us understand and interpret the work with groups in conflict. Insofar as memory plays a crucial role when groups in adversarial relations come together, we will need to address some of the power, pain, and problems related to memories as they surface in reconciliatory processes. Importantly, when I work with groups in conflict, memory is treated with deep sensitivity as regards its emotional content, but it is not put on a pedestal as an untouchable and undisputable truth. Memory is not a monument. It is, rather, malleable and develops its own dynamics within group processes. Though we are intimately linked to memories, we are not enchained to them as passive bodies. We can—within some limits—make choices.

The ability to make choices regarding painful memories (our own or those transmitted generationally) is related to what is known in the psychotherapeutic world as a *working-through, a *Durcharbeiten* in Sigmund Freud's terminology.[3] Originally referring to individual therapy, it has come to be applied to social experiences, especially in light of Holocaust memories and their transmission to subsequent generations.[4] It is a kind of memory work that is part and parcel of working with groups in conflict.

## RECONCILIATION AND MEMORY WORK

Before outlining a better understanding of what I mean by *memory work, I return briefly to the distinction of social and political reconciliation. Since reconciliation is not needed unless wrongdoing has occurred in the past, memory and remembering play a critical role in the processes of social and societal healing. Because the inflicted and received injuries may have been suppressed or otherwise have remained publicly unacknowledged, the act of remembering is as important as it is burdened by unresolved emotions.[5] Depending on the degree and extent of the harm inflicted, we can speak of traumatic memories (in cases of intolerable harms) or injurious memories (in cases of harms that do not lead to psychic disintegration and fragmentation). In either case, activating memories—whether in public settings like truth commissions or in more intimate settings like intergroup dialogue—is emotionally painful. A vital part of the task of acknowledging the harms inflicted and endured is, then, to engage in memory work.

When it comes to memory work in the mode of political reconciliation, the record is checkered at best. Some national truth commissions, for example, restrict themselves to legal frameworks and proceed perfunctorily. They neither offer psychological support services to victims nor do they consider the emotions accompanying injurious and traumatic memories to be relevant for the reconciliatory mechanisms they employ. This can lead to a loss of credibility in the eyes of victims, as in the case of Zimbabwe's Commission of Inquiry. In other cases, like the South African Truth and Reconciliation Commission, mental health assistance has been provided.[6] And yet, "truth commissions," as Priscilla Hayner reminds us, "do not offer long-term therapy; they offer survivors a one-time opportunity to tell their story."[7]

In the case of social reconciliation, memory work—and I would further add the qualifier *emotional* memory work—is a core element in addressing fractured and injured interpersonal and intergroup relations. Space is provided to express anguish. Emotional memory work opens doors to those unforgiven zones of human agony where people have experienced manifestations of human cruelty and grave immorality. Confronted with moral injury and physical trauma, an instinctive reaction might be to recoil from facing it or to leave such labor to the professional intervention of psychiatrists and psychotherapists. Within intergroup settings, however, the task of emotional memory work is not therapeutic healing of individuals; instead, it is geared toward the integration of human agony in the presence of the other.

Mechanisms of political reconciliation might be criticized for neglecting the value of emotions; practices of social reconciliation, on the other hand, might need to be cautioned against giving emotions too much weight. In the latter case, such caution is prudent in order to avoid giving emotive responses *a priori* credibility. It is important to remind ourselves that the power of anguished personal testimony lies in its immediacy, which renders it instinctively persuasive. It has a direct impact on the listener. A personal narrative in intergroup settings might be compelling precisely because it articulates strong emotions. Participants, however, may not be sufficiently alert to how personal memories are shaped by, and actively shape, affective identifications with large-group identities. Thus, personal stories may reproduce rather than repair the injurious memory of a group's social identity.[8] In other words, to face memories productively, we need critical distancing devices that allow us to engage our emotions cognitively as well. This necessary balancing between acknowledgment and judiciousness in reconciliatory process constitutes what elsewhere I referred to as "cultural therapy."[9] As cultural therapy, reconciliatory work in group settings reaches beyond political and legal frameworks (even when those pursue alternative forms of justice)[10] as it also reaches beyond individual therapy (where traumatized clients benefit from direct therapeutic intervention). The practice of memory work in group settings is one in which the psychosocial, psychopolitical, and emotional dimensions are addressed that underlie and feed specific conflicts.[11]

Memory work—as opposed to memory in and of itself—refers to an active process of working through the past. Simply put, we all have memories, but not all of us are willing to engage them critically. Whereas memory itself remains largely uninterrogated, memory work is an "active inquiry into the past," as Jewish studies scholar Nina Fischer proposes.[12] We find a number of different conceptions of memory work in the literature: for example, Iwona Irwin-Zarecka's broad understanding of memory work as "giving order and meaning to the past" (politically, intellectually, or individually), Nina Fischer's definition of it as an "individual's conscious, voluntary, and methodical interrogation of the past" (applied to Jewish second-generation literature), or Annette Kuhn's personalized search of family memories through photographs. There is also James Young's application of this idea to national memorials and memorialization, Barbara Gabriel's study of memory work as a national effort against forgetting, and Gabriele Schwab's study on delayed memory work in societies with violent histories.[13] The spectrum is fairly wide; yet all these different conceptions agree that memory work is a deliberate and active working-through—in contrast to a simple consumption and regurgitation of memories. It is not an acting-out. On the contrary, the "processes of working through," historian and trauma scholar Dominick LaCapra writes, "counteract the force of acting out."[14] In Annette Kuhn's words, "memory work is a practice of unearthing and making public untold stories."[15] It is a practice of wrestling with these stories between people for whom, due to adversarial relations, memories and their embedded messages resonate differently.

Memory in and of itself is not a moral good, and there have been a number of critical voices cautioning us about the potential danger and pitfalls of an overabundance of and overreliance on memory and about an almost fetishized embrace of memory in recent decades. Many of these critical studies touch on three salient points: the virtue assigned to memory in the current memory boom is a modern phenomenon; memory and forgetting are not antidotes but are inextricably linked to each other; memory can serve separatist national mythologies that freeze people into hostile relations, though it can also give voice to the voiceless when governments want to cover up grave injustices.[16] Such criticism is useful, and active memory work can integrate it when facilitating groups in conflict. In the best circumstances, memory work is cognizant of the interplay between the traumatic content of memories, the narrative form it takes to get communicated, and the sociopolitical context within which it gets a hearing.[17] "Memory work," Kuhn writes, "makes possible to explore connections between 'public' historical events, structures of feeling, family dramas, relations of class, national identity and gender, and 'personal' memory."[18] Memory work, hence, is a form of both critical and empathetic inquiry.

## I WISH THE SOAP WOULD BURN YOUR HANDS

In an experimental nine-day workshop that included several layers of facilitation, over sixty Israelis, Germans, and Palestinians gathered to explore levels of personal and collective pains, past and present. The multifariously organized workshop was divided into a student group led by a team of mentors, an adult group (including additional counselors) led by me, and combined large-group meetings run alternately by different facilitators. On the morning of the fifth day, about midway through the workshop, Yigal, one of the Israeli students, caused irritation in the larger group when it was his turn to speak. Every morning we started with a *reflection circle for the whole group before we would separate into the student and adult units. In these circles, each of us had a chance to briefly share a thought, insight, dream, or feeling. Whatever was shared was not up for discussion or questioning. We just listened, no matter what it might trigger in us.

When it was Yigal's turn, he said: "In my family, when we gather for a Jewish holiday, my grandmother passes a bar of soap around the table." Yigal explained, in a voice both somber and indignant, that in his family of Holocaust survivors everyone had to hold the soap in his or her hands, then pass it on to the next person. The soap, his grandmother said, was made of the human remains and bones of people murdered in the Nazi concentration camps. It was supposed to remind them of the trauma and continuous threat that Jewish people endure.[19]

As if this recollection was not chilling enough, Yigal, after a moment of hesitation, added: "I wish Germans would pick up the soap and it would burn their hands."[20]

Since Yigal disclosed this memory during the morning circle of reflection, no one was allowed to respond. Simply having to listen to it intensified the discomfort that many people—and especially German participants—felt at that moment. It was a story of compounded emotions and multiple memory layers. Yigal had shared a personal memory of an intimate family setting in which the collective memory of the Holocaust assumed a ritualized form of remembrance. He had made himself vulnerable by opening a window into the privacy of his family's home, exposing a discomforting domestic ceremony to a large, heterogeneous group. Yigal was also distressed, a distress caused perhaps as much by the anguish of growing up in a family of Holocaust survivors as in his audacity of revealing this private vignette to a group of Germans and Palestinians. Yigal was also angry. On a less-than-conscious level, he might have acted out an aggressive impulse against people who, representatively, stood for a past trauma (Germans) and a current menace (Arabs).

The fact that Yigal shared this story does not yet constitute what I call memory work. Perhaps it is at this juncture that my approach differs from those who emphasize that the unearthing and recovery of untold stories in the context of family secrets or a traumatic past already *is* memory work. The emergence of such stories and the courage to tell them in mixed-group settings is a necessary initial step, but it is merely the beginning of a working-through process. For a fragile and fraught story like Yigal's to emerge, some trust must have already been established in a group. It is no coincidence that the story was not told early on but midway through the workshop. Even then, it took courage. Yigal elicited immediate sympathy, with people feeling bad for the burden of the Holocaust passed on in his family. Yet he also confronted the group with a grim desire: "I wish Germans would pick up the soap and it would burn their hands."

This is the moment when emotional memory work begins. We could, hypothetically, imagine a number of reactions and outcomes to Yigal's story. Someone could have responded instantaneously, perhaps angrily or defensively, thus breaking the "listening-only" directive for the morning circle. Or someone from the leadership team could have taken Yigal aside after the session and chided him for obstructing the spirit of peace. The larger group could have ignored Yigal's memory for fear of its explosive potential. It is also conceivable that the memory could have triggered counteraggression acted out by the other participants by shunning Yigal for the remaining days. Or some Israelis could have flocked around him privately without backing him up publicly. Needless to say, I would consider any of the above scenarios unproductive. They would have ignored the resurfacing of a potentially volatile memory. The haunting quality of this family's ritual as well as the *ressentiment*[21] expressed in Yigal's harsh wish would have remained suppressed for the sake of collective harmony.

After the morning circle, the large group divided into its subunits. Yigal stayed with the student group, and I continued working with the multiage adult group. What I summarize below happened, hence, without Yigal being present. Because his recalled memory resonated with many people due to identifying with their respective historical burdens, it took on a life of its own.

Germans, Israelis, and Palestinians had shared a number of significant personal insights during the morning's reflection circle. There was no guarantee that Yigal's input would be picked up by the group of adults and counselors I was facilitating—although, when it was picked up, I was not surprised. In a first round of reactions to the morning session, the overall tone among the adults was cautious and polite. Several people mentioned that it would be better to stop being strategic and tactful and that we shouldn't be afraid of bringing up uncomfortable topics. But these sentiments were voiced only in the abstract, without anyone willing to take a risk. Two Israeli participants stated that they were not yet "feeling" the presence of the German participants. The Germans, they said, come across as guarded, and they keep the dark side of their legacy at bay. Another Israeli requested he not be called a "Jew" but an "Israeli." There were subdued tensions, but this is as far as it went.

To move deeper, we created a *witnessing circle—a spatial constellation in which select members of a social group enter into a conversation while other participants become attentive listeners (the so-called witnesses). In a trilateral meeting, like this workshop, such witnessing could be a circle of people listening in to a conversation between Israelis and Palestinians or between Palestinians and Germans; this group chose to start with a German-Israeli conversation.

What topic would they address? To determine this, we conducted a simple exercise (*topic selection). Each of the German and Israeli participants in the inner circle received a large index card, and everyone was asked to write down one (and only one!) topic that seemed most urgent at that moment.[22] To preserve anonymity, each card was put face-down on the floor, shuffled, and then spread across the floor, face-up. Among the suggested topics, we read: "chosen people syndrome," "how to be authentic around each other," "antisemitism," "the horror," and also "the soap should burn your hands." To select among those topics, everyone had to walk around the index cards on the floor and, when ready, step on a card of their choice. Several people could, of course, step on the same card. Any card with only a few votes was removed. People whose card of choice had been taken away joined one of the remaining groups. When this is repeated three or four times, a clear majority for a particular topic card is usually found in less than ten minutes. It is a simple and time-efficient way of making the group responsible for its choices. The index card selected read, "The soap should burn your hands."

Once the German and Israeli interlocutors were seated, facing each other and with the listening witnesses sitting behind them, it was the Germans who began to speak about the "soap." Someone wondered why Jewish Israelis still befriend Germans. Someone else mentioned that the Holocaust was such a major event that it is hard to speak about it without adopting a submissive attitude. Would young Germans, another German wondered, have to shoulder the burden of making things OK again? A few indicated that their families, one way or another, were connected to the Holocaust and the war. Overall—as a note-taker recorded in her report—the Germans spoke very tactfully but somehow seemed blocked.

The Israeli group, after initially approaching the soap topic in similar cautious ways, addressed the Germans more deliberately. "In some circles in Israel, the Holocaust is not very deep. It is still unfinished business, and it can never be 'unfinished.' People need to stop tiptoeing around it." Another person chimed in: "Not all Israelis have a grandmother or grandfather who survived the Holocaust, and though everyone knows the history, it is not necessarily a big issue." "You know," someone else added, "not everyone is a soap-maker. We don't need everyone to get hurt over memory. I appreciate that Germans take responsibility and come over here to help"—to which another Israeli replied: "Germans are tough; they follow rules. There is a connection between the Holocaust and German culture."

Then it was the Germans' turn again. Because there is a deep shame about the Holocaust in Germany, someone said, we have a need to come to this seminar in Israel. "When we arrived here, the Palestinians welcomed us warmly, but there always seems to be this 'glass' separating us from you. This is especially true for left-wing Israelis. Right-wing Israelis at least say exactly what they think." Someone else changed the conversation: young Germans would be happy to give up their national identity because they see evil in German national feelings. A German man in his sixties wondered how he could take on more responsibility: "I am not a member of the soap-making generation," he said, "but it is imprinted in our national heritage. Still, I refuse to crawl with a burden on my back. I want to stand strong."

As the exchange thickened, an Israeli challenged the German dialogue partners directly. The soap, he said, is like the last resort, a radical image of what the Holocaust means to Israelis. "We want to put it behind us and move forward, but we cannot, and so we move forward as best as we can. I don't think Germans understand how we feel about it. Yes, we need to see the soap burning in your [German] hands as it is burning in ours." For another Israeli, a memory surfaced: "I have tried to write about the Holocaust," she recounted, "but where do you start when people are treated like objects? This is what the soap symbolizes. I remember an Israeli musician who told me that his father, when still living in Greece, was told, 'It is too bad the Nazis did not make soap out of you.' I want to know whether the Germans know these things."

Back to the German group. A man, responding to the last statement, replied that he wasn't sure what to do. After the war, he said, he lived as a child in the former concentration camp of Dachau, which had become a camp for displaced persons.[23] "As a child," the German man said, "I was constantly confronted with victims and perpetrators. My father was involved in transports. I want to ask him, 'Father, was the soap made of . . . ?'"

At this point, I need to interrupt the description for some interpretative observations about what had transpired so far. It did not take much to notice that, initially, the Israelis and Germans talked past each other. Over time, however, they began to respond more thickly to each other. It is quite important for groups in conflict to move from making general statements to engaging each other with *direct statements. It makes a difference, for example, if Germans lament generally the immensity of the Holocaust or if they address their discomfort when meeting Israelis today ("there seems to be this 'glass' separating us"). This is a move in the right direction, but it is still not as direct as it could be. A direct statement, for example, is to stop talking about Israelis in general and, instead, respond to a particular person. I imagine the following possibility: "Chava, when we first met, you kept me at arm's length. I thought to myself, 'Here is yet another typical Israeli, suspicious only because I happen to be German.' Now I wonder whether Yigal's soap has something to do with it. I almost don't dare to ask: does it?" Reversely, an Israeli would not say, "I want to know whether the Germans know these things" but might ask: "Gerd, you said that you are not a member of the soap-making generation. I don't fully understand what this means to you, or why you said it. Are you afraid we see you as a soap-maker?"

In this witnessing circle, we did not get to that level of directness. What was shared was still largely within a safe zone. If there were any raw emotions, they remained controlled and did not break through the surface. As a consequence, a few clues for deepening the conversation were missed. For example, no one asked the German man to clarify what he meant by living as a child in Dachau's "displaced persons" camp or by him mentioning that his father had been involved in "transports." His elisions and allusions begged for completion and rectification: it probably was not a DP camp but the temporary refugee camp for German expellees that the Bavarian government opened in Dachau in 1948; but no one asked.[24] Another example would be the Israeli woman who recounted the story of a musician whose father had been accosted in Greece ("too bad the Nazis did not make soap out of you") and then wondered whether "the Germans know these things." Her recollection was less about sharing information than seeking acknowledgment of the hatred directed at Jews. It was not so much meant to add to the group's knowledge about antisemitism but felt like a plea for someone to take personal responsibility. Because the comments were addressed to "the" Germans in general, no individual German felt addressed.

Despite these shortcomings, the group inched closer together. Israelis and Germans started to use a common vocabulary and relied on a shared reference system, which imperceptibly bonded them. Outside this group situation, the shared language that evolved would have made little sense. In the conversation summarized above, this is best exemplified by the terms "soap-maker" and "soap-making"—not exactly words that come up in regular conversation. "Not everyone is a soap-maker," an Israeli said. "I am not a member of the soap-making generation," a German later stated. "Too bad the Nazis did not make soap out of you," an Israeli woman recalled an antisemitic insult. And a German man imagined confronting his father with a question that trailed off, "Father, was the soap made of . . . ?"

How deeply this shared new language resonated among the participants is difficult to convey to people who were not present. Analytically, though, we can note that such shared language is essential. Dan Bar-On and Fatma Kassem, who have worked with groups in protracted conflicts, observed that during a "joint working-through process, the group developed a common emotional and conceptual language that differed from the separate languages" characteristically employed by their respective communities.[25] In our case, soap and soap-maker became symbolically charged and overdetermined words that created a reference system, bonding the participants in ways that probably went unnoticed by them.

Let us return to the process itself. As part of a witnessing circle, the witnesses—those who were not part of the conversation itself but active listeners—eventually had a chance to share their observations. The Palestinian witnesses felt that the Germans remained guarded. Germans, they said, feel guilty and burdened, and now they wish to prevent evil everywhere. But have they not already done enough to make up for it? Regarding the Israelis, the Palestinians were surprised how friendly they were toward the Germans.

Among the Germans who were witnessing the conversation, a few expressed feelings of guilt. "My father was very antisemitic," someone confessed. "My family could not get over it, and so it is up to the younger generation to overcome this legacy." Another German said that the soap ought to burn: "I feel that Yigal wants it to burn in my hands. The image is so strong and truthful. It is like, forever, a knife in my heart."

The Israeli witnesses felt unease about much of the conversation, especially regarding their fellow Israelis, who, they thought, were too judgmental. One observer felt that it was hard for Israelis to have a normal life and that both sides needed to learn how to live with the Holocaust. Another Israeli witness disagreed: "The knife may not be in my heart," she said, "but it is always over my head, ready to slice my throat."

We took a short break. Afterward, we moved to a final round. A bar of soap, taken from one of the bathrooms in the guesthouse, was placed on the floor in the center of the group. Yigal's memory was now manifestly present, a material object to touch. Yigal's morning input had set into motion an intensifying process of reflection, moving from cautious remarks to direct declarations, from testimonial recollections to testy disapprovals. Now, in the final round, the memory was in our midst in the form of a tangible presence. If people wanted to touch it and hold the bar of soap in their hands, they could.

Only two German men of the generation born during World War II took up the challenge. The first man stepped into the circle, picked up the soap, closed his eyes, took a deep breath, and said: "When my father returned from the war, he attempted to burn himself. He survived his suicide attempt, and I am grateful for it." He then passed the soap to another German of his generation. Cupping it in his hands, it was his turn to speak: "I want to throw the soap away. My father . . . my father said after the war that the gas chambers were not enough—I am so ashamed." Silently, he slipped the soap off his hands, back on the floor.

We let "shame" resonate in the space we occupied, and we stayed silent for a while. None of the Israelis picked up the soap to hold in their hands. "It is just a piece of soap," an Israeli said somberly. "And yet it means so much to the Germans, it makes me feel ashamed."

Experiencing shame is deeply distressing and can, when fully felt, be shattering to the self. It is different from guilt insofar as it arises from one's own consciousness of having done something so dishonorable that reintegration into a social community cannot be imagined. Guilt, on the other hand, is tied to feeling responsible for a particular wrongdoing or offense, and it can be redressed through remorse or acts of repentance.[26] I am not claiming that we reached in this witnessing circle a level of shame that was self-shattering—for in common parlance people often do not distinguish between feelings of shame and guilt. But it did get us to a place where the participants owned their feelings, which the "soap" had triggered; they no longer kept Yigal's memory at bay as another person's issue. Breaking through the defensiveness of generalized statements, individual Israelis and Germans allowed their own memories to emerge and to respond to each other. Their assumptions about "the" Germans or "the" Israelis became unsettled—enough so that they could empathetically respond to each other's feelings of shame. As an Israeli said at the end: "It means so much to the Germans, it makes me feel ashamed."

Coda: I have had opportunities to meet Yigal over the years at other occasions. His own professional and personal life has taken an unexpected turn; he now moves between Israel and Germany and he lives in both countries. At some point, perhaps four years after he had shared the story about the soap in the morning circle, he took me aside and told me that the passing of the soap at family gatherings happened only once. "When I told this story in the morning circle," he admitted, "it might have come across as if it were a recurring event. But it wasn't."

As always, I appreciate honesty. His belated admission does not change the soul-searching that his memory triggered among the German and Israeli participants at that workshop. Yigal's recollection had made people realize the complexity of the emotional weight of memory when addressing a traumatic history in the presence of descendants of both victim communities and perpetrator societies. Nor do I think that Yigal was intentionally deceiving the group on that day. His memory was real, chilling even if it happened only once. If remembering is "never solely reporting on the past so much as to establish one's relationship toward it," as anthropologist Michael Lambek argues,[27] then Yigal's retelling established this relationship, not only for himself but vicariously for descendants of Holocaust survivors in Israeli society. Belatedly admitting an inaccuracy did not take away from the message Yigal wanted to convey: that some of the pain of his community needed to be felt by members of the community who had caused the pain.

The emotional memory work that ensued—incomplete as all memory might be[28]—helped Israelis and Germans in each other's presence to work through aspects of a past that has continued to divide them. This is what unsettling empathy entails: to be confronted with the unexpected, with something that challenges how a social community has one-sidedly come to terms with the past—yet only on and in their own terms while forgetting to take into consideration the other side. Within the context of unsettling empathy, emotional memory work does not limit itself to unearthing memories in one's own family and community but includes doing so together in the presence of others and their memories. Such reciprocity transcends boundaries of communal belonging. Not only do we choose what memories we divulge; we also choose to render our memories vulnerable to the judgment of others—who, we hope, will not react contemptuously but respond supportively.

## POST-SHOAH JEWISH GENERATIONS

Yigal's recounting of a family event was not the kind of memory that represented an objective, impersonal truth but a memory that was "intersubjective and dialogical" as it unfolded through an act of remembering.[29] Even though it was a personal recollection, it wasn't Yigal's memory alone—for it was, at its core, a memory of a collective trauma enacted through a distinctive ritualized gesture. On one level, the act of remembering happened within the protectiveness of a family, and there was no doubt about ownership about this Shoah memory.[30] It belonged to his grandmother and his family and, by extension, to the Jewish community as a whole. When scholars talk about the transmission of traumatic memory from one generation to the next, here we see an example of how the transference had taken on a tangible, embodied quality (the passing of the soap) in the presence of three generations: a Holocaust survivor, the second generation (Yigal's parents), and the third generation (Yigal himself). Eva Hoffman, in her remarkable cultural and psychological meditation on her parents' memory of the Holocaust, writes in *After Such Knowledge*: "The guardianship of the Holocaust is being passed on to us . . . [t]he second generation"[31]—and with the passing of time, we need to add to Hoffman's observation, the third and fourth generations.

Such guardianship cannot be ensured when the circle of remembrance is widened. The act of remembering, in Yigal's case, did not only take place intersubjectively between three generations. It also took place dialogically with people external to the protective frame of familial and generational ownership. By expanding the circle, a generationally transmitted familial memory of the Holocaust, fragile and precious to the Jewish community, had been rendered vulnerable to the views of outsiders: Germans and Palestinians. The guardianship evoked by Hoffman was no longer iron-clad. By moving beyond the familial, Yigal chose to take a step into the unknown. What had been safeguarded by a community sharing a cohesive ethos was now vulnerable to contestation.[32] Yigal thus opened doors to creating new layers of trust between communities.

Most of what has been written about the generational transmission of Holocaust memories could be coded as memory work that happens within one's own community. The therapeutic literature on descendants of Holocaust survivors focuses, understandably, on interfamilial and intersubjective processes; similarly, the quite extensive body of literary and autobiographical works produced by the second and third generation as well as literary criticism of these works stay within intragroup relations.[33] Critical scholarship in the last twenty years, however, has pushed back against limiting our understanding of the workings of memory to what sociologists and social psychologists would call an "in-group."[34] Two influential studies come to mind: Marianne Hirsch's work on postmemory and Michael Rothberg's study on multidirectional memory. In *The Generation of Postmemory*, Hirsch, a literary critic and child of Jewish survivors, writes in her introductory chapter that at "stake is not only a personal/familial/generational sense of ownership and protectiveness, but an evolving ethical and theoretical discussion about the workings of trauma, memory, and intergenerational acts of transfer." Such an ethical inquiry, almost by necessity, cannot stay insular but must account for a

variety of memories. Consequently, Hirsch moves in her book from focusing on postmemory among Jewish generations to integrating "other
massive historical catastrophes."[35] Similarly, though with a different in-
vestigative objective, Michael Rothberg argues that claiming ownership
of memories leads to "competitive memories," and those are antithetical
to thinking of memories as coming "into being through dialogical interactions with others." Rothberg calls for a "multidirectional memory" that
allows for conversations about "multiple traumatic pasts" in the public
sphere. "Memories," he writes, "are not owned by groups—nor are
groups 'owned' by memories."[36]

Rothberg's critique of claiming memory as one's own, or of being
claimed by memory, is helpful in the context of memory work in mixed
groups. It reminds facilitators and participants alike that we have agency
when it comes to memory and that we can make choices regarding acts of
remembering. Rothberg's critique does not take away from the severe
impact memories of traumatic events have on survivors, who often feel
bereft and paralyzed and who, often throughout their life, struggle with
regaining a voice and pulling together a fragmented self. Such hardships
are real—but they are not exclusionary. We will return to these issues in
the chapter on trauma; for now we are concerned with the descendants of
survivors and the transmission of memories to the next generation.

Children growing up in survivor families carry with them the remnants of their parent(s)' trauma, which can seriously affect their ability to
make uninhibited choices. In their families, the Holocaust was a daily
companion, whether incessantly verbalized or silently communicated.
"There are legions of Holocaust survivors who never speak of the scars
cut too deeply," writes Erin Einhorn, a descendant of Polish Jewish survivors. "But there are others . . . who tend to speak of them constantly."[37]
The children got to know intimately the wounded memories in the
homes they were growing up in. Nina Fischer, in her study of second-
generation writings, refers to Helen Epstein's vivid description of her
childhood as an example of the difference of wounding memories and
active memory work.[38] Around the dinner table, Epstein's father, a survivor, would hunch down and swallow his food as quickly as he could. He
would fly into a rage when his children refused to eat or did not eat
enough. The past was present at every meal, even though the father's
starvation during the Holocaust was never explicitly stated to Helen as a
child. Only later does Epstein recognize, in Fischer's interpretation, that
"anything that endangered the health of [her father's] children was a
personal threat." There is a difference, Fischer explains, between the raw
material of Helen's childhood memory and the memory work of an intentional literary text that the adult Epstein engages in, transforming a confounding old memory into a new understanding of family relationships.[39]

In the early 1980s, children of survivors organized themselves in "second generation" self-help groups and in "children of survivors" associations, especially in the United States and Israel. Some worked through
their experiences of growing up in survivor families artistically, intellectually, and scholarly. Marianne Hirsch's concept of postmemory draws
attention to the fact that the memory of survivor parents, which was
based on actual lived experience, was so strong that it became a vivid and
vital part of the memory of the second generation. [40] Hirsch further distinguishes between "familial postmemory," referring to biological descendants of survivors (like Yigal), and "affiliate postmemory," referring to a
generation that grew up within a culturally affiliated milieu and in the
vicinity of survivors without being direct descendants themselves (like
some of the Israelis in the witnessing circle described above). [41] As to the
question of being claimed by memory, it is safe to presume that affiliate
postmemory allows for a wider range of agency and choice than being in
the grasp of familial postmemory.

## MEMORY OBJECTS

One way that familial memories are passed on is through objects that are
either literally or symbolically representative of the past. This happens
far more often than we acknowledge. Most of us have experienced some
version of it when, for example, a close relative dies and a remembrance
object is handed down to the next generation, or when during family
gatherings—including religious holidays—a particular object is placed
on a table or hung up as a special decoration to recall or make present the
past. "Objects as carriers of memory," writes Nina Fischer in her study of
the Jewish second generation, "evoke group history and social identity
across generations as they link back to family members, family history,
and cultural history." [42] Ethnographer Andreas Kuntz, in a chapter titled
"Object-Related Ritualizations," studied the centrality of objects in postwar German families for rendering manifest their war experiences. He
calls them *Erinnerungsobjekte*, *memory objects. In some cases, these objects generate types of conversations at family gatherings that are often
constrained by unspoken taboo zones, while, in other cases, they function
as silent witnesses of a fraught past and smother all further conversation.
Kuntz mentions the case of a "shabby wooden horsey" that a family put
as an ornament on their Christmas tree every year. This horsey was a
silent reminder of the tragic death of the couple's infant daughter in the
immediate aftermath of World War II. It happened when the mother
briefly left the infant unsupervised when visiting her husband in an Allied prison camp for SS members. The wooden horsey ornament thus tied
together memories of personal feelings of guilt (leaving the infant unsupervised) and national guilt (the husband's SS membership). If "silence

is one of the most exhausting forms of remembering," Kuntz writes, then "memory objects" within a ritualized family setting could be called the "most popular form of narrating" among postwar Germans.[43]

Kuntz also mentions the *Fluchtkoffer* as another recurring memory object in German families, the symbolically charged "suitcase" that Germans took along when fleeing the advancing Soviet forces in 1945. His observations are specific to postwar German culture, but the centrality of objects that contain painful, ambiguous, and incommensurable memories applies to other contexts as well. In terms of the function of a memory object, the soap in Yigal's family was not so different from the wooden horsey and the *Fluchtkoffer* in German families, except that in the former case, it played a ritual role in a family of Holocaust survivors and in the latter in a family of Nazi perpetrators.[44] In families of survivors and their descendants, sometimes it can be a surviving photograph or small artifacts that take on a testimonial or numinous quality. Such objects are preserved not for their material value or aesthetic beauty but because they hold intrinsic value to a person or a family. Among Palestinian families who were expelled or fled from their villages during Israel's 1948 War of Independence, a central memory object is the key. These keys are symbolic reminders of their lost homes to which Palestinians would like to return. They are treasured by families and handed down to the next generation.[45] As "numinous objects," these artifacts evoke reverence and awe, loss and hope. Their "mnemonic value" is intangible and psychological, because the stories they tell hold emotional weight for those who own them.[46] Such memory objects might eventually be discarded as they are passed on, or they might find their way into museums or into a politicized public sphere.[47]

Imbued with memories, the passing of these objects to the next generation comes with implicit or explicit obligations. To those to whom they have been passed on, they tell a story without the need for this story to be told: it is the tactility of these objects that holds emotional meaning. Whether it is the soap or the horsey, the *Fluchtkoffer* or the key to a lost home, these objects can be touched. Within a cohesive community, such memory objects have a stabilizing function. They are the containers of horror, grief, loss, and yearnings; and because they "contain" the past (both in the sense of storing it and controlling it), they need not be examined in the affected families. But when we work in mixed, interactive seminars, those containers can be "opened": we can take a closer look at what is inside and loosen the restraint (and taboos) around them.

Memory objects are one of the entryways into the memory work that needs to be done with groups in conflict. As testimonial and numinous objects, they facilitate access to a group's narrative of grief and loss. As material objects, they visualize and spatialize memory. For example, a group can be asked to find the right distance to a memorial object. Physically moving either away from or closer to such an object if placed in a room can reveal the degree to which participants identify with the memory the object represents.

In my facilitation work, I do not overwhelm people with materials but frequently introduce a core symbolic object that either a group member or I bring to a meeting. Working with such an object can be as simple as asking teachers in an interactive seminar on Holocaust education to position themselves physically in relation to an object to indicate their relationship to this history. In one particular workshop in New York, I asked the attending educators to find the right distance for themselves in relation to a portrait of a Holocaust survivor in whose honor the seminar was held.[48] Their spatial relation was meant to indicate their motivation for teaching the Holocaust: the closer they stood to the portrait, the stronger their emotional attachment to the Holocaust; the farther away, the stronger their historical and intellectual interest in teaching it. This exercise visualized differences they had struggled with in the seminar. In a non-threatening way, they recognized a source of their earlier frustrations when circular argumentation about teaching strategies seemed to go nowhere. Now that they could visually see different motivations spaced out in the room, those differences were productively addressed.

The example about this educator seminar is fairly straightforward. Such work, however, can get quickly complicated and thorny when social identities are intimately tied to memory objects and contested by others. The example of the "soap burning hands" gave us a taste of such complexity. Over the course of this book, we will encounter other occasions where a tangible object helped a group to keep their focus and channel or amplify their experiences.

When memory objects become part of the emotional labor in groups, it is important to understand the context within which this takes place. It makes a difference whether we work with memory objects in a homogeneous setting, in which a largely cohesive ethos is shared, or in a heterogeneous group shot through with adversarial relations. In homogeneous settings, working with memory objects seeks to address the silences, secrets, omissions, pains, and delegated obligations contained in these objects.[49] The aim in this scenario is to support group members in the difficult task of mourning but also to challenge their acceptance of certain time-honored, communal assumptions about acts of remembering. In the case of working with memory objects in heterogeneous settings, a prime task is to avoid turning intimate memories into competitive memories, and, instead, to allow multiple acts of remembering to emerge through dialogical interactions.[50]

## POSTWAR GERMAN GENERATIONS

Memories—whether in the form of transmitted stories, silences, emotional messages, or objects—feed the narratives we tell about ourselves. It is important to realize that our family narratives about the past are governed by transindividual patterns and strategies that are contingent on social forces of legitimation. Though true for all family narratives, the legitimation pressures are more prevalent in bystander and perpetrator families. It is to German family history that I will now turn.

The truism that family histories are characterized by silences and selective memories takes on a moral quality when applied to generational patterns of communication within families of bystanders, enablers, beneficiaries, accomplices, and perpetrators. Here the silences and omissions are not innocent but often conceal levels of complicity and culpability. Whereas a certain myth of innocence characterized the official versions of German family history for many decades following World War II, the more recent flood of family biographies written by post-1945 German generations indicates a shift to more awareness of their families' entanglements with Nazism.[51] Still, many members of the postwar generations can only work with fragments when trying to reconstruct an image of parents, grandparents, and extended families during the Nazi regime. Those fragments are rarely value-neutral, and they must be approached with a healthy dose of suspicion. They often hide more than they reveal. Some research also suggests that the grandchildren themselves render the narrative fragments they were told even more "innocent" than they were originally conveyed in families. A study at the turn of the twenty-first century concluded that in Germany, "children and grandchildren . . . use even the most far-flung clues in family stories about the good deeds of their parents and grandparents to invent a version of a past that configures them as good people." In the process of transmission, Nazi party members were changed into people with anti-Nazi attitudes, or bystanders into resistance fighters.[52] This distortion has characterized many reconstructed family histories until the beginning of the twenty-first century and can be found to some degree even today.

The reconstruction of most life stories among nonpersecuted Germans does not start with Hitler's seizure of power in January 1933 but with the last years of the war and the immediate postwar period. Emphasizing those years over the earlier period shifts the focus from complicity to victimhood. Stories about German refugees and expellees, about Allied bombing raids and German prisoners of war in the Soviet Union, and about the hunger and cold experienced in war-ravaged Germany in 1946 move to the foreground of what is remembered. German people thus became the subject of descriptions of suffering—a perspective fostered by German historiography of the 1950s. What remained out of sight were the years prior to 1944.[53]

When German retellings of a family's past begin at the end of the war, Jews and other victims of Nazi ideology disappear from sight. What remains obscured are any contacts that members of one's family may have had with the European Jewish population and other victimized communities. Had they been neighbors or friends? Colleagues or teachers? Did someone in the family watch Jews being deported without intervening on their behalf? Did they actively lend a hand in the persecution? Did they participate as civilians or soldiers in the bloody *Aktionen* in the occupied territories in the east? These are the kind of questions that, for many decades, have not been part of the memory transmitted in German families.[54]

Growing up in Germany, fourteen years after the war ended, I, like others in my postwar generational cohort, have been exposed to similar patterns, not because my parents intentionally wanted to keep secrets but because we partook in an accepted cultural conversation. To understand and resist such discursive practices requires active memory work among postwar generations. What I knew about my father's boyhood, for example, was for many years limited to a few stories about his conflicted identity as a devout Catholic altar boy and a member of the Hitler Youth movement. Because of his continued loyalty to the church, he could not rise in the ranks of the local Hitler Youth. I was also familiar with a few events that occurred toward the end of the war after he had been drafted into the German army at age sixteen, which ended with his eventual imprisonment as a POW by the Czech government. I did not learn about other aspects of his story until I was in my midthirties and already living in the United States. It came about accidentally and only because I had earlier befriended Edward Gastfriend, a Polish Jewish survivor. Born in Sosnowiec, Gastfriend had survived several concentration camps, including Auschwitz, the slave labor camp of Blechhammer in Upper Silesia, Gross-Rosen, and Buchenwald. A conversation with my father in the mid-1990s revealed, unexpectedly, that he had been stationed as a teenage soldier less than three miles away from the Blechhammer camp where Gastfriend had been imprisoned. Both Gastfriend and my father were at this place at the same time for about one year, and both were of the same age. One was behind the fence as a slave laborer while the other manned antiaircraft guns to protect the nearby industrial complex from Allied war planes. The unearthing of this part of my father's past I have described in more detail elsewhere.[55] What is important here is how this coincidental discovery added to and changed a typical postwar narrative to include memories linked to the Shoah.

Unearthing this part of my family history did not yet constitute—as I hope has become clear in this chapter—the moral labor of memory work. But it was a precondition for the choices I would have to make. Should I duly take notice of what I discovered and then shelve it away? Should I let my friend Edward Gastfriend, the survivor, know about my father's military service in Blechhammer? Should I make my father's past public? I eventually told Edward about my dad. I also asked my father to join me on a journey back to places of his past. He promptly said yes, and a few months later, during the summer, the two of us traveled together for several days back to his hometown in the Sudentenland (Czech Republic) and other sites related to his life in the 1940s, including Blechhammer in Poland, the Nazi labor camp previously buried in my family's memory. During our journey, my father did not hold back in remembering the past. He told me anything I wanted to know, and I audiotaped our conversations. For the first time in his recollections, Jews of his former hometown and a Jewish childhood friend emerged. He remembered having seen inmates in striped uniforms being marched to the industrial complex at Blechhammer. When we stopped at Terezin to visit the former ghetto/labor camp, he told me about Jewish survivors lining the streets of Terezin the day after liberation in May 1945, when he retreated from the front as an eighteen-year-old soldier.

I am recounting these personal recollections to emphasize the necessity of active memory work if we want to expand our self-understanding of our place among postwar German generations. As long as I relied on the repeatedly told stories of my father's childhood ambiguity (torn between Hitler Youth and the Catholic Church), I identified as a *postwar* generation. With the newly discovered proximity of a Jewish slave labor camp in my family history, I began to see myself also as a *post-Shoah* generation. The distinction I am drawing here may not be obvious at first. It may even be misleading, as if I were adopting the term "post-Shoah" to claim some sort of victim identification. Quite to the contrary, though, this shift ruptures the reliance on selectively transmitted war memories of nonpersecuted German families; it thereby creates space for incorporating memories of the genocide. The limited cache of war and postwar stories would thus be counteracted, complicated, and augmented by familial ties to the history of genocidal antisemitism. The Shoah would stop being a pursuit of merely historical and intellectual information and, instead, become an intimate wrestling with unwieldy aspects of one's family biography. In contrast to societal evasions, the Shoah thus reclaimed would become part of a personal past—which, of course, it always has been, and frequently in more intimate ways than previously realized by post-1945 German generational cohorts.

I made my choices. Making these choices was a privilege, not a burden. This may sound strange, but the truth is that descendants of families of bystanders, enablers, and perpetrators can live perfectly well without ever having to confront the past. I could have chosen to ignore Blechhammer and let my discovery fall back into oblivion. No one would have made me accountable for such forgetfulness. Having the choice to ignore the Shoah as part of one's personal history and to remain, instead, content with the one-sidedness of postwar storytelling regarding German hardship must be considered a privilege. Children of Jewish survivors have had less choice in this matter. They could not opt out of a Holocaust memory imprinted on them in the many ways we know today from the literature.[56] Descendants of survivors did not have the option of not knowing the Holocaust intimately. Ironically, it is the "privilege" of living in the land of perpetrators where descendants of bystanders, enablers, beneficiaries, accomplices, and war criminals do not have to confront the various levels of culpability in their family histories. This continuing and perhaps maddening inequality between the descendants of different sides is one of the disturbing legacies of the Shoah—and it reminds us of power asymmetries that characterize most groups in conflicts, an asymmetry that memory work also needs to account for.[57] The descendants of beneficiaries and perpetrators can, however, choose to confront their family legacies and thus take on the intergenerationally transmitted obligations that come with the unresolved emotions of a selectively silenced past.[58]

If descendants of nonpersecuted German families continue to understand themselves exclusively as a *postwar generation*, then emotionally charged stories of German anguish during the last war years will dominate personal memory, such as stories of *Flucht und Vertreibung* (flight and expulsion) or the Allied bombing of German cities—the kind of stories that get entombed in memory objects like wooden horsey ornaments or the *Fluchtkoffer* (suitcases used for fleeing from the East). Understanding oneself also as a *post-Shoah* generation calls Germans born after 1945 into the responsibility of facing up to the challenges of a perpetrator history. The moral labor now requires us to critically investigate affective identification with memories transmitted in one's German family and to do so in the presence of members of victim communities. Those who have taken steps in this direction report that they have been able to replace the burden of vague personal guilt feelings with, for example, commitments to explore the ethical and juridical dimensions of genocidal and post-genocidal situations.[59] "However unspeakable the truth appears to be, knowing almost always liberates," observes Gabriele Rosenthal, who researches the psychological effects on children and grandchildren of perpetrators.[60] People committed to integrating difficult knowledge seem better prepared to counter the tendency to objectify victims. Surprisingly, a radical departure from the myth of innocence of one's family history seems to generate more openness toward the testimony of others.

## OUR TWO-HUNDRED-YEAR PRESENT

With these general reflections on postwar German generations, I now turn to an example of German family history in a mixed Jewish-German setting. Utilizing the concept of a "two-hundred-year present," which sociologist and peace researcher Elise Boulding has expounded on many occasions,[61] we will witness some of the gaps that exist in families marked by secrecy and complicity.

When our lives are not interrupted by war, premature death, or genocidal violence, we live in a *two-hundred-year present. This is a presence measured by physical touch. This must surely be impossible, a skeptical reader might quickly object, since our individual life expectancy certainly cannot span two hundred years. The two-hundred-year present by physical touch, however, is a span that reaches from those who have touched us when we were born to those who we will touch before we die. I have been touched by my grandparents, who were born around 1900. With some luck, I may be able to touch the yet-to-be-born children of my daughters, my future grandchildren, who, if they have auspicious lives, may reach into the decade of the 2090s. From the 1900s to 2090s, this is the two-hundred-year present of my life.

Once we become aware of the people we are connected to by physical touch, we may realize that we are not just autonomous, independent beings floating outside of history. History neither begins with us nor does it end with us. Traumatic histories also do not begin with us or end with us. We live in a continuum of relationships, and we do so through our families and through the communities we inhabit and that we bequeath to our children and children's children. Aware of how far we stretch backward and forward, we can recognize the responsibility that comes with a two-hundred-year present: we are called to account for the past as well as to imagine the future.

Those who have touched us may have done so with the love and caring they were bringing to their families. But the touch we have received from the generations before us can also be burdened by the wrongdoings of previous times. Their touch may have marked us with hurt or shame. At times, a touch can be poisonous, and we can spend a lifetime in convalescence. In such cases we have no choice but to find ways to repair the damage done by those who have touched us so that we do not pass on the poison to our children and grandchildren.

Every family, every community, every nation has skeletons in their closets. These hidden bones can be of minor or major social importance, but if left silenced and denied, they will impair future relations. On a smaller scale, a skeleton in the closet can be a child born out of wedlock; it can be the homosexuality of an uncle in the 1950s or the bigotry of a grandmother during the civil rights movement. On a larger scale, we can think of how national histories intersect with individual lives. In the United States, for example, awareness of living in a two-hundred-year present makes slavery not a remote event but reveals a presence to which Americans are very much connected. In Germany, it is the Holocaust that exudes a strong presence in families and communities.[62]

On several occasions, I have been able to introduce the idea of a two-hundred-year present through embodied constellations, where workshop participants create a generational chain of their family histories in the context of intercultural encounters. The mechanics of such an exercise are fairly simple: a participant volunteers to show his or her family history. As protagonist, he or she is asked to stand in the center of a line, representing him- or herself at the current stage of life. The protagonist then invites four additional people, each representing a parent and a grandparent to stand on one side of the protagonist, and a child and grandchild to stand on the other side. A generational chain thus becomes visible as a constellation in space. Whether the protagonist already has children or grandchildren does not really matter: they can be imagined, as we always have to imagine our future.

In mixed groups of Germans and Jews, the constellation of a two-hundred-year present can be very compelling because it conveys tangibly the effects of troubled histories in families belonging to either victimized communities or a perpetrator society. In the example below, I focus on German family history. I will describe one German woman's display of her family's generational chain. As in most cases when Germans reconstruct their family histories, hers also revealed a gap in the intergenerational chain related to World War II and the Holocaust. The disrupted or broken link usually occurs in the transition from the generation that lived through the war and the Holocaust to those born after 1945. This gap is often marked by muddled emotions, turmoil, darkness, silence, and fear.[63]

The particular constellation I will describe below happened in a mixed German-Jewish workshop on memory, with a focus on intergenerational relations.[64] For this one-day workshop in Germany, about twenty participants had signed up, including non-Jewish German university students, children of Holocaust survivors living in Germany, people born in the final years of the war and the 1950s, and a few people who had been adults during the 1940s, including a Holocaust survivor. Midway through the workshop, we approached the topic of German family history, a delicate issue in heterogeneous groups of Germans and Jews. It is not easy for Germans in the presence of Jews to open a window into their family that might reveal a perpetrator perspective and mentality; it is also not easy for Jews to witness their German peers struggling with the ambiguities of loyalty and love in families touched by moral failure and criminal complicity.[65]

## *FRAUENGESCHICHTE*: A WOMAN'S FAMILY CONSTELLATION

After I briefly introduced the idea of a two-hundred-year present, a German woman, who was born not long after World War II, volunteered to present her family's generational chain. What she showed us left her, by the end, deeply disturbed, so much so that she almost regretted having stepped forward. Later, in a letter I received a few weeks after the workshop, she took back ownership of her choice. She had been profoundly unsettled by the experience, she admitted in the letter, with the result of suffering for days from symptoms of withdrawal, nightmares, unprovoked sobbing, and speechlessness. But she no longer felt any anger about these symptoms. Rather, she said, she now realized that something must have her to sign up for this workshop in the first place, perhaps to cope with something still unresolved in her family. "The moment I had decided to attend the seminar," she wrote, "I had already made a choice without being fully conscious of it. This was even truer for my spontaneous decision to volunteer for creating a generational chain. I was clearly not forced to do it."

What happened? In a first step, the woman, whom I will call Annette, picked from among the participants a representative for each of the generations. With herself in the center of the generational link, she chose two people to represent her daughter and granddaughter (both standing to her right and representing future generations), then her mother (standing to her left and representing past generations). So far, these were only women. Only for her grandparents' generation, Annette picked a man to represent her grandfather.

In a second step, Annette provided some information about each of the characters in her family chain, just enough to know who was who and what their relations to each other might be. Intriguingly, she only placed her grandfather into the context of German history. We learned that he had been raised at the end of the German *Kaiserreich* (Wilhelmine Empire) and remained *kaisertreu* (loyal to the monarchy). Described as unapproachable, stern, and cold, the grandfather remained nameless. It is not that Annette wanted to keep his name a secret; she just couldn't remember it.

In contrast to the nameless grandfather, the women in her family chain were all characterized in relational terms. We learned what kind of relations they had with each other and how close or distant their personal-emotional ties had been. An image emerged in the room that presented her German family as women's history. This impression was bolstered when each of the five people in the generational chain was asked to express physically how they related to the person next to them. All four women spontaneously created a gesture that connected them by physical touch; only the grandfather stood isolated. It was a striking image of strength and solidarity among the women, with the man lost in his own space.

To show a constellation of one's family biography is, for the protagonist, something personal and unique: it reveals intimate details about specific family dynamics. At the same time, such a constellation also

gives insight into the dynamics and representation of a large-group identity. The individual and the collective levels merge and interact. What is
deeply personal for the protagonist in a constellation of a generational
chain is, at the same time, profoundly illuminating for the group participants at the collective level. To maintain a balance between personal
insight and collective dynamics is what distinguishes such sessions from
individual therapy and what makes them beneficial for groups in conflict
in reconciliatory settings.

In a third step, we invited the group participants who were watching
the constellation from outside to offer some feedback on what they were
witnessing. A range of small observations was shared, expressing some
unease about a sculpture that so ostensibly portrayed women's solidarity. "It feels like a postwar reconstruction of German women's history,"
someone said. "I like it because it acknowledges the labor of the
'*Trümmerfrauen*' [women who cleared the rubble after the war in the destroyed German cities[66]] and women's stride toward emancipation."

"Yes, I see this too," someone else added, "but the image also seems to
suggest women's innocence. I don't see the war or the horrors of the
Holocaust, and I do not see how women were involved in this history."

Indeed, the constructed generational chain seemed to convey that
only men—in the person of the grandfather—were "historical" figures
related to Germany's national history. Women were characterized only
by their internal relationships and seemed to float outside of the realm of
polity. Isolated as the grandfather was from the four generations of wom-
en, with no physical touch between him and them, the message seemed
to be that *Tätergeschichte* (history of perpetrators) is *Männergeschichte*
(men's history). It preserved the myth of the innocence of German wom-
en.[67] With the disappearance of fathers in Annette's generational two-
hundred-year present, the perpetrators seemed to have disappeared too.

"The fact that we created this chain of women," Annette later wrote,
"seemed natural to me, because I am a woman, and so are my daughter
and granddaughter. It was also clear to me that my mother had to be
there. I did not even think about my father." During the workshop itself,
after being prompted by the group's feedback, Annette revealed a few
remembered details about the Nazi past. But her memories remained
vague and merely suggestive. She talked about brothers of her nameless
grandfather, who had apparently died during the war. As it turned out,
though, she had initially misspoken, since the brothers she had mentioned were actually her father's brothers. In other words, these brothers
were her uncles and, hence, young men during the Nazi regime. One of
her uncles, we learned in passing, was a member of the feared SS. Shadows of the Nazi past entered into the constellation, but only in muddled
ways—like a dark presence refusing to take on a clear shape or form.

"The whole time," Annette said, "I was in charge of keeping the generational chain together." When she shared this insight, it became clear

how strenuous her position had been: much effort had been invested into keeping up an image of women's bonding and strength. In a fourth step, then, we invited Annette to remove herself from the generational chain. After a moment of hesitation, she vacated her place. As soon as she left, something unexpected happened. The four generations remaining in the generational chain spontaneously started to move without being prompted to do so. They rearranged themselves anew in space. No longer lined up in a generational chain, the three women surrounded the grandfather. He suddenly found himself in the center of the family constellation, encircled by the women representing Annette's mother, daughter, and granddaughter.

Annette watched this unexpected change with visibly growing anxiety. She was almost in a state of panic, pacing back and forth. She finally settled in a place far away from the newly formed sculpture, her body exuding mental and emotional turmoil. She looked frightened. The solidarity among women, which she had so carefully maintained and for which she had felt responsible, had collapsed right in front of her eyes. The isolated, stern grandfather had become the center of attention. "I was shocked to the depth of my soul," Annette would later say, recalling the new sculpture. "Under no circumstance would I have returned to this sculpture, even if my refusal to join would have cost me the loss of my daughter and granddaughter." Danger and calamity, Annette said, emanated from her grandfather, and a deep sense of darkness. She remembered that when she had been seven years old and her grandfather died, she stood at his open casket and thought, "It is good that he died."

In a fifth step, we asked the people representing Annette's family members how they felt standing in the spontaneously formed new sculpture with the grandfather in the center. The daughter mentioned how uncomfortable it made her. She needed more distance from the grandfather. We invited her to move. The participants representing the daughter and granddaughter stepped away together, leaving a large spatial gap between themselves and the older generations (Annette's mother and grandfather). We asked the daughter to acknowledge the gap between them and to describe it to us. Lowering her eyes and looking down to the floor, as if looking into an abyss rather than across to the preceding generations, Annette's daughter was at a loss for words. "I do not see much. I do not know what to say." It was an empty space for her. Though not entirely. She also said that she had little interest in finding out about the abyss, this Nazi past. She did not want to do her mother's work.

Annette was still watching, anxiety-filled, from a distance. Yet, the new constellation also freed her from her paralysis. She rejoined the sculpture and placed herself next to her granddaughter and daughter. But she did not step into the gap in order to fill the empty space. She was no longer trying to hold the intergenerational chain together. She no longer tried to connect to her mother and bridge the gap—an abyss of "darkness," as she would later write in a letter. The chain was broken, separating the postwar generations from the war generation of mother and grandfather.

## THE TRUTH ALMOST DROVE ME MAD

In the final round of conversation between Annette as protagonist, her family "representatives," and the group at large, we shared our observations, but we could push our interpretations only so far. Annette was mentally exhausted and needed time and space to digest all that had happened. Clearly, something deep and unsettling had occurred, not only for Annette personally but for the group as a whole. The German participants identified with various aspects of the two-hundred-year present in German families. The question was raised whether the unresolved task of acknowledging the gap or abyss between the generations was delegated to Annette's daughter and whether it was fair to burden the new postwar generation with this task. The participants of Jewish background, however, responded differently. Though they were largely grateful for having been allowed to witness an intimate moment in German family history, they were nevertheless uneasy. Because it is so rare that groups that are separated and yet united by a shared antagonistic past reveal to each other guarded aspects of their own culture and family, the Jewish participants reacted defensively.

What happened? Whatever the specific darkness was that remained unnamed in Annette's family constellation, the session still humanized the onerous struggle that marks so many German families after the Holocaust. In other words, the Jewish participants were able to peek into the intimate struggles of German families regarding their social identity embedded in a perpetrator legacy. Revealing *cultural secrets in the presence of the other can break down protective barriers by which we define ourselves against the other. When those old identity boundaries get threatened, we often reflexively call on mental defenses and build up new walls. As a matter of fact, we can often observe that if one side opens the wall too much, the other side builds up its own wall. Psychologist Dan Bar-On calls this the "double wall phenomenon."[68]

In this particular workshop, an instance of strong defensive discomfort erupted during the last round of conversation, shortly before we were about to part ways. It happened when the only attending aging Holocaust survivor accused one of the young German participants of harboring pro-Nazi sentiments. The accusation was unprompted and very much unwarranted. Feeling deeply insulted, the young man yelled back at the survivor and was ready to leave the room in anger. Only the intervention of other group participants prevented further escalation.

This interaction between the Holocaust survivor and the German man of the postwar generation was brief but nevertheless loaded with suspicion and anger. It operated on several complex and interwoven levels that cannot be fully unpacked here. In the context of our discussion, it is sufficient to read it as a defensive reaction to having been unsettled by the breaking down of social identity boundaries, which, it seems, was triggered when witnessing Annette's struggle with her German family history. In the workshop, empathetic understanding emerged between and among German and Jewish participants tied to each other by a traumatic past. But for the survivor, such gestures of empathy were too much to observe and absorb. His unprovoked accusation against the young man, rooted in his own fears, can be read as an attempt to quell anxieties over the loss of old, familiar boundaries. Those boundaries had neatly kept apart the narratives of victims and perpetrators in the post-1945 public discourse in Germany. Such separation guaranteed a publicly accepted moral equilibrium that would not touch more ambiguous zones of human interactions during the years of war and genocide. These boundaries of discourse in the public sphere would keep in check mistrust, recriminations, and suspicions; a loosening of those boundaries would stir an existential anxiety and moral panic—and the attending survivor angrily expressed just such fear.

## CODA

During this workshop itself, we never learned what the gap represented or what the abyss symbolized in the intergenerational German family chain that Annette had shown us. Presumably it had to do with secrets kept about the Nazi past. Given that the gap in Annette's family constellation occurred precisely at the period that separated the postwar generations from the war generation, it seemed to suggest a silencing and veiling of the Nazi past. We can't be sure, though. What was hidden might have been a family secret altogether disconnected from Nazism. Or it could have been a mixture of both. From Annette's story we knew for certain that the grandfather had played an important role in the family. In a correspondence a few weeks after the workshop, Annette told me that she had consulted with other family members to find out her grandfather's name. No one remembered! Her extended family, she wrote, recalled him as tall, hard, cold, penny-pinching, commanding, never giving gifts, and never touching anyone. Only a sister-in-law, who had never met him personally, eventually remembered his name.

In our ensuing correspondence, I gently encouraged Annette to place herself in the gap that had been created in her generational chain during the workshop and to imaginatively explore what she might find there. She wrote back, saying she could not do so. "I imagine sitting right at the edge of this gulf and looking down," she wrote. What she discovered at the edge, however, was anything but pleasant. It was an "enormous, dark, sharp-edged, dangerous abyss. You could neither place yourself in it, nor could you jump across it. It would only be possible to descend into it and ascend on the other side—that is, if you were able to make it across. You would have to go into the midst of hell. From the abyss emanated flames, smoke, stench. And dreadful screams, sobbing—the whole abyss nothing but a nameless horror."

For more than ten years in her life, Annette added, she had made efforts to descend into the abyss to find out the truth about her family. "I eventually found the truth in the abyss," she wrote, "and the truth almost drove me mad." Whatever she found, it remained her secret.

## RESPONSIBILITY TOWARD THE FUTURE

To return to troubled times is not meant to reinscribe what is already known historically but to change and transform contemporary relations. In this sense, it does not really matter that Annette did not reveal the exact nature of the truth she had found and that this truth remained her knowledge alone. What does matter is that Annette had been willing to risk vulnerability in the presence of others, including those who might have been victimized as Jews by members of her own extended family. This is what it takes to move into a posture of unsettling empathy. In a chapter on "History and Memory" in the shadows of the Holocaust, Dominick LaCapra, professor of the humanities, emphasizes that working through the past is a process and "not an accomplished state." Rather than seeking a "definitive closure," it is the effort of linking "critical memory-work to the requirements of desirable action in the present."[69] Active memory work compels us to reconsider our assumptions; it renders us vulnerable in the presence of the other. Our memories might be incomplete and selective—"shot through with holes," as Henri Raczymow famously articulated in 1986[70] —but memory work activates the internal tensions in the social body of one's own community, especially when those with whom we live in conflict are present. This conflict can lie in the past, like the Holocaust. In this case, becoming aware of our two-hundred-year present makes those historical traumas far less removed than we sometimes assume. Or the conflict is ongoing—as is the case today with the long-simmering, low-intensity new warfare of the twentieth and twenty-first centuries.[71] In this case, our two-hundred-year present calls us into responsibility toward the future. We have been touched by the generations before us, but what do we want to pass on? People can make choices, and we need to empower people to choose what must be left behind on the rubble of history and what needs to be carried forward. Of the touches we received from previous generations,

which ones need to stop with us so as not to contaminate future generations? What generational embraces can we accept, and which ones do we
need to reject? Emotional memory work is unsettling because it opens us
up to the past anew and asks us to be more purposeful about the future.

There are no magic bullets in this line of reconciliatory work that
brings memory into play. Transformative change does not rely on miracles. I have described two exceptionally intense scenarios (Yigal's soap;
Annette's family chain) that played out in the presence of those with
whom the protagonists were in conflict. I have suggested, prudently and
cautiously, some interpretive possibilities without plumbing the full
depth and complexity of those involved in these settings. These scenarios—I hope—indicate possibilities for building up trust between groups
in conflict.

## NOTES

1. For example, Pierre Nora's multivolume work, *Realms of Memory* (1996); Maurice Halbwachs, *On Collective Memory* (1992); Jan Assman, *Cultural Memory and Early
Civilization* (2011a); Aleida Assman, *Cultural Memory and Western Civilization* (2011);
and Jenny Edkins, *Trauma and the Memory of Politics* (2003).

2. Jan Assman, "Communicative and Cultural Memory" (2011b); Ellen Fine, "The
Absent Memory" (1988); José van Dijck, *Mediated Memories* (2007); Peter Leesem and
Jason Crouthamel, *Traumatic Memories* (2016); Alison Landsberg, *Prosthetic Memory*
(2004); Leo Spitzer, "Back through the Future: Nostalgic Memory and Critical Memory
in a Refuge from Nazism" (1999); Froma Zeitlin, "The Vicarious Witness: Belated
Memory" (1998); Marianne Hirsch, *The Generation of Postmemory* (2012); Anastasia Ulanowicz, *Second-Generation Memory* (2013); and Michael Rothberg, *Multidirectional Memory* (2009).

3. Sigmund Freud, "Remembering, Repeating, and Working-Through" (1914).

4. See Dan Bar-On and Fatma Kassem, "Storytelling" (2004, 290); Yael Danieli,
"Confronting the Unimaginable" (1988). For a comprehensive volume, see Yael Danieli, *International Handbook of Multigenerational Legacies of Trauma* (1998). See also note 20
in Chapter 3.

5. See, for example, Pumla Gobodo-Madikizela, "Remembering the Past" (2012).

6. Priscilla Hayner's study (2002) of various truth commissions list significant differences. Among those with little credibility are, for example, Zimbabwe's Commission of Inquiry, which was never made available to the public, and the nonrelease of
the Burundi investigations. The *Nunca Mas* report of the National Commission in
Argentina, to name another example, which was politically contested but effective,
explicitly shunned reconciliation because, in Argentina's context, "reconciliation" was
perceived as a code word for doing nothing. In the case of South Africa, Brandon
Hamber arrives at a more positive assessment, *Transforming Societies after Political Violence: Truth, Reconciliation, and Mental Health* (2009). Hamber, born in South Africa, is a
clinical psychologist and director of a conflict research institute in Belfast. He has been
involved with the South African Truth and Reconciliation Commission and has written about the process of reconciliation and the psychological implications of political
violence.

7. Hayner, *Unspeakable Truths* (2002, 135).

8. Wolf Schmidt, in "Peace Making by Storytelling" (2000), writes: "Storytelling,
the academically unfiltered relating of personal experience of violence and politics, is
not superior to academic historiography itself, either in respect to its truthful content
or even its power of judgement. For all the authenticity of personal experience, it is

generally unavoidably woven into the prevailing pattern of tradition and political-historical cliché. . . . The historical images of enmity and hatred are probably more lastingly formed at the kitchen table than simply through academic efforts. . . . [Yet] personal storytelling leads to potential enlightenment and reconciliation if it takes place in the form of a cross-border dialogue" (15). See also Chapter 5.

9. Krondorfer, *Remembrance and Reconciliation* (1995, 91).

10. Alternative forms of justice can be transitional, traditional, or restorative justice. See Naomi Roht-Arriaza and Javier Mariezcurrena, *Transitional Justice* (2006); Neil Kritz, *Transitional Justice* (1995); Jennifer Llewellyn and Daniel Philpott, *Restorative Justice, Reconciliation, and Peacebuilding* (2014a); and John Braithwaite, "Traditional Justice" (2014).

11. See, for example, Vamik Volkan, *Enemies on the Couch: A Psychopolitical Journey* (2013); Brandon Hamber and Elizabeth Gallagher, *Psychosocial Perspectives on Peacebuilding* (2014).

12. Nina Fischer, *Memory Work: The Second Generation* (2015).

13. Iwona Irwin-Zarecka, *Frames of Remembrance* (1994, 145); Nina Fischer, *Memory Work* (2015, 2); Annette Kuhn, *Family Secrets* (1995); James Young, *At Memory's Edge* (2000); Barbara Gabriel, "The Unbearable Strangeness of Being" (2004); and Gabriele Schwab, *Haunting Legacies* (2010, 1–40, esp. 26). Although many studies on memory work focus on the legacy of the Holocaust and World War II, it also finds application in the context of Palestinian memory; see, for example, Lia Abu-Lughod and Ahmad Sa'di, "Introduction: The Claims of Memory" (2007), and Lena Jayyusi, "Iterability, Cumulativity, and Presence: The Relational Figures of Palestinian Memory" (2007).

14. Dominick LaCapra, *Writing History, Writing Trauma* (2001, 22). "Working through the past," he writes in an earlier work, is a "process . . . to relate accurate, critical memory-work to the requirements of desirable action in the present" (*History and Memory after Auschwitz* 1998, 42).

15. Annette Kuhn, *Family Secrets* (1995, 8).

16. For a critique on memory's modern ubiquity, see, for example, Lea David, "Against Standardization of Memory" (2017); David Berliner, "The Abuses of Memory" (2005); Andreas Huyssen, *Present Pasts* (2003, esp. Chapter 1); Tzvetan Todorov, "The Abuses of Memory" (1996); Harald Weinrich, *Lethe: The Art and Critique of Forgetting* (2004); and Jay Winter, "The Generation of Memory" (2000). Arguing for the value of certain forms of forgetting, see Marc Augé, *Oblivion* (2004); Leonard Grob, "'Forgetting' the Holocaust" (2008); Mordechai Gordon, "Between Remembering and Forgetting" (2015), who suggests that forgetting is also an educational and moral good; and Krondorfer, "Is Forgetting Reprehensible?" (2008a). For cultural and literary criticism, see Susan Rubin Suleiman, *Crises of Memory of the Second World War* (2006), and Gunnthorunn Gudmundsdottir, *Representation of Forgetting in Life and Writing Fiction* (2017). For a historical study, see Patrick Geary, *Phantoms of Remembrance* (1994). For a defense of memory (against forgetting), see Yosef Hayim Yerushalmi, *Zakhor* (1996), and Avishai Margalit, *The Ethics of Memory* (2002).

17. My inquiry into memory through the practical lens of "memory work" is guided not by an interest in the scientific basis of memory or its philosophical foundation. Rather, my interest falls into the field that Jeffrey Olick calls "social memory studies," in *The Politics of Regret: On Collective Memory and Historical Responsibility* (2007, 9). It is the kind of inquiry in which memory is regarded, as Michael Lambek and Paul Antze put it in a different context, as a "collective and individual practice" coming "into play in society and culture" (1996, xv).

18. Kuhn, *Family Secrets* (1995, 4).

19. For inserting Holocaust memories into family rituals at Jewish holy days, see Liora Gubkin, *You Shall Tell Your Children: Holocaust Memory in American Passover Rituals* (2007).

20. There is plenty of misinformation on the question of whether Nazis produced soap from the corpses of murdered victims in the camp (especially from body fat), as a quick check on the internet will demonstrate. Though this rumor has been circulated

widely, most historians are skeptical since hard facts cannot be established. The United States Holocaust Memorial Museum in Washington, D.C., and Yad Vashem in Jerusalem keep largely silent on this issue. Some cautiously concede that German researchers tried to develop such a product but also insist that soap from human bodies was never produced on an industrial scale. There is an interesting dramatic play written on this controversy by Jeff Cohen, *The Soap Myth* (2012). Be that as it may, Yigal never claimed that anyone in his family believed that the bar of soap passed around among them was made of human bodies. The significance of his story lay in what the soap symbolized.

21. *Ressentiment* differs from resentment insofar as it refers to a psychological state resulting from buried feelings of hostility and envy that cannot (easily) be satisfied. This differentiation can be traced to the philosophies of Søren Kierkegaard and Friedrich Nietzsche.

22. For a variation of the "topic selection" cards, see also "loaded word" cards (Chapter 8).

23. For the problematic use of "displaced person camp" in this context, see note 24 below.

24. The use of the term "displaced person camp" for describing his time as a child in Dachau is historically inaccurate. Displaced person camps (DP camps) have a specific meaning: they were set up by the Allies in Germany after 1945 to house liberated camp inmates and refugees from Eastern Europe. In 1948, due to housing shortages, the Bavarian government turned part of the former Dachau concentration camp into a temporary refugee camp for German expellees; this is probably what the German man referred to. As regards the phrase "involved in transports," it is highly suggestive of Nazi criminal activity (conducting deportation trains? putting people on transport to the killing centers?), but no one asked in this setting, and the group never found out.

25. Bar-On and Kassem, "Storytelling" (2004, 292).

26. "Whereas guilt refers to punishment for wrongdoing," writes Donald Nathanson, "shame is about some quality of the self" (*The Many Faces of Shame* 1987, 4). For shame as a political emotion, see Sara Ahmed, *The Cultural Politics of Emotion* (2004, 101–121).

27. Michael Lambek, "The Past Imperfect: Remembering as Moral Practice" (1996, 240).

28. Memory, writes Lambek, "is perspectival" and hence "*essentially* incomplete" (1996, 242; emphasis in original).

29. Lambek argues for conceptualizing memory as a function of social interaction rather than insisting on "excessive subjectivity" or "excessive objectivity" of memory (1996, 238).

30. In this book, I am using the terms "Shoah" and "Holocaust" as synonyms. The Hebrew term "Shoah" has been introduced to refer specifically to the genocidal anti-semitism unleashed by Hitler's Germany, rejecting both the overusage of "Holocaust" (as it has come to be applied to other kinds of mass violence) and its biblical roots (*holo kaustos* refers to wholly burnt sacrifice in the Bible).

31. Hoffman (2004, xv).

32. I define ethos—in distinction to discursive practices—as a community's belief "that their assumptions, choices, and behaviors are correct and valid"; an ethos is what is deeply felt by people and shared as an unquestionable truth in social units (*Remembrance and Reconciliation* 1995, 47–70, 48). Daniel Bar-Tal defines ethos as "the configuration of shared central societal beliefs that provide a particular dominant orientation to a society at present and for the future" ("Sociopsychological Foundations of Intractable Conflicts" 2007, 1434).

33. See, for example, Nina Fischer's *Memory Work* (2015), a study on published life writings and fictional texts by children of Holocaust survivors. See also Marianne Hirsch, *Family Frames* (1997); Eva Hoffman, *After Such Knowledge* (2004); Aaron Hass, *The Aftermath: Living with the Holocaust* (1995); Marita Grimwood, *Holocaust Literature of the Second Generation* (2007); and Victoria Aarons and Alan Berger, *Third-Generation*

*Holocaust Narratives* (2016). See also Esther Faye's complex meditation on "writing shame" ("Being Jewish after Auschwitz: Writing Modernity's Shame" 2003) and the intellectual-philosophical memoir by Martin Beck Matuštík, *Out of Silence: Repair across Generations* (2015). On psychological approaches, see Martin Bergmann and Milton Jucovy, *Generations of the Holocaust* (1990); Yael Danieli's work on children of Holocaust survivors and multigenerational legacies of trauma (1988; 1998; 2017); and Ilse Grubrich-Simitis's earlier psychoanalytic observations when treating descendants of survivors ("Vom Konkretismus zur Metaphorik" 1984).

34. For in-group/out-group distinction, especially as it concerns in-group favoritism and out-group exclusion, see Henry Tajfel, *Differentiation between Social Groups* (1978), and Miles Hewstone and Ed Cairns, "Social Psychology and Intergroup Conflict" (2001, 324–325).

35. Hirsch, *The Generation of Postmemory* (2012, 1–2). Her book progresses from chapters on *familiar* postmemories (Jewish generations) to *affiliate* postmemories (on art, photography, and testimonial objects) to *connective* histories, which, she writes, is "more explicitly comparative memory work" (24) and includes Palestinian, Kurdish, and Polish stories. On postmemory from a Palestinian perspective, see Lila Abu-Lughod, "Return to Half-Ruins: Memory, Postmemory, and Living History in Palestine" (2007).

36. Rothberg, *Multidirectional Memories* (2009, 4–5).

37. Erin Einhorn, *The Pages in Between* (2008, 41–42).

38. This is based on Helen Epstein's book *Children of the Holocaust* (1988). See also Epstein's fleshed-out account of her family history, *Where She Came From: A Daughter's Search for Her Mother's History* (1997).

39. Fischer, *Memory Work* (2015, 162). She cites many examples of such daily interactions in the life writings of the second generation, situating them in what she calls "nodes of family memory" (8). Such nodes are memorial objects, names, food, and physical and emotional embodiment (scars, tattoos, nightmares), where memories get bundled and intensified. See also Alan and Naomi Berger, *Second Generation Voices* (2001), and Melvin Jules Bukiet, *Nothing Makes You Free* (2002).

40. Marianne Hirsch, *The Generation of Postmemory* (2012), and ibid., "Past Lives: Postmemories in Exile" (1998).

41. See also Chapter 3 on trauma.

42. Fischer, *Memory Work* (2015, 32).

43. Andreas Kuntz, "Objektbestimmte Ritualisierungen" (1991, 225–226). His ethnographic research dates to the 1980s, when the war generation (Germans who were adults or young adults during the 1930s and 1940s) still dominated family life.

44. Cf. Kurt Grünberg's critique on psychologizing traumatic memory, especially when comparing descendants of victims and perpetrators ("Zur Tradierung des Traumas der nationalsozialistischen Judenvernichtung" 2000).

45. On Palestinian memory and narratives of the year 1948, in which they were expelled from Palestinian land, see especially Chapter 5.

46. On testimonial objects, see Hirsch's chapter "Testimonial Objects" in *The Generation of Postmemory* (2012); on numinous objects, see Rachel Maines and James Glynn, "Numinous Objects" (1993); on the "mnemonic value" of these objects (mnemonic = something that assists in retrieving memory), see Fischer, *Memory Work* (2015, 32).

47. On the debate over the value of memory objects in museums, see Monica Eileen Patterson, "Teaching Tolerance through Objects of Hatred" (2011), and Oren Baruch Stier, "Torah and Taboo" (2010). Objects of memory can move from the private to the political sphere where they represent a collective symbol of loss or resistance. The Palestinian "key," for example, has come to stand for resistance in the current Israeli-Palestinian conflict; it is featured, for instance, in an over-dimensional size on top of the entry gate to the Palestinian Aida Refugee Camp in the West Bank.

48. These workshops were held for educators from across the United States during a New York Summer Seminar at the Olga Lengyel Institute for Holocaust Studies and Human Rights, https://www.toli.us/sponsored-programs/summer-seminar/.

49. Within homogeneous groups, such memory work is more self-referential and could be compared to the kind of critical memory work we find, at times, in family-biographical or autobiographical explorations such as, for example, Annette Kuhn's *Family Secrets* (1995), where she dives (psycho)analytically into her past through a family photo album.

50. Within heterogeneous groups, such memory work can quickly turn controversial, as, for example, in the case of "testimonial projects" organized by dissident groups within Israel—which led to real dialogue but also to acrimonious exchanges; see Tamar Katriel, "Showing and Telling: Photography Exhibitions in Israeli Discourses of Dissent" (2011, 109).

51. Since the late 1990s, a plethora of biographical reckonings of and studies on German family complicity in Nazism has appeared. These children, grandchildren, and personally invested scholars clearly have made a choice to confront the past on the familial level. Among the many titles, see Martha Keil and Philipp Mettauer, *Drei Generationen* (2016); Oliver von Wrochem, *Nationalsozialistische Täterschaften: Nachwirkungen in Gesellschaft und Familie* (2016); Alexandra Senfft, *Der lange Schatten der Täter* (2016); Jennifer Teege, *My Grandfather Would Have Shot Me* (2015); Silke Gahleitner et al., *Das ist einfach unsere Geschichte: Im Dialog mit der zweiten Generation nach dem Nationalsozialismus* (2013); Barbara Cherish, *The Auschwitz Kommandant: A Daughter's Search for the Father She Never Knew* (2011); Beate Niemann, *Mein Guter Vater* (2008); Katrin Himmler, *Die Brüder Himmler: Eine deutsche Familiengeschichte* (2005); Ernestine Bradley, *The Way Home: A German Childhood, an American Life* (2005); Claudia Brunner and Uwe von Seltmann, *Schweigen die Täter, reden die Enkel* (2004); Jens Pyper, *Uns hat keiner gefragt: Positionen der dritten Generation zur Bedeutung des Holocaust* (2002); Stiftung für die Rechte zukünftiger Generationen, *Was Bleibt von der Vergangenheit?* (1999); Ulla Roberts, *Spuren der NS-Zeit im Leben der Kinder und Enkel* (1998). See also Erin McGlothlin, *Second Generation Holocaust Literature: Legacies of Survival and Perpetration* (2006).

52. Salomon Korn, "Schlicht als Deutsche: Erinnern an den Holocaust," *Süddeutsche Zeitung* (January 26, 2001). See also Harald Welzer, Sabine Moeller, and Karline Tschuggnall, *"Opa war kein Nazi": Nationalsozialismus und Holocaust im Familiengedächtnis* (2002); a condensed version of some of the book's findings also appear in Welzer, *Grandpa Wasn't a Nazi* (2015). Also Oliver Fuchs, "An Exploration of German Subjectivity" (2013; esp. 152–155).

53. Norbert Frei, *Vergangenheitspolitik* (1999); Robert Moeller, *War Stories* (2001), and ibid., "Die Vertreibung aus dem Osten und westdeutsche Trauerarbeit" (2002); Nicolas Berg, *Der Holocaust und die westdeutschen Historiker* (2003). For general information about postwar Germany's tangled attitudes toward the past, see Charles Maier, *The Unmasterable Past* (1988), and Siobhan Kattago, *Ambiguous Memory* (2001).

54. See Harald Welzer et al., *"Opa war kein Nazi"* (2002); Christian Schneider, "Noch einmal 'Geschichte und Psychologie'" (1997); Gabriele Rosenthal, *Der Holocaust im Leben von drei Generationen* (1997); Jürgen Müller-Hohagen, *Verleugnet, verdrängt, verschwiegen* (1988); Krondorfer, *Remembrance and Reconciliation* (1995).

55. "Afterword," in Edward Gastfriend's *My Father's Testament* (2000); a longer version in German, "Eine Reise gegen das Schweigen" (2002).

56. See note 33 above.

57. On the question of asymmetry, see Chapter 7.

58. For a philosophical inquiry into the question of obligations for postwar Germans, see Doris Schroeder and Bob Brecher's theoretical systematization in "Transgenerational Obligation" (2003). For a different approach to obligations among third-generation Germans, focusing on affective attachments and narrative framings, see Oliver Fuchs, "An Exploration of German Subjectivity" (2013). For post-1945 Germans who made the choice to confront the past in familial settings, see the select list of publications in note 51 above.

59. See, for example, the intellectual and self-investigatory study by Gabriele Schwab, *Haunting Legacies* (2010).

60. Quoted in Doris Schroeder and Bob Brecher, "Transgenerational Obligations" (2003, 48).

61. See, especially, the chapter "Expanding Our Sense of Time and History" in Boulding, *Building a Global Civic Culture* (1990).

62. For a fascinating study of the intersection of memory work regarding race in Germany and the United States, see Susan Neiman, *Learning from the Germans: Race and the Memory of Evil* (2019).

63. See, for example, Wolfgang Neumann, "The Presence of the Past: Using Memory Work to Search for Psychological Traces of the Nazi Past in Contemporary Germans" (2002); his list of references cites important titles in the field of memory work in German families.

64. The Study Group on Intergenerational Consequences of the Holocaust (formerly PAKH) invited me to lead this workshop. The group was founded in 1995 by Jewish and non-Jewish German members, most of them psychotherapists, with the aim to raise awareness of the impact of traumatic histories through personal confrontation, especially with respect to the Holocaust and World War II. http://www.pakh.de/EN/index.html.

65. See Claudia Berens, *"Coming Home" from Trauma* (1996).

66. For biographies of *Trümmerfrauen*, see Trude Unruh, *Trümmerfrauen* (1987); for the genesis and historicization of the myth of *Trümmerfrauen*, see Leoni Treber, *Mythos Trümmerfrauen* (2014).

67. Recent historical scholarship has countered the myth of German women's innocence. See Wendy Lower, *Hitler's Furies* (2013); Elizabeth Harvey, *Women and the Nazi East* (2003); Gudrun Schwarz, *Eine Frau an seiner Seite* (1997); Angelika Ebbinghaus, *Opfer und Täterinnen* (1996). On Holocaust and gender, see also Krondorfer and Ovidiu Creanga, *The Holocaust and Masculinities: Critical Inquiries into the Presence and Absence of Men* (2020).

68. Dan Bar-On, *Legacy of Silence* (1989, 328). Bar-On has used the "double wall" to describe the interactions between the German perpetrator generation and their children with respect to confronting the Nazi past. In postwar Germany, Bar-On observed, the parents build a wall "around their feelings about the atrocities" and the children a protective wall in reaction to their parents' past. "If those on one side try to find an opening, they encounter the wall on the other side" (328). Similar dynamics can be observed in group interactions between Jews and Germans. I have often encountered it when facilitating intercultural groups that are in tension or antagonism with each other.

69. Dominick LaCapra, *History and Memory after Auschwitz* (1998, 42, and esp. Chapter 1).

70. First delivered as a lecture at the Sorbonne in 1986, it was subsequently published by Henri Raczymow as "Memory Shot Through with Holes" (1994).

71. See, for example, Mary Kaldor, *New and Old Wars* (2012).

# THREE

## Trauma

### *Straddling a Line*

The Angel of History, as described by Walter Benjamin, might represent a melancholic view of history, but we can also imagine this angel traumatized. With rubble piled ceaselessly upon agonizing rubble, the disasters and sorrows of history are overwhelming and paralyzing. Such traumas cannot be healed—at least not in any meaningful way that we commonly associate with healing—that is, a full recovery or restoration of health. We might be able to live with trauma, or despite it. We might be able to learn how to cope with it.[1] And we might seek, perhaps over a lifetime, to express a wounding so deep that it defies language. "Healing trauma," however, sounds like an oxymoron.

Despite the widespread use of the term since the 1980s, which couches just about any severe or unjustly received harm in the language of trauma,[2] trauma is an experience qualitatively different from other forms of hurt and wounding. When working with groups in conflict, historical and cultural traumas might be lingering in the background and feed mistrust, suspicions, and defensiveness among participants. Only in rare circumstances do such group processes touch the deepest and most recalcitrant recesses of a traumatic experience wherein individuals, inflicted with the self-shattering and disintegrating force of trauma, are left fragmented and without a voice intelligible to the external world.[3] I am making this point at the onset of this chapter to remain realistic and humble. Insofar as traumatic content enters into the facilitation of groups in conflict, it is different from medical and therapeutic care provided to individual trauma survivors.

Yet, my work as facilitator of intercultural encounters often straddles the line between different understandings of trauma as they variously apply to the repairing of broken relations between social groups in conflict. In adversarial group settings, the long-term effects of endured wounding and culpable wrongdoing are present, and we need to pay attention to the eroding power of injurious experiences and traumatic memories in social relations. In this sense, the theoretical frames of historical and cultural trauma are relevant for both our conceptual comprehension as well as the practice of group facilitation. In this chapter, I will look at examples in which historical and cultural trauma became part of the dynamics of reconciliatory processes.

## TRAUMA DISCOURSE

The current ubiquitous usage of the word "trauma" in academic writing, public discourse, and the media requires a few words of clarification. This brief exercise is helpful on two accounts: for one, it helps to distinguish medical and psychological definitions of trauma from investigations that speak of historical and cultural trauma; second, it helps to differentiate between traumatic experiences with respect to severity, duration, agency, and morality.

Trauma definitions generally agree on two elements: trauma is caused by a severe violation of integrity (often described as a shattering of self and the world), and it has a lingering, long-term impact. But beyond this general agreement, descriptive and theoretical investigations differ significantly. For example, does the violation of integrity only concern the physical and psychological wounding of the individual (as medical and a majority of therapeutic models suggest), or does it equally apply to social groups and communities in the form of transmitted injurious memories and sustained malicious discrimination (as historical and cultural theories argue)? Is traumatization a uniform and universal reaction to violence-induced rupture (akin to a biologically innate regulatory mechanism), or is it a culture-dependent response? In the case of the latter, theorists in the humanities and social sciences argue that trauma gets crystallized through existing cultural frames that give the severity of an assault its specific meaning.[4]

Severity: What determines the gravity of the harm experienced? Is it individual or social factors? In the mental health field, the authoritative tool to diagnose disorder (the DSM) remains focused on the psychobiological timelessness of trauma's destructive impact, independent of the individual's ethnic or cultural background. Theorists of cultural trauma, in contrast, emphasize that it is the social environment that largely determines whether an event is experienced as traumatic.[5] Disparity of theoretical perspective can also be observed between those that see trauma as the result of a single, forceful event (like the medically defined sudden, blunt, radical impact on the body) and those that look at trauma as the result of an insidious web of abiding social injustices, such as colonialism, apartheid, or racism.[6]

Duration: Despite differences, there are multiple overlaps among the definitional fields, among them the observation that secondary traumatization is possible. For example, historical and psychological trauma theories have found some common ground in assuming that witnessing someone else's trauma can be traumatizing to the witness[7] and that trauma can be transmitted across generations.[8] Some psychoanalysts and therapists have joined historical and cultural theorists in affirming that the effects of trauma can transcend individual life spans and continue on as subterranean anxieties and pathologies in subsequent generations. Such continuities of *transmitted traumas can be traced *inter*generationally as well as *trans*generationally. The difference between these seemingly interchangeable terms is that "intergenerational" refers to traumatic patterns and memories transmitted *within* a family system, while "transgenerational" refers to traumatic patterns and memories transmitted *across* unified social identities, independent of personal family histories.[9]

Agency: There is also the issue of agency, which, here, refers to the situational and social position that people inhabit vis-à-vis trauma-inducing events. This is particularly relevant in terms of treating people and communities suffering from post-traumatic stress disorder (PTSD). It is known that extraordinary violence not only threatens, disrupts, and shatters the integrity of victims but also disintegrates people who are actively participating in violent events (such as soldiers in war). Even the culpable wrongdoer—the person inflicting severe harm—can suffer from PTSD injury in a post-violent or post-genocidal situation, an observation that has been helpfully expanded by the concept of moral injury to grasp the effects of violence on people who have committed state-sanctioned violence under duress or in morally ambiguous situations.[10] Thus, ironically, the whole spectrum of agency vis-à-vis world-rupturing and self-shattering violence—victims, witnesses, bystanders, accomplices, perpetrators—may require therapeutic treatment or rely on broad support systems for their social reintegration.[11]

Morality: While medical and mental health professionals (and also clergy) are, to a large extent, required to treat everyone equally and independent of their agency, historical and cultural trauma theorists pay attention to the ethical and political dimensions of the long-lasting social impact of traumatized communities. Those theorists remind us not only of the staying power of trauma but also of the danger of the ubiquitous use of trauma terminology. In the case of the latter, undifferentiated trauma talk may lead to a facile equation of all traumatized people, thus erasing the ethical difference between *harm inflicted* and *harm endured*. Ironically, despite the medical and moral necessity of recognizing war trauma as real harm (in opposition to regarding traumatized soldiers during World War I as "constitutionally feeble" men with "hysterical symptoms"),[12] the broadening and popularizing of a psychological understanding of trauma has the effect of weakening moral and ethical concerns. "By applying the same psychological classification to the person who suffers violence, the person who commits it, and the person who witnesses it," Fassin and Rechtman lament in *The Empire of Trauma*, "the concept of trauma profoundly transforms the moral framework of what constitutes humanity."[13] Other critics point to the contemporary fixation on trauma in Western academic circles and public parlance that has led to entrenched identity politics in a "wound culture." Such a wound culture not only zooms in on shock and trauma but also commodifies pain and violence.[14] And when pain is commodified and trauma language inflated, the wounds of other people get treated like a public spectacle at a nonthreatening distance for the spectator. "Being a spectator of calamities taking place at another country," writes essayist and cultural critic Susan Sontag, "is a quintessential modern experience."[15] Voyeuristic consumption turns trauma into a "sentimental political discourse," which, as a consequence, prevents an effective call to political action from being articulated.[16] To mitigate such ethical dilemmas, a critical trauma theory would need to negotiate the right balance between fostering (individual) repair and pursuing (communal) justice. It is a quandary that not only affects processes of social reconciliation but also requires sustained transnational discussion about the value of retributive justice versus restorative justice, especially in transitional societies.[17]

The seminars and workshops I have conducted over the years take place within a circumscribed, condensed time frame. We have already seen in the previous chapter how memories of historical trauma enter into these social processes. Other forms of trauma, however, also come into play. Sometimes, the traumatic or traumatizing experiences are severe and direct, at other times hidden and subtle. They reach from individually endured severe harm (victims of torture; victims of rape) to the psychological effects of secondary witnessing;[18] from cultural memories of genocide to personal paralysis in damaged families; from repetitions of politicized communal trauma narratives to unacknowledged losses passed on intergenerationally; from the postmemories imprinted on family members to the felt memory of continuous threats to one's physical and emotional integrity.

Occasionally I have in a group participants who are traumatized without them being aware of it. The lack of individual awareness is often rooted in a lack of communal language because social and political circumstances are such that any acknowledgment of damage to one's own soul and body is communally spurned as aggrandizing self-pity. This is particularly true for individuals and groups that are in the throes of current conflicts and for whom any trauma talk seems like an emotional luxury they cannot afford. Why would an individual claim trauma for him- or herself—a community under duress might wonder—aren't we all suffering under the same conditions? In these environments, claiming to be traumatized can be judged as being disloyal to a large-group political identity. It is therefore important to distinguish between historical trauma and cultural trauma in conflict settings.

The difference between historical and cultural trauma, as it applies to working with groups in conflict, can be described in the following terms. In settings where *historical trauma is the primary source of contentious social relations while the actual conflict has subsided, there is generally a stronger willingness to consider trauma a paradigmatic model for restorative efforts. The temporal distance to the past serves as a buffer that allows the conflicting parties to approach agonistic memories with greater emotional and political freedom. But in settings where chronic or unresolved conflicts determine large-group identities, there is a less-developed ability to understand the situation through trauma for the people affected. For continuous events of suffering to become trauma, a cultural crisis must occur in which collective pain is perceived, and then represented, as a fundamental threat to a large-group identity. It is in this setting that we can speak of *cultural trauma. People who live in such volatile situations may, however, not describe their experiences as trauma and, instead, rely on political modes of communication to voice their grievances and seek solutions. The immediacy of lethal treats or the adaptation to unending duress may put people into survival mode. The temporal and mental distance is missing to read one's situation as traumatic. Yet, independent of whether the affected individual actors or communal bodies acknowledge trauma, looking at it through the lens of cultural trauma helps to name and comprehend the severity of threats and harm to communal and personal integrity.

Let us now consider a scene where a particular expression of historical trauma surfaced in a group setting.

## WHEN I WALKED IN MY GRANDMOTHER'S SHOES

In chapter 1, we saw Dafne acting out a subliminally transmitted obligation by throwing a piece of meat across a dinner table the first night in a guesthouse in Berlin; in chapter 2, we saw how a memory-object (Yigal's soap) triggered and deepened an exploration between Israelis and Germans on (family) memories related to the trauma of the Holocaust. In the example below, we will accompany Oren in a mixed Israeli-German setting, where, at some point, he embodied his grandmother who had escaped the Holocaust.

In my work—and this comes out of my study of and experience with the third generation[19]—I differentiate between continuities that, as I mentioned above, can be traced *inter*generationally (traumatic patterns and memories transmitted *within* a family system) and *trans*generationally (traumatic patterns and memories transmitted *across* unified social identities, independent of personal family histories).[20] This distinction helps us to remain aware of the different levels of intensity that memories have in people's lives. It makes a difference, for example, if a person soaked up the "black milk"[21] of the Holocaust in an intimate family setting or if a person encountered it through stories in the larger social environment or through cultural artifacts (films, books, speakers, museums, etc.). In the first case, a good facilitator would have to be alert to the nuances and silences in what is being communicated; in the second case, a facilitator can probe more boldly a person's emotional and intellectual identification with a national or communal narrative.

An *inter*generationally transmitted memory of a traumatic past is intimately tied to a person's identity, while a *trans*generationally transmitted memory is related to a person's social identification. And while the boundaries between identity and identification are diffuse, to differentiate between them conceptually provides some tools to remain aware of different levels of vulnerability and how to process individual stories within group dynamics. With Oren, we get introduced to an example of the intergenerational transmission of a traumatizing past, this time not through a memory object, as in the case of Yigal's soap, but through an embodied enactment.

The setting within which Oren's story played out was a multigenerational workshop for German and Israeli educators, therapists, teachers, and community organizers. It was held in a German retreat center near Bonn. Ranging in age from midtwenties to early seventies, the participants wanted to get a better grasp on their relations as Jews and Germans with respect to the legacies of the Holocaust and World War II. I worked with them for three days. The workshop's title, "Restorative Forgetting/ Necessary Remembering," indicated the general direction we wanted to take. It was an ideal setting for bringing a symbolically dense, polyvalent, and evocative object to this gathering. A simple cardboard container the size of a shoebox was the *symbolic object at this workshop. Painted pitch-black inside and outside, it was placed in the center of our meeting space to guide us through the next three days. It was our memory box — and, as memory goes, it contained as much of what was remembered as what was forgotten. It functioned as storage and archive; as an advocate for the forgotten and an uncomfortable reminder for what needed to be remembered; as a retainer of familial remembrances and a black hole into which memory disappeared. This memory box will have another appearance in Chapter 6, but for now we will turn our attention to Oren.

Oren, in his midtwenties, was among the younger participants in this group of about twenty people. I do not remember at what point he told the group that his grandmother, still alive at the time, was the only member of her Polish Jewish family who had survived the Holocaust. Among the many personal background stories the group exchanged, it was somehow clear that Oren had a familial connection to the Holocaust. This mixed group of German and Israeli educators, therapists, and community leaders went about the task of learning from each other with great sincerity and honesty. Honesty is a necessary step in these processes, but honesty in itself is not yet a working-through. As a matter of fact, in the beginning of a process, participants often confuse honesty with getting permission to ask the other group whatever they never dared to ask before. Those questions, at times, linger somewhere between innocuous ignorance and biased beliefs, and they can provoke strong emotional reactions. Since such "honest" asking is almost always taboo in the public sphere, a protective space can offer opportunities to ask uncomfortable questions—no matter how contentious.

To understand this better, I will give a small taste of what happened in this group during an open forum on the first day. Eavesdropping on the group's conversation at this particular moment will bring into sharper focus Oren's physical embrace of his grandmother on the last day of the workshop.

Some of the statements voiced by participants were intended as "informational" questions, but they all carried strong emotional overtones. At the risk of simplifying complex layers of emotions, I will indicate in brackets the primary emotion that was expressed so as to make it easier for the reader to grasp the mood in the room. An Israeli woman in her midthirties, having served in the army and considering herself on Israel's political left, said: "The world hates us. If one day, we would leave to a different planet, no one would care. But the Germans, we trust you: YOU would not do it again" (fear). A German woman responded: "Should we feel guilty? You know, it is not in our German genes or nature. All of humankind can do it—it is not just a German problem" (defense against guilt). A woman psychotherapist, whose father belonged to the German soldier generation, responded pensively: "I feel the guilt intensely" (guilt/shame). Yet another German woman chimed in, directing her question at the Israelis: "Have you ever asked yourself why you have always been persecuted for thousands of years?" (passive-aggressive). That comment-question drew immediate angry responses from two Israelis. A German man, wanting to ease the tension, tried to mediate between the positions. Rebuking the Israeli woman's self-defeating statement about "the whole world hating Jews," he veered off into a somewhat convoluted educational lecture: "Peace researchers say that it is all geography. It is not the fault of the people who live there [in Israel]. It is the meeting point of all the world's trade routes, and where the first humans from Africa traversed and spread over the whole world . . . " Somewhere during this conversation, Oren intervened in a muted voice: "Maybe we Israelis can help you. Perhaps we can help Germans carry the guilt, not to get rid of it, but help carry it."

During the next two days the group was able to replace the asking of "honest" (i.e., problematic) questions with owning their own stories and being receptive to others. On the last morning, Oren voiced a strong interest in bringing his grandmother into our space. Rather than just narrating her story, we asked Oren to choose among the Israeli participants one person to guide him. He chose Aaron.

"Tell us about your grandmother," Aaron prompted. "What is her name?"

"Maya," Oren responded. Maya was born in Poland. She was the only survivor of a large family, except for her brother—but Maya rarely talked about him because he later died in one of Israel's wars. In Poland Maya had joined the Hashomer Hatzair, a secular-socialist Zionist youth group.[22] As an active member of this group, she left Poland at age twenty-four, before the Shoah. She arrived in Israel when immigration was still illegal under the British mandate. Almost everyone else in her family died. According to Maya, she survived because she had joined the Zionist movement while the others stayed "religious."

Oren yearned for something more than merely telling Maya's story, and so we sent him briefly out of the room with his guide. "When you are ready to come back in, we will ask Maya herself," I suggested. Soon after, Oren and Aaron returned. Seated on blankets in the middle of our circle, they started a conversation. Aaron asked: "How do you feel today, Maya?" Oren's whole demeanor changed immediately. His English took on a heavy Polish-Hebrew inflection, his hand gestures were those of an old woman, his lips shivered, and his eyes filled with tears: "I am alone. I feel so lonely."

After some silence, Aaron asked: "Do you mind being with us this morning in the presence of Germans?"

"No," Maya/Oren responded. "I don't mind being here. But I do not like to sit in the circle."

"Do you have any message for us?" Aaron wondered.

"No, I have no messages. I have no lessons for you to learn."

Other people jumped in to ask questions. Some were more intellectual in content, and Maya stumbled over them and grew silent. When Israelis asked more direct questions, Maya/Oren was drawn back into the trauma of separating as a young woman from her family in Poland. "Tell us about your father, Maya." Maya's tears were about to overflow. We no longer saw Oren sitting on the blanket in our midst. Every part of his body was the body of an old woman, the voice not his but that of his grandmother, facial expressions not of the Oren we knew but of Maya whom we got to know.

A German man in his midsixties asked gently: "Can you tell us about the last time you saw your father?" (This would have been Oren's great-grandfather, whom he never knew.) Maya was just about to respond when a German woman, also in her midsixties, turned to the German

man in protest: "You cannot ask such a painful question. Stop asking such painful questions"—to which yet another German participant reacted angrily: "Let Maya talk. I would like to know."

The angry exchange almost derailed the precious moment of Oren's *mimetic enactment. The narrative thread about Maya's father got dropped, but Maya responded to whether she minded that her grandchild (Oren) was in Germany with other Germans in the room. "I don't mind. I just want them to succeed in what they do."

"Maya, why do you want us to succeed. Why?" an Israeli wondered.

"Because I long for my home, my home in Poland," Maya responded.

When Oren was gently moved out of his role—*de-rolled, as I call it—people shared their reactions to Maya's story. Her loneliness was a strong trigger for Israelis and Germans alike. Several confessed to feeling flooded with guilt when listening to Maya's story. Oren—being fully Oren again—explained that when his grandmother complains about loneliness, she forgets to tell about the regular visits she receives from her three children and six grandchildren. He also said that Maya, now in her nineties, believes that the first kibbutz she had joined in Israel in her youth was her home back in Poland and that family members from Poland would come to visit her.

Marianne Hirsch describes postmemory carried by later generations as "experiences . . . transmitted to them so deeply and affectively as to *seem* to constitute memories in their own right." The connection to the past, she writes, is not "mediated by recall but an imaginative investment, projection, and creation."[23] Oren's physical enactment certainly was such an imaginative investment. By mimetically embodying his grandmother, he evacuated his own life's story to become (like) her. As a group, we no longer saw Oren in our midst but Maya. Insofar as the transmission of historical trauma is a conflation of past and present, we saw this conflation being played out right in front of our eyes.[24]

Other layers of conflation transpired during this session as well. There was the spatial-temporal conflation of Israel and Poland in the grandmother's recounting of home (in old age), when she began to confuse the locations of home. There was also a kind of emotional conflation when each side (German and Israeli) found a shared ground of empathy regarding Maya's loneliness. And there was a kind of moral conflation concerning the weight of history, when Oren offered to carry the burden of guilt *with* the Germans. To bear such conflations without defensiveness—and not insist on asking "othering" questions or building up walls to forcefully differentiate oneself from the other—is part of what I call unsettling empathy.

There was yet another level of conflation of past and present that had to do with the merging of a childhood memory with the present workshop. This, however, was not revealed during the workshop itself but in an email I received from Oren later. I will return to this last instance of conflation shortly, but let us first listen to what Oren had to say about his perception of becoming his grandmother.

A few weeks after the workshop, Oren wrote in an email: "The impersonation of my grandma left a great impact on me. Several days before we left Israel to go to Germany we met with the Israeli group. Aaron asked each of us to tell what kind of emotional or cognitive luggage we bring with us to the seminar . . . I said that I am interested in the connection between my family's and my people's past, and how it relates to my own personality and collective identity." Oren continued to say that his grandmother's story was always important to him because "it is part of who I am and how I see the world." He wondered whether he felt so strongly about the German guilt early in the workshop—even offering to help them carry it—because he knew what it means to carry an emotional burden. "When I walked in my grandmother's shoes it became clearer to me," Oren wrote. "When I told her story I felt that I'm very truly speaking her words—I was very confident in everything I said in her name, I knew exactly what she would say and how it will make her feel. . . . I felt very connected; I felt like her experience is to a great extent mine. Those feelings of helplessness and guilt that she carried all these years, the disability to feel pride despite everything she achieved in her life: I could see all these emotions, not just the story, the pure emotions."

And then, in the same email, Oren added that the black memory box accompanying us throughout the workshop triggered something else, a memory of fear from his childhood: "We had a session in which everyone wrote a dangerous memory and put it in the black box. I wrote 'childhood trauma.' When I was a child—maybe eight or nine years old—two older boys locked me inside a dark closet and didn't let me out. It was very stressful, and I felt helpless and humiliated. For many years I haven't shared it with anyone. . . . I realize now that the way I chose to deal with this experience as a child, the fact that I didn't tell anybody, wasn't incidental. It was a pattern [in my family] that this painful experience only reinforced."

The workshop resuscitated those memories, Oren wrote. It helped him to connect some dots between transmitted patterns in his family and his own coping mechanisms. Here we see another level of conflation: triggered by the presence of a symbolic and polyvalent object in the workshop, a humiliating childhood memory overlapped with memories of a past not his own. "Today I'm no longer in this place," Oren wrote at the end of his email, "but I think what I felt during the seminar is that there is a part of me who always remembers what it feels like to be in this place. And today I look at it as a strength."

## NOW I KNOW WHAT TO DO

In the summer of 2014, when the Israel Defense Forces (IDF) and Hamas in Gaza fought a lethal fifty-one-day war, I met with Israelis, Palestinians, and Germans in a location in the West Bank, close enough to the border with Israel to be within relatively safe reach for Jewish Israeli citizens. The political tension and military conflict had begun weeks earlier—first with the abduction and killing of Israeli youths, then a Palestinian teenager—and they unabatedly continued during our gathering. Rockets and artillery caused death, harm, and fear; equally fierce was the media war fought by politically motivated parties on domestic and international levels. It made it difficult to distinguish fact from fiction, myth from reality-on-the-ground, propaganda from human tragedy.

No one knew for sure how many, if any, Israelis, Palestinians, and Germans would be willing to attend our meeting in the West Bank. Germans could not easily ascertain the degree of danger when traveling to Israel; Palestinians and Israelis feared for their physical safety and were afraid of the social consequences of breaking with the codes of loyalty to their own communities. This war pushed Palestinians and Israelis even further apart, with each side demanding allegiance along national lines and group loyalty. Internally, each community ostracized and punished individuals who dared to stay in touch with people from the other side. And yet, a group of eighteen Israelis, Palestinians, and Germans met for four days during this tense summer.[25]

Originally, the meeting had been planned to design a curriculum for an international student program and to develop tangible concepts for implementing a dialogical-educational encounter. Given the extraordinary circumstances, however, it was difficult to focus on this self-set task. The nearby war along the border to Gaza—a mere forty-five miles away—left little mental and emotional space for future planning. In a charged climate of violent conflict, the future fades away.

During actual violent conflict, a call for a dialogical meeting seems counterintuitive. Violent conflicts produce traumas in the present moment—medical trauma (physical injuries), psychological trauma (witnessing people being killed and homes destroyed), severe emotional distress (loss, mourning), and mental agony (realization of political and existential instability). In the midst of conflict, the outcome is unpredictable and the infliction of traumatizing injuries uncontrollable. Unlike historical trauma, where temporal distance alleviates some of its pains (even when it leaks into the present, as we have seen above in Oren's story), violent conflicts don't have the luxury of a mediating space. They are immediate. Thus, current and ongoing violent conflicts bring into sharper relief the concern that reconciliatory or dialogical processes are fundamentally antithetical to trauma treatment. Since trauma is a severely destructive, disruptive, and disorienting force, any restorative effort would seem to work best if done in a safe space, where caretakers can pay undivided attention to repairing the physical, mental, and emotional integrity of the survivor, and where trauma victims learn to mobilize their own resources for coping and reintegration. Bringing different sides to such a process of repair would only cause detrimental emotional reactions (like anger, guilt, self-blame) or trigger retraumatizing flashes that would delay the process of restoring trust in oneself and the world.

These concerns are valid. Protection is crucial in the medical and psychological treatment of traumatized individuals. But those rules and precautions do not apply equally to historical and cultural trauma settings. Here, principles of committing to working-through take precedent—and in the case of working with groups in conflict, it requires the presence of the other. Cathy Caruth, one of the early pioneers of expanding trauma theory to cultural, literary, and ethical investigations, claims that trauma not only roots us in our historical situatedness but also calls us to acknowledge the ways in which historical trauma links individuals and cultures. "The notion of trauma . . . is aimed not at eliminating history but at resituating it in our understanding," she writes in *Unclaimed Experience*. "History, like trauma, is never simply one's own." Rather, "history is precisely the way we are implicated in each other's trauma."[26] In other words, communicating across cultural divides about the effects of trauma not only crystallizes the perception of our boundedness to our respective histories but also reaches beyond the one-sidedness of parochial history retelling. Applied to working through historical and cultural trauma, we can say that the realization of being "implicated in each other's trauma" calls for creating pathways for cross-cultural understanding.

What the group needed in the midst of the Israel-Gaza war in the summer of 2014 was a safe space that allowed all three nationalities—Israelis, Palestinians, Germans—to share deeply wounded stories and to express their feelings about the brute force of ideological entrenchment during military conflict. War correspondent Chris Hedges, who has reported for years from some of the most vicious war zones around the globe, observes that nations in violent conflict create myths that paint their opponents in the most unfavorable, horrid, less-than-human light. Such a mechanism is needed to first construct an image of the enemy and then to justify and proceed with the violence enacted upon people declared as enemy. The first victim of such myth-making, Hedges notes, is the ability to recognize our shared humanity and our propensity for empathy. [27] If our opponents are declared less than human, then their pain and suffering does not affect us. In a situation of war, efforts of reconciliation are seen by the warring parties as weakness, disloyalty, and, at worst, betrayal. And those who are perceived as "betraying" their own community are ostracized and punished. The Israelis and Palestinians who together with their German peers met this summer understood these risks. They feared not only the destructive force of weapons of war but also the social tension in their own families and communities—a tension that can potentially spill over into violence. Several of our participants had remained elusive and secretive about the purpose of our meeting even to their spouses and families. By choosing to participate, they chose to be present to the moment—and that in itself was already a step toward imagining a future beyond the current stalemate.

Because we were working together in the midst of an actual conflict, the participants arrived without having had a safe space to acknowledge trauma, hatred, fears, and the loss of human life. The feelings and experiences we brought to the seminar were raw, crude, unprocessed. The *safe space we created was for many the first time to account for their feelings after weeks of violent conflict. They had not admitted the severity of their feelings to themselves, let alone to others. Surprisingly, it was precisely the presence of the other that made possible such self-awareness.

We began the meeting in a basic way: we simply shared what had affected us most during the ongoing war. We listened to the fears, the hate, the grief, the dead, and the emotional paralysis. The mood was muted, if not outright depressed. There was also an air of disbelief in the room. It seemed unreal to meet with people declared "enemies" by the media and by their respective communities while hearing the occasional booms of artillery in the distance. In the evening, we created a quiet space, allowing each person to gather their thoughts, then write down on a piece of paper what they considered the "darkest aspects" of this violent conflagration. When everyone was done writing, one person at a time stepped into the circle, where an empty box had been placed. The person read his or her paper aloud, to which the group, in unison and almost liturgically, responded: "We heard you." The paper was then crumpled and thrown into the box. When it was Amal's turn, he stepped into the circle, hesitated, then shared with us that he had been unable to tell his Palestinian family—his wife, his children, or anyone else—about meeting Israelis. "They only know that I am meeting with Germans," he said. Revealing anything more would have had repercussions he'd rather not predict. Amal, from a large West Bank town, had been engaged for many years in improving Palestinian livelihoods as well as reaching across the Israeli-Palestinian divide. He held his paper in his hands. "I cannot read it to you now," he said. He folded the paper and, instead of throwing it into the box, he slid it into his back pocket.

Though disappointing at the moment—it seemed as if Amal did not trust us with his emotions—the group forgot about the incident as we continued our sessions over the next days. Over time, however, we did learn that among Amal's relatives in Gaza, several had lost their lives. Because of the war, Amal could neither help nor attend their funerals. At our closing session, Amal returned to the paper he had stashed away the first evening when he was supposed to put it in the box.

For our closing circle, we arranged a small mound of soil, stones, and a flower in the room's center. People remarked on the beauty of this arrangement. One person commented that it looked like a grave. As we went around the circle with everyone telling what the last four days meant to them, Amal eventually spoke. "You remember, I did not read you my paper on the first day," he said in his broken English. "I want to tell you what it is." He pulled out his paper. "I wrote on this paper the names of my relatives who were killed in Gaza by Israel." Amal did not share those names with us but continued: "I know what to do with the paper now." He placed the paper on the arrangement on the floor, then covered it gingerly with the soil and stones. He backed away from it. The arrangement had indeed become a symbolic grave. Several in the group cried silently.

In the midst of violent conflict, wounds are fresh and fear is ever-present, with little hope for any immediate improvement. In these settings, one frequently meets people who have been exposed to traumatizing incidents that fall squarely into the medical and therapeutic definition of trauma. There is immediacy of trauma that historical trauma settings do not have to deal with to the same extent. Such immediacy can condemn people into silence. Continuing threats, losses not yet mourned, fears not yet tamed—those resist language. Amal had not been able to speak, neither to his family when leaving home to join us nor during our initial circle of people deemed "enemies" by the outside world. It is difficult to know whether Amal considered himself a traumatized person, but his inability to speak was clearly a sign of being emotionally asphyxiated. There was no forum where speech was possible. With both the public and the familial spheres poisoned by admonitions to express only national grievance and patriotic anger, there was little room for more complex expressions of grief and fear.

Amal was not alone in this paralysis—most of his fellow Palestinians and Israelis shared or related to his feeling of powerlessness. During the course of our meeting, where we blended soul-searching with open conversations and ritually structured events, Amal found a form into which to pour his grief. What the group had named on the first day as obstacles for pursuing constructive work on a future student program—namely the fear, the dead, the hate, the paralysis—returned in the final circle of our meeting. By symbolically burying the names of his family members, Amal opened a space for all of us to mourn.

## FEAR IS CONTAGIOUS

The last day in this 2014 summer seminar, which concluded with Amal's gesture of grief, had started very differently. An external disruption almost ripped the group apart. On the morning of that last day, the retreat center hosting our group in the West Bank received an unexpected call from the Palestinian Authority, claiming that we had no permission to gather and that we had to leave immediately. Any meetings with Israelis and Palestinians were, at the time, prohibited. As it turned out, the order was not exactly true, since it was a German organization that had planned the meeting. International organizations are not required to inform the Palestinian Authority, who, in turn, would have informed the Israeli security about our presence.[28] Though we were able to clarify this and get clearance to complete our seminar, the phone call triggered turmoil and confusion among the participants. A young Israeli psychologist and grandchild of Holocaust survivors no longer felt safe and accused the leadership of failing to provide security. He got so frightened that his whole body began to shake. He asked why the Palestinian Authority even knew about our gathering. He accused the German organization for not having secured a permit and that it "colossally failed" to make the appropriate security arrangements. This young man was not pretending. Existential fear and anger had him in their grip. "Fear," critical race and queer theorist Sara Ahmed writes, "responds to what is approaching rather than already here."[29] When the group tried to seek solutions, he got up, left the room, and slammed the door behind him.

His fear spread like wildfire through the group, threatening to unravel everything we had painstakingly accomplished during the last days. Other Israelis began to panic.[30] The German participants were also surprised to learn that the Palestinian Authority knew about our presence. Palestinians participants shrugged it off, welcoming the group to the realities of "the holy land." Everyone watches out for everyone in this neighborhood, they explained, and that is precisely the reason why we are safe here. A meeting like this, the Palestinians exclaimed, would never be a secret.

I too began to feel anxious. Fear is contagious. Once it entered our room, it was hard to contain. Our frantic discussion veered around the question of whether a security risk was real or just a formal misunderstanding. It took us over an hour to come up with a solution amenable to everyone (the Israeli psychologist eventually joined us again): we would end the day earlier than planned with a closing session immediately after lunch.

By the time lunch was over, everyone had calmed down. Those Israelis who in the morning had wanted to leave immediately when learning about the phone call by the Palestinian Authority were now comfortably mingling with everyone over coffee. The fear that had spread like a destructive force in the morning—threatening to undo everything we had worked for in the last days—dissipated the moment the group returned to the concluding session with stones, soil, and a flower in our midst. With Amal's gesture of grief that turned the arrangement into a symbolic grave, fear lost its power. Fear, because it is so real, can be so easily manipulated. But this group had the foresight and strength to contain it.

## BETWEEN TRAUMA AND POLITICS

In the fall of 2013, I conducted a trilateral, four-day seminar for Israelis, Palestinians, and Germans who had been engaged in peace-building in-itiatives in the Middle East. The seminar—bearing the title "Between Trauma and Politics"—was billed as a mentor-training program. It of-fered participants a chance to explore and reflect on the multidirectional ways that traumatic memories impel and impede social trust between these three national groups.

The fine line we walked in this seminar was between dialogical en-gagement with historical trauma while being attentive to the urgency of the political situation. We negotiated the variously triangulated bonds between Palestinians, Israelis, and Germans.[31] Both individual and large-group identities crossed and overlapped at the axis of historical and cul-tural trauma. Indeed, the participants of this meeting were strongly indi-viduated people as well as representatives of larger social identities: grandchildren of Holocaust survivors, children of Nazi war criminals, Palestinians living under the occupation of the West Bank, Israelis having served in the military, and educators, activists, and therapists. Further-more, the participants brought a number of generational and age per-spectives to the table, stretching across a whole spectrum of unresolved pasts and present tensions. Deeply personal experiences that were marred by traumatic content blended with collective narratives of suffer-ing and guilt. Since the Israeli and Palestinian participants came from living situations marked by acute anguish, discrimination, violence, death, and mutual recriminations, the exchange was often volatile and fragile.

Settings that straddle the line between historical trauma and unre-solved political conflict can be understood through the lens of cultural trauma. As mentioned above, the identification of a particular situation as cultural trauma does not depend on whether it is recognized as such by the affected individuals or communities. People in politically explo-sive situations may speak about the suffering they endure—for example, as a result of unjust treatment by a superior power or as the inevitable price one pays for resistance—but the use of the term "trauma" is hardly pervasive in these settings or is carefully sidestepped. Claiming traumati-zation for oneself might actually erode social solidarity since it could be perceived as undue self-pride in one's own injuries over the common-weal or as an excuse for not fully participating in the defense of one's people and nation.

Our trilateral meeting included participants who had been in Israeli prisons for years; who witnessed neighbors being fatally shot; who served in the Israeli army; who had been involved in the militant Palestinian resistance; who survived rocket attacks launched from Gaza; and who, on the other side of the Gaza border, were faced with the war-wounded in understaffed Palestinian hospitals. Previous trilateral meetings also included Israelis who had lost friends to Palestinian suicide bombings and Palestinians who had been tortured in Israeli prisons.

When we asked the group during our four-day meeting to recall and share individual stories of traumatizing or near-traumatic experiences, several Palestinian men looked quizzical at first. They weren't sure what was asked of them. But then they started talking about their experiences: about being struck by a rubber bullet still lodged in his neck, threatening to paralyze him at any time; about being arrested at age fourteen and spending the next ten years in an Israeli prison; and about witnessing the incineration of a whole family when a rocket hit an apartment building in Gaza. They hastened to add that they never thought about these experiences as traumatic. "It's just how it is; everyone is exposed to it."[32]

In cultural trauma settings, not enough time may have passed between event and memory for the affected people to read it as a traumatizing environment. Or a conflict has been going on for so long that it has taken on an air of normalcy, thus resulting in underestimating the extent to which communities have been shattered and fragmented. In "chronic psychic suffering," as in the case of postcolonial trauma or the so-called post-traumatic slave syndrome, the root cause is not a sudden, blunt force threatening to disintegrate a person (like a car accident) but collective structural violence (like slavery or apartheid).[33] Hence, another fine line that needs to be attended to in cultural trauma settings is to work with people who recover from recent medical trauma or suffer from untreated mental trauma while simultaneously being attuned to the trauma-inducing structures that are long-term and chronic. A person with a rubber bullet lodged in his neck is both a case of medical trauma as well as one incident in a long line of incidents in an ongoing conflict.

Communities living under the daily stress of politically volatile and violent environments tend to tell, as a psychic defense, nostalgic tales of innocent suffering or heroic tales of resistance.[34] To move away from these tales toward an understanding of cultural trauma requires an active framing of such events. "Disorganization, displacement, or incoherence in culture," writes sociologist Piotr Sztompka, are the conditions that lead to "cultural trauma."[35] To be recognized as trauma, those conditions need to be framed as such by social actors. A rubber bullet lodged in a neck could be understood as the inevitable cost of resistance (and the affected person might be praised for his bravery), or it could be read as part of a cultural trauma if socially framed as such. Trauma becomes comprehensible, writes psychiatrist Judith Herman, only when it is supported by a "political movement" that can "counteract the ordinary social processes of silencing and denial."[36] Similarly, the sociologists Jeffrey Alexander and Piotr Sztompka argue that for cultural trauma to be recognized some narrative mediation needs to occur and some social conditions must be met. "Cultural trauma," according to Alexander, "occurs when members of a collectivity feel they have been subjected to a horrendous event that leaves indelible marks upon their group consciousness, marking their memories forever and changing their future identity in fundamental and irrevocable ways." And Sztompka writes that it needs "the condition of cultural disorientation, accompanied by social concern and expressed by intensified emotional, intellectual, organizational activism."[37] To regard a rubber bullet lodged in one's neck as part of a larger cultural trauma requires an environment that supports and provides a language that brings this into articulation.[38]

At the 2013 trilateral meeting, such emotional and intellectual awareness coalesced around the recognition of cultural trauma. I want to illustrate this briefly with respect to the Palestinian participants, who, each in their own way, had the ability to act and think in nonlinear ways—that is to say, in ways that were not predetermined by loyalty to a particular political agenda. Their readiness to try out new communicative patterns became obvious early on in the seminar when a Palestinian man not only recalled his years in an Israeli prison but also explained why he had been arrested. As a teenager he had plotted to grab a weapon from an Israeli soldier in the occupied territories by stabbing him with a knife. By telling this memory in a mixed-group setting, this man took the risk of revealing a part of himself related to accountability, and he did so in the presence of Israelis and fellow Palestinians. He abandoned the frame of a national master narrative in which Palestinian suffering is almost always couched in terms of innocence and resistance. Instead, he admitted to being part of a wider system of violence, locked into a fatal cat-and-mouse game between an occupying army and an occupied population.

Recalling stories about one's own suffering and listening to stories of the suffering of others are important steps in reconciliatory processes. In this seminar entitled "Between Trauma and Politics," we went a step further and asked each group to think about obstacles in their own community. We wanted each group (Israeli, Palestinian, German) to think about their own blind spots that impede intercultural understanding. We wanted each group to name three such obstacles, none of which could explicitly or implicitly blame anyone but oneself. This, admittedly, is a difficult task in volatile situations of prevailing power asymmetries. And yet, in this seminar each group was able to name three such obstacles. To everyone's surprise, one of the internal obstacles the Palestinian group identified on a note card read, "national aspirations." Both the Israeli and German participants had assumed that "national aspirations" would not be perceived by Palestinians as an obstacle but would be defended as a non-negotiable cornerstone to their large-group identity.

In a later session, we invited the Palestinians to unfold the meaning of this obstacle for the whole group. We asked them to sit together in the center of our circle, allowing the German and Israeli participants to eavesdrop on their conversation. It quickly became a lively debate among four Palestinian men, especially since not everyone in the group had agreed to pick "national aspirations" as an example of an internal impediment to peace. The debate eventually went around in circles, losing steam and coherence. To the outside observer, it seemed that the increasingly convoluted discussion veered around two separate issues—namely, "national identity" and "political aspirations." When made aware of this, the Palestinians felt that it made sense to separate these two issues. In a next step, we wrote these two phrases on separate cards and placed them apart in the room. I then invited the Palestinians to create a group sculpture for each phrase by using their bodies. Improvising spontaneously, they represented "national identity" as a close circle of interlocked bodies, arms around each other's shoulders, and backs turned to the outside world. It was an image of internal unity and solidarity. The sculptural representation of "political aspirations," however, showed a very different image. The Palestinians quickly scattered in the room, and there was absolutely no contact nor connection between them.

The Palestinians themselves seemed most surprised by the striking difference between their improvised sculptures. They were equally surprised that they had taken the risk to show these sculptures in the presence of Israeli Jews and Germans. It unsettled them. It caused a profound moment of cultural disorientation—the very condition that sociologist Sztompka theorized as essential for the active framing of a cultural trauma. A shift from "disorientation towards cultural trauma," he argues, manifests itself when "tensions and clashes are perceived and experienced as problems, as something troubling or painful that demands healing."[39] It was as if we just witnessed a resituating of understanding of history and a reframing of grievances by an oppressed group. The sculpture of "national identity" anchored the Palestinians in a tight-knit circle of communal support. This, it was clear, was non-negotiable. Though we might be tempted to read this spontaneous sculpture as a self-conscious political statement of solidarity, perhaps even of an enforced national unity, I would like to suggest an alternative reading. We can understand the sculpture of interlocked bodies as a symbolic gesture of "national identity" that shoulders a history of accumulated anguish and generationally transmitted fragmentations—something akin to cultural trauma. Perhaps the emotional weight of recognizing a wish for unity under the constant threat of fragmentation resisted the deliberate verbalization in the earlier round of discussion. Their bodies, however, spontaneously performed a symbolic expression of a community under duress.

Yet, the pressure for unity does not produce stability. The other sculpture, of "political aspirations," split them apart. It literally displaced the Palestinian bodies across space, leaving them in a state of political disjointedness. This seemed like a candid image of the internal frictions among Palestinians, perhaps also reflecting the political turmoil in the leadership in the West Bank territories and beyond.[40]

The difference between the earlier wordy and directionless discussion among the Palestinians and, subsequently, the clarity of their physical sculptures was arresting. Their bodies were able to express something that seemed inaccessible to language—at least on that day. It was as if an underlying anxiety was waiting to be "translated into symbolic language," a phenomenon that is well known in trauma studies.[41] More important for our purposes was the fact that this group of Palestinians was willing to expose an internal tension in the social body of their community to a group of Israelis and Germans. Revealing such tensions in the presence of those with whom one lives in enmity is part of the posture of unsettling empathy. It requires risk-taking. It unsettles what we perceive as reality as it also unsettles what others expect of us. Merely describing how each party perceives reality is not enough; it must be followed with a working-through that adjusts and revises each person's perception of one's being-in-the-world in pursuit of (re)establishing trust. Such processes, to use Cathy Caruth's words, require us to get implicated in each other's histories and traumas.

## NOTES

1. Rather than looking at trauma as an event, it might be more accurate to view it "as a process with lifelong consequences" (Julia Chaitin and Shoshana Steinberg, "'You Should Know Better': Expressions of Empathy and Disregard among Victims of Massive Social Trauma" 2008, 201).

2. See Didier Fassin and Richard Rechtman, *The Empire of Trauma* (2009, esp. 1–23). See also Wulf Kansteiner's critique of the popularity of the trauma metaphor in cultural and literary studies in "Genealogy of a Category Mistake" (2004).

3. On the difficulty of finding verbal representation of traumatic experiences, see, for example, Dana Amir, "Traumatic Miss and the Work of Mourning" (2017).

4. In *Trauma: A Social Theory* (2012), Jeffrey Alexander argues that "events are not inherently traumatic" but that "trauma is a socially mediated attribution" (13).

5. In "Cultural Traumas" (2019) cultural sociologist Giuseppe Sciortino briefly delineates distinctions of trauma theories among scholars in the humanities, social psychologists, and cultural sociologists. Sciortino argues that "extreme forms of suffering become traumatic only if they are interpreted and made meaningful to an audience in terms of wider symbolic structures" (136).

6. Wulf Kansteiner, in "Genealogy of a Category Mistake" (2004), criticizes the "liberal use of the trauma metaphor" as seemingly "epistemologically sound" but "ethically [not] responsible" outside a therapeutic setting (213). In contrast, in *Postcolonial Witnessing* (2013), Stef Craps, though also critical of trauma theory, widens the scope to non-Eurocentric settings to include the devastations of colonialism. See also Sonya Andermahr, "Decolonizing Trauma Studies" (2015).

7. The *Diagnostic and Statistical Manual of Mental Disorders* (DSM) recognizes that exposure to trauma can come about through direct experience to self or witnessing such harm to others: "The person has been exposed to a traumatic event . . . [when] the person experienced, witnessed, or was confronted with an event or events that involved actual or threatened death or serious injury, or a threat to the physical integrity of self or others" (DSM-IV-TR, 467). On witnessing, see Shoshana Felman and Dori Laub, *Testimony* (1992); for critical views on witnessing, see Gary Weissman, *Fantasies of Witnessing* (2004); Stef Craps, *Postcolonial Witnessing* (2013); and Robert Meister, *After Evil* (2012, 212–231).

8. For a good discussion of the generational transfer of memory and associated terms such as "postgeneration," see Marianne Hirsch, *The Generation of Postmemory* (2012, 1–36). For a study outside the Holocaust context, see Burcu Münyas, "Genocide in the Minds of Cambodian Youth: Transmitting (Hi)stories of Genocide to Second and Third Generations in Cambodia" (2008).

9. As mentioned in Chapter 2, Hirsch distinguishes between "familial" and "affiliative postmemory" (*The Generation of Postmemory* 2012, 36). This distinction largely, though not completely, overlaps with the difference I am drawing here between *inter*generationally and *trans*generationally transmitted memories.

10. On moral injury, see David Wood, *What Have We Done? Moral Injury of Our Longest Wars* (2016), and Robert Emmet Meagher and Douglas Pryer, *War and Moral Injury: A Reader* (2018). Both books are for a general readership, and they cite the relevant scholarly literature.

11. For arguments to acknowledge the trauma of perpetrators, see Saira Mohamed, *Of Monsters and Men: Perpetrator Trauma and Mass Atrocity* (2015); Nurit Shnabel and Arie Nadler, "A Needs-Based Model of Reconciliation: Perpetrators Need Acceptance and Victims Need Empowerment to Reconcile" (2010); Zahava Solomon, Nathaniel Laor, and Alexander McFarlane, "Acute Posttraumatic Reactions in Soldiers and Civilians" (2017); and Rachel MacNair, *Perpetration-Induced Traumatic Stress: The Psychological Consequences of Killing* (2002). Ditte Marie Munch-Justice is skeptical about some of MacNair's claims; in "Perpetrator Disgust: A Morally Destructive Emotion" (2018), Munch-Justice wonders whether scholars interpret too eagerly certain behaviors among violent perpetrators as signs of moral qualms. Looking at "disgust" as a moral emotion, she argues that the disgust perpetrators express during acts of atrocity is not a sign of moral stirrings but a weakness they strive to overcome.

12. Paul Lerner, *Hysterical Men: War, Psychiatry, and the Politics of Trauma in Germany* (2003, 1); also Judith Lewis Herman, *Trauma and Recovery* (1992, esp. Chapter 1).

13. Fassin and Rechtman (2009, 21). Similarly, cultural critic Lauren Berlant, in "The Subject of True Feeling" (1999), argues that the "tactical use of trauma to describe the effects of social inequality . . . overidentifies the eradication of pain with the achievement of social justice" (54). See also Robert Meister, *After Evil* (2012, Chapters 2 and 5).

14. See Mark Seltzer, "Wound Culture: Trauma in the Pathological Public Sphere" (1997); also Sara Ahmed, *The Cultural Politics of Emotion* (2004). For a different take on "wound culture," see Gabriele Schwab, *Haunting Legacies* (2010), especially her chapter "Identity Trouble: Guilt, Shame, and Idealization."

15. Susan Sontag, *Regarding the Pain of Others* (2003, 18).

16. Stef Craps, *Postcolonial Witnessing* (2013, 125). See also Robert Meister, *After Evil* (2012, 212–231).

17. See, for example, Mark Amstutz, *The Healing of Nations* (2005).

18. On psychological effects of witnessing, see Shoshana Felman and Dori Laub, *Testimony: Crises of Witnessing in Literature, Psychoanalysis, and History* (1992). For a fuller discussion of witnessing and secondary witnessing, see Chapter 10.

19. Krondorfer, *Remembrance and Reconciliation* (1995). These programs are documented in edited magazine-style reports that contain student essays and reflections: *Memory Work and Post-Holocaust Identity: Confronting the Past as a Third Generation* (2003); *Confronting Memory, Tolerating Differences: Encountering the Holocaust as a Third Generation* (2000); *Living in a Post-Shoah World II: Reflections of American, German, Jewish*

*and Christian Students* (1997); *Living in a Post-Shoah World I: Reflections of American, German, Jewish and Christian Students* (1994); *The Third Generation after the Shoah between Remembering, Repressing and Commemorating* (1992); and *A Journal of a German/American Student Exchange Program: Encountering the Holocaust as a Third Generation* (1990).

20. When I employ terminology related to "generationally transmitted trauma," I mostly think of social mechanisms of transmission. New research also suggests a psychobiological foundation regarding the transmission of trauma through the generational chain. In the field of epigenetics (the study of changes in organisms that are caused by modified gene expression rather than by alterations of the genetic code itself), scientists explain the epigenetic transmission of trauma as a blend of environmental and hereditary factors. In his short survey article, "Epigenetic Transmission of Holocaust Trauma: Can Nightmares Be Inherited?" (2013), Natan Kellermann concludes that transmitted (or secondary) traumatization is the result of "inherited (genetic) dispositions that can be either turned on or off, and thus activate either overwhelming anxiety or sufficient coping in the same person at different times, according to certain aggravating and mitigating (environmental) factors" (38). Concretely, when, for example, children of Holocaust survivors dream about the Holocaust, they might be genetically disposed to having nightmares, but the content of their nightmares (the Holocaust) is soaked up from their family environment.

21. This trope is a reference to Paul Celan's famous poem "Todesfuge" (Death Fugue). For the German original and an English translation (with contextual interpretation), see John Felstiner, "Paul Celan's Todesfuge" (1986).

22. The Hashomer Hatzair was founded in 1913 in Galicia as a youth movement that studied Zionism, Jewish history, and socialism. It is still in existence in Israel with international branches. For its history, with particular focus on gender relations, see Ofer Nordheimer Nur, *Eros and Tragedy* (2014).

23. Marianne Hirsch, *The Generation of Postmemory* (2012, 5; emphasis in original).

24. This workshop may have activated Oren's (dormant) anxieties due to environmental and inherited factors. Given Natan Kellermann's survey on the epigenetic transmission of Holocaust trauma (see note 20 above), it is possible to explain Oren's emphatic and embodied identification as a result of his family environment and genetic disposition, both of which were stimulated in the intergroup encounter.

25. See also Krondorfer, "Notes from a Field of Conflict" (2015).

26. Caruth (1996, 11, 24).

27. Chris Hedges, *War Is a Force that Gives Us Meaning* (2003).

28. When groups of Israelis and Palestinians officially meet in the West Bank without an international organization, permission needs to be granted by the Palestinian Authority and the Israeli security. The Palestinian Authority is the governing body of the Palestinian autonomous regions of the West Bank and, technically, also the Gaza Strip, though the latter has been ruled and governed by Hamas since 2006.

29. Sara Ahmed, *The Cultural Politics of Emotion* (2004, 65).

30. "Once fear is aroused," Neta Crawford sums up her reflections on fear as an emotion in world politics, "there is no simple way to disentangle thinking from fear and fear from thinking" ("Institutionalizing Passion in World Politics: Fear and Empathy" 2014, 540). On fear in intractable conflicts, see Daniel Bar-Tal's notion of a "collective fear orientation" ("Sociopsychological Foundations of Intractable Conflicts" 2007, 1439–1440). On the difference between fear and panic, see Rose McDermott, "The Body Doesn't Lie" (2014, 561).

31. On the issue of triangulation, see Chapter 9.

32. In a similar vein, Lila Abu-Lughod and Ahmad Sa'di write that "the problem in the Palestinian case seems to be more about collective memory than individual memory of trauma"; they do not, however, interpret this as an expression of cultural trauma but as a result of "powerful nations" not wanting "to listen" to Palestinian stories ("Introduction" 2007, 11). On trauma in the Palestinian context, see Didier Fassin and Richard Rechtman's chapter on Palestine in *The Empire of Trauma* (2009, 189–216).

33. Stef Craps, *Postcolonial Witnessing* (2013, 25–26); Sonya Andermahr, "Decolonizing Trauma Studies" (2015); and Ron Eyerman, *Cultural Trauma: Slavery and the Formation of African American Identity* (2001). For a fierce argument against the concept of cultural trauma, see Wulf Kansteiner and Harald Weilnböck, "Against the Concept of Cultural Trauma" (2008); their criticism is mainly directed against a deconstructionist discourse of trauma, which, in their assessment, valorizes a metaphorical, aestheticized, and anti-narrative view without grounding it in empirical and interdisciplinary scholarship. Their critique zooms in on, among others, Jenny Edkins's *Trauma and the Memory of Politics* (2006) and Cathy Caruth's *Unclaimed Experience* (1996). See also the controversial book by Joy Degruy, *Post Traumatic Slave Syndrome* (2005); for critique of Degruy, see Peter Wood's review, "Post Traumatic Slave Syndrome" (2014; www.nas.org/articles/post_traumatic_slave_syndrome; accessed February 16, 2019), and Ibram X. Kendi's essay "Post-Traumatic Slave Syndrome Is a Racist Idea" (*Black Perspectives*, June 21, 2016; www.aaihs.org/post-traumatic-slave-syndrome-is-a-racist-idea; accessed February 16, 2019).

34. See, for example, Pumla Gobodo-Madikizela, "Remembering the Past" (2012).

35. Piotr Sztompka, "Cultural Trauma" (2000, 453).

36. Judith Herman, *Trauma and Recovery* (1992, 9); what Herman particularly refers to in this passage is the need for political support for the "*study* of psychological trauma" (9; emphasis added).

37. Jeffrey Alexander, "Toward a Theory of Cultural Trauma" (2004, 1); Piotr Sztompka, "Cultural Trauma" (2000, 456).

38. See also Chapter 5 on "chosen trauma."

39. Sztompka, "Cultural Trauma" (2000, 455).

40. For an interesting historical account of the political tensions between the Palestinian Authority in the West Bank and Hamas in Gaza (as well as the Palestinian population), told through the documents and perspectives of these groups, see Tareq Baconi, *Hamas Contained: The Rise and Pacification of Palestinian Resistance* (2018).

41. Deirdre Boyle, "Traumatic Memory and Reenactment in Rithy Panh's *S-21*" (2009, 99). Differentiating between ordinary narratives and traumatic memory, Bessel van der Kolk and Onno van der Hart, in "The Intrusive Past" (1995), observe that while the former is a social act that can be integrated, the latter often defies language and can be recalled only if accompanied by a physical reenactment. I am not claiming that the "national identity" sculpture was an instance of traumatic recall, but I wish to point out similarities in terms of the power of embodied improvisation and symbolic physical gestures when language fails.

# FOUR

# Empathy

## *Transforming Certitudes*

The issue of empathy will be the last broad concept introduced in this book to help us frame the thorny and sometimes perplexing work with groups in conflict. "Empathy" is no less contested and complex than the terms "reconciliation," "memory," and "trauma." Like them, it has received plenty of attention in fields as diverse as social psychology, philosophy, history, sociology, art theory, political sciences, and international relations as well as primatology, anthropology, theory of mind, medical care ethics, and neurosciences.[1] In humanities scholarship, we find a number of descriptors that point to different ways of dissecting or explaining the value of empathy, such as "belated," "narrative," "imaginative," "realistic," "mediated," "empty," or "postmodern" empathy, or such phrases as "empathy fatigue," "fragility of empathy," or "empathic sadism."[2] This chapter will touch on some of those discussions, always with an eye on the usefulness of empathy when facilitating groups in conflict. As mentioned in the introduction, the qualifier "unsettling" adds an essential dimension to empathy, and the phrase "unsettling empathy" is vital to recognize the transformative potential when working in mixed-group settings.

When we get to the end of a workshop or interactive seminar, I often share observations about the process we have been through together. Occasionally I mention *unsettling empathy, which seems to be instantly intelligible and persuasive to participants. It helps them digest their encounter with the other and to understand how the labor they invested in each other has moved them—against all kinds of mental resistance—to a different place.[3] The examples described in the previous pages may have already provided a taste of what unsettling empathy might entail, and this chapter will elaborate on it in more depth. Instead of jumping straight into a definition, I will first wade through some of the ambiguities that "empathy" and related terms evoke.

## TWO POLES OF EMPATHY

In her book *A Human Being Died That Night*, Pumla Gobodo-Madikizela relates her encounter and conversations with Eugene de Kock, one of the white South African apartheid perpetrators. Dubbed "Prime Evil" by the post-apartheid media, de Kock had been sentenced to over two hundred years in prison for crimes against humanity as the commanding officer of a counterinsurgency unit of the South African police. Gobodo-Madikizela, a clinical psychologist, had served on South Africa's Truth and Reconciliation Commission as an expert on dealing with gross human rights violations. While visiting de Kock in prison for an interview, she unexpectedly began to see him as a human being. She felt he deserved some kind of recognition and perhaps even a chance at rehabilitation—a realization that she found deeply troubling but that she nevertheless proceeded to explain and affirm. Her thoughts on the value of empathy toward the end of the book are worth quoting at length:

> For the absence of empathy, whether at the communal or personal level, signals a condition that, in subtle but deeply destructive ways, separates people from one another. . . . In addition to an external context that makes reconciliation normative through the language of restoration—a truth commission, for example, or a counseling agency that focuses on victim-offender encounters, or a national dialogue that begins to put in place the symbols and vocabulary of forgiveness and compromise—there are internal psychological dynamics that impel most of us toward forming an empathic connection with another person in pain, that draws us *into* his pain, regardless who that someone is. . . . We cannot help it. We are induced to empathy because there is something in the other that is felt to be part of the self, and something in the self that is felt to belong to the other.[4]

Gobodo-Madikizela describes empathy as a deeply human trait that almost inevitably pulls us into each other's pain,[5] and she probes its limits at perhaps the most difficult crossing of human relations—namely, between perpetrators and victims. There is something compelling and touching about this passage, for what Gobodo-Madikizela describes is not an act of moral magnanimity—an act that could easily slide into a self-congratulatory gesture of sympathy from a position of power—but an encounter into which one is drawn almost against one's will and against one's better knowledge.[6] Similar stories of such unlikely encounters—which we could call "intersubjective" empathy—can be found in perhaps more places than we expect. For example, there is Michael Scott

Moore's reengagement with his former Somali kidnapper who had held him captive for more than two terrifying years.[7] We can mention Nasser Salhoba's struggle with an "intimate enemy"[8] in Libya, seeking to recognize bits of the humanity in the now-imprisoned torturer Marwan Gdoura. We can also think of Eva Mozes Kor's willingness to forgive the Nazis despite the fact that she had suffered through cruel medical experimentation in Auschwitz and lost many family members in the Holocaust. In Cambodia, the *genocidaire* Duch, who was responsible for the deaths of thousands, tearfully expressed his remorse in front of victims and survivors at the site of a killing field. In Israel and Palestine, parents from both sides who have lost loved ones due to killings caused by the respective other side have been meeting since 1995 in a forum of bereaved families to work together for peace. In a *New York Times* op-ed piece, to name a last example, the American right-wing radio host Glenn Beck expressed empathy with the Black Lives Matter movement, writing that "empathy is acknowledging someone else's pain and anger while feeling for them as human beings—even, and maybe especially, when we don't agree or understand them."[9] Any of these and similar instances can quickly draw ire from people who disbelieve the sincerity of such encounters. Skeptics can discredit motivations, such as in the case of Cambodian victims and witnesses who accused Duch of shedding "crocodile tears" during his public remorse, or in the case of Glenn Beck's melodramatic tears as another ruse of his populist public performances.[10] Critics also dispute the moral right of an individual to extend a hand to those who have committed grave harm, as in the case of Eva Mozes Kor's gesture of reconciliation reviled by other Holocaust survivors and their descendants.

On the opposite end of the spectrum of empathy is not the absence of empathy, and not even the erosion or blocking of empathy,[11] but what can be called the dark side of empathy. Generally judged as a social and moral good,[12] empathy has received its share of criticism by scholars who point to its disingenuous spirit, its slippery and ambiguous nature, and its negative and harmful sides.[13] Devoid of a moral dimension and a political grip on justice, empathy can be turned into a manipulative tool to tease, embarrass, shame, and betray others. In some academic circles, empathy is met with such a high degree of suspicion that it is generally assumed to be disingenuous—so much so that the wholesale dismissal of empathy has become its own trope of a presumed self-evident truth. This can certainly be observed in critical writings on the representation and historiography of the Holocaust.[14] Another oft-invoked case to address the dark side of empathy is torture. If empathy is defined as the imaginative ability to feel like someone else, to intrude, so to speak, into the intimate world of feelings of the other, it could very well be used against a person. In the most extreme case, it is part of a torturer's skill set. The "torturer," writes Gabriele Schwab in a chapter on deadly intimacy, must "sustain empathy to access intimate knowledge about the victim's pain." Similarly, philosopher Martha Nussbaum, in her study on the intelligence of emotions, posits that for a torturer to be successful at his art of cruelty, he "must be aware of the suffering of the victim . . . all without the slightest compassion."[15] Of course, just the opposite argument can be made about torture—namely, that torture is a violent act of political power that necessitates a complete absence of empathy.[16] But here is not the place to argue over the correct analysis of the dynamics of torture. Rather, the purpose of listing these examples is to illustrate the range of scholarly views on empathy. We must take note of those who caution against uncritically embracing empathy for its presumed redemptive value; they argue that empathy, when defined merely as the ability to feel what someone else feels, is not an inherently moral good. But we must also listen to those who affirm empathy as a deeply rooted human response that compels us to validate the humanity of even those who have harmed us and our communities.

Another way to approach empathy is to distinguish it from the related terms "pity," "sympathy," and "compassion" and from more complex terminology such as "vicarious and idealized identification" or "voyeuristic appropriation." It might be easy to distinguish empathy from pity and voyeuristic appropriation, but it is more difficult to clearly demarcate the lines between the triad sympathy-compassion-empathy, not least because they are often used interchangeably. In the end, a battle over words might be less productive than adopting a practice in which we listen carefully to the context within which a particular word is employed and to the weight it is given by a particular person. Yet, to grasp the importance I ascribe to "unsettling empathy" in this book, we cannot avoid striving for more definitional clarity.

Feeling pity is usually understood as the most superficial level of relating to someone else's pain and distress. Pity presumes that the distance between us and the person to be pitied remains intact, so much so that this person becomes an object of our fleeting concern with whom we do not wish to establish a relationship. The classic example is the viewing of graphic photographs of human beings in distress from conflict zones around the world. We might react emotionally to those images, but we do not take our emotional reaction any further, let alone act on it.[17] Empathy, on the other hand, asks us to enter into a relation. Such a relation, however, cannot bear the characteristics of voyeuristic appropriation, a manner by which we gain a certain aesthetic pleasure by seeing the pain of others while imagining ourselves in their place. This attitude has been amply criticized as being akin to a pornographic consumption of misery, not in the sense of sexualized gratification but of indulging in cruelties suffered by others.[18] The aesthetic-emotional sensations we might feel remain solipsistic, centered on us, not the other.

Identifying with a subject is another way of relating to someone other than ourselves. Contrary to voyeuristic appropriation, where spectators orbit around their own pleasurized distress, in vicarious and idealized identification we wish to abandon the self and *become* the other. It could be described as a way of sympathizing with someone else to the extent that boundaries between self and other get blurred. The other ceases to exist as "other." In vicarious and idealized identification, we imagine that by becoming the other we will fully know and understand the other and hence be able to speak in their voice. Often, though, we have formed the other in our own image and end up speaking not in their voice but in their stead.

*Vicarious* identification refers to people's desire to identify with an aspect of their own legacy that they themselves did not experience directly. In this sense, it is related to the phenomena of inherited trauma and postmemory addressed in the previous two chapters. Critics, like humanities professor Ruth Leys, dispute such notions, arguing that the conflation of boundaries between history and memory leads individuals to erroneously believe that they can inhabit "the same psychology" as the social group they belong to.[19] *Idealized* identification refers to identifying with people who are different from ourselves, usually in the context of real or imagined power imbalances; as such, it is related to sympathy.[20] In situations of sustained social conflict, idealized identification can go two ways: victimized and colonized people can idealize their aggressors and oppressors, or people in power and descendants of perpetrators can idealize victims.[21] Especially for descendants of wrongdoers, it is tempting to avoid carrying the weight of their ancestors' guilt and, instead, to identify with those who have been victimized. We could say that in contrast to empathy, which respects boundaries and aims at seeing the other as the other, vicarious and idealized identifications blur boundaries. Painting identification in such negative terms seems to leave little room for any redemptive qualities in identifying with the other. However, when working with groups in conflict, vicarious or idealized identifications can be productive stepping-stones in the process of trust- and awareness-building.[22]

If we consider pity, voyeuristic appropriation, and vicarious/idealized identifications to be problematic expressions of feeling with, for, or about the other, it is less easy to distinguish empathy from compassion and sympathy. If pity can be described as a feeling *about* people, the other three terms (compassion, sympathy, empathy) have been variously, but inconsistently, described as feeling *with* or *for* people.[23] The prefixes *com-* (Latin: with/together) and *sym-* (Greek: with/together) seem to point to some intrinsic similarity between com/passion and sym/pathy. It is feeling "with" someone's situation, or "together with" someone. "Passion" (Latin: *passio*) and "pathy" (Greek: *pathos*) also hold alike meanings, though *pathos* refers to emotions more generally (including suffering), whereas *passio* denotes suffering specifically. Where does this leave us with empathy? The prefix *em-* refers to "putting something into a certain state"; it indicates an active component.[24] "Empathy," which entered the English language only about 120 years ago and is derived from the Greek *empatheia* (a state of emotion) is the ability to actively put oneself into the emotional state of another.[25]

Whether this brief etymological exercise is helpful, I am not certain, but it provides a few clues as to why scholars and practitioners generally regard sympathy and compassion as feeling for someone else's situation from a place somewhat removed. This distance could be described as a "unidirectional" flow of feelings from those in a safe and neutral position to those who find themselves in a less fortunate situation.[26] Empathy, on the other hand—at least when it is accepted as a moral good rather than dismissed as disingenuous affectation—contains a dimension that is less about one's own feelings and more about the state of others. Social psychologist Daniel Batson, for example, calls empathy the ability to recognize "the internal states of others" *and* to respond "with sensitivity to their suffering." Bioethicist Jodi Halpern and human rights advocate Harvey M. Weinstein define "empathy [as] imagining and seeking to understand the perspective of another person." Comparative literature professor Gabriele Schwab defines empathy as a "form of intersubjective relationality—a gift of emotional connection to the other." Similarly, the historian Carolyn Dean emphasizes that empathy operates in a "mode of intersubjective relations [that keep] healthy boundaries and [respect] the otherness of the other." And social policy analyst Elizabeth Segal persuasively argues that empathy, though neurobiologically hardwired into our human fabric, can be (and must be) trained and developed.[27] I find myself among those voices. *Empathy, as a positive force, is our imaginative ability to understand the experience of someone other than ourselves by entering into a relational process that is both affective and cognitive. Empathy pursues, as philosopher Amy Coplan argues, an "other-oriented perspective."[28] Although rooted, located, and activated in the self, empathy is not about the self but about the other.

## WHAT DO YOU (NOT) SEE?

To illustrate the difference between pity and empathy—and everything in between—I want to use an example from my university courses in which I teach issues related to violence and trauma to (mostly) American students. Part of my teaching philosophy in these courses is to get students to comprehend the human dimension of historical trauma. This includes awareness of our *moral emotions (such as embarrassment, guilt, shame, anger, disgust, contempt, but also gratitude and pride) when we respond to or make sense of human-made disasters.[29] One of the more difficult and sensitive issues in the U.S. context is the history of lynching, and in particular the showing and exhibiting of lynching photographs. I do not spare my students the sight of those photographs. Together, we look at some select images in class, and I ask them: What do you see?

This particular unit is embedded within a larger discussion on collective forms of violence and visual representations of cruelties. Sessions on racialized violence in the United States are proceeded by an examination of communal violence in other places. We will have read, for example, parts of Sudhir Kakar's *The Colors of Violence* about the ferocious history of Hindu-Muslim riots in India. Kakar, an Indian psychoanalyst and cultural psychologist, opens his book with his reactions to a photograph of a two-year-old girl with a deep gash across her face—a victim of the communal hatreds he is about to analyze. Kakar pulls us into the all-too-familiar situation of consuming photographs of violence as they stream in daily on multiple media platforms. He confronts us with the very site where pity usually rules our reaction: we see the photo of the disfigured girl with a mix of diffuse emotions, but we don't really see it. Kakar writes:

> I cannot empathize with the child because I must defend myself against her pathos. It is far easier for me to pity her. Pity is distant. The girl's face, then, is not haunting but nagging, . . . evoking an angry guilt. . . . The core of the analyst's sensibility does not lie in clinical expertise or in a specific way of observing and interpreting people's words and actions. . . . The core is empathy. Empathy is the bridge between the serene reserve of the clinician striving for objectivity and the vital, passionate, and vulnerable person who inhabits the clinician's body. . . . Without its vital presence, I fear that the creative tension between objectivity and impassioned involvement, between the stoic and the emotionally responsive perspectives, will be lost.[30]

In my class, we discuss this passage in depth, grasping the difference between pity and empathy and also addressing what "learning" at a university level entails. In addition to teaching unaffected objectivity (which allows us to respond to suffering with technical knowledge and professional skills), do we need awareness of our own vulnerability when responding morally and emotionally to what we see? By the time we get to viewing select photographs of lynching, we have already been sensitized to the ways people respond to violence.

Many lynching photographs eerily resemble each other.[31] The camera focuses in on the contorted, tortured, cut, whipped, and oft-times burned bodies of predominantly black men, hanging from trees or lamp posts. Encircling and surrounding this body are white onlookers. There is a visual center and a periphery, inverse to the real power relations: the mutilated black body is central, the white onlookers peripheral. The photo I use in class when asking, "What do you see?" is the lynching of Rubin Stacy in Fort Lauderdale, Florida, on July 19, 1935. It shows the body of a young black man hanging from a tree with a rope around his neck and his hands handcuffed in front of him; he is surrounded by a group of smiling white men and women in their fine Sunday dresses, including several teenage and younger girls. [32]

After a few moments of silence, students hesitantly begin to speak. Their responses cover the whole spectrum associated with empathy as detailed above. If it is pity, a typical expression goes like this: "I have seen pictures like this before. It is a terrible part of our history," or "I feel very sorry. Is this what you ask us to feel?" There is defensiveness in these replies, keeping "our history" at arm's length or assuming that they ought to "feel sorry" (in response to the question of what they *see*, not what they *feel*). Other students articulate their distress over the graphic violence depicted, a response I call *spectacular* distress (which is of course related to the originary act of spectacular violence). [33] It can be interpreted as a form of sympathy, a suffering "with" the victim. Eventually, the focus of the students' comments shifts away from the victim to the on-lookers on the periphery. Students now express distress at the smiling faces of the white crowd, especially the children. This response I call *moral* distress. It is a reckoning with the amorality of the situation, per-haps an expression of compassion insofar as it is triggered by a reckoning with a diversity of feelings represented in this photo. We also get re-sponses of identification, when, for example, an African American stu-dent identifies with the body of Rubin Stacy and says, "This could be me." We can call this response a manifestation of an empathetic *vicarious* identification. [34] It also happens that we get responses that approximate a kind of *idealized* identification, when, for example, a white student insists on being able to understand only the pain of the unjustly tortured black victim while claiming not to be able to relate to any of the white onlook-ers. [35]

What, then, about empathy? If empathy is, as I suggest above, the imaginative ability to understand the experience of someone other than oneself by entering into a relational process that is both affective and cognitive, the student responses so far have not yet reached the level of empathy. They are still unidirectional, articulating the affective impact of the photograph on the self. Empathy's relational quality is not yet activat-ed: students are not interacting with each other regarding the impact of showing this photograph in class, nor do they make connections to mem-ories passed on (or not passed on) in their familial and communal envi-ronments.

A series of questions will guide the students into a more relational engagement. For example, I ask what they think about the identity and motivation of the photographer. Or I ask with whom (if anyone) they identify when looking at the photo and what this tells them about themselves today. The latter question usually triggers levels of discomfort because it makes the students aware of their identities within the racialized context of American history. It makes them aware of whom they wish not to be identified with. They also become alert to the diversity in the classroom. Some students react defensively, pointing out, for instance, that their grandparents arrived in the United States only after the period of lynching or that their families lived in places where lynching did not occur. When adding those layers to our class discussion, distress over the graphic content of a historical photo morphs into tension over identity politics in the current environment. What until now has been a visually unsettling experience (looking at the photograph) is moving into the unsettling terrain of current relationships (in the classroom). Often, our first class session on lynching photographs ends on such an unsettling note.

When, a few days later, we meet again in class, we expand the discussion by asking how present the memory of lynching is in our respective communities of belonging. Predictably, most students of white European ancestry say it is not present, while black American students say it is. Students of more recent immigrant families, especially from Asia, have little knowledge, while Mexican American and Native American students in Arizona report a range of familiarity with the topic.[36] To help with the conversation, I often tell them briefly about the buried and selective memories in my family of origin when growing up in postwar Germany. I then ask: Where is the memory of lynching in the white community?

In *Regarding the Pain of Others*, Susan Sontag writes:

> A trove of photographs of black victims of lynching in small towns in the United States between the 1890s and 1930s . . . tell us about human wickedness. About inhumanity. They force us to think about the extent of the evil unleashed specifically by racism. Intrinsic to the perpetration of this evil is the shamelessness of photographing it. The pictures were taken as souvenirs and made, some of them, into postcards; more than a few show grinning spectators . . . posing for a camera with the backdrop of a naked, charred, mutilated body hanging from a tree.[37]

Where did the memory of white spectators go? What happened to the memory of those who were children in the photo? Witnessing a lynching in 1935, for example, these children must have still been alive at the turn of the twenty-first century. And what happened to the perpetrators' memory objects—those postcards, souvenirs of collected body parts, and framed photos with pubic hair of the victims glued to them? Historian Amy Louis Wood reports that lynching was "often deliberatively performative and ritualized" and "frequently made public . . . through displays of lynched bodies and souvenirs" as well as "photographs," "songs," and "lurid narratives" long after the killings were over.[38] Were these souve-

nirs and objects passed on, hidden, or discarded? These concerns intensify our class conversation. Interactions between the students become
both weighed down and enriched by the emergence of moral emotions
that are difficult to process: embarrassment and guilt about the silencing
of this history among some students, pride in the resilience of their communities among others.

Only once did it happen in the numerous classes I have taught on this
subject over the years that a white student came forward with an unexpected admission. In an almost classical case of psychic resistance, he had
earlier attracted the ire of his fellow students when spouting insensitive
remarks about the lynching photographs. He questioned the value of
showing them, claimed he could not relate to them, and suggested that
we accept that bad things happen in history and move on. In the follow-
up session, when we inquired about the presence and absence of lynching memories in different communities, he took a deep breath, then announced: "My family told stories about a lynching. I think it was one of
my great-uncles who was there. I don't know much about it. But I know
my family was involved." It was the only time a student admitted that
family members of an earlier generation had been part of a lynching—
perhaps one of the onlookers in the white mob so ever-present in these
photos, or worse.

Admitting the complicity and culpability of one's extended family is
not the linchpin in defining empathy. The student's admission merely
illustrates the candor that can be reached when a learning environment
does not limit itself to the dissemination of historical facts or to critical
analysis of representation but also engages students on the level of empathy. We could have used those photos merely as illustrations in a lecture
on the history of lynching. Or we could have chosen not to use them at all
for all the problematic reasons of voyeurism and numbing sensationalism
that scholars and educators have addressed. Countering such concerns,
Susan Sontag writes: "It has become a cliché of the cosmopolitan discussion of images of atrocity to assume they have little effect, and that there
is something innately cynical about their diffusion." It "is absurd," she
continues, "to generalize about the ability to respond to the suffering of
others" based on those who are consumers of images or remain distant
spectators. Yes, images of suffering may evoke mere pity or feed our
sensationalist appetites, but, as Elizabeth Segal asserts, empathy is something that must—beyond being part of our neurobiological makeup—be
learned and developed. [39]

Moving from knowledge dispensation to acknowledgment requires
additional steps of *Durcharbeiten* (working-through). In the example
above, asking "What do you see?" was only a first step for students to
realize their unconscious preferences when looking at the photo of Rubin
Stacy's body. It helped them to analyze the image's content, framing, and
context but also to become aware of their emotional attachments and

defenses. The initial round of "seeing" remained unidirectional insofar as the flow stayed between spectator and image. Steered by pity, sympathy, and identification, students reported and reflected on how the photograph affected them, but they did not yet adopt an other-oriented perspective. Moving from "this is what I see" to "what we do not see" opened up the process to the relational quality of empathy that I consider so vitally important. When this happens, it is always an unsettling experience—but it opens the possibility of acknowledging how we are implicated in each other's histories and lives.

## EMPATHY THAT UNSETTLES

If empathy as an other-directed orientation is our imaginative ability to understand the experience of someone other than ourselves by entering into a relational process that is both affective and cognitive, why do we need the additional qualifier "unsettling"? In the example above, the class discussion could have stopped when the students realized how differently they identified with the lynching photograph, or after recognizing and absorbing their different cognitive perspectives and emotional attachments. Perhaps this is all that can be expected to happen in an academic environment. Most educators would not push any further for curricular, pedagogical, or political reasons. In an increasingly risk-averse educational environment, with its trigger warnings and administrative oversight, there are fewer and fewer incentives for instructors to take the risk of employing discomfort as a tool of learning. The fact that I occasionally allow such "unsettling" to happen in my courses I admit with some trepidation (as I imagine some of my colleagues' negative comments), but stronger than any trepidation is my belief that these moments are a benefit to my students.[40] Be that as it may, an academic environment is not the same as working with groups in conflict, and it is the latter where more is at stake and where alternative forms of exploration are not only welcome but necessary.

*Unsettling* empathy, in addition to our imaginative ability to understand the experience of someone other than ourselves, requires a willingness to be challenged and the ability to embrace such a challenge. As an ethical posture toward the other, it shakes up ("unsettles") our foundational assumptions about the world, compelling us to fully validate the existence of the other as the other is, not as we wish them to be. Unsettling empathy is a relational commitment to caring responsiveness in the face of past injustices and power asymmetries. It requires taking the risk of vulnerability in the face of the other.

I coined the term "unsettling empathy" a few years ago, for it sharpens and clarifies elements that I perceive as essential in reconciliatory processes. Unsettling empathy, I suggest, requires two elements: a willingness to be challenged by the other, and the ability to turn this challenge into a positive disposition. Put differently: unsettling empathy is a *willingness* to be unsettled by the presence of the other regarding our own attitudes and assumptions about the world, our identification with large-group identities, and, to some extent, regarding our deeply held beliefs and values. As Halpern and Weinstein put it, the "cognitive" and "emotional openness" of empathy "tolerate[s] ambivalence."[41] Unsettling empathy is also the *ability* to embrace such a challenge as beneficial and enter into "productive engagement" with "memories, histories, and identities" of the other without having to give up who we are.[42]

In the field of trauma studies, Dominick LaCapra has developed the concept of "empathic unsettlement" to make a similar point. He views empathy, like I do, as a "counterforce to numbing."[43] When I speak about unsettling empathy, which reverses the order of his wording, I am gesturing toward LaCapra's alike-sounding phrase. The concepts, however, are not identical. Whereas LaCapra is interested in empathic unsettlement as a theoretical concept to analyze trauma in relation to the problem of history, historiography, and representation, I am interested in unsettling empathy primarily as an ethical practice that can be learned and acquired. Let me briefly elaborate on this difference.

According to LaCapra, it is not sufficient to respond to historical trauma merely through the lens of "objective reconstructions of the past," as many historians do. Equally problematic would be to appropriate historical trauma through a "vicarious" and "unchecked identification" by secondary witnesses. While the first (objective) response errs on the side of neglecting the subjectively experienced traumatic impact, the second (vicarious) response errs on the side of a well-intended, but ultimately facile, "surrogate victimage." Vicarious witnessing can lead to an overidentification with victims so that the boundaries between self (witness) and other (victim) get blurred.[44] The concept of empathic unsettlement, according to LaCapra, avoids such traps. "Resist[ing] full identification with . . . the experience of the other," empathic unsettlement creates a "desirable affective" relation with the other in order to understand their traumatic suffering. It allows us to respond to trauma without seeking closure, thus recognizing "unsettling possibility" contained in traumatizing events.[45]

LaCapra's theorizing about empathic unsettlement takes place, according to one of his interpreters, "primarily in the context of aesthetic representations by historians or 'secondary witnesses' . . . based on the experiences of the Holocaust."[46] There is, of course, nothing wrong with doing so. My concern, however, does not rest in aesthetic, literary, or cultural representations but seeks to understand the practice of reconciliatory processes. Nevertheless, there are two key components of LaCapra's theoretical insights—identification and closure—that relate to my own observations.

First, the issue of identification. The kind of empathy LaCapra and I pursue resists an equation of empathy with identification. To empathize with someone else should not be confused with becoming the other person, as is often assumed when empathy is commonly translated into the image of "stepping into" or "walking in the shoes" of another. We do not need to become the other in order to empathize. When LaCapra cautions against vicarious overidentification, he criticizes the unhelpful blurring of boundaries between secondary witnesses and victims.[47] It is a wrong-headed narcissistic fusion with the other, he asserts, in which the other ceases to exist as other. For example, in one of my workshops with Israelis and Palestinians, an attending Israeli human rights lawyer accused a Palestinian participant of collaboration because he had voiced an interest in reaching out to Jewish settlers in the West Bank. The lawyer's intention was to show undivided political solidarity with the plight of the Palestinian people. Hence, she dismissed the Palestinian's wish to step outside the boundaries of a politically correct narrative. Despite her well-intentioned gesture of idealized identification, her undifferentiated fusion with an imagined political correctness erased the other as other. She did not invest curiosity in understanding where the wish of this Palestinian man came from. In another situation, where the issue of trust and mistrust was on the table, a Palestinian told Israeli participants that they could only gain his trust if they agreed with his political position. Here, too, the difference between self and other was erased. In both cases, empathy and identification became fused in unhelpful ways. Requesting from either Israelis or Palestinians an empathetic conformity with particular political positions expunges the "otherness" of the other. Empathy in reconciliatory processes does not work in such unidirectional ways.

Unsettling empathy requires the willingness to question assumptions about ourselves and presuppositions about the other—but it does not ask us to become the other. Amos Goldberg, an Israeli Jewish Holocaust scholar working in the field of trauma, history, and representations, grapples with a similar issue in the context of the Nakba (the 1948 expulsion of Palestinians from their land) and the Holocaust as "defining events" for Palestinians and Israelis.[48]

> Empathy does not ask subjects to put themselves in the victim's shoes, to take the victim's place, but to identify specifically with the traumatic core of the victim's existence, thereby recognizing the *separateness*, lack and radical otherness that are inevitable components of relations with trauma victims and, in fact, of social relationships in general.[49]

Goldberg's recognition of empathy as separateness rather than identification coincides with my understanding of unsettling empathy. Not surprisingly, he employs a similar term in the context of the Palestinian-Israeli conflict: "disruptive empathy."[50]

Second, the issue of closure. LaCapra's insistence that empathic unsettlement is a response that seeks no closure but accepts unsettling possibilities parallels my assertion of the affective and cognitive openness of empathy and of the open-endedness of reconciliatory processes in general. "Empathic unsettlement," LaCapra writes, "poses a barrier to closure and places in jeopardy harmonizing or spiritually uplifting accounts of extreme events."[51] Not limited to the trauma context within which LaCapra operates, the same can be stated for moments of unsettling empathy as they occur in intergroup encounters. Unsettling empathy in reconciliatory settings resists closure; its efficacy is not measured by achieving harmonious unity. It does not prove its success when people hold hands and sing "Kumbaya,"[52] regardless of how often these clichés get repeated in the media or are reenacted in less rigorous settings.

Unsettling empathy, then, plays a crucial role when working with groups in conflict. It is a posture that needs to be learned and practiced by people who, because of identifying with large-group identities, have come to distrust each other. It is neither just a pedagogical tool or didactic element nor simply a skill or method. Instead, unsettling empathy is a posture insofar as it is a kind of practiced awareness and a relational commitment to caring responsiveness.

As opposed to compassion and sympathy, unsettling empathy calls us into the presence of objective differences without negating the vitality of human interaction. The posture of unsettling empathy allows for the inclusion of both a critical perspective on power asymmetries (regarding injustices and trauma) *and* a building-up of relational trust with the other, despite wrongdoing in the past and contentious memories in the present. This is not a recipe that populist politicians or national leaders promote. It is, however, a central element for working with groups in conflict on a grassroots level, for it blends the critical and political dimension with the affective and intersubjective dimension of empathy.

Being aware of the transformative potential of unsettling empathy has very practical implications, and it can be trained, learned, and refined. It is also an ethical vision. It is a deliberate ethical stance that, ideally and over time, might become an acquired disposition and sensibility that eventually informs, guides, and structures our attitudes toward life.[53] Because it demands our willingness to engage with others as they are, not as we wish them to be, it is costly. It questions the certitude[54] with which we tend to operate when we hold on to identitarian memories, fortify our familial and national narratives, try to legitimize violence, or frame unjustly endured harms as trauma in order to secure large-group solidarity. The moment unsettling empathy occurs is not a pleasant experience, but it is a transformative one.

## WE ARE IN THIS HISTORY TOGETHER

The language I employ to describe the transformative potential of unsettling empathy might set high expectations about working with groups in conflict. Surely some dramatic climax ought to occur! Surely the participants, as if caught in an act of conversion, would emerge from a crisis reborn! Reality, however, is more humbling. Working through mistrust, injurious memories, and traumatic histories requires emotional and cognitive labor that mostly unfolds in small steps. The seminar-workshop I will describe below to illustrate the posture of unsettling empathy will dampen high expectations. I do so deliberately in order to show the small steps groups can take toward unsettling empathy. In this particular interfaith meeting, the participants sidestepped passionate engagement with moral emotions because they were more comfortable with a cognitive approach to understanding differences. What this example will demonstrate, then, is that an unsettling of certitudes and beliefs can transpire even when a group is not ready or willing to render themselves vulnerable in more personal terms.

The three-day workshop-seminar took place in Weimar and Buchenwald in January 2002. A group of Jewish religious leaders and rabbis from the Chicago area was visiting Germany for a nine-day, government-sponsored tour, meeting with politicians, diplomats, and community leaders to learn about contemporary Germany. It was organized by the (now-defunct) Bridge of Understanding, whose director invited me to develop, plan, and facilitate a workshop on interfaith dialogue. For those three days, German religious leaders from the Catholic and Protestant traditions met in Weimar with their Jewish counterparts from Chicago. The goal was to lay a foundation for more trusting relationships between religious professionals from the United States and Germany. Given the strained relationships between Jews and Christians over the long history of Christian anti-Judaism, and particularly between Germans and Jews in light of the recent history of racial and genocidal antisemitism, we called this workshop-seminar "Our Faith in the Face of the Abyss."[55] The twenty-seven participants understood that we would address the following questions in a conversational and interactive setting: What do we need from each other in order to renew our relationships as American Jews and German Christians? Is it possible to bridge differences that are the result of political and religious history? Can faith traditions sustain us in the face of a traumatic past so that we can work together for a better future?

The significance of meeting in Weimar and Buchenwald was not lost on the participants. The two locations are fraught with historical and symbolic significance. Weimar had been a center for German literary and avant-garde culture before World War II (Goethe and Schiller lived there, and the city is remembered for its 1920s Bauhaus school). The city was also politically important. The first German democracy after World War I was called the Weimar Republic, and when Hitler set out to destroy it, it was not accidental that the Buchenwald concentration camp was built nearby. Buchenwald is a site of Germany's darkest hours, a place of terror for political prisoners from Germany and numerous other nations, and later a death trap for Jews who survived the brutal evacuations and death marches from labor camps farther to the east. The geographic choice of our meeting location added weight to the necessity of starting a conversation across religious, cultural, and national differences.

The American group consisted of male and female rabbis and community leaders, representing a diversity of age and religious outlook (reform, conservative, reconstructionist, and modern orthodox). Many worked as congregational rabbis, others in leadership positions of Jewish community organizations. The German group consisted of Protestant and Catholic clergy, theologians, religious educators, and interfaith directors; their group composition also reflected gender, age, and regional diversity. It included East and West Germans. Among them, for example, were two young theologians still in training as well as pastors who for many years have brought awareness of the importance of Jewish-Christian dialogue to their local parishes. Most of those leaders promoting Jewish-Christian relations in Germany had had no prior opportunities to discuss issues of faith with a large group of American rabbis.

Before the official beginning of the workshop-seminar, the American group and some early German arrivals got a tour of the city by the director of Weimar's Goethe Institute. To the amusement of the group, he led us to some of the locations where Goethe pursued his amorous affairs. He also divulged that the famous singer and actress Marlene Dietrich had spent time as a student in the building now occupied by the Goethe Institute. The Bauhaus, too, was of special significance. Mies van der Rohe, the director of the Bauhaus architecture school, left Germany after the Nazis seized power and found his way eventually to Chicago.

During the seminar's opening sessions, the participants introduced themselves, revealing the group's rich diversity. Many of the Jewish religious leaders from Chicago had not been to Germany before, and they forthrightly expressed their concerns about being here. They also told the group that members of their families and congregations had misgivings about their travel. The German group, as a whole, was a little more cautious and guarded, with some veiled expressions of guilt feelings.

To involve as many participants of this fairly large group as possible, we distributed colored index cards. Every participant wrote down what she or he considered the most pressing religious or theological issue today. These anonymous topic cards were collected, redistributed, and then read aloud. The spectrum of issues was as broad as the group's diversity: Torah learning—theology after Auschwitz—community—compassion—religious teachings of tolerance—reconciliation—serving

God—Jews as chosen people—can Jews and Christians pray together—
dialogue for peace—never again; and so forth. The group listened to the
concerns as presented on these index cards. Since no one was identified
by name, the conversation never became defensive. To everyone's surprise, many of the listed theological and religious concerns could not
easily be identified as either Christian or Jewish—except for a few, like
the card on "reconciliation." At least this is what Arnold Jacob Wolf
assumed, an American reform rabbi who was part of the Chicago group.
Born in 1924, Wolf had been a champion of peace and progressive politics
in the United States. He passed away in 2008, six years after we met.[56]
When looking at the reconciliation card, Rabbi Wolf was certain that it
could have only been written by a Christian. For Jews, Wolf was convinced, the concept of reconciliation in the shadows of Buchenwald was
*treyfah* (forbidden). Only much later did a Jewish male participant reveal
that it was him who had penned the word "reconciliation" on the card.

On the second day, we created a *fishbowl. This is a technique in
which a few people sit in an inner circle to talk about a given topic while
a surrounding larger group eavesdrops on the conversation. The fishbowl exercise is particularly effective in large groups when discussions
tend to lose focus. The fishbowls I conduct usually have a tap-in, tap-out
option. If a person wants to join the conversation, he or she can tap
someone in the circle on the shoulder, thus requesting that person to
vacate the seat for someone else. The topic for the inner circle was "Never
again!" Someone had written it earlier on one of the index cards. Six
people, half of them American, the other half German, started the conversation in the small circle. They wondered: How do Jews and Christians
use the phrase "Never again"? It slowly dawned on them that "Never
again" (in German, "Nie wieder") has been used quite differently in each
community. Whereas in the German discourse it usually refers to a call to
pacifism after the two world wars (*Nie wieder Krieg*—Never again war), in
the Jewish community it refers to "never again the Holocaust." For the
Jewish community, it is a call to vigilance and political strength: Never
again will we walk like sheep to the slaughter! The Jewish and Christian
religious leaders realized that their employment of this phrase had little
do to with ethical or theological reasoning; instead, it was shaped, and
perhaps dictated, by the different ways each group had learned to interpret the lessons of history.[57]

In the evening, before the group's trip to the memorial site of Buchenwald, we addressed our worries concerning the visit. Would this place
bond American Jewish leaders with their Christian German peers, or
would it pull them apart? Participants were asked to jot down notes
about their fears and expectations of visiting this site as a mixed group. In
a next step, we asked whether it was desirable to create a liturgical moment of commemoration together as Jews and Christians at the site of the
former concentration camp. A consensus slowly emerged that it would

be important to do so. After everyone had a chance to suggest one key element they would like to see as a part of a commemoration, the task of finding a commemorative format was delegated to a smaller group.

The day we toured Buchenwald was cold, cloudy, and rainy. The drabness of January added to the gloomy mood emanating from the camp's remains. Daniel Gaede, the educational director of the Buchenwald memorial, who had been with us throughout the workshop-seminar, served as our guide. He balanced sensitively the need for information with time for emotional processing. A particularly sensitive place was the pathology room next to the crematory where flayed and tortured bodies had been dissected. Some rabbis connected it to Rabbi Akiva who, in ancient times, had been tortured to death by the Romans. Others raised questions about God: at this place, they said, we Jews are confused about God—but deep down we are more bitterly disappointed by human beings. A female rabbi, whose husband, she said, was the great-grandchild of Leo Baeck, a leading German rabbi of liberal Judaism in the early twentieth century,[58] was particularly appalled by the porcelain insulators used for the electric barbed-wire fences surrounding the camp. These insulators were produced by the Rosenthal porcelain company. "I now understand why my grandmother refused to buy Rosenthal porcelain," she exclaimed. German participants struggled with their own issues of faith, several of whom disagreed vehemently with each other. "The senseless death of Christ on the cross," a woman pastor from Berlin stated, "helps us to meditate the senseless death in Buchenwald." A Dominican priest disagreed: "We know that some SS guards had crucifixes in their homes and taught their children to pray. What does this say about the power of the cross? Where was God?"[59]

Arnold Jacob Wolf made a discovery that became particularly meaningful to him. He came across a plaque remembering the Jewish Austrian prisoner Bruno Bettelheim, who had survived and then emigrated to the United States. Bettelheim later settled in Chicago, where he became a famous and controversial child psychologist. During his lifetime, people accused Bettelheim of inaccurately describing the conditions of camp life due to the fact that he was in Buchenwald "merely" for a short time in 1939. Bettelheim committed suicide in 1990.[60] "Bettelheim was my neighbor in Chicago," Rabbi Wolf said. "Our kids played together." Now standing in Buchenwald himself, Wolf continued, he realized how wrong his accusers had been. What did they mean when they attacked Bettelheim for "merely" being in Buchenwald? "I feel the need to honor him, now that I've seen this place."

At the remaining stone foundation of a barrack, the group pulled together for their commemoration. It was a cautious liturgy, reduced to the bare bones of reading a biblical psalm in Hebrew, English, and German, humming a song in Hebrew, and reciting the *kaddish*, the mourning prayer. Brief as it was, it was utterly meaningful to the participants. What they had feared before their visit did not come true. German religious leaders had feared that they might not feel anything in Buchenwald or be tempted to wrongly identify with the victims; Jewish religious leaders had feared being constantly observed by others or that they might become upset and angry in the company of Germans.

When we gathered at the hotel for reflection that evening and the next morning, the earlier anxieties had dissipated and been replaced with (theological) confusion and (personal) sadness. We processed our experiences in witnessing circles. In the first circle, everyone from the American Jewish group was in the center talking about their impressions, while the Christian Germans were listening. In the second circle, we reversed the roles. Each group responded to the same question: "How can our faith traditions sustain us in the face of the Holocaust?" Arnold Jacob Wolf shared his utter surprise about a German participant of a younger generation who had helped him walk across some icy spots in Buchenwald. "A complete stranger—he helped me over the ice!" he said incredulously. "I expected to be angry yesterday; instead I was overcome by sadness." Later, Rabbi Wolf added a memory from thirty years ago. He had been invited as a rabbi to attend a Christian ecumenical world conference, and there he met pastor Martin Niemöller, one of the few Christians resisting the Nazi regime.[61] "Those days were a highlight in my life," he said, "and these days in Weimar are my second highlight." A German participant confided that in previous meetings with only Christian participants she had never experienced "such sincerity when discussing questions of faith in the shadows of the Holocaust." A Jewish participant said: "I realize now that we, as Jews and Germans, are in this history together."

When we departed, we were not quite the same people. The liturgical framing of a traumatic and divisive past provided a shared language that defied prior expectations and doubts. Rudimentary as the liturgical moment had been, it was a focal point: it gave the group direction to their more anxious moments *before* the visit of the memorial site, and it generated trust and mutual acknowledgment *after* the visit. The shared liturgical moment was not a closure; quite the opposite, it opened new possibilities. As one of the Chicago rabbis stated at the very end: "Perhaps we just got to the point where we might dare to look at the really scary issues."

In those short three days, we may not have gotten to the truly "scary issues," but the safe and interactive environment we created enabled these religious leaders to engage each other as American Jews and German Christians, entering into conversations that blended personal anxieties, religious concerns, and theological issues without the defensiveness that dominates so many public debates.

## UNSETTLING AS A CRITICAL PRACTICE

The degree to which particular groups, or individuals within a group, feel unsettled by the encounter with the other varies widely. The interfaith encounter described above may seem relatively innocuous and safe when compared to working with groups who find themselves in intractable violent conflicts. But this is not a competition of who dares to be unsettled most. Each group calls for its own guidelines and parameters, and each will move as far as its participants are willing to go in a given situation. In this book, we come across different scenarios, from slightly more cerebral approaches in educational settings to moments of haunting that push the boundaries of what seems endurable.

In educational theories concerned with social justice, the notion of unsettlement has been used to refer to a critical pedagogical practice of remembrance that "initiate[s] a continual unsettling."[62] To be attentive to the actual dynamics of empathy in intercultural group settings is such a critical practice.[63] A posture of unsettling empathy can be actively incorporated within a protective space; and insofar as the Latin *corpus* refers also to the anatomical body, the in*corpo*ration of unsettling empathy includes embodied, nonverbal approaches when facilitating groups in conflict.

The protective environment that needs to be provided for unsettling empathy to occur has been variously referred to as third space, liminal space, transitional space, or intermediary space. Importantly, it is an intentional space created outside of ordinary rules that individuals and communities impose on themselves. It is conducive to hold and handle high social tension within groups while creatively exploring what Cathy Caruth might call a "resituating [of] our understanding," or Roger Simon calls a "reworking [of our] notions of community, identity, embodiment, and relationships."[64] In a similar vein, Pumla Gobodo-Madikizela—with respect to apartheid's historical trauma—speaks of the necessity for dialogical engagement with "testimonies [that] are unsettling" within a frame of "making public spaces intimate."[65] Her spatial metaphor mirrors what I consider essential when working with groups in conflict where large-group identities are at stake: to express and reveal the intimate wounds of historical and cultural trauma in spaces that surpass the purely intersubjective and address the political emotions that dominate the public domain. "At the core of what unfolds in these encounters," Gobodo-Madikizela writes, "is a *reciprocal mutual engagement.*"[66]

The posture of unsettling empathy has yet another advantage over a less-differentiated notion of compassion. A compassionate attitude has the tendency to erase some of the objective differences of agency vis-à-vis traumatic history. In the name of a common humanity, compassion too quickly glosses over the ethical difference between harm inflicted and harm endured, presenting all sides as victims of circumstances they could not control. Unsettling empathy, on the other hand, calls us into the presence of objective differences without negating the vitality of human interaction. For example, when a descendant of a perpetrator society cannot fully acknowledge the extent of pain inflicted (note: not endured!) and hence fails to address the issue of vicarious accountability, the injustices and abuses of the past remain ignored, with the result of potentially stalling any dialogic progress in the present. When, on the other hand, a descendant of a victimized community identifies vicariously with his or her family's trauma to the extent that it disallows the full humanity of the other side to emerge, dialogic progress is equally blocked. The posture of unsettling empathy allows for the inclusion of both a critical perspective on power asymmetries (regarding historical and cultural trauma) as well as compassion with the other despite historical injustices and contentious memories. Unsettling empathy blends the critical/political dimension with the affective/interpersonal dimension of working through historical and cultural trauma, and as such it is a vital element in reconciliatory processes.

I will conclude with a summary of the central features of unsettling empathy:

Unsettling empathy costs something, whereas compassion can too easily be mistaken as the kind of civil discourse that uses polite forms of rhetoric to mask underlying tensions.

Unsettling empathy requires the risk of vulnerability, of courage, and of being shaken to one's foundations and assumptions about the world and the other.

Unsettling empathy calls us into the presence of objective differences without negating the vitality of human interaction, whereas compassion may tempt us to erase some of the objective differences in the name of a common humanity.

Unsettling empathy allows for the inclusion of both a critical perspective on power asymmetries as well as the empathetic stance toward the other despite unresolved historical injustices.

Unsettling empathy describes a posture that blends the critical/political with the affective/interpersonal.

## NOTES

1. For brief overviews, see Amy Coplan, "Understanding Empathy" (2011); Aleida Assman and Ines Detmers, *Empathy and Its Limits* (2016); and Fritz Breithaupt, "A Three-Person Model of Empathy" (2012).

2. On belated empathy, Aleida Assman, "Looking Away in Nazi Germany" (2016); on narrative empathy, Suzanne Keen, "A Theory of Narrative Empathy" (2006); on imaginative empathy, Lynn Hunt, *Inventing Human Rights: A History* (2007, 32); on realistic empathy, Brewster Smith, "Realistic Empathy: A Key to Sensible International Relations" (2004); on mediated empathy, Assman and Detmers, "Introduction" (2016, 3); on empty empathy, Gabriele Schwab, *Haunting Legacies* (2010, 166), and E. Ann

Kaplan, *Trauma Culture* (2005; esp. Chapter 4); on postmodern empathy, Amos Goldberg, "Empathy, Ethics, and Politics" (2016), where Goldberg also introduces "liberal" and "conservative empathy." On empathy fatigue, often synonymously used with compassion fatigue, Susan Moeller, *Compassion Fatigue* (1999); Assman and Detmers (2016, 3); and Carolyn Dean, *The Fragility of Empathy* (2004, 1, 57–58). On empathic sadism, Fritz Breithaupt, "Empathy for Empathy's Sake" (2016).

3. When facilitating workshops, I do not provide lengthy introductions and I refrain in the opening sessions from explaining the kind of building blocks and dynamics detailed in this book. Select conceptual explanations are sprinkled throughout seminars and workshops, especially when people clamor for some cognitive frameworks to organize their insights, feelings, and struggles. Mentorship trainings reserve time, of course, for a more systematic look at those frames and dynamics.

4. Gobodo-Madikizela (2004, 127; emphasis in original).

5. In the same passage, Gobodo-Madikizela actually alludes to empathy as "a learned response embedded deep in our genetic and evolutionary past" (2004, 127).

6. For a critical appraisal of Gobodo-Madikizela's *A Human Being Died That Night*, see Ross Truscott, "A South African Story of Disavowal: Toward a Genealogy of Post-Apartheid Empathy" (2015). Truscott reads the encounter through the lens of a (post)colonial condition of psychoanalytic interpretations, suggesting that empathy can pull a person into complicity. For an appraisal of Gobodo-Madikizela's book through the lens of "rehumanization," see Jodi Halpern and Harvey M. Weinstein, "Rehumanizing the Other: Empathy and Reconciliation" (2004, 572–575).

7. Benjamin Weiser, "Held Hostage, Then Befriended, by a Somali Who Is Now Charged" (*New York Times*, November 9, 2018).

8. For the term "intimate enemies" that describes the psychic relationship between torturer and victim, see Gabriele Schwab, *Haunting Legacies* (2010, 166).

9. Nasser Salhoba's story is told and interpreted in Orna Ophir, "Looking Evil in the Eye/I" (2015, 113–118). For Eva Mozes Kor, see the 2006 documentary *Forgiving Dr. Mengele*, the books she has cowritten, and any number of articles online. Duch's, whose full name is Kaing Guek Eav, public remorse is told in Saira Mohamed, "Of Monsters and Men" (2015, 1199–1200). For bereaved Israeli-Palestinian families, see the official website The Parents Circle–Families Forum (theparentscircle.org/en/about, accessed February 21, 2019). Glenn Beck's op-ed, "Empathy for Black Lives Matter" appeared in the *New York Times* (September 7, 2016).

10. For Duch, see Mohamed, "Of Monsters and Men" (2015, 1200), and David Chandler, "Coming to Terms with the Terror and History of Pol Pot's Cambodia" (2003). For Glenn Beck, see Scott Loren, "Tears of Testimony: Glenn Beck and the Conservative Moral Occult" (2016).

11. For the absence, blocking, and erosion of empathy, see, for example, Gerben A. van Kleef et al., "Power, Distress and Compassion: Turning a Blind Eye to the Suffering of Others" (2008), which is a study on the correlation between people in power and their lack of compassion; and Shelley Berlowitz, "Unequal Equals: How Politics Can Block Empathy" (2016). Simon Baron-Cohen, in *The Science of Evil: On Empathy and the Origins of Cruelty* (2011), suggests the term "empathy erosion." For empathy that is disabling, see Neta Crawford, "Institutionalizing Passion in World Politics: Fear and Empathy" (2014).

12. Amy Coplan and Peter Goldie, *Empathy: Philosophical and Psychological Perspectives* (2011), and Elizabeth Segal, *Social Empathy: The Art of Understanding Each Other* (2018).

13. For a discussion on the disingenuous nature of empathy, particularly as it relates to representations of the Holocaust, see Carolyn Dean, *The Fragility of Empathy* (2004); also Steven Aschheim, "The (Ambiguous) Political Economy of Empathy" (2012); Nils Bubandt and Rane Willerslev, "The Dark Side of Empathy" (2015); Fritz Breithaupt, "Empathy for Empathy's Sake" (2016); and Robert Meister, *After Evil* (2012; esp. Chapter 7).

14. Carolyn Dean, in *The Fragility of Empathy* (2004), questions the late-twentieth-century scholarly critique of empathy with respect to Holocaust representations and historiography. My "essays," she writes, "take apart self-evident presumptions in mainstream . . . [about] the recently perceived precariousness of empathy" (15).

15. Gabriele Schwab, *Haunting Legacies* (2010, 165), especially her chapter on "Deadly Intimacy: The Politics and Psychic Life of Torture"; Martha Nussbaum, *Upheavals of Thought: The Intelligence of Emotions* (2001, 329). In *Inventing Human Rights* (2007), Lynn Hunt moves with ease from imagined empathy to torture: "[Empathy] is imagined, not in the sense of made-up, but in the sense that empathy requires a leap of faith, of imagining that someone else is like you. Accounts of torture produced this imagined empathy through new views of pain" (32). See also Fritz Breithaupt's "Empathy for Empathy's Sake" (2016), where he asserts that "empathic sadism" is a way to exert control over others, which moves in the direction of torture, even though he does not extend it to torture; he mentions torture explicitly in "A Three-Person Model of Empathy" (2012, 86).

16. In my analysis of torture, I arrive at this conclusion. Because torture is a process that absolutizes the "truth" of the torturer, "empathy has been methodically dislodged from the vocabulary of torturers" (Krondorfer, "Torture" 2017, 33). See also Elaine Scarry, *The Body in Pain* (1985), and Jean Améry, *At the Mind's Limits* (1980).

17. In an oft-quoted sentence, Susan Sontag expresses this idea of action, though she relates it to compassion rather than pity: "Compassion is an unstable emotion. It needs to be translated into action, or it withers" (*Regarding the Pain of Others* 2003, 101).

18. See Carolyn Dean's chapter on "Empathy, Suffering, and Holocaust 'Pornography,'" in *The Fragility of Empathy* (2004, 16–42).

19. Ruth Leys, *Trauma: A Genealogy* (2000, 285). Leys specifically critiques the claim of transgenerational trauma. See also the discussion of memory and transmission of trauma in Chapters 2 and 3.

20. In "Rehumanizing the Other," Jodi Halpern and Harvey Weinstein make the connection between sympathy and identification (as different from empathy): "Sympathetic feelings," they write, "involve an idealized or at least strategically incomplete view of the other" (2004, 580).

21. A classic text about the identification with the colonizers is Frantz Fanon's *Black Skins, White Masks* (1967). An exemplary case of idealized identification with victims is Germany's postwar philosemitism; see Frank Stern, *The Whitewashing of the Yellow Badge: Antisemitism and Philosemitism in Postwar Germany* (1992); also Robert Meister, *After Evil* (2012, 186–192).

22. For a discussion of idealized identification in the colonial imaginary and how this dynamic could be employed to counter harmful legacies, see Gabriele Schwab's chapter "Identity Trouble: Guilt, Shame, and Idealization" (*Haunting Legacies* 2010, 108–112).

23. For example, Tania Singer and Claus Lamm, in "The Social Neuroscience of Empathy" (2009), write that "empathy denotes that the observer's emotions reflect affective sharing ('feeling with' the other person), while compassion [and] sympathy . . . [denote a] 'feeling for' the other person" (84). Note that the prefixes "com" and "sym," which translate as *with*, are here equated with "feeling *for*." Jodi Halpern and Harvey Weinstein define sympathy to be "*about* experiencing shared emotion" ("Rehumanizing the Other" 2004, 568; emphasis added). Emy Koopman, a literary theorist, shows how sympathy used to be considered to be of higher moral value than empathy: "The general sense in which sympathy has come into use is that one is affected by, understands, and/or has a strong concern for the feelings of another, while empathy is used to express that one is experiencing similar feelings, but without necessarily feeling 'concern'" ("Reading the Suffering of Others: The Ethical Possibilities of 'Empathic Unsettlement'" 2010, 242). Against this view, Koopman argues for the validity of empathy by embracing LaCapra's concept of "unsettling empathy" (see further below in this chapter).

24. That empathy is active and promotes prosocial behavior has been variously pointed out; see, for example, Kirsten Monroe, *The Heart of Compassion: Portraits of Moral Choice during the Holocaust* (2004); Neta Crawford, "Institutionalizing Passion in World Politics" (2014); C. Daniel Batson and Adam Powell, "Altruism and Social Behavior" (2003).

25. Though the etymological origin of empathy is the Greek *empatheia*, the term came into the English language via the German late-nineteenth-century word *Einfühlung* (feeling into, feeling-in) to describe how to feel one's way into a work of art. Around the 1900s, it was picked up by the German psychologist Theodore Lipps and American psychologist Edward Titchener, the latter translating it as "empathy." See Mark Davis, *Empathy* (2018, 3–11), and Carolyn Dean, *The Fragility of Memory* (2004, 141 n. 25).

26. Assman and Detmers, "Introduction" (2016, 4).

27. Daniel Batson, "These Things Called Empathy" (2009, 12); Jodi Halpern and Harvey Weinstein, "Rehumanizing the Other" (2004, 568); Gabriele Schwab, *Haunting Legacies* (2004, 17); Carolyn Dean, *The Fragility of Memory* (2004, 14); Elizabeth Segal, *Social Empathy* (2018). That empathy can be taught is also argued by Neta Crawford, "Institutionalizing Passion in World Politics: Fear and Empathy" (2014), and Norma Deitch Feshbach and Seymour Feshbach, "Empathy and Education" (2009).

28. Amy Coplan, "Understanding Empathy" (2011, 13). Coplan calls empathy's other-oriented perspective a "mode of intersubjective engagement" where our imaginative "simulation" remains focused on "the other's experiences and characteristics rather than reverting to imagining based on our own experiences and characteristics" (13). Assman and Detmers also speak of an "other-directed orientation" ("Introduction" 2016, 6).

29. For moral emotions, see June Price Tangney et al., "Moral Emotions and Moral Behavior" (2007), and Jonathan Haidt, "The Moral Emotions" (2003). See also Ditte Marie Munch-Jurisic's critical reflections on disgust as a moral emotion when applied to violent, genocidal perpetrators ("Perpetrator Disgust: A Morally Destructive Emotion" 2018); for a discussion of disgust as a political emotion, see Sara Ahmed, *The Cultural Politics of Emotion* (2004, 82–100).

30. Sudhir Kakar, *The Colors of Violence: Cultural Identities, Religion, and Conflict* (1996, 3).

31. See the book and catalogue by James Allen, *Without Sanctuary: Lynching Photography in America* (2000); also Dora Apel and Shawn Michelle Smith, *Lynching Photographs* (2008); and Bettina Messias Carbonell, "The Afterlife of Lynching" (2012).

32. For a reproduction of this photo, see https://www.withoutsanctuary.org/ (photo #51). Accessed February 14, 2019.

33. The spectacular distress a viewer feels today is directly related to the original spectacular violence—though, at the time it took place, the white mob was not distressed but rather joyous. Spectacular acts of violence are cruelties performed publicly and deliberately. As the word "spectacular" indicates, this modality of political violence rests on the fact that it must be seen. Spectacular violence is a deliberately ritualized display of extreme violence. The lynching of African Americans did not happen in secret. It was publicly announced locally and regionally. "Hundreds, sometimes thousands of white spectators gathered and watched their fellow citizens tortured," writes Amy Louis Wood in *Lynching and Spectacle* (2009, 1).

34. Recall that I defined *vicarious* identification as a person's desire to identify with an aspect of his or her legacy that was not experienced directly.

35. Above, I defined *idealized* identification as identifying with people who are different from oneself, usually located on different ends of a real or imagined power scale.

36. More recently, the lynching of Latinos and Hispanics is getting more attention. See, for example, Simon Romero, "Latinos Were Lynched in the West. Descendants Want It Known" (*New York Times*, March 3, 2019); also Ken Gonzales-Day, *Lynching in the West* (2006) . The fact that about fifty Italians—portrayed as "sneaking and coward-

ly Sicilians" and "descendants of bandits and assassins"—were lynched in America between 1890 and 1924 is largely unknown; see Frank Viviano, "Atrocities America Forgot" (2019, 50).

37. Sontag (2003, 91).

38. Amy Louis Wood, *Lynching and Spectacle* (2009, 2).

39. See note 27 above.

40. There are, of course, higher education advocates who, like me, defend the necessity of the challenging nature of learning. In the article, "Administration, Faculty, and the Hard Free-Speech Questions," Jonathan Alger and Mark Piper state that "opposing viewpoints . . . may be unsettling for some students, but effective learning and the advancement of knowledge is not secured by closing off viewpoints because of worries that students will be unsettled" (2019, 17). At the time of their essay's publication, Jonathan Alger was president and Mark Piper faculty senate speaker at James Madison University.

41. Jodi Halpern and Harvey Weinstein, "Rehumanizing the Other" (2004, 569).

42. Bashir Bashir and Amos Goldberg, "Deliberating the Holocaust and the Nakba" (2014, 78). Their point is similar to Amy Coplan's insistence that a "clear self-other differentiation" needs to be maintained in empathy ("Understanding Empathy" 2011, 5, 15–17).

43. Dominick LaCapra, *Writing History, Writing Trauma* (2001, 40).

44. LaCapra (2001, 40–41).

45. LaCapra (2001, 78–79); he cautiously extends such "unsettling possibility" also to perpetrators (41, 79).

46. Amos Goldberg, "Narrative, Testimony, and Trauma" (2015, 17). See also Emy Koopman, who states that LaCapra is more interested in "historiography," though his concept is beneficial to analyze literary texts ("Reading the Suffering of Others" 2010, 243); also Pumla Gobodo-Madikizela, "Psychological Repair" (2015, 1102f).

47. "Objectivity should not be identified with objectivism or exclusive objectification that denies or forecloses empathy, just as empathy should not be conflated with unchecked identification, vicarious experience, or surrogate victimhood" (LaCapra, *Writing History, Writing Trauma* 2001, 40).

48. Bashir Bashir and Amos Goldberg, "Deliberating the Holocaust and the Nakba: Disruptive Empathy and Binationalism in Israel/Palestine" (2014, 77).

49. Goldberg, "Narrative, Testimony, and Trauma" (2015, 16–17; emphasis added).

50. Bashir and Goldberg, "Deliberating the Holocaust and the Nakba" (2014).

51. LaCapra, *Writing History, Writing Trauma* (2001, 41).

52. The spiritual "Kumbaya" is a popular folk song; it has come to refer to an artificial holding of hands in groups under the pretense of harmony and agreement while deep-seated discord remains.

53. Similarly, Hava Shecter and Gavriel Salomon, in "Does Vicarious Experience of Suffering Affect Empathy for an Adversary?" (2005), state that "the disposition for empathy, perhaps like other dispositions and skills, can be strengthened or weakened as a function of experiences or training one undergoes" (127); they cite additional literature supporting this notion. See also note 27 above.

54. The term "certitude" is intentionally chosen here over the almost synonymous term "certainty." Whereas certainty refers to something that is clearly established (as in factually certain), certitude refers to a state of feeling absolutely convinced. It is the difference between being personally convinced of something that one considers factually or emotionally true (certitude) or having certainty about an established fact that has an evidentiary and empirical base. That there are no clear boundaries between these terms; that contestation always happens at these boundaries is self-understood.

55. The literature on interfaith encounters between Christians and Jews is immense. Both the Holocaust and an increasing religious tolerance in civil society have motivated the improvement of Jewish-Christian relations after 1945. For select readings, see Mary Boys, *Seeing Judaism Anew* (2005); Edward Kessler, *Introduction to Jewish-Christian Relations* (2010); Marc Krell, *Intersecting Pathways* (2003); Philip Cunningham,

Norbert Hofmann, and Joseph Sievers, *The Catholic Church and the Jewish People* (2007); Donald Dietrich, *God and Humanity after Auschwitz* (1995); Richard Rubenstein, *After Auschwitz: History, Theology, and Contemporary Judaism* (1992); Zachary Braiterman, *(God) After Auschwitz: Tradition and Change in Post-Holocaust Jewish Thought* (1998); Manfred Görg and Michael Langer, *Als Gott weinte: Theologie nach Auschwitz* (1997); Katharina von Kellenbach, Björn Krondorfer, and Norbert Reck, *Von Gott reden im Land der Täter* (2001). For critical studies on interreligious issues, see Catherine Cornille, *The Impossibility of Interreligious Dialogue* (2008); and Cornille and Christopher Conway, *Interreligious Hermeneutics* (2010).

56. For more information, see the obituary by Margalit Fox, "Arnold Jacob Wolf, a Leading Reform Rabbi, Is Dead at 84" (*New York Times*, December 29, 2008) www.nytimes.com/2008/12/30/us/30wolf.html (accessed February 22, 2019).

57. For a variation on this theme, see David Rieff's comment: "Since 1945, 'never again' has meant, essentially, 'Never again will Germans kill Jews in Europe'" ("The Persistence of Genocide," 2011, n.p.)

58. Regarding interfaith relations, see Leo Baeck's essays *Judaism and Christianity* (1958).

59. For a working-through in the context of pastoral care in postwar German churches, see Thomas Beelitz, "Pastoralpsychologisches Arbeiten im Land der Täter" (2013).

60. A short biography of Bettelheim is published on the website of the Buchenwald memorial, https://www.buchenwald.de/en/1193/ (accessed February 22, 2019); any number of websites provide information on the controversy over his professional credentials.

61. For a brief but solid overview on Martin Niemöller, see the United States Holocaust Memorial Museum's webpage, https://encyclopedia.ushmm.org/content/en/article/martin-niemoeller-biography (accessed February 20, 2019).

62. Roger Simon, Sharon Rosenberg, and Claudia Eppert, *Between Hope and Despair: Pedagogy and the Remembrance of Historical Trauma* (2000, 6).

63. Intriguingly, the idea of empathy as a critical practice has been discussed not only in education but also in museum studies, where it is being applied to intentionally created spaces. See the work of Elif Gökçiğdem, *Fostering Empathy through Museums* (2016), and ibid., *Designing for Empathy: Perspectives on the Museum Experience* (2019).

64. Cathy Caruth, *Unclaimed Experience: Trauma, Narrative, and History* (1996, 11); Roger Simon et al., *Between Hope and Despair* (2000, 6).

65. Gobodo-Madikizela, "Remembering the Past: Nostalgia, Traumatic Memory, and the Legacy of Apartheid" (2012, 262), and ibid., "Transforming Trauma in the Aftermath of Gross Human Rights Abuses: Making Public Spaces Intimate" (2008). On safe spaces, see also note 33 in Chapter 5.

66. Gobodo-Madikizela, "Remembering the Past" (2012, 262; emphasis in original).

# 2

# Dynamics and Approaches

# FIVE

## Taking Risks, Telling Stories

Yael, a Jewish Israeli woman, had joined a four-day workshop to explore the strained relations between Israelis and Palestinians. The workshop took place in the summer of 2015 in the territories of the West Bank, at a location easily reached by non-Palestinians. Yael, in her midthirties, teaches in a school for troubled Jewish Israeli teenagers from the vicinity of Jerusalem, including Jewish settlements. Yael describes herself as leaning toward the political left. She is committed to countering a nationalist Israeli narrative that legitimizes an expansionist land ideology in which Palestinians are seen, at best, as a nuisance and, at worst, as mortal enemies. As a teacher, Yael is confronted daily with teenage students who, by and large, come from Israel's economic lower-income class and who have to cope with additional challenges, ranging from behavioral and emotional health issues to dysfunctional families. Most of her students, Yael told our group, embrace uncompromising right-wing attitudes. Many of the adolescent boys are part of La Familia, a fan group associated with the Jerusalem Beitar soccer club. Notoriously, members of La Familia chant insults against Arab Palestinian players and occasionally wave flags of the violently racist and ultranationalist political Kach party, a party banned in Israel since 1994.

Yael talked about her professional life to a group of Palestinians, Germans, and Jewish Israelis. Most of the participants were secular, identifying with their Muslim, Christian, or Jewish backgrounds only culturally, while a few adhered to their faith traditions more stridently. It was Yael's turn to tell us something about her life. Sitting in a chair and facing the group, she shared her struggle with her students' right-wing attitudes.

From an Israeli perspective, there was nothing spectacular to Yael's story, although she could be admired for working in an educational environment in which her own values and political beliefs were challenged

daily by the people she was serving. This challenge was not particularly
different from social workers in any society dealing with a recalcitrant
clientele whose views and attitudes have been shaped by their lives'
exacting circumstances.

Yael, however, told her story to a mixed Israeli-Palestinian-German
group within a politically volatile context. Inevitably, her personal narrative got politicized. Her experience was perceived not only as that of an
individual but also as someone representing a collective. From the perspective of Palestinians, her story confirmed the complicity of all Israelis
in the Zionist enterprise that limits Palestinian freedom of movement
and, some would say, threatens the very existence of Palestinians. Whereas for Yael her story was an expression of her individual life choices that
reflected her ambivalent attitude toward current Israeli politics, for the
Palestinian listeners her story mirrored the larger Zionist experience. Put
differently, in Yael's mind her account laid bare her criticism of Israel's
national master narrative while in the perception of Palestinians her personal story was part and parcel of the Zionist narrative.

## MASTER NARRATIVES

On a basic level, we can define a *master narrative as a story in and
through which a collective (social, religious, national) recognizes and
understands itself. A master narrative offers coherence to varied experiences of individual members belonging to a larger social group. Group
cohesion and master narrative are tightly interwoven, which accounts for
the fact that a master narrative can accommodate a wide-ranging multiplicity of individualized stories. Despite all these individual variations,
similar overall patterns are discernible that provide social meaning to
events that would otherwise remain a conglomeration of discreet and
fragmented experiences. In this sense, master narratives do remove complexity and ambiguity from real-life experiences. A master narrative thus
provides legitimacy to large-group experiences from which people derive
truth and fundamental certainties about themselves. For example, German family memories of World War II vary widely in their specificity,
but most stories allude to instances of one's family's noncompliance with
Nazi ideology and to the hardships that befell Germans at the end of the
war and the immediate postwar years. This postwar West German narrative, which dominated family stories for a good fifty years after 1945,
carried the message, "We suffered, too!"[1] This leitmotif bundled and
organized a whole spectrum of events that are specific to individual family histories. In homogeneous settings, the normative power of master
narratives functions precisely because their discursive operations remain
largely unrecognized.

In mixed settings—and this is true especially for groups in conflict—the cohesion and legitimacy of a group's master narrative are punctured and questioned. A group's master narrative no longer functions smoothly because it clashes with competing claims of another collective narrative. Social and political conflicts are almost always accompanied by competing claims maintained and iterated by national grand narratives.

Because of the persuasive and unifying force of a master narrative, individual storytelling, as important as it is, is not necessarily an antidote to a meta-narrative; rather, it can be an extension of it. Individual stories cannot easily defy the mold within which they are cast by dominant narrative frames. In this sense, individual storytelling in situations of conflict is rarely innocent.

Suggesting that personal storytelling is not innocent does not imply that the individual teller has malicious intent. The opposite might be closer to the truth. When Yael shared in honest and straightforward ways important aspects of her life, she did not want to insult her Palestinian listeners. If anything she wanted to bridge a gap between them by revealing her own personal conflicts. But because her story was told in a context of past and ongoing conflict, it could not be divorced from the psychopolitical dynamics that are activated when large-group identities are at stake. The Palestinians in our group did not suspect Yael of not telling the truth. They did not doubt the accuracy of her experience. Rather, the truth she told about her right-wing students confirmed, in their perception, the very grand narrative that Yael herself intended to deflate.

In workshops, we deliberately set up a format that fosters and encourages intergroup dialogue. Compassionate listening to individual stories, however, does not miraculously change the attitudes of the respective other group. It does not organically humanize the other. To approach dialogue with groups in conflict with an overly sanguine presumption about the benevolent power of storytelling, no matter how well-intended, is tantamount to wishful thinking, for it underestimates the persuasive sway of master narratives. Yael revealed an inner conflict to our group. As a socially conscious teacher, she dedicated her educational labor to a segment of Israeli society that embodies a nationalist mentality she abhors. A third-party listener would have had little difficulty appreciating the nuances of her inner conflicts and respecting (or even praising) her personal courage. The Palestinians, as an affected group in the conflict, could not, however, hear her story in quite the same way. Since a master narrative can be told in manifold variations, Yael's story just confirmed their expectations of a normative story that a community likes to tell about itself. In Yael's case, this is the story of a "politically correct" Israeli who wishes to stand in solidarity with Palestinians.

I have observed those dynamics in many workshops. Just as Palestinian participants reacted with reservation to Yael's case, Israelis have responded with similar caution when listening to a Palestinian story. When, for example, a Palestinian individual speaks of his or her hardship, many Israelis dismiss it as just another version of the Palestinian grand narrative of suffering. The moment an Israeli or Palestinian recounts a personal experience in a mixed-group setting, the story may have already lost its credibility. Such loss of credibility is not synonymous with an allegation of lying; rather, the recounting of a personal experience is perceived as selective, reductive, insincere, and manipulative.[2] This dynamic is, of course, not particular to the Palestinian-Israeli case; it can be observed in many situations where groups in conflict try to reestablish trust and renew their relationships. Individual storytelling in and of itself cannot defuse the tension and mistrust that have accumulated as the result of collective injuries and traumatic memories.

If storytelling remains on the level of a reciprocal exchange of accounts of suffering, the lines between compassionate listening and feeling manipulated are thin. "On the parts of the Israeli participants, I felt a lack of sensitivity [and] an inability to listen to the Palestinian pain and suffering," Fatma Kassem recalls about an Israeli-Palestinian encounter led by a different organization. Fatma was shocked to learn that an Israeli participant, after the seminar had ended, declared that "the shows were very well produced."[3] Compassionate listening that is limited to each side foregrounding a history of suffering is prone to entering a cycle of competitiveness. What is needed is not competition but a "productive interplay of disparate acts of remembrance" and recognition.[4]

With each side attached to its particular narrative framing of events, and with each side—as in the case of Israelis and Palestinians—having mastered to perfection the telling of such a narrative, the result is an inability to listen to individual stories with empathetic understanding. We can call this situation a failure of testimony, or *testimonial injustice.[5] Testimonial injustice occurs particularly in conflicts rooted in asymmetrical power relations when the testimonial voice of an individual is not acknowledged. Such nonacknowledgment can occur in the form of being ignored, belittled, doubted, dismissed, discredited, legally challenged, and so forth. One "suffers testimonial injustice," philosopher Barrett Emerick writes, "when [someone's] actual or potential testimony is not given the degree of credibility that it deserves, in virtue of some prejudice on the part of the hearer."[6] This can take the form of outright denial and malicious dismissal of victim perspectives, as we have seen in Radovan Karadžić's self-defense at the ICTY (chapter 1). In the context of practices of social reconciliation, which often work on the basis of self-select participation, such outright denial rarely happens, although I have witnessed it too. Testimonial injustice surfacing in these intergroup encounters expresses itself in gestures of polite disregard and inattentiveness—and this I have observed frequently in the initial phase of Israeli-Palestinian encounters. No matter how harrowing and sad a personal story might be, the other side absorbs and acknowledges it only partially or not at all.

The reason for such an inability is not to be sought in a person's moral failure or empathy deficiency. Testimonial injustice—in the context of guided reconciliatory processes—cannot be explained simply as individual lack of the empathetic imagination.[7] Rather, the cause must be located in a master narrative's proclivity to press the multitude of human experiences into a story of victimization in which the respective other is portrayed as being insensitive to collective suffering or accused of causing it.[8] A parochial focus on the suffering and victimization of one's own group—a phenomenon I will explore below as "chosen trauma"—activates defensive shields dormant but ever-present in the clash of competing master narratives. "At the heart of narratives of struggle," writes conflict resolution scholar Robert Rotberg, "is collective memory. Such memory need not reflect truth; instead, it portrays a truth that is functional for a group's ongoing existence."[9] In the Palestinian-Israeli conflict, a simplified version of such competing grand narratives might look like this: We/my family arrived as desperate refugees from the Holocaust in Europe with two suitcases at the shores of Israel, where we were greeted by Arab-Palestinian hostility. Or: We/my family were expelled in the 1948 Nakba[10] from our Palestinian villages by European Jews, whom we had welcomed at first but who left us with nothing but hurtful memories and the keys to our former homes. Given this setup, the deep existential insecurity left by the Holocaust and the deep wounds of uprootedness caused by the Nakba get played out endlessly in the media and in personal and social narratives as mutual recriminations regarding the Israeli occupation and Arab terrorism.[11]

## DEATH TO THE ARABS

Yael's story about teaching students affiliated with La Familia had not come to an end yet. At first, the Palestinian participants did not listen to her with much empathetic understanding. Rather, they seemed to merely endure her story. We witnessed, in other words, a mild case of testimonial injustice. While the Palestinians mustered sufficiently polite self-restraint necessary not to derail the early phase of the encounter, some of their body gestures sent unmistakable signals: occasional yawning, frequent checking of iPhones, sitting slumped in their seats. Their initially detached attitude did not change until Yael, almost in passing, mentioned that her adolescent students frequently use the "d.t.t.a" phrase. Some in our group immediately caught the significance of the abbreviation, others not. "What does d.t.t.a stand for?" I asked when noticing the sudden nervousness in the room. Yael responded: "It stands for 'Death to the Arabs.'"

Yael's daring admission caught everyone's attention. I say "daring" because Yael must have been aware of the risk she took when mentioning the hate phrase. By telling us about working in an environment where "Death to the Arabs" is frequently proclaimed, she risked being identified with the slogan through proximity to it. How did she distance herself from it? Did she confront her students? Would she consider quitting her job at the school? Perhaps she responded to her students as teachers often do in comparable situations: they try to reason with students by providing different viewpoints. Or perhaps she responded like social workers do, approaching the conflict indirectly by trying to alleviate her students' living circumstances, thus hoping to change their minds in the long run.

By deviating from the grand narrative that depicts Israelis as "peace-loving persons compelled only by circumstances beyond their control to engage in violent conflict,"[12] Yael opened up the national narrative to its darker side. If a master narrative is defined as a normative account that a community likes to tell about itself, it glosses over, ignores, hides, or makes invisible moral ambiguity and contradictions in relation to people defined as the other, whether in terms of class, gender, nationality, sexuality, or ethnicity. The highly problematic "dark side of narratives," Daniel Geiger, an organization studies scholar, argues, is that their "normative state cannot be questioned within the narrative mode" itself. Rather, "narratives always amplify themselves by conveying normality and the criteria for normality at the same time."[13] For example, more radicalized segments in the Palestinian population might judge Yael's story as normative because they assume that "Death to the Arabs" is *the* core of the Israeli-Zionist narrative. Israelis, on the other hand, might fervently disagree with such a negative assessment and point to the positive nature of the Jewish narrative. A benevolent Israeli version would be a story of deliverance from destruction (Shoah) and the realization of the Zionist dream for national autonomy. Such a story would extol Israel's national-collective virtues of turning arid land into agricultural success and upholding democracy in a region dominated by illiberal Arab nation-states.[14]

When Yael mentioned that she was working in an environment where her students spouted "Death to the Arabs," she risked being accused by Palestinians of upholding an untenable status quo. But she also risked being verbally rebuked by her fellow Israelis for undermining the moral uprightness of the national Israeli narrative, because so doing would play into the hands of Palestinian paranoia about Zionism's ultimate goal: to make Palestinians disappear.[15]

The courage to take personal risks moves reconciliatory processes forward. It is an essential building block for creating a base of trust and empathy.[16] Enriching individual stories with a critical and discomfiting edge makes it possible for wounded and wounding memories to leak through the fortified borders of master narratives. Unless we allow ourselves to become sensitized and pay attention to the presence of wounded and wounding memories—and then investigate how these memories express themselves in interpersonal encounters and through the subtleties of intrapsychic realities—we easily slip into forums of compassionate listening where the exacting nature of working through the past is avoided. As a matter of fact, compassionate listening alone, without the valor of querying the limitations of one's own master narrative, may just lead to iterations of patterns embedded in those narratives, with which each group affirms and defends its large-group identity. Psychoanalyst Vamik Volkan, who has facilitated groups in various global conflict zones, observes that participants coming together to discuss their "conflictual relationship between their respective large groups" almost always feel "under personal attack and [are] compelled to defend their large group. The personal stories that emerge typically reflect what 'others' did to 'us.'"[17] In productive reconciliatory processes, feelings and perceptions of being attacked are to be acknowledged, but one also needs to move beyond them.

Yael's admission touched on the historical and cultural traumas that underlie the conflictual relations between Palestinians and Israelis. The political hatred voiced in the "Death to the Arabs" slogan embodied (and also masked) collective fears on each side. On the Palestinian side, it feeds into the collective traumatic memory of the Nakba and the continuing dispossession of Palestinian lands by Israeli settlers. Indeed, the ultimate fear of Palestinians is the total erasure of their national identity through the loss of political autonomy and land ownership.[18] On the Israeli side, the d.t.t.a phrase constitutes the most virulent expression of a fear that Jews might face destruction again just like in the Holocaust unless they remain forever vigilant and always keep the upper hand over their real and perceived enemies through military prowess. Those mutually dependent—and simultaneously mutually exclusive—fears are rooted in traumatic memories; they sit deeply in the collective psyche of each people, feeding their actions, motivations, and narratives.

It may not yet be evident to the reader how Yael's story about her students—with which I am illustrating the dynamics of risk-taking and storytelling—contributed to activating collective trauma. To make this more apparent, I need to back up for a moment and explain how this particular group got to the point where Yael was able to talk about her life as an educator.

A day earlier (the first day of the workshop), the group had discussed what it would mean personally to them to cross borders—real and imagined borders as well as political and intimate boundaries. The discussion meandered in various directions, but several participants voiced their concern that attending this workshop would undermine the semiofficial Palestinian "anti-normalization" campaign. This is a campaign designed to deter any interactions between Israelis and Palestinians that might normalize the occupation, the latter a shorthand for a generally unacceptable political situation of Israeli economic and military control of Palestinian territories. Unless meetings would lead to real political change, Palestinians were not to convene or cooperate with Israelis anywhere.[19] What, then, would we be doing in this workshop, people wondered. Would we work for political change or merely engage in polite dialogue? At some point during this early discussion, the topic of Israeli settlements in the West Bank came up. When one Palestinian in his twenties professed that he would be interested in "crossing borders" into settlements to talk to settlers, he met resistance from both his fellow Palestinians and from (secular) Israelis who identified politically with the Palestinian plight. Rapprochement between Jewish settlers and Palestinians? This was *haram*, forbidden, taboo! Overall, this round of discussion remained within the discursive mode of political barter. It did not yet touch on the psychosocial and emotional dimensions that motivate, below the surface, the many verbal exchanges between people in conflict.

The next morning, each national group (Germans, Israelis, and Palestinians) was given the task to elect one member of their in-group to tell a story to the whole group on the theme of "borders of exclusion and fear." In other words, we put responsibility and agency back into the hands of each national group, entrusting each with the charge to select one of their own to represent them. The Israeli group chose Yael. This is why Yael ended up telling us about the right-wing mentality of her students. We can, therefore, say that Yael represented not only herself but also, in that moment, the Israeli large-group identity. It is probably no accident that her story included the unresolved issue of Jewish settlements from the previous day. Many of Yael's students, we need to recall, were coming from such settlements.

It is also no accident that on the following day—after Yael had shared her story—collective trauma became the prominent topic in the group. On that day, all three national groups consented to explore together their respective collective traumas. Other themes and subjects had been suggested, but "collective trauma" became the prime topic of choice. Yael's remarks about d.t.t.a contributed to this choice, not so much on a conscious level as on the level of emotional resonance. Her story constituted a link between the unresolved issue of Jewish settlements of the previous day and the topic of collective fears rooted in trauma on the following day.

## THE KEY: CHOSEN TRAUMA AND LARGE-GROUP IDENTITY

When Yael mentioned the hateful phrase, she not only rendered herself vulnerable to being associated and identified with a dark side of the

Israeli master narrative but also rendered the narrative susceptible to the harmful effects of her country's *chosen trauma. We cannot say that Yael was doing any of this intentionally or that she was thinking of the technical term "chosen trauma" when telling her story. On the other hand, she had been selected by her own group to represent the Israeli perspective on "borders of exclusion and fear," and she knew very well that sharing the d.t.t.a phrase with this group would have repercussions. Willingly taking the risk of vulnerability, she opened venues for the group as a whole to go beyond rehearsed national narratives and beyond chosen traumas.

What is a chosen trauma? According to Vamik Volkan, chosen traumas and large-group identities are closely linked. They support and reinforce each other, providing social groups with shared common roots and a present sense of belonging. Large-group identities provide a feeling of "we-ness" and "sameness" in which shared "subjective experiences" foster social cohesion and provide security.[20] As a psychoanalyst, Volkan came to realize that historical events are one of the most important amplifiers that constitute large-group identities (other amplifiers include language, shared physical characteristics, food, etc.). The power of historical events, Volkan observes, does not depend on whether they are imagined or real, factual or misperceived: they always constitute a strong motivational force.[21] As such, historical events are remembered and retold by groups as "chosen glories" or "chosen traumas." Chosen traumas are psychologically more complex than chosen glories. While the latter increases "collective self-esteem," a chosen trauma is a resilient identity marker because it connects people to shared experiences of suffering and perceived injustices. A chosen trauma refers to those historical events that a group collectively remembers as a time of having "suffered catastrophic loss, humiliation, and helplessness at the hands of its enemies." It can be transgenerationally transmitted, especially when "linked to the past generation's inability to mourn losses of people, land or prestige."[22]

In order to avoid any misunderstanding, Volkan asserts that no group "chooses" to be victimized. The victimization of groups is imposed on them, not chosen. Yet, groups of people come to agree on a tragic or harmful event in their past, which they grant the foundational status of a trauma. As a foundational event, it secures group cohesion and is dwelled upon in the spheres of politics, culture, and family. Once isolated and identified, a chosen trauma becomes culturally adopted and accepted as a reference point for understanding oneself within collective history.[23]

At this point, I like to introduce Fahed, a Palestinian man in his forties who resides in a West Bank town under the governance of the Palestinian Authority. He is a man who has found a way of living precariously with multiple contradictions: a faithful Muslim, he still enjoys a secular lifestyle; assisting the Palestinian Authority in negotiations, he still nurtures contact with Israelis outside the Palestinian Authority's purview; a family man proudly showing photos of traditionally dressed relatives, he defies traditional Arab family values; sincere and honest in his intentions, he sometimes does not tell his family that he joins meetings with Israelis. Over several workshops and seminars he attended, I have come to appreciate Fahed's fine sensibility. Almost never thrashing overt political slogans, he is deeply identified with the Palestinian cause. When he was a medic at a younger age, he took care of injured teenagers who were hurling stones at the Israeli security forces. Once, when picking up an injured boy, he inexplicably fell down and collapsed on the streets where the rioting was taking place. He fell into a coma. When he woke up several days later, he was told that he had been struck by a rubber bullet.

Fahed knows the chosen trauma of his people. He can speak the language of resilience and of loss.[24] When it comes to political resistance, he is unwavering in his opposition to the occupation of Palestinian territories by the Israel army. He will not shy away from telling you that the Oslo Accords of the early 1990s, which had been celebrated as a milestone in the peace process, just worsened the occupation, limiting Palestinian self-governance to ever-shrinking parts of the West Bank. When solidarity is demanded, he complies. For example, during the 2015 workshop that Yael also attended, Fahed left us for an afternoon. The day before, religious Jewish extremists had firebombed a Palestinian home in Duba, West Bank, killing the toddler Ali Dawabsheh and severely burning his parents and brother (Ali's parents died a few weeks later from their burns). Fahed decided to join a demonstration near Duba to protest the killing and to support members of his extended family residing nearby.

Fahed is equally aware of loss, symbolically condensed in the keys to the former homes of Palestinians who had been expelled or fled during the Nakba. As mentioned earlier (chapter 2), many Palestinian families literally have kept their keys to their former (and today mostly destroyed) homes as precious memory objects, investing them heavily with memories of loss. It is to this symbolic key—charged with personal memories of loss as well as the political emotions of pain and anger—that we will now turn.

In one of the workshops Fahed attended, we had tasked each national group (Palestinians, Israelis, Germans) with showing us how they would publicly memorialize their collective plight in a living sculpture. Living sculptures are a particularly effective way to connect people to their deeply held assumptions, or, as is often the case, to make them realize discrepancies between cognitive and affective levels of knowing. Living sculptures are a means of scenic improvisation, approaching individual and collective identity conflicts through theme-centered and embodied presentations of a "monument." In small teams, participants prepare a sculpture with their own bodies that represents the thematic task given to them. Those sculptures can neither move nor talk. One can think of them as monuments displayed in a public square. Each team has limited time for preparation (usually about twenty minutes) in order to preserve the improvisational spirit of this exercise. Each team is encouraged during the brief preparation time to spontaneously experiment with constellations and not to overthink intellectually how to approach the given theme. Eventually, each team's sculpture is presented to the whole group. The scenic improvisation will then undergo a careful analytic probing by means of amplification, mirroring, replacement, intensification, vocalization of feelings, sound, and gestural adjustments.

In the Palestinian national sculpture, Fahed was a central figure. Bent over and carrying another person on his back, he held out one hand in front of him, clutching a key. He was surrounded by other people, either touching him or watching him. It was not obvious whether these figures added to his burden or alleviated it. At some point, I tried to pry loose the key from Fahed's hand. This happened in the working-through phase when unpeeling the various psychosocial and emotional layers of the sculpture. Fahed desperately clung to the key with all of his might. He would not let go of it.

The sculpture's connotation, from a Palestinian perspective, was obvious. The key as memory object represented the traumatic legacy of the Nakba. Central not only in family stories of Palestinian refugees, the key appears also in artistic performances and public monuments. The vigor with which Fahed held on to the key embodied also the virtue of *sumud* (Arabic for steadfastness). In the Palestinian context, *sumud* can refer to holding on to one's land (against enforced dispossession), creating alternative institutions (against occupation policies), or developing strategies of nonviolent resistance.[25]

The power of living sculptures lies in the fact that they visually present variations of large-group identities, mostly in subconscious ways. The bodies arranged in a particular *gestalt*[26] reveal aspects of the seemingly obvious master narrative but also contain plenty of unintended ambiguous elements. In the case of Israeli and Palestinian sculptures, time and again they represent a range of Nakba and Holocaust motifs, from stark symbolization to faded echoes. Time and again it seems that both groups are drawn by or pulled into their respective chosen traumas when presenting their sculptures.

When critical trauma scholars speak of "chosen trauma" or of constructed trauma narratives, an unsuspecting reader might wrongly assume that, according to these scholars, traumas are invented. That, of course, is not the case. The Holocaust really happened; and the Nakba really happened. Each lingers strongly in their collective mentality and memory. The intent of those studies is not to diminish or trivialize acts of wrongdoing and injurious memory but to interrogate the discursive formations that turn historical events into highly charged collective memories. From such an analytical point of view, one may ask, for example, whether the 1948 Nakba was indeed the most disruptive force that Palestinians experienced in the Israeli-Palestinian conflict. The Nakba (Catastrophe) had already been preceded by skirmishes and dispossessions of Arab lands under British colonial rule, and it intensified after the 1967 "Six-Day War," which Palestinians call the Naksa (Calamity). The year 1967 was the beginning of the military occupation of the remaining Palestinian territory, a development that has continued (rather than ceased) after the Oslo Accords in the 1990s. Other significant events might include the 1970 "Black September" with the defeat of Palestinian *fedayeen* fighters in Jordan, the continuing ambiguous legal status of Palestinian refugees in neighboring countries like Lebanon, or the political strife between the Palestinian Authority and Hamas.[27] Yet, it is the Nakba that today is the reference point in the master narrative of Palestinian suffering.[28]

The argument that "events are not inherently traumatic" but that "trauma is a socially mediated attribution," as sociologist Jeffrey Alexander puts it, is not helpful when inserting it into the practice of working with groups in conflict. It is bound to be misunderstood as diminishing the severity of the felt experience of pain.[29] Yet, the sociological argument contains an important insight for facilitators because they need to stay alert to the persuasive force of personal storytelling that can easily be swept up by national narratives of a chosen trauma.[30] For historical events of suffering to become trauma, a cultural crisis must occur in which collective pain is perceived, and then represented, as a fundamental threat to a large-group identity. Alexander suggests—contrary to an aura of factual and forensic inevitability that leads a group to name a painful event "trauma"—that cultural trauma emerges through compelling frameworks of representation. Value-added factors such as the nature of the pain, the nature of the victim, the role of the wider audience in relation to the victim, and the identification of responsible perpetrators lead to the creation of a trauma narrative that becomes persuasive and meaningful to a collective group. Hence, facilitators need to remain aware of two levels: the real and transmitted experiences of pain as well as the constructed nature of trauma narratives.

When hawkish Israelis, for example, complain that Palestinians create and inflate their narrative of suffering, they are, in light of insights gleaned from critical trauma studies, not altogether wrong. The Nakba has become the chosen trauma narrative of Palestinians, and they are not willing to let go of it given the continued threat to their group identity. Yet, the same voices that criticize the Palestinian narrative as politically manipulative get it wrong in other ways. For one, they reduce the Palestinian trauma narrative to being merely a political tool, devoid of actual experiences of injustice. Second, they remain blind to processes that have turned their own historical experience (the Holocaust) into a chosen trauma narrative that organizes their century-long histories of persecution and statelessness.[31] Since unsettling empathy aims at reversing a unidirectional flow of self-centered compassion, it does not nestle in a place where one group can charge another group with manipulating narratives of suffering while safeguarding one's own narrative against such criticism. Diminishing, trivializing, or dismissing the legitimacy of each other's chosen trauma narratives—as persistently happens in the Israeli-Palestinian conflict, with Palestinians questioning the extent of the Holocaust and Israelis questioning the severity of the Nakba—leads to endless rounds of mutual recriminations and feeds an inexhaustible source of mistrust.[32]

Where does it leave us? If we ought not to question the legitimacy of a chosen cultural trauma, are we caught in irreconcilable clashes of master narratives, with no hope of breaking through the safeguarding of borders that secure our large-group identities?

One answer can be found in the creation of safe spaces where groups in conflict can experiment with alternative options.[33] Safe spaces provide opportunities to leave aside—at least temporarily—the visible and invisible chains that tie individuals to large-group identities. It allows us to gain perspective on trauma while it also defuses identification with our in-group's chosen trauma narrative.

Fahed, as mentioned above, is a complex man. He can fully embody the Palestinian narrative of suffering, but he can also step away from it. When I tried to pry loose the key in his hand as he represented the Palestinian plight in the living sculpture, he held on to it with all his strength. But then he said: "You should know, this is not me, this is not 'Fahed' protecting the key. I am just showing what Palestinians would do. I do not fully agree. Sometimes we need to let go if we want to move forward."

I cannot assure the reader which version of Fahed to believe more: Fahed defending the key to his last breath, or Fahed taking a step back and saying that the key's charged symbolism is not his own view but represents his community's mentality. Perhaps the difference does not matter so much because both sides can be equally true, depending on time and place. Importantly, Fahed's ability to step back from the trauma narrative of his community demonstrates that people have the capacity, if provided with a safe environment, to gain critical perspectives on their emotional-political investments in large-group identification. As a matter of fact, focusing exclusively on the level of national narratives of trauma disregards "local biographical memories" that reveal contradictions and tensions with "top-down collective memory," as Daniel Monterescu and Haim Hazan have convincingly demonstrated in their microlevel analysis of life stories of Palestinian and Jewish Israeli residents of Jaffa.[34] When Fahed distanced himself from the symbolically charged key, he took, like Yael, the risk of being accused of disloyalty by his own people.

Defusing the sway of a community's chosen trauma is not cost-free. But when explored, practiced, and trained in protective spaces, it strengthens resilience against one-sided national narratives and moves reconciliatory processes forward.

A final word on Fahed: the last time I met him in an Israeli-Palestinian encounter, he confided to the group that he has been called a normalizer, collaborator, and traitor by some of his Palestinian neighbors and on social media. Stepping back from a collective's chosen trauma does, indeed, cost something—minimally an accusation of disloyalty. Sometimes Fahed receives hostile messages on Facebook from fellow Palestinians; at other times, it is his family that is worried. His mother, Fahed said, is afraid for his life when he travels to Israel. She fears that he will be imprisoned; she also fears that he will be poisoned when sharing meals with Israelis—a material fear with its own antisemitic twist.[35]

Chosen traumas, like master narratives, might be indispensable insofar as they are the backbone of social cohesion. They provide meaning to collectives. They help us understand ourselves and the world around us. Yet, they are also problematic and can be stumbling blocks for reconciliatory and bridge-building efforts between groups in conflict. Clinging to a chosen trauma, like clinging to iterations of master narratives, cements the past in order to score points in the present. "Social groups can, and often do, refuse to recognize the existence of other's trauma," Alexander writes, and hence "diffuse their own responsibility for the suffering."[36] Like the dark side of master narratives, there is a dark side to chosen traumas, for often they tempt us to proclaim legitimacy only to the historical and culture traumas of our own people but blind us to the traumatizing experiences of other people who are not "like us."

As an antidote to such moral blindness, steps can be taken to defuse chosen traumas so that a space opens up for considering the experiences of others. "Defusing" means to investigate self-critically our investments in our own chosen trauma: What stories of suffering do we hold on to? What memories of injustice do we take to be indisputable truth? What do we feel we need to defend, and why? What do we fear? How do we employ our collectively chosen trauma in our present lives? What discomfiting truths about our own community do we refuse to see? Time and again, political-emotional investment in our trauma narrative translates into testimonial injustice toward people with whom we are in conflict. The presence of the other, I contend, is essential for defusing stumbling blocks in reconciliatory processes.

## THE CONFINING EFFECT OF MIRRORS

The function of mirrors can illustrate how master narratives operate when they are stumbling blocks in reconciliatory practices. Mirrors exclude the other, for they are unidirectional and reflect only an image of the self. When groups in conflict meet each other with the intent of moving toward greater mutual understanding, a caricature of a compassionate listening exercise might look like this: Members from each group sit across from each other with individual participants taking turns telling their story of hardship and suffering. The listeners are not to intervene in the process but are supposed to validate and not question the story. Some awkward silence follows, some tears flow, and some polite enquiry is permissible. Perhaps a ritual gesture, like holding hands or lighting a candle, signals the end of one story before someone from the other group begins to tell his or her story of anguish and victimization.

Keeping the concern of testimonial injustice in mind, it is important to validate each other's stories of personal and collective pain in the opening phase of an encounter.[37] Yet, when personal storytelling remains unchallenged, it is in danger of becoming a solipsistic exercise rather than a relational interaction, replicating the unidirectional flow of mirrors. Instead of seeing the other, a mirror is held up which only reflects the plight of one's own group. A mirror's perplexing disposition is that it makes us believe we see reality accurately reflected when we actually can see only the space behind us, not in front us. Similarly, unchallenged and uncritical storytelling that remains framed within a master narrative tends to see only the space-time behind us. It always harks back to the past. Compassionate listening thus tends to remain caught in its own mirror image of the past, more invested in validating and legitimizing the in-group account of one's injurious past rather than seeking pathways with the other in the present and the future.

As we look at the other person across from us, we see a reflection of our own narrative instead of relational possibilities that might emerge from our encounter. This *mirroring effect replicates a self-contained (rather than other-directed) "narrative identity," wherein a personal story remains caught in the trappings of a collective narrative.[38] With respect to the national narratives of Palestinians and Israelis, many scholars and scholar-practitioners concerned about their narratives' mutual exclusiveness are trying to escape the confining effects of mirrors; they are invested in overcoming the antagonistic relations between these narratives and challenging, mitigating, and bridging the narrative gaps.[39]

Taking risks and rendering ourselves vulnerable are some of the steps we can take to stop gazing into mirrors. Safe spaces open venues for stepping away from chosen cultural traumas and chosen national glories. They allow us to work through psychopolitical and psychosocial stumbling blocks. We cannot presume, as I have argued above, that our individual stories are automatically an antidote to master narratives. Within our individual stories that circumambulate a historically or culturally traumatic core reside a number of smaller mirrors that reflect particularized personal anxieties, such as Yael's educational challenge with her nationalist-minded students, or Fahed's complex relation to the key as a collective memory object. Becoming attentive to the confining, self-refe-rential effects of those smaller mirrors can be hard emotional labor on intersubjective levels (between individuals) and on intrapsychic levels (within one's mind). When working through these anxieties deliberately and prudently, it is possible to switch from well-intended but often inef-fectual modes of compassion to a posture of unsettling empathy. Unset-tling empathy leaves salutary cracks in the mirror image we have of ourselves as well as in the biases we carry about the other. A sequential series of monologues in the presence of the other has to morph into dialogical engagement with the other.

## I WAS AFRAID OF BEING KIDNAPPED

We can now return to Yael's story. We might be at a better place to interpret the nervousness that spread in the room when she mentioned "Death to the Arabs" as an unsettling experience. It unsettled expecta-tions about what can or cannot be shared in a mixed group; it unsettled the anticipated framing of a personal story within the patterns of a master narrative. Something was now at stake for the Israeli and Palestinian participants. The group became energized and attentive.

Rather than entering into a prolonged debate with the whole group about the d.t.t.a phrase, I asked Yael whether she would be willing to approach her dilemma nonverbally. To switch to a different mode of working-through was, at this moment, important in order to stay with the emotional urgency of the situation. In general, the use of *nonverbal communication reaches what psychiatrist Irvin Yalom calls the "core" of group therapy, or—when applied to facilitating groups in conflict—the core of the potential for change and transformation in reconciliatory pro-cesses.[40] To get behind and underneath the comforting familiarity of our master narratives requires, at times, modes of exploration that do not limit themselves to verbal communication. Participants are encouraged to challenge themselves and others on affective and cognitive levels of communication, including creative, body-centered, and nonverbal com-ponents. Though such work is deeply personal and relational, I always keep the focus on the dynamics of the group process. Vamik Volkan calls such processes "psychopolitical."[41]

Yael hesitantly agreed to switch to nonverbal expressions. She later confided that she was highly skeptical of my suggestion, not sure wheth-er to trust my guidance and whether to adopt nonverbal forms, which, she said, she generally dislikes. Yael consented nevertheless. In the first round, I invited her to get off her chair and repeat two hand gestures. The first gesture related to an earlier session when she had stepped into the center of a roped-off circle and assumed the pose of a boxer, with two clenched fists. The other hand gesture related to her telling us about her students: there, she had repeatedly and nervously flipped her hands up and down. While the first gesture was a deliberate representation of strength, the other gesture was an inadvertent movement mirroring her story's trepidation. I asked Yael to augment and repeat both gestures for us, switching back and forth between them several times: clenched fists/ flipping hands, strength/trepidation, assertiveness/doubt, boldness/inde-cisiveness, power/fear . . . or whatever else resonated with people when watching her amplified gestures.

When Yael stopped, I asked her fellow Israeli participants whether they could relate to the ambivalence expressed in her hand gestures. The first person to respond was an enthusiastic young man from Tel Aviv. It was his first time attending a workshop in which he was exposed to direct contact with Palestinians. Instead of sharing with us how he related to Yael's ambivalence (after all, she had been chosen to represent the whole Israeli group), he went into a lengthy speech—an anthropological mini-lecture of sorts—about why and how all Mediterranean cultures use lots of hand gestures. His long-winded speech missed the point, and its evasive nature threatened to drain the group's vitality. The unsettling experience of watching Yael's wordless struggle, it seemed, had to be pressed back into the safety of academic discourse.

In a second round, I invited Yael to repeat the phrase "Death to the Arabs" while looking intentionally at the Palestinian participants. Perhaps some readers might object that this would be asking too much of her and that it would unfairly expose her. The intent, however, was to move a narrated line from her story into the full emotional presence of the group. It was important not to brush aside the affective impact of this phrase but to feel more deeply the political emotion as well as the inter-subjective weight of this utterance in the physical (rather than abstract) presence of the other. I knew I was asking a lot of Yael—perhaps to lay bare part of her soul. As always, participants are free to opt out of any part of the process of exploration. Yael said that she wanted to try; she forewarned us that it would probably make her cry.

Softly, with a quivering, almost failing voice, she repeated: "Death to the Arabs"—"Death to the Arabs"—"Death to the Arabs"—"Death to the Arabs." A pin could have dropped in the room, that's how quiet and apprehensive it was. Yael started crying. She got embarrassed about her tears. Her tears—as cliché as it might sound—softened the hearts of her Palestinian listeners.

Some of my readers may intuitively understand what happened in this exchange. Others may remain skeptical, wondering whether individual tears in asymmetrical political conflicts contribute anything worthwhile to the need of social repair and restorative justice. Let me, hence, rephrase the above scene in more erudite prose. Beyond the mere mirroring effect of compassion, which is devoid of critical moral reasoning, what transpired in Yael's embodiment was the power of unsettling empathy. As a relational commitment to caring responsiveness in the face of past injustices and power asymmetries, unsettling empathy requires us to risk vulnerability in the face of the other. Yael literally looked at the face of the other. It can be interpreted as an ethical posture toward the other, compelling everyone to fully validate the existence of the other.

I will conclude the chapter with Yael. Toward the end of the workshop—after shedding tears when realizing the emotional weight of the d.t.t.a phrase in the presence of Palestinians—Yael spontaneously decided to join one of the Palestinian male participants on a nightly walk. He lived in Bethlehem in the West Bank, not too far from the center where the workshop was held. He had asked a few Israelis to join him walking his dog in his Palestinian neighborhood. This excursion happened on the same day that Israeli extremists had firebombed a Palestinian home that, as mentioned above, killed the toddler Ali Dawabsheh. Everyone in Israel and the Palestinian territories was on high alert, fearing another round of widespread violent protests. Notwithstanding the security risk, Yael accompanied the young Palestinian man that night, crossing into Area A, which Israelis are not permitted to enter. [42]

The next morning, during a group session, Yael turned to the Palestinian man who had, against regulations, taken her into Area A. She looked into his eyes and admitted that she had been gravely frightened when he made several phone calls in Arabic while they walked together through his neighborhood at night. "I was afraid you make calls for arranging our kidnapping," she told him candidly, "or do some other harm to us." Surprisingly, the Palestinian man did not get upset. Instead, for the first time in our four-day seminar, he finally relaxed. He loosened his arms, which had been tightly crossed around his chest, protecting himself for most of the seminar. He thanked Yael for her honesty. He said that he expected all along such fear and mistrust among Israelis. He could see her now as a human being, fearful in her own ways, and no longer simply a representative of a "politically correct" Israeli.

## NOTES

1. The brevity of this example is meant only as an indication of how a master narrative operates. It is not meant to do justice to the nuances of the discursive structure of German war memories. See also the cited literature in Chapter 2, especially notes 51–53. For a case study of a detailed discursive analysis of dealing with the past in postwar German memoirs, see Krondorfer, "Nationalsozialismus und Holocaust in Autobiographien protestantischer Theologen" (2006).

2. Those who have followed the politically contested terrain of memory narratives between Israelis and Palestinians are familiar with the clash and seeming incompatibility of those narratives; hence there is an incessant mistrust vis-à-vis personal stories of suffering. Among the extensive literature, see the Jewish Israeli and Palestinian contributions in Robert Rotberg's *Israeli and Palestinian Narratives of Conflict* (2006a); Meir Litvak, *Palestinian Collective Memory and National Identity* (2009); Idith Zertal,

*Israel's Holocaust and the Politics of Nationhood* (2005); Rashid Khalidi, *Palestinian Identity: The Construction of Modern National Consciousness* (1997); Neta Oren and Daniel Bar-Tal, "The Detrimental Dynamics of Delegitimization in Intractable Conflicts: The Israeli-Palestinian Case" (2007); and, on personal political history, Omer Bartov's "National Narratives of Suffering and Victimhood" (2019).

3. Fatma Kassem, "A Step to Make My Dream Come True" (2000, 99–100); her personal reflection is about one of Dan Bar-On's TRT meetings ("To Reflect and Trust").

4. Michael Rothberg, *Multidirectional Memory* (2009, 309).

5. "Testimonial injustice" was explored extensively by feminist philosopher Miranda Fricker, *Epistemic Injustice* (2007).

6. Barrett Emerick, "Empathy and a Life of Moral Endeavor" (2016, 172).

7. Often, we narrowly locate a deficient attitude toward hearing a victim's testimony in individual moral agency. See, for example, Barrett Emerick (2016). Emerick discusses the more individualized implications of testimonial injustice in the larger context of an epistemic failure that occurs in less overt forms of "civilized oppression" (172).

8. See Hava Shechter and Gavriel Salomon, "Does Vicarious Experience of Suffering Affect Empathy for an Adversary? The Effects of Israelis' Visits to Auschwitz on Their Empathy for Palestinians" (2005); Julia Chaitin and Shoshana Steinberg, "'You Should Know Better': Expressions of Empathy and Disregard among Victims of Massive Social Trauma" (2008); Michalinos Zembylas, "The Politics of Trauma: Empathy, Reconciliation and Peace Education" (2007); Daniel Bar-Tal et al., "A Sense of Self-Perceived Collective Victimhood in Intractable Conflicts" (2009).

9. Robert Rotberg, "Building Legitimacy through Narrative" (2006b, 4).

10. The Nakba (Arabic: catastrophe) refers to the 1948 mass expulsion of Palestinians from their homes. See also the discussion further below.

11. In *Twilight Nationalism*, Daniel Monterescu and Haim Hazan write that the "main relationship between Israeli memory and the Palestinian memory is that of negation and mutual exclusion. This frame of reference creates a one-sided paradigm of liberation versus victimhood that nourishes biographical narrative, which in itself can either adopt it, reject it, or alter it to suit its own needs" (2018, 14). Herbert Kelman addresses the struggle over "national identity" as a central problem in Israeli-Palestinian encounters. "The zero-sum view of identity and the mutual denial of the other's identity," he writes, "create serious obstacles in conflict resolution" ("The Role of National Identity in Conflict Resolution: Experiences from Israeli-Palestinian Problem-Solving Workshops" 2001, 193). See also Robert Rotberg, "Building Legitimacy through Narrative" (2006b).

12. Robert Rotberg, "Building Legitimacy through Narrative" (2006b, 4).

13. Daniel Geiger, "The Dark Side of Narratives" (2008, 74).

14. For a liberal-reformist affirmation of the Zionist narrative that also aims at doing justice to the Palestinian plight, see, for example, Ari Shavit, *My Promised Land: The Triumph and Tragedy of Israel* (2013).

15. I am not suggesting that the Palestinian fear is unfounded or pathological but that it is *perceived* by hawkish Israelis as "paranoid." For a moderate affirmation of the Palestinian narrative that also aims at affirming the rights of Israelis, see, for example, Elias Chacour, *Blood Brothers: The Dramatic Story of a Palestinian Christian Working for Peace in Israel* (2013); his account suffers from occasional self-aggrandizing elements.

16. Daniel Bar-Tal and Ilai Alon connect trust and risk-taking. In "Sociopsychological Approach to Trust (or Distrust)" (2016), they propose the following definition of trust: "lasting expectations about future behaviors of the other (a person or a group) that affects the own welfare (of one person or of own group) and allow for a *readiness to take risks* in relation to the other" (312; emphasis added).

17. Volkan, "Transgenerational Transmissions and Chosen Traumas: An Aspect of Large-Group Identity" (2001, 83).

18. This fear is, for example, expressed by Elias Sanbar, when he writes that "the contemporary history of the Palestinians turns on a key date: 1948. That year, a country and a people disappeared from maps and dictionaries" ("Out of Place, Out of Time" 2001, 87).

19. For a critique of Israeli-Palestinian dialogue work as a continuation of normalization, see Stephen Sheedi, "Psychoanalysis under Occupation: Nonviolence and Dialogue Initiatives as a Psychic Extension of the Closure System" (2018); he states: "Dialogue, intended to naturalize 'co-existence' without genuine restorative justice, is traditionally seen by the Palestinian political groups as a means of *tatbi* or 'normalization'" (356).

20. Vamik Volkan, *Enemies on the Couch* (2013, 77), and ibid., "Transgenerational Transmission and Chosen Traumas" (2001).

21. Similarly, Bruce Edwards, in "History, Myth, and Mind" (1998), observes: "It is not necessary for the historical or popular accounts of these past events to be accurate, consistent, logical, or indisputable. . . . What is important for the group is that the mental doubles of these traumas . . . are shared by all members of the group . . . and support the group in times of collective stress" (1).

22. Vamik Volkan, *Enemies on the Couch* (2013, 158), and ibid., "Transgenerational Transmission and Chosen Traumas" (2001, 87).

23. Alon Confino speaks of "foundational pasts" (*Foundational Pasts: The Holocaust as Historical Understanding* 2012). See also the discussion of cultural trauma in Chapter 3.

24. For an analysis of narratives of resilience in relationship to historical trauma, see Aaron Denham, "Rethinking Historical Trauma: Narratives of Resilience" (2008). Denham discusses the value of such narratives as a response to historical trauma among marginalized communities in a postcolonial context, specifically Native Americans.

25. From a performance transcript of Gabi 'Abed: "I remember that in 1948 our peace of mind vanished all at once. . . . [People] abandoned everything . . . and took the key with them. They keep the keys to this day . . . and fifty-five years have now passed and they still hope to return" (cited in Daniel Monterescu and Haim Hazan, *Twilight Nationalism* 2018, 1). On *sumud*, see Monterescu and Hazan, *Twilight Nationalism* (2018, 2, 14), and Stephen Sheedi, "Psychoanalysis under Occupation" (2018, 365–367); on *sumud* and nonviolent resistance, see www.holylandtrust.org/index.php?option=com_content&task=view&id=122&Itemid=96 (accessed March 9, 2019).

26. See Chapter 1, note 45.

27. For political infighting, see Tareq Baconi, *Hamas Contained: The Rise and Pacification of Palestinian Resistance* (2018).

28. For example, Lila Abu-Lughod and Ahmad Sa'di write in their "Introduction: The Claims of Memory" (2007): "For Palestinians, the 1948 War led indeed to a 'catastrophe.' A society disintegrated, a people dispersed, and a . . . communal life was ended violently. The Nakba has thus become, both in Palestinian memory and history, the demarcation line between two qualitatively opposing periods. After 1948, the lives of the Palestinians at the individual, community, and national level were dramatically and irreversibly changed" (3); see also Saleh Abdel Jawad, "The Arab and Palestinian Narratives of the 1948 War" (2016).

29. Jeffrey Alexander, *Trauma: A Social Theory* (2012, 13). See also Didier Fassin and Richard Rechtman's chapter on Palestine in *The Empire of Trauma* (2009, 189–216), where they discuss the links between humanitarian aid discourse and trauma constructs in Palestine: "Trauma then offers not a last resort in the absence of physical wounds, but a significant added value in the construction of testimony" (197).

30. Jeffrey Alexander calls it "a new master narrative of suffering" ("Toward a Theory of Cultural Trauma" 2004, 15).

31. The denial of the Nakba in Israeli society is strong. It reaches from the extreme end of *Nakba-Nonsense*, a booklet published by a right-wing nationalist group, to the 2011 law to cut governmental funding to any Israeli organization commemorating the

Nakba; see Bashir Bashir and Amos Goldberg, *The Holocaust and Nakba* (2019, 2). For a critical Israeli perspective on the Holocaust as chosen trauma, see Avraham Burg, *The Holocaust Is Over* (2008). In addition to the Holocaust as national trauma, Ari Shavit argues in *My Promised Land* for the centrality of the Masada trauma/triumph narrative in early modern Zionism (2013, 71–97). The Roman siege of the Jewish fortress Masada ended with a mass suicide by the beleaguered Jewish rebels. One might argue that the Masada narrative moved from a chosen trauma (insofar as it ended tragically) to a moment of chosen glory (insofar as the suicide today is interpreted as national pride and resilience).

32. Robert Rotberg, in "Building Legitimacy through Narrative" (2006b), writes about Palestinians and Israelis that they are "locked together in struggle, tightly entangled, and enveloped by a historical cocoon of growing complexity, fundamental disagreement, and overriding misperceptions of motives" (2). See also Neta Oren and Daniel Bar-Tal, "The Detrimental Dynamics of Delegitimization in Intractable Conflicts: The Israeli-Palestinian Case" (2007). In *The Holocaust and the Nakba*, Bashir and Goldberg speak of "oppositional narratives" (2019, 4); see also Bashir and Goldberg, "Deliberating the Holocaust and the Nakba: Disruptive Empathy and Binationalism in Israel/Palestine" (2014); Amos Goldberg, "Empathy, Ethics, and Politics in Holocaust Historiography" (2016); Meir Litvak, *Palestinian Collective Memory and National Identity* (2009); and Meir Litvak and Esther Webman, *From Empathy to Denial: Arab Responses to the Holocaust* (2009).

33. Ilan Pappe suggests a "third space" as a relational approach in which alternative narrative options can emerge. "The third space seeks to reconstruct an individual story within the collective story produced by the national narratives of the occupier and the occupied. The reconstruction, or narrative, should reveal the fluidity of the structure that compose the communities of individuals" ("The Bridging Narrative Concept" 2006, 200). Safe spaces have been recognized as essential for a facilitated environment in which human relations can be rebuilt; they are also called "intermediate spaces" or "potential spaces." Pumla Gobodo-Madikizela speaks of "making public spaces intimate" ("Transforming Trauma in the Aftermath of Gross Human Rights Abuses" 2008); see also ibid., "Psychological Repair" (2015, esp. 1115f).

34. Daniel Monterescu and Haim Hazan, *Twilight Nationalism* (2018, 15). They write: "A close examination of personal life stories unravels a whole universe of contradictions . . . that have been systematically censored by the hegemonic national register" (14). From a different angle, but with a similar intent, Keziah Conrad argues in the context of Bosnia and Herzegovina that recovery from trauma does not happen within a grand scheme but in the everyday and ordinary life ("Dwelling in the Place of Devastation: Transcendence and the Everyday in Recovery from Trauma" 2014).

35. The suspicion of poisoning goes back to Christian medieval charges of Jews poisoning wells. After the period of the Black Death, "the accusation became part and parcel of antisemitic dogma and language. It appeared again in early 1953 in the form of the 'doctors' plot' in Stalin's last days, when hundreds of Jewish physicians in the Soviet Union were arrested and some of them killed on the charge of having caused the death of prominent Communist leaders. . . . Similar charges were made in the 1980s and 1990s in radical Arab nationalist and Muslim fundamentalist propaganda that accused the Jews of spreading AIDS and other infectious diseases" (Walter Laqueur, *The Changing Face of Antisemitism* 2006, 62).

36. Jeffrey Alexander, "Toward a Theory of Cultural Trauma" (2004, 1).

37. For a nuanced conceptual study on personal and collective memories on the Holocaust and *al-Naqba*, including an alternative to master narratives through "my-their" memory that positively assists reconciliation and peace-building, see Julia Chaitin and Shoshana Steinberg, "'I Can Almost Remember It Now': Between Personal and Collective Memories of Massive Social Trauma" (2014); on the positive effects of storytelling in social and political contexts, see Dan Bar-On, *Bridging the Gap: Storytelling as a Way to Work through Political and Collective Hostilities* (2000); on the integrity of personal narratives, see Julia Chaitin, *Peace-Building in Israel and Palestine* (2011).

38. On narrative identity, see Maureen Whitebrook, *Identity, Narrative, and Politics* (2001). For the constraining effects of narrative identity in intergroup meetings between Israeli and Palestinian students and Germans and Israeli student groups, see Julia Chaitin and Shoshana Steinberg, "'You Should Know Better': Expressions of Empathy and Disregard among Victims of Massive Social Trauma" (2008).

39. For bridging the national narratives, see Ilan Pappe "The Bridging Narrative Concept" (2006), and Mordechai Bar-On, "Conflicting Narratives of Narratives of Conflict: Can the Zionist and Palestinian Narratives of the 1948 War Be Bridged?" (2006); on overcoming the role of Palestinians and Israelis as "antagonists of each other's history," see Edward Said, *Freud and the Non-European* (2003, 55); on challenging and mitigating seemingly intractable differences, see Bashir Bashir and Amos Goldberg, *The Holocaust and the Nakba* (2009, 5). For limits of bridging narratives in Israeli-Palestinian intergroup dialogue, see Shelley Berlowitz, "Unequal Equals: How Politics Can Block Empathy" (2016). For an excellent study on the unproductive recycling of visual and narrative similarities when comparing Jewish suffering during the Holocaust and Palestinian suffering in Gaza, see Michael Rothberg, "From Gaza to Warsaw: Mapping Multidirectional Memory" (2011); Rothberg argues that instead of using comparative analysis for the purposes of "equation and symmetry," we need to pursue a "reflexive justice" when "decentering" parochial or nationalized memories (538, 540).

40. In the context of group therapy, Irvin Yalom helpfully distinguishes between the "front" and the "core": "The *front* consists of the trappings, the form, the techniques, the specialized language, and the aura surrounding each of the ideological schools; the *core* consists of those aspects of the experience that are intrinsic to the therapeutic process—that is, *the bare-boned mechanisms of change*" (*The Theory and Practice of Group Psychotherapy* 1995, xii; emphasis in original). See also Elliot Leffler's support of the importance of touch in intercultural encounters, "Rechoreographing Intercultural Encounters: The Power and Limits of Dramatic Play in Segregated Communities" (2016, 148).

41. Vamik Volkan, *Enemies on the Couch: A Psychopolitical Journey through War and Peace* (2013).

42. Neta Oren and Daniel Bar-Tal, "The Detrimental Dynamics of Delegitimization in Intractable Conflicts: The Israeli-Palestinian Case" (2007). The West Bank is divided into Area A under the control of the Palestinian Authority, Area B under Israeli security control but civil matters under the control of the Palestinian Authority, and Area C in Israel's control.

# SIX

## Haunting

For a transformative quality to transpire in reconciliatory processes, the encounters need to move beyond the surface of friendly conversation, beyond the comfort zones of rehearsed opinions, beyond the limitation of a culture's master narrative and chosen trauma, and beyond the loyalties that communities impose on large-group identities. Occasionally, a process moves even beyond our ordinary experience of linear time through the intrusion of a *haunting presence. This chapter will describe such an occasion. We will get a glimpse at how intensified memory work can lead a group into the presence of a haunted past that becomes temporarily embodied in a returning ghost.

I conducted a three-day seminar for a group of German and Israeli educators, therapists, teachers, and community organizers on the long-lasting legacies of the Holocaust and World War II. It was the same group in which Oren impersonated his survivor grandmother through a mimetic enactment, which exuded its own haunting quality (Chapter 3). This multigenerational group had already worked together for some time on peace-building activities, but the repercussions of disruptive and traumatic memories kept obstructing their present-day relationships. They hoped that this seminar on "Restorative Forgetting/Necessary Remembering," which took place in a small town near the Rhine in Germany, would allow each side to explore the complexity of memory's abyss. A cardboard box painted pitch-black served as a symbolic core object to guide us through these three days. It was our symbolic container of what was forgotten and remembered.

Because the participants of this German-Israeli encounter showed an extraordinary ability to take personal risks and to respond to each other straightforwardly without breaking the trust that had been built up over time, they were ready to confront directly the ghosts of the past. On the evening of the last day, I proposed to enter with them hitherto uncharted territory. When we met after dinner, the November darkness had already descended around us, hushing the sounds rising from the German town at whose edge the retreat center was nestled.

Some of the German participants were born during the final years of World War II or in the immediate postwar years. They carried early childhood memories of fear and deprivations. Those were the years of destruction and chaos reaching civilians in every major German city, but also of hunger and misery after 1945. These German descendants also bore conflicting emotions toward their fathers. Snippets of stories of their fathers emerged during previous sessions, intruding on our space like a spectral presence, never tangible and never the focal point of any of our conversations. Yet they kept seeping through the cracks of people's narratives and memories. An Israeli participant—herself a peace builder and conflict-resolution expert—wrote after the seminar: "The Germans in our group tended to talk about the Nazi perpetrators of their past that often haunt them, leaving an inner darkness that never quite dissipates. We Jews spoke more about the voices of the victims from the past that accompany us at different times through life. These voices cause sadness and loss, and they sometimes warn us about putting our trust in other peoples, that is, in non-Jews." Her recollection captured well the perspectival differences with which each group came to the seminar, perspectives resonating with the (chosen) traumas of their national histories as experienced in the intimate setting of the emotional lives of their families.

The seminar eventually took a turn for which no one was prepared. "For over twenty years," the Israeli scholar and peace-building activist continued in her letter, "I have been engaged in the psychosocial significance of the Holocaust in the lives of the victims, their children and grandchildren, and sometimes the perpetrators as well, and their children and grandchildren. I have written a lot about this in academic articles and books. I have interviewed hundreds of survivors, children, and grandchildren, and run seminars for the second and third generations in Israel, and also with German colleagues in Germany. I thought that I had pretty much heard it all, thought about it all. Wrong."

## FATHERS

Several German participants articulated their wish that their fathers should have been present in this encounter of Jewish Israelis and Germans. There was a sense of anger at their parents' generation for not confronting the past sufficiently and, instead, for delegating it to subsequent generations. They also bemoaned their fathers' lack of courage to expose themselves to the presence of Jews and Israelis after 1945. Their fathers, they surmised, might have benefited from such an encounter—a subtle wish, as I understood it, to redeem the fathers who had been implicated in National Socialism and also a desire to break through the unyielding silence that encased so many postwar German families.

The fathers of these particular Germans had identified with the Nazi regime to various degrees of complicity, including war criminals. This was the case for Alois Schintlholzer, who had joined the SA (Stormtroopers/Brownshirts) in Austria in 1933 and later the SS (Schutzstaffel/Hitler's Elite Defense Units). Still later, Alois took part in the killing of partisans and Jews in Italy. Tried as a war criminal in 1961, he spent only eleven months in prison. He remained a lifelong unrepentant National Socialist. In 1950, he helped Adolf Eichmann escape to Argentina by driving him personally in the family car to the Austrian border. This man was Ursula's stepfather. Ursula, born in 1947, participated in our seminar. The details of her stepfather's story were not shared in any of the group sessions, but Ursula had a chance to tell us about him in broad strokes. I did not learn the full story until Ursula published the reckoning with her family legacy four years later.[1] Alois Schintlholzer, as well as other fathers, remained invisible figures in the midst of our Israeli-German encounter, absent and present at the same time. Despite their uncanny presence, they remained elusive. Without flesh and blood, we could not get hold of them.

Prior to the evening session, we had used the black box in multiple ways, including two exercises that signaled different temporal-emotional movements. In the first exercise, every participant wrote something about the past on a note card, and these cards were placed inside the box with the purpose of retrieving them later. In this case, the idea was to pull something out of the black box of memory/forgetting and bring it into the present, something that each person was ready to explore in our group. The second exercise asked participants to do the reverse: write something on a note card that would remain in the box, something that each person would rather forget or keep secret. In this case, we deposited something back into the past that we were aware of in the present. Those cards were discarded at the end of the seminar and no one, including myself, learned what was written on them. Whatever these cards contained was inaccessible and yet somehow in our midst. This seemingly innocuous twofold approach provided safety because it allowed individuals to make decisions about the extent to which they were ready to share disturbing memories. "Merely uncovering memories is not enough," write psychiatrist Bessel Van der Kolk and psychotherapist Alexander McFarlane, unless they are "modified and transformed . . . in an act of creation." Van der Kolk and McFarlane advise that exploring traumatic memories for their "own sake has no therapeutic benefits unless it becomes attached to other experiences, such as feeling understood, being safe . . . or being able to empathize with and help fellow sufferers."[2] When working with groups in conflict, it is important to know a group's limitations and to let a group decide for itself how far it is willing to go.

## GHOSTLY APPEARANCE

On the last evening of the seminar, I suggested that we needed to visit the absent German fathers who had been with us in our prior sessions. Better still, I suggested, we allow them to visit us. After making sure that there was consensus for moving into a sphere we had not dared to enter previously, we placed the black memory box in the wide open circle. The task was simple: let us invite one of these spectral German fathers into our midst. Nervousness and incredulity spread. How would we do this? We unfurled a blanket next to the black box and asked for a German participant to volunteer. Hildegard, who had experienced the war as a child in the eastern German provinces, stepped forward.[3] When she was comfortably resting on the blanket, we dimmed the lights and opened the top of the black box—symbolically representing the opening of buried memories or of a grave. I slowly guided her into letting go of her own self and imaginatively taking on the figure that she felt might emerge from the black box.

Hildegard took time to transition into her role. She closed her eyes; her body eventually began to squirm, wriggle, and twist. She seemed to resist a presence that was taking over her being. When she finally opened her eyes and looked around in the circle, she was no longer play-acting. Rather, she appeared to be—for the lack of a better term—possessed: a ghostly presence had taken hold of her. If a ghost is "something lost or invisible or seemingly not there [but] makes itself known or apparent to us," sociologist Avery Gordon writes,[4] then we were visited that evening by the ghost of one of the German fathers. Hildegard had become a German soldier returning from the grave. It was not her own father, though, and the ghost remained nameless throughout the evening.

We are, of course, not talking about a literal ghost apparition that populates folklore, movies, and the popular imagination but about a haunting presence of a figuration that a social or collective body has been unable to resolve or put to rest. The trope of a "haunting presence of the past" is frequently invoked to describe the intrusion of traumatic memories or of memories that are unwelcome and unresolved. While the initial impetus of thinking about haunting in psychosocial terms traces back to Freudian psychoanalytic terminology and to individual therapy,[5] the concept has been enlarged to address recalcitrant memories and buried histories in social and collective groups. "The ghost is not simply a dead or missing person, but a social figure," and this figure is "tangible and tactile as well as ephemeral and imaginary."[6] Unresolved memories and histories "often come to us as ghosts, demanding attention, looking for justice, [and] challenging the way we know, act, and feel," argue Debra Ferreday and Adi Kuntsman.[7] As social figures, ghosts transmigrate across generations. That which haunts—like the dead "who took unspeakable secrets to their grave"—is passed on to subsequent generations until it eventually fades away if and when it is worked through individually and collectively.[8]

As if waking up from a long, deep sleep, Hildegard—in her new persona—stared into space and asked: "What do you want from me? Why did you call me?" Slowly, the group began to verbally interact with the ghost. The specific questions and answers do not really matter here, and I am not sure they really mattered during the session itself. The eerie presence of a resurrected German soldier-father filled the room, putting everyone under a spell. Questions were asked, but many remained unanswered. The ghost reluctantly offered fragmented bits of information and stubbornly refused to provide specifics. He had returned from the grave with his silence intact. This frustrated and infuriated the group. Hypnotized by the ghost's unsettling aggressiveness, we were in the presence of a dead man teasing and threatening us by hinting at a secret and violent past.

When he unexpectedly led us to an execution site, putting bullets into his victims, we almost preferred his previous silence rather than having to imagine this scene. In a matter-of-fact style, almost catatonically, the soldier-father told of "things" that just needed to get done. He showed no emotional remorse. The group prodded but failed to elicit any small gesture of sorrow or any recognition of culpability. Now that a door had opened to a scene at the killing fields, how could any meaning emerge from this? The group grew impatient.

As is always the case when reporting about the dynamics of such group sessions, words cannot adequately describe what transpired during that evening. Time stood still (we were in the presence of the ghost for more than an hour).[9] It seemed the group had been transposed to a historical trauma that, in our imaginary, felt so real that it took on an aura of reality. We came close to witnessing what religious language knows as spirit possession.[10]

## CONTAINING THE GHOST

There is a "stain on the soul" of second-generation Germans, Eric Santner writes. "Legacies—or perhaps more accurately: the ghosts, the revenant objects—of the Nazi period are transmitted to the second and third generations at the site of the primal scene of socialization, that is . . . the postwar family."[11] Santner, in his study on German postwar films, did not have in mind a "literal" embodiment of the ghosts he referred to, but Hildegard had led us to the site of a primal scene that haunts German postwar generations. In *Haunting Legacies*, Gabriele Schwab, professor of comparative literature, traces "the psychic life of violent histories," especially with regard to the Holocaust and German family history, including her autobiographical reflections of growing up in Germany in the immediate postwar years. For Schwab, "'haunting legacies' are things hard to recount or even to remember, the results of violence that holds an unrelenting grip on memory yet is deemed unspeakable." [12] To have a ghostly father return and speak to a group of Germans and Israelis was nothing short of extraordinary. It was not an easy encounter.

The German group was split in half regarding its attitude toward the ghost. One half was angry at his refusal to speak and at his unrepentant attitude; the other half was supportive, gently prodding the ghost to show signs of insight and regret. Both sides, it seemed, acted on the two primary impulses that descendants of perpetrator generations have at their disposal when responding to culpable wrongdoing. On the one hand, they can take a firm and angry stance toward their parents' generational silence about the past (which is also an angry reaction to being burdened with the atrocious legacy passed on by their fathers and nation); or, on the other hand, they can adopt a soft and sympathizing stance toward their parents' shameful silence, perhaps hoping to find points of connection. Questions directed at the ghostly father in our midst fell in either of the two categories: trying to get him to talk by coaxing him with an attitude of nonjudgmental curiosity or querying him about his choices in a more moral-confrontational style. The ghost, however, remained immune to his "children's" angry rejections as well as their tenuously therapeutic gestures of inclusion—which made his appearance so hypnotically powerful and threatening.

The Israeli group remained mostly silent throughout the whole sequence/séance. A few dared to ask him questions but largely left the inquiry to the Germans. The Israelis felt the need to put distance between themselves and the ghost and to reduce their engagement with him to a minimum. They observed skeptically their German peers' efforts to interact with him. The longer the German interaction lasted, the more anxious and threatened the Israelis became. "What a shame," wrote the Israeli scholar-activist quoted above, "that one people is haunted by demon-like, terrifying ghosts, and one people (the group to which I belong) is fraught with existential fear about potential enemies just waiting to annihilate us. These are not good ways to live." For the Israelis, after an hour of watching the scene unfold, it was time to bring the session to an end.

But how do you return a ghost? If "ghosts are a form of calling, a *refusal* to disappear, and an insistence on presence," how do you exorcise *die Geister, die ich rief?* [13]

Our father-ghost of this evening refused to go back into the black memory box from which he had emerged. His resistance was strengthened by those in the German group who did not want him to leave yet.

They were still trying to reach out to him. My signals (both nonverbal and verbal) to relieve Hildegard from her ghostly possession were simply ignored. The German participants who sought an entry into the entombed emotional state of the ghostly father protested my attempt to end the session. They felt that I was interrupting their psychopolitical efforts of understanding the mentality and soul of the perpetrator generation.

The ghost himself, now that he was among us, had begun to enjoy himself. He seemed to get a certain pleasure from the fact that he was emotionally attended to without having to change. He yielded power as a bearer of terrifying secrets (which he hinted at sparingly), and he held sway over us by revealing little about himself. I reminded the group several more times that we had already exceeded the allotted time for the evening, but each attempt at bringing the session to a close was unsuccessful. Eventually I had to physically recapture the space that the ghost inhabited, assertively asking for a moratorium on further questions. I turned to the means of *direct intervention, which is at the disposal of facilitators when a group begins to spin out of control in potentially detrimental ways. I put my hands on the ghost's shoulders, gently but firmly making him/her lie down on the blanket. Slowly, Hildegard's body relaxed. She sighed. Finally, we were able to close the lid of the black box.

The "séance" had come to an end. When we took a break, the Israelis lost no time rushing out of the room, while many in the German group continued with an animated debate. In the ensuing group discussions that evening and the next morning, the issue of putting the ghost back into the box remained contentious. The half of the German group that had wanted to extend the session voiced frustration. They felt that I had deliberately ignored a critical moment. They argued that we missed out on a chance to approach Germany's legacy not with the usual confrontational attitude but with a more nuanced view of their fathers' mentality. They thought that their valiant efforts to move toward a platform of shared grief were prematurely interrupted. The other German half, however, felt that it made no sense to keep investing so much energy and effort into the ghost. In their view, he was as irredeemable as the history he represented. It was time to stop the ghost from spreading any more of his poison. They felt more than ready to have the ghost disappear.

It is possible to interpret these two German responses through the lens of transference and countertransference, a dynamic known in therapy when strong feelings, like guilt and anger, judgment and fascination, are projected from therapist to patient and vice versa. The mental contagion effect of recalcitrant traumatic content is, I believe, especially active when working with perpetrator trauma, or the haunting presence of perpetrator trauma. Allan Young, in his study on self-traumatized perpetrators, writes perceptively that a "patient who is a perpetrator" creates the "potential of undermining the solidarity of the therapeutic regime, by splitting the staff into conflicting factions: one side identifies with the patient's victim and longs to punish the patient, while the other side identifies vicariously with the patient's violent acts and aggressive urges."[14] Young's observation may shed some light onto what we witnessed that evening in our group. There was no unity, no solidarity in the German group; instead, two conflicting factions were responding differently to the ghostly father-soldier appearance.

The Israelis had yet another response. For them, the ghostly presence had become unbearable. Had the situation continued any longer, they confessed afterward, they would have left the room. For them, what was threatening was not only the appearance of the ghost itself but also the German group's seemingly tireless efforts to engage him. They viscerally began to understand how frustratingly difficult it was for a perpetrator society to work through the past. But they also wondered whether, by trying so hard to understand the ghostly father, Germans began to err on the side of sympathetic identification rather than historical and moral judgment. They felt like uninvited guests witnessing a family feud, like eavesdropping on an intense moment of *cultural intimacy.[15] It frightened them, and yet they were grateful for it.

When we finally turned our attention to Hildegard, who had volunteered to channel the ghost, she started crying. Although she could not put words to her tears at the time, she later conveyed in emails that these were tears of grief for her father and his generation. "After the session," she said, "I had a profound feeling for having failed. I thought of it as a personal failure, but Björn offered the possibility that this feeling of failure belonged to the perpetrator ghost. That felt right to me. Fact is: the Nazi perpetrators failed as humans in a most extreme form. Perhaps, we can hardly even speak of a 'human' failure. This is what I felt in my role." What Hildegard impersonated was less an individual memory than a collective spirit. Anthropologist Michael Lambek, in his observations about "spirit possession" as culturally alternative forms of memory work, writes that "spirits do not memorialize private suffering so much as they speak to the wider family and community."[16] This collective dimension is perhaps the reason why Hildegard could find a healthy distance to the evening's experience. Later, in another letter, she wrote: "When I volunteered, I had no idea about the scope and impact of what was to follow. I do not feel burdened but I am still thinking about it. . . . I think for now everything has been said."

Being haunted is "to be in a heightened state of awareness."[17] The ghost session had managed to unsettle everyone that evening, though not for the same reasons. For some, the dialogical and emphatic engagement with the ghost unsettled them because they tried but failed to understand the perpetrator's mentality; for others, it was the act of secondary witnessing of a reimagined and reenacted scene of harm inflicted (and, by extension, harm endured) that was deeply disturbing; for yet others, a posture of unsettling empathy allowed them to witness and share a fragile moment of cultural intimacy.

The posture of unsettling empathy also led to particular investments into present relationships. For example, those Germans who had reproached the ghostly father with anger quickly grasped how threatened the Israelis felt by the ghostly presence; they, like the Israelis, were ready to end the session. Those frustrated about the too-early disappearance of the ghost, however, had lost touch with the emotional state of the Israelis. Deeply absorbed in their own history and in their attempts to find a compassionate (though not exonerating) understanding of their fathers' generation, they were too busy with their own *Vergangenheitsbewältigung* (coming to terms with the past) to notice the emotional upheaval of their Israeli peers. They were surprised to hear how frightened the Israelis had been.

These fluctuating layers of unsettling empathy demonstrate that memory is multidirectional and that such multidirectionality must be valued and validated in intercultural encounters. A younger German participant wondered afterward why the Israelis did not express more anger toward the Germans (this person belonged to those who wanted to end the ghost session). Another German shared a passage from a German author who had written about how the soul of perpetrators can be positively affected and transformed when physically touched by victims (this person belonged to the group that wanted the ghost to stay longer among us). Another German woman, in a letter, thanked Hildegard for her vicarious role-playing of the unknown German perpetrator, for it moved her to hitherto unknown places in her own working through the past. Ursula, the stepdaughter of Alois, the Nazi war criminal, sent a letter years later when the chapter about her family history got published. She wrote that when she participated on a panel for a public reading in Berlin, "it felt as if a steel brace that coiled around my chest had finally cracked." An Israeli participant stated: "We can never be completely free of our traumatic past. There will most likely always be a part of us Jews that see Germans and think 'Nazi,' for a fleeting moment, and most likely always be a part of the Germans who see a Jew and think 'stay away—danger,' for a fleeting moment. But facing our connected pasts together, we Jews and Germans can look these demons and fears in the eye and not succumb to their hatred, nor feel lost in an endless black hole of total loss." The many attitudes toward memory and remembrance do not cancel each other out but enrich each other in a "shared moral and political project."[18]

Lest I be misunderstood, I want to make clear that I do not advocate inviting the ghosts of the past on a regular basis. In fact, I would rather caution about such an approach in intercultural groups that work through historical trauma. In exceptional circumstances, one might dare make a haunted, invisible past known in some embodied form, but one needs to know one's limits. There is valid intellectual criticism about bringing ghosts back from the past, relating to the problem of vicarious identification[19] as well as to the ethical conundrum of trying to redeem and rehabilitate the memory of former perpetrators.

Calling on ghosts, however, does not need to lead to attempts at reconciliatory exoneration or at healing a genocidal past. To the contrary, it may be conducive to pursuing justice. "Ghosts are about a possibility of justice," argues legal scholar Christiane Wilke. "They are reminders of a need for justice and can point to the impossibility of justice within the constraints of the law."[20] The Israeli peace-building scholar-activist, whom I had quoted earlier, ended her letter with the following words: "I learned that the demons and the fears of the past still linger in all of us, even if they have become more and more faint, at least on the conscious level. . . . It's not completely true, but after this weekend seminar, I can more honestly say: I ain't afraid of no ghosts."

## NOT THE DEAD BUT THE GAPS HAUNT US

Matthew, an American student from a college in Maryland where I was teaching at the time, was neither German nor Israeli. He nevertheless attended this seminar in Germany with permission from the group. I had invited him because he had sought me out for conversation after one of my classes on the Holocaust. He wanted to talk about his troubled American family and especially about his German grandfather. He was looking for an opportunity to begin making sense of family secrets. Predictably, throughout the Israeli-German seminar, Matthew felt like an outsider and did not engage as actively as others. His journey was just beginning.

When we returned to the United States, Matthew got very quiet in the Holocaust course for the remainder of the semester. When I asked him to speak to his fellow students about our seminar in Germany, where we had encountered the German father-soldier ghost, he said he couldn't do it. After returning from Germany, he explained, he had visited his grandfather in New York, and this visit had shaken him up.

This is what Matthew told me: While at lunch in New York to tell his grandfather about his experiences in Germany, the grandfather blocked all conversation. He refused to talk, exploded in anger, and point-blank told Matthew that he would not tell him anything about the past. Of the little that Matthew knew from his family about his grandfather, he now wondered, what was false or true or incomplete? Matthew's father showed no interest in the past, and so Matthew continued to live with a family biography filled with insinuations and contradictions.

Born in 1921, Matthew's grandfather had fought in Königsberg (East Prussia) as part of the German *Wehrmacht* (army). He might have even been in the SS, but, as Matthew admitted, this was more conjecture than based on certainty. Once, when his grandfather was a little drunk, Matthew learned that he had taken on a new name. But no one in the family seemed to know (or wanted to know) when and why he had assumed a new name. His original German family name remained unknown. Apparently, his grandfather had immigrated to the United States in 1945. Matthew remembered a slideshow at his grandfather's birthday, showing him as a twenty-five-year-old man in America in 1946. The slides did not include a single picture of him as a baby or a child. No one in the extended family was surprised about this absence or asked any questions.

In old age, his grandfather began to identify with U.S. veterans and to spend most of his time in veteran homes assisting returning Iraqi soldiers. Matthew recalled him speaking incessantly about the war, but in such general and vague terms that everyone around him assumed he had fought in World War II as an American GI, not in the German army. He even donned a purple heart on his jacket when visiting veteran homes or his extended family. He was also on a religious quest to embrace Judaism, a fact that many family members disliked, especially when he exhibited fervent pro-Zionist religious ideas. To top it all, his grandfather had married a woman in the United States from a Jewish German family whose roots in America dated back to the migration wave of the 1880s. Matthew wished he could speak to her, but she had passed away many years earlier.

This was Matthew's story. This is why he had retreated into silence when he returned from the seminar in Germany. "What haunts us are not the dead but the gaps left within us by the secrets of others," writes French psychoanalyst Nicolas Abraham.[21] Matthew was left frozen: he was angry and confused. By the time I lost contact with him, he was still haunted.

## OUTLOOK

The ghostly appearance in this Israeli-German seminar demonstrates how complex, difficult, and intense intercultural memory work can become. When the collective identity of one group fills up the space and even moves into an achronological experience of intimate conversations with the dead, the other group either builds up defenses and sabotages such conversations or it seizes the opportunity to eavesdrop on family secrets of a different culture that are usually not shared in mixed settings. We saw a variety of responses in the encounter with the German father-soldier ghost. Intercultural meetings bring up defensiveness, fears of betrayal of family secrets, and a desire to withdraw into protected and familiar mental territory, but these forces can also be transformed into deepening and exploring cultural and interpersonal moments of intimacy and witnessing the exploration of uncanny cultural secrets. When these encounters work well, they compel us to reconsider our assumptions and render us vulnerable in the presence of the other, which is an indispensable seed for any personal and social transformation to occur.

## NOTES

1. Ursula Sperling-Sinemus, "Unglaubliche Lügen und unfassbare Wahrheiten— Wissen, um weiterzuleben" (2015). Because her story is published and hence in the public domain, I am using Ursula's real name here. In the seminar, it took some effort to get the group to listen to her story. She had been quiet for long stretches; when she was finally ready to speak, she got interrupted twice by other participants. Only after she got upset and threatened to leave the room did the group finally give her some space to talk about her SS stepfather.

2. Bessel Van der Kolk and Alexander McFarlane, "The Black Hole of Trauma" (2007).

3. Note that this German woman was not Ursula who is mentioned above in relation to her stepfather.

4. Avery Gordon, *Ghostly Matters: Haunting and the Sociological Imagination* (1997, 63).

5. Stephen Frosh, *Hauntings: Psychoanalysis and Ghostly Transmissions* (2013); on haunting in relation to the uncanny, see Sigmund Freud, "The Uncanny" (1919/1974); also Adrienne Harris, Margery Kalb, and Susan Klebanoff, *Ghosts in the Consulting Room* (2016).

6. Avery Gordon, *Ghostly Matters: Haunting and the Sociological Imagination* (1997, 8, 201).

7. Debra Ferreday and Adi Kuntsman, "Haunted Futurities" (2011, 1).

8. Nicolas Abraham, "Notes on the Phantom: A Complement to Freud's Metapsychology" (1994, 171). See also Nigel Williams's exploration of his Anglo-German family history: "being haunted . . . in psychoanalytical terms" means that "such traumas . . . are not amenable to symbolization and hence deplete and haunt the psyche of more contemporary generations" ("Anglo German Displacement and Diaspora in the Early Twentieth Century: An Intergenerational Haunting" 2015, 139); for a third-generation Jewish woman's story, see Nirit Pisano, "Ghosts in the Mirror: A Granddaughter of Holocaust Survivors Reflects the Faces of History" (2015); for a comparative study on imagined conversations with the dead in the wake of genocide, see Carol Kidron, "Resurrecting Discontinued Bonds: A Comparative Study of Israeli Holocaust and Cambodian Genocide Trauma Descendant Relations with the Genocide Dead" (2018); for the ghostly presence of "replacement children" as a result of war and genocide, see Gabriele Schwab's chapter on "Replacement Children: The Transgenerational Transmission of Traumatic Loss" (*Haunting Legacies* 2010, 118–150); for a therapeutic case study of an intergenerational ghostly haunting, see Heather Ferguson, "Ghostly Intrusions" (2016).

9. "Haunting . . . alters the experience of being in linear time," states Avery Gordon ("Some Thoughts on Haunting and Futurity" 2011, 1).

10. For the healing role of spirit possession after violent conflict in a different cultural context, see the work of Victor Igreja et al., "Gamba Spirits, Gender Relations, and Healing in Post-Civil War Gorongosa, Mozambique" (2008), and ibid., "The Epidemiology of Spirit Possession in the Aftermath of Mass Political Violence in Mozambique" (2010). On spirit possession as an alternative form of working through difficult communal memory, see Michael Lambek, "The Past Imperfect: Remembering as a Moral Practice" (1996).

11. Eric Santner, *Stranded Objects: Mourning, Memory, and Film in Postwar Germany* (1990, 35).

12. Gabriele Schwab, *Haunting Legacies* (2010, 1); her book is not about intergroup encounters but about tracing these legacies in "literary texts, memoirs, and creative nonfiction" (3). Similarly, Jonathan Schorsch, in "Jewish Ghosts in Germany," writes about the impact of "ghostly haunting by society's victims" on postwar Germans as a "complex relationship between the personal psyche and the national imaginary" (158).

13. Debra Ferreday and Adi Kuntsman, "Haunted Futurities" (2011, 6; emphasis in original). The German quote is a reference to a verse in Johann Wolfgang Goethe's *Der Zauberlehrling* (1797; *The Sorcerer's Apprentice*); translated, it means "the spirits that I called," which refers to someone being summoned to help who later cannot be controlled.

14. Allan Young, "The Self-Traumatized Perpetrator as a 'Transient Mental Illness'" (2002, 640).

15. Cultural intimacy refers to situations when a group renders itself vulnerable in the presence of the other at the risk of being misunderstood. "Cultural intimacy is the recognition of those aspects of a shared [collective] identity that are considered a source of external embarrassment but that nevertheless [assure] insiders [a] common sociality," writes anthropologist Michael Herzfeld. "It can even be dangerous for those who reveal the cultural secrets of their nation-states, or of their particular interest-groups, to outsiders" (*Cultural Intimacy: Social Poetics and the Real Life of States, Societies and Institutions* 2016, 2, 7). See also "cultural intimacy" and "cultural secrets" in the Glossary.

16. Michael Lambek, "The Past Imperfect" (1996, 236).

17. Ferreday and Kuntsman, "Haunted Futurities" (2011, 9). For hauntings related to violent histories in the Israeli-Palestinian context, see Yehudit Kirstein-Keshet, "Of Ghosts and Dybbuks: The Haunting of the Israeli Imagination" (2011); for a case study on a daughter-father relationship in the postcolonial context of Egyptian/Muslim-British identity, see Amal Treacher Kabesh, "On Being Haunted by the Present" (2011); for the Cambodian auto-genocide, see Cathlin Goulding, "Living with Ghosts, Living Otherwise: Pedagogies of Haunting in Post-Genocide Cambodia" (2017).

18. Michael Rothberg, *Multidirectional Memory* (2009, 132).

19. On the problematics of vicarious identification, see my discussion in Chapter 4; on vicarious witnessing, see my discussion in Chapter 10.

20. Christiane Wilke, "Enter Ghost: Haunted Courts and Haunting Judgments in Transitional Justice" (2010, 77). For Avery Gordon, haunting is distinct from trauma precisely because it is about "something-to-be-done": a "repressed or unresolved social violence is making itself known" with the possibility of some kind repair ("Some Thoughts on Haunting and Futurity" 2011, 2).

21. Nicolas Abraham, "Notes on the Phantom" (1994, 171).

# SEVEN

## Frustrations

When introducing new ideas that pertain to the implementation of a social practice, authors typically select examples that highlight specific dynamics: these examples must be persuasive in their clarity and demonstrate the particular points that need to be conveyed. It is no different in this book in which I argue that unsettling empathy is a core component for working with groups in conflict. The examples I have chosen aim at communicating with lucidity the kind of personal and social dramas that unfold when people encounter each other in deliberately arranged safe spaces. Therein lies, of course, the peril of misrepresentation, for these examples might make it look as if these processes consist of a series of successive crescendos that inevitably lead to a climax in which a group experiences some form of relief and redemption. Yet, the reality of working with groups is more complicated. What is easily overlooked are those long and nondramatic sessions in which conversations go around in circles, hit dead ends, and seem to lead nowhere. Zooming in on highlights can be distortive insofar as actual processes are tedious at times and can test the patience of a group. Since participants arrive with widely divergent expectations, individuals get frustrated at various moments, sometimes not until weeks or months later. This chapter is about those moments—when external pressures and internal resistance stall a process and when individual frustrations cannot be resolved.

To take the risk of being vulnerable and interacting intimately with people with whom one lives in a tense or adversarial relation is not everyone's cup of tea. We all deal with stress, anxiety, fear, and injustices differently. Human beings, in general, seem to have a high capacity for enduring hardship and for living resiliently in the face of what they cannot imagine can change. But for people drawn to experimenting with processes in which moments of unsettling empathy transpire, it is different: they hunger for change and do not want their imagination restricted by external forces. Within this spectrum, though, motivations differ widely. Some participants hope for cathartic healing that comes with a dusting of new-age spirituality, while others seek solutions that can be swiftly translated into political action. For some, it is their first time stepping into an adversarial-intimate space, but others have grown tired of these kinds of encounters, though they would like to give it one last chance. Some people welcome fresh approaches to stale politicized discourse or simply want their activist batteries recharged, while others seek out professional and educational development opportunities. Such divergent expectations and backgrounds inevitably lead to individual impatience and dissatisfaction. For understandable reasons, not everyone can handle with ease the tension between the experience of an intimate group setting and external social-political pressures when reentering the public sphere. Weeks, months, and sometimes years later, a few people distance themselves from those experiences with disillusionment because they see no tangible results in their communities or because they are pulled back into group loyalty. Many more, however, stay in touch via networks, form lasting friendships, or create initiatives inspired by what they experienced in these processes.

## MISSING CUES

In the summer of 2017, fourteen students from Ben-Gurion University in the Negev and Northern Arizona University met for three weeks to study and travel together in southern Israel and northern Arizona. The student group was deliberately diverse. On the Israeli side, it included Bedouins and Jews of Ashkenazi and Mizrahi backgrounds;[1] on the American side, students came from Mexican, Polish, Jewish, Navajo, Latina, Mexican German, and White Mountain Apache Mormon family origins. The students met for ten days in southern Israel, followed by ten days in northern Arizona to address the theme "Borders, Identities, Social Repair: Majority Cultures & Indigenous Lives in Arizona and Israel." Led by a team of three facilitators, the students were guided through this cultural encounter with open-forum discussions, guided interactive sessions, presentations by experts and scholars, and field trips. The students explored how their diverse social identities have been shaped by geographic, historical, and political boundaries. Learning how different communities inhabit, allocate, and manage their respective environments and how real and perceived injustices are negotiated in different communities, emphasis was given to the experiences of Bedouin cultures in Israel's south and Native American tribes/nations in America's southwest.[2]

For most students, it was their first time visiting Israel or the United States, respectively, especially the American southwest. In addition to participants being introduced to a different country's culture and national history, the program addressed the complex and contentious issues of land use and land rights, indigeneity, dispossession, history-based claims to ownership, power imbalances, invisible privileges, and resilience. Select readings and a broad range of scholars and experts introduced the students to different perspectives and interpretations. Most of the field trips were organized around the theme of innovative community initiatives and resilience. They included visits to recognized and unrecognized Bedouin villages, the Ben-Gurion archive at Sdr Boker, a workshop on traditional medicinal healing by a Bedouin women's cooperative, the Resilience Center in the economically struggling Israeli town of Ofakim, and a kibbutz near the Gaza border frequently targeted by Hamas's cross-border shelling; in Arizona, they included a day trip to a Hopi pueblo to attend a sacred Kachina ceremony, an intertribal environmental institute, a visit to a renowned Navajo artist in his Flagstaff studio, and a trip to a grassroots sustainable farming initiative in the Navajo Nation. We thus created a tapestry of different learning experiences in which cognitive units alternated with interpersonal sessions and hands-on workshops.

The goodwill and enthusiasm of the first few days came to a sudden halt early on. A crisis erupted on the fourth day. Initially, the conflict seemed to be a healthy sign of a group deepening their engagement with each other. It could have been a step toward more direct communication. Instead, this student group never quite recovered from the confrontation of that day. For the remainder of the program, students tiptoed around divisive issues, withdrew into silence, and regressed into what, at times, came across as immature defiance. Only during the last two days, when there was no time left for reengaging some of the divisive issues, were people willing to voice regrets and frustrations about having missed out on opportunities that this program had offered.

What happened? On the afternoon of the fourth day, the group attended a series of short presentations at Ben-Gurion University of the Negev, among them an Israeli government representative from the Bedouin Authority Office.[3] He talked about issues relating to the plight of Bedouin communities from an Israeli government position, insinuating at various points that "problems" lay within the Bedouin communities themselves rather than resulting from governmental policies. When two Bedouin women of our group countered his narrative with a few pointed questions, he quickly dismissed them. Here is how one Jewish American student remembered the event in her reflection essay:

> While at Ben Gurion University, we heard from a handful of presenters covering topics ranging from transitional justice to plans from the Bedouin Authority Office. We explored the concept of the "other" and political discourse among Israeli students. It was really interesting, yet

the moment we all took away from that day was a conversation, if you can call it that, between one of my fellow Bedouin students and a representative from the Israel Bedouin Authority Office. He presented a government proposal to bring better access to education and utilities to the Bedouins in the Negev. However, it would require them to be uprooted from their homes. Throughout the presentation he suggested that Bedouins were unwilling to compromise because they did not wish to be moved from their current lives in the unrecognized villages. He even made comments like "it takes two to tango" and "they want what they don't have."

After he was done, the Bedouin student moved to the front row and shared her skepticism. She was well-spoken and brought up valid points, only to be rudely shot down. The conversation ended when the representative asked her: "Who lived in the Negev first?" She said, "the Bedouins," and he replied "the Jews." Another Bedouin woman attempted to reason with him, but she too was constantly interrupted. None of the other students took part in the conversation.

Another American student remembered the situation in similar terms, leading her to question her own silence.

Seeing confrontations between minority and majority cultures, I began to question my place within different communities. For example, when the Israeli government official blatantly disregarded the voices of my Bedouin peers, I stood idly by, unsure of my role. Do I stand and scream, demanding they be heard? Or was this not my place to speak— after all, I knew very little about the argument at hand. I began to uncover the passive attitudes I held. This was where my privilege was most prevalent: I am in the majority group, therefore I had always assumed that the issues and fights of the minority were of little concern to me.

The self-questioning attitude conveyed in the quote above, with which this American student asked herself why she was unable to speak up for her Bedouin peers, could not be called upon at the moment the contentious exchange had occurred. She was able to articulate her thoughts in writing retrospectively, only after the program had ended. During the program itself, the dismissive attitude of the government official left the group in a state of unease.

Equally strong was the discomfort regarding the silence among the participants during the session with the government official when no one in the group jumped into the debate to support the two Bedouin peers. This was all the more disquieting since in the days prior to the fiery exchange the group had begun to create strong bonds. They were curious about each other's different backgrounds and affirmed their common cause of creating a just world. After the exchange with the government official, the group entered into an obstructive mode of accusatory and defensive attitudes that blocked a more rewarding comprehension of how power dynamics in majority-minority relations were mirrored and echoed among their own group-internal differences.

The group's internal implosion happened the following evening during an open forum when Morissa, a Mexican American student, asked the Israeli Jewish participants why they had not interfered the previous day on behalf of their Bedouin peers. "Why did you not say anything? Why did you stay silent?" Her questions were expressed with some irritation and bafflement but still within the boundaries of respectful discourse. They were not hostile; yet they were perceived as accusatory by the Jewish Israeli participants, perhaps even more so since two of them had just opened up to talk about their own fears living in a society under siege. The increasingly terse exchange led to slamming of doors, counter-accusations, tears, individual declarations of mistrust, and refusals to verbally participate.

In the following days, we, the facilitators, offered the group a number of ways to realize that such conflagrations are part of processing tough issues. We arranged sessions that employed distancing devices (such as analysis of how macrosocial conflicts get reflected in microsocial settings) and, in parallel, led the group into nonverbal exercises to unearth the underlying emotional turmoil. But the broken trust between the American and Israeli groups never quite healed—with the Bedouin participants caught somewhere in the middle.[4] Mistrust manifested itself in guarded talk and unusually long stretches of silence during group sessions. A willingness for critical self-reflection surfaced only in the last two days and later in the reflection essays.[5]

Our facilitator team deliberated a number of interpretations and explanations as we realized that the distrust would not vanish.[6] Various factors seemed to play a role: the numerical and gender imbalance in the group, differences in student expectations, variations in leadership style, and the nature of a pilot program on complex social conflicts.[7] We also discussed the unsettling effects of making a group pay attention to its own imbalances of power and privilege. We asked ourselves whether a mostly undergraduate student population had the maturity to handle the complexity of the program's multipronged design. We wondered how threatening it might have been to Israeli students to be berated by an American minority student on their failure to support Bedouin minorities in their own midst. Perhaps the Israelis were unaccustomed to being so directly confronted by someone from a minority group, for Morissa felt free to articulate a concern on behalf of the Bedouin minority. Bedouin students themselves might have couched those concerns in more cautious terms in the presence of Israeli Jews. A statement by an Israeli student after the program seemed to confirm this explanation. "I learned," she wrote, "that perhaps I needed to travel to the other side of the globe in order to deepen my relationship with my own Bedouin neighbors."

Morissa, the Mexican American student, felt emboldened to speak her mind on minority issues perhaps because she was speaking up for others not in her own country. When she voiced her frustration at the session in Sdr Boker (Israel), it was easier to share her exasperation on behalf of the publicly demeaned Bedouin women rather than standing up for herself at her own American university campus. When the American and Israeli groups met separately for a session—devised by the facilitator team to address the issue of trust in each national group within the comfort zone of everyone's mother tongue—Morissa's concerns garnered the most attention by her American peers. Morissa talked about how she was taken off-guard by the strong Israeli reactions when questioning their silence. She then switched to the American context, adding that, perhaps, she should not have been surprised at all: the Israeli reactions were exactly what she would have expected from white students in the United States if she had dared bring up her Mexican minority experience. "And so I don't bring it up on campus," she said. When encouraged by her fellow Americans in the group to say more, Morissa mentioned how exhausting it was to convey to privileged people the daily struggles of her immigrant family or the effects of poverty on her labors to persevere and succeed in her studies. When telling of her immigrant background, her body was uncontrollably shaken by grief and rage. Whatever had accumulated over years—the silences of her peers, her inability to communicate with them, and the unspoken injustices of a system not made for advancing people like Morissa—poured out into our American circle in Israel.

During the remainder of the program, Morissa felt inhibited to approach the Jewish Israeli students and vice versa. The moment of vulnerability and trust she was able to share with the American group was not transferable to the larger mixed group. Neither side moved, and Morissa remained silent for long stretches in the remaining twelve days of the program.

Sometimes, there is little that can be done in such situations. When a group gets so deeply stuck, it will run its course until the end. It is a discomfiting experience, a different kind of "unsettling" that needs to be borne rather than resolved.

This does not mean, however, that no learning takes place. Perhaps we can speak of delayed reactions that unfold in such situations and that lead to insights and acknowledgments only after a program has ended. In her final essay, Morissa reflected on missing cues and risking vulnerability:

> It all began the night I asked the Jewish Israeli students why they didn't speak up against the government official the day before. I wanted to get them and others in the room thinking of a different reality and the privileges they possess. However, this caused me to be blinded to the fact that the Jewish Israelis were just opening up and expressing their realities. They expressed the fears they face in Israel.

As I listened, I was doing my best to understand and empathize with them, but I couldn't help but compare. How did their realities and fears compare to the Arab Bedouins? How was it that their experience as a majority in Israel was harder than that of Arab Bedouins? It was in that moment that I interrupted them to ask my question, which in the end caused the Jewish Israelis to feel as though I was not listening.

In that moment I didn't feel as though I had caused them to shut down. I thought I had posed a question that would just make them think about it. It wasn't until the next day that I realized how much I hurt them. I immediately noticed their distance. I understood that it was best to give them space, but the following day the distance was even greater. I realized that I had hurt them, and it had cost me their trust.

Culturally speaking, when Latinos hurt someone with words we step back and give them space until we gain back their trust. For me, that was a natural response. I stepped back and gave them space. It wasn't until the last day of the program that I was able to explain my distance to them. It allowed me to understand that we cannot compare the fights of others. We all experience our own struggles, but when we compare them, we can blind ourselves from understanding where others are coming from.

Morissa continued to describe how, before joining this program, she did not like sharing her experiences with white Americans at home. What she had directed at the Jewish Israeli students that evening, she realized, was also meant for the white American students at her university. Thus motivated, Morissa had opened up to the American group in the separate session in Sde Boker, telling them what it meant to be an independent Latina woman, a first-generation American, and a first-generation college student. "I understood early on in life that this was my reality, that my parents were undocumented immigrants, and that if I wanted to go to college I had to make it happen on my own." Morissa noticed that those around her had not been exposed to such difficulties. "They were only now seeing the privileges they had. At that moment I realized how our experiences can help others learn something about their identities. It felt as though I was repurposing a negative and difficult experience into something positive. That is what makes the cost of becoming vulnerable worth it."

Morissa's delayed insights were perceptive and compelling—and so were many others that were shared in essays when looking back at the program. Once the students had left the charged atmosphere of the program itself, they could write reflective and self-critical papers. This was encouraging, but it did not lessen the fact that a palpable degree of empathy failure stalled the process during the cultural encounter itself.

## IMBALANCES

In her chapter on "Dialogue, Forgiveness, and Reconciliation," social psychologist Barbara Tint lists five salient points that are challenges to dialogical processes in which groups seek some transformational change to conflict. First, tensions arise from power imbalances between different social groups; this is amplified by the discrepancy when individuals are treated as equals in the dialogue work while outside they remain on unequal footing. Second, peace-building efforts pursued in dialogue work occur "slowly through relational change rather than structural change," which can frustrate those who are eager to jump into political action or want to analyze systemic injustices. Third, acknowledging *power asymmetries requires people to assume different responsibilities, depending on whether they belong to "high-power" or "low-power" groups. Fourth, many conflicts cannot be placed into a neat binary of perpetrator and victim; hence, processes must carefully wade through convoluted layers of complicity, culpability, historical guilt, competitive victimhood, and moral accountability. Finally, reentry into society after an intense group process can be emotionally and socially taxing because people may encounter "estrangement" and "hostility" from their communities or may be left with a "feeling of betrayal" when social reality clashes with the more intimate character of human encounters in reconciliatory processes.[8]

These challenges have some bearing on explaining the difficulties we experienced in the program with the Israeli Bedouin and ethnically diverse American students. With the stated aim of exploring relations between majority society and minority communities, the student program intentionally addressed concerns about power imbalances, but the socioemotional weight of this complex theme overwhelmed the students. During the initial bonding phase of the group, the students ignored those imbalances in favor of learning about each other's different backgrounds with an open mind. People were curious. It was exciting and prompted the sharing of personal details. The unspoken motto might have been, "Our differences make us equal" or, similarly, "Our shared interest in justice makes us equal."

Such initial excitement is not unusual. Many groups in the early phase of an encounter exhibit abundant curiosity about the people they meet and are eager to share bits and pieces of their lives. A deep-seated wish for accepting people as they are, mixed with a sprinkling of exoticism about the other's otherness, sustains those initially unguarded encounters—almost as if they are still in the Garden of Eden before the Fall. This excitement, however, also masks the different expectations that people of majority and minority populations carry with them.[9] Hence, the expulsion from a state of innocence is inevitable, especially when privilege and power asymmetries are prominent in these encounters.

A number of critics of dialogical or reconciliatory work take those power asymmetries that obfuscate structural injustices (Tint's first two challenges mentioned above) as their launching pad for dismissing or invalidating these peace-building efforts. Educational anthropologist Zvi Bekerman, for example, criticizes "intergroup encounters between Jews and Palestinians" as initiatives that are undertheorized and "echo modern white, Western, totalizing conceptualizations" of psychologized treatments for social ills. Though he grants those encounters "short term effects on intergroup attitudes," Bekerman deems them largely futile because they fail to "influence attitudes in society at large." Even more importantly, he argues, "differences are set in the realm of meaning and not in the realm of power relations."[10] Similarly, Middle East studies scholar Stephen Sheehi launches a critique of Israeli-Palestinian dialogues from a psychoanalytically informed perspective, arguing that they operate within a colonial mindset that traps Palestinians into "forsak[ing]" their own practices of protection and resilience as a disempowered minority while keeping "political, economic, and psychological *structures* of oppression" intact.[11]

Such metacritique is not without its merits if measured by the standards of an ideal outcome that establishes two equally empowered and equally secure nations sharing their resources. Scholar-critics like Bekerman and Sheehi seem to prefer large-scale political solutions that address structural and systemic problems rather than investing in small-scale grassroots initiatives that seek pathways beyond the social, political, and military confines imposed on identitarian politics. Yet, in the meantime, people in conflict zones around the world (not just in Israel/Palestine) are stuck in mutual recriminations and mistrust, and they express their misgivings with the different means at their disposal, depending on access to resources and power. Such stuckness on a national or societal level is not entirely unlike the microlevel stuckness that the Israeli-American student group experienced in the summer of 2017.

Existing research offers evidence that microlevel encounters are positive and reduce prejudices when the conditions are optimal.[12] But let us not forget that political life—real life—does not unfold under ideal conditions set up in controlled environments. The messiness that accompanies the work with groups in conflict is just part and parcel of the challenges that need to be tackled.[13] Ideally, a dialogue ought to unfold with equal partners around the table. Some dialogues are constructed this way, like interfaith meetings with religious leaders and scholars. However, to be able to sit together as equal partners is often already the result of privilege: it is the reward for belonging to a privileged professional class. Most communities living in conflict, in contrast, have neither the time nor the resources to wait for such an optimal environment to arrive. As a matter of fact, they are in conflict because there are imbalances of power and privilege and because there are inequities and injustices related to access to and distribution of material, educational, health, and spiritual resources. It is within such unequal situations where working with groups in conflict frequently takes place and where acquiring an empathetic posture can lead to a softening of entrenched positions.

Power asymmetries are a "significant challenge" to dialogue work, Barbara Tint admits, but in conflicted societies "equal status rarely exists."[14] In other words, facilitating groups in conflict is, almost by definition, a commitment to working with and through the messiness of existing power imbalances. It is an investment in slow relational change that does not show immediate effects on macropolitical levels. "While dialogue is certainly not an infallible process," Tint suggests, "it is still one of the most useful and successful methods of dealing with groups in conflict."[15] With Dan Bar-On I would argue that the "microsettings" of dialogue groups "are important for identifying undercurrents, working through painful emotions, and experimenting with metaphors and verbal expressions that are necessary for understanding macroprocesses."[16] Intergroup encounters offer spaces in which people can experiment with and imagine alternatives in the presence of the tangible pains, anxieties, and struggles that each group brings to the table.

## RESPONSIBILITIES

Barbara Tint's third and fourth points of challenge to dialogue work concern the issue of responsibility. Depending on where people find themselves on the power scale, when they participate in conflict resolution they need to become aware of their position and learn to assume different responsibilities. Those responsibilities become more diffused in settings where complicity, culpability, and victimhood cannot be neatly separated. In such ambiguous settings, moral accountability is in constant flux.

Both of these challenges were operative in the 2017 student program on majority-minority relations. On the more obvious level, each group consisted of members of the majority society (Israeli Jews and white Americans) and minority communities (Bedouins and Americans of Mexican, Native American, and mixed ethnic backgrounds). Hence, each national group had to address issues of privilege and power in their own midst. On a less acknowledged level, the "imperial might" of America led to defensiveness in the Israeli group. American students dominated the discussions due to being the numerically stronger group and as a result of their culturally distinct ways of expressing themselves and their command of English, the program's *lingua franca*. On a third level, power asymmetries were further complicated due to status differentiations within the Israeli majority group and within the American minority group. In the Israeli group, we had students from Ashkenazi and Mizrahi backgrounds. The Mizrahim, sometimes referred to as Oriental Jews, immigrated to Israel from Middle East countries (like Syria, Iraq, Yemen, Iran, or Azerbaijan) and the North African region (like Algeria, Tunisia, or Morocco). They generally belong to an economically underprivileged stratum within Israeli society. In the American group, individuals with mixed ethnic backgrounds struggled with identities simultaneously privileged and nonprivileged, like those with Jewish-Hispanic, Native American white Mormon, or first-generation Polish-American family backgrounds.

This broad mix of identities defied easy labels regarding privilege and power. It obscured political and moral responsibility for past and current injustices as it also impeded acts of political solidarity across national boundaries. If, perhaps, one could have expected an indigenous alliance between Native Americans and Bedouins, this did not really happen; or if one suspected stronger bonds along gender identity, this also did not happen (an American woman later expressed it thus: "I was surprised to hear Bedouin and Jewish women say they are afraid of each other"). The multiple belongings and identities complicated discussions about political accountability, historical legacies, complicity, and victim status. Such multiplicity contributed to a lack of empathetic identification. But it was not all negative; it also resulted in productive confusion: a complex reality was not pressed into a simplified black-and-white mold.

Regardless of the diffusion of political and moral responsibilities due to the students' multiple identities, broader psychopolitical dynamics of high-power and low-power differences did not vanish. A number of studies show how unequal power in groups can lead to anxieties and to upward and downward resentments. These dynamics can play out in a variety of ways. For example, dominant groups can feel threatened when they perceive other people's claims to power as illegitimate; anxieties are triggered when low-status members openly confront high-status members; and efforts of reconciliation are hampered when a group is perceived to be homogeneous (even when it is not). A lack of compassion and empathy can be the result of high-power status, since high-power members generally respond less emotionally to "individuals disclosing an experience of suffering" (though the same people may not be insensitive to their plight). A lack of empathy can also be the result of the inability of victims to be compassionate to other people's suffering because they are preoccupied with their own. Furthermore, a purely emotional experience in the presence of an adversarial group (such as Palestinian and Israeli students visiting together the memorial site of the Auschwitz-Birkenau camp in Poland) does not automatically lead to "emotional empathy" with a minority; it can nevertheless lead to greater understanding if and when "cognitive interpretations" are complementing the learning process.[17]

I have observed these dynamics in the Israeli-American student group as well as in other settings. For instance, Morissa's challenge to the Jewish

Israelis' lack of support of their Bedouin peers could have been perceived
as an illegitimate claim to high power; as such, it was experienced as a
threat that triggered defensiveness. Vice versa, the perceived homogeneity of the Israeli group by the American students resulted in missing cues
about their social differentiation and thus blocked reconciliatory gestures. With rising anxieties, neither minority nor majority groups risked
an open conflict. It is possible that Bedouin and Native American, Mizrahi and Latina participants were preoccupied with their own specific
struggles that made it difficult for them to form alliances or relate to each
other with more empathetic understanding. Yet, despite the lack of displayed emotional empathy during the program, weeks later students reported a greater appreciation of each other, probably because we had
included numerous sessions that offered cognitive interpretations to off-
set their emotional turmoil.


## WHO BENEFITS?

An example from another context will shed additional light on the perplexing issue of power asymmetry and responsibility in heterogeneous
groups that include minority populations. This example pertains to the
departure of an esteemed colleague from a collaborative project that we
cofacilitated. Together she and I offered a few multiday "racial reconciliation retreats" for ethnically diverse students within the context of
American higher education.

Sybol and I had been colleagues at St. Mary's College of Maryland for
many years before we started working together. The initial impetus for
organizing retreats on racial(ized) identities for undergraduate students
occurred at an unlikely place: the department's photocopier. I was pre-
paring class materials for my course on "Religion and Violence," particularly for the units on lynching. I was photocopying a few pages from
James Allen's exhibit catalogue, *Without Sanctuary: Lynching Photography
in America*.[18] When my African American colleague entered the room to
do her own photocopying, my routine class preparation turned into a
moment of moral embarrassment. Sybol peeked at the copied photographs. She did not say anything or react in any discernible way, but her
presence jolted me out of my perfunctory chore and into the unsettling
awareness of the sheer brutality of the images I was reproducing. I wondered: What does Sybol think about what I am doing here? I felt compelled to justify and to explain the educational purpose of these photographs. In her presence, it felt as if I had been caught in an amoral activity. I felt white. In an instant, my professional identity vanished and so
did my German immigrant status (since, at that time, I was not yet an
American citizen).

None of that had anything to do with Sybol herself. These were my projections, my transferences, my anxieties. The coincidental meeting at the photocopier led to longer conversations, and those gave rise to the idea of inviting American students from diverse backgrounds to multi-day retreats. These retreats were meant to assist them in learning how to talk to each other across their ethnic and racial divides—because, as we learned in these encounters, students on U.S. campuses persistently tip-toe around those issues.

Later, when Sybol and I were in the process of planning yet another retreat, this time in Flagstaff with students from both Maryland and Arizona, I received an unexpected email from her. It was in the wake of the killings of Trayvon Martin, Michael Brown, and Eric Garner. We were in the final stages of organizing the retreat before sending out invitations to students when Sybol announced that she would leave the project. She wrote:

> In my heart of hearts, I feel that we should revisit the objectives and intentions of the retreat in light of the current and very painful racial climate. I personally need time and space to diagnose this climate, figure out my own relationship to it, and lick my wounds. Something big has shifted in the culture, and shifted in me, and my intuition is that the retreat might need to become something different.
>
> I think white students need safe spaces to confront and come to terms with whiteness, and I think they need to do it on their own. I think that in the presence of people of color, it becomes something else. Whiteness becomes the center, but in a strangely deflected sort of way.

In my response I acknowledged her doubts and her personal decision, but I also shared my sadness over losing her as an ally for a project that, as far as I could tell, was not offered in quite the same way anywhere else. "I feel that we are still at the beginning of a project which—as we might continue to improve it—can become a source of awareness and culturally healing for our students." Receiving Sybol's letter triggered an uncertainty not too dissimilar from what I had felt years earlier at the photocopier. I understood her reasoning but disagreed with her conclusion. In my disagreement, I felt "white" again. People with privilege and power, Sybol argued, ought to do their homework and begin thinking about their whiteness with people like them. Otherwise, there would always be the danger of displacing the emotional labor of bringing attention to inequalities onto minorities.[19]

This made sense to me in light of the "homework" I had done over many years concerning my German origins and faith tradition (work that continues to this day). Doing this homework, I realized that what had really propelled me out of cultural complacencies and misconceptions was my parting with enclaves of sameness when intentionally reaching out to the other. No matter how well intended, homogeneous groups, left to their own devices, can neither fully grasp the perspective of others nor understand the joyous and pained ties that other people have to their histories and traditions. The presence of the other, I learned, is essential.

I am detailing the exchange with Sybol because it illustrates the problematics of addressing power imbalances between minority-majority relations in intergroup settings when the larger society barely changes or, periodically, undergoes convulsive public struggles to rectify unjust and, for many, unbearable conditions of discrimination and repression. The criticism that "racism" (like other forms of inequality and injustice) "will not change by contact" but only "by collective action" has been voiced in different national contexts.[20] It raises questions about responsibilities to ourselves and to the people we chaperone through difficult processes.

Sybol, in her email, concluded that retreat settings are too problematic, at least at the time she announced her decision. The Black Lives Matter movement had just garnered strength, and it was predictably countered by a backlash of white *ressentiment*.[21] Implied in Sybol's reasoning was also the question of who is benefiting from such interpersonal encounters. Do low-power or high-power groups, majority or minorities benefit? In his critical analysis of contemporary human rights discourse, political science professor Robert Meister argues that human rights workers have transformed themselves into "compassionate witnesses" of evil, who enter into relationships with victims with the aim of making the victims feel better—moving them from feeling "depressed" and "wounded" to feeling "elated" and "healthy." Those processes, according to Meister, neglect to touch structural injustices. Who then, he asks, benefits from them? It is the human rights community, Meister replies, that "finds security in *self*-approach" by adopting a stance of "melancholic" compassion. "By containing the other [the victim, a minority, the disempowered] within himself, the melancholic feels sadder but also safer than he otherwise would."[22] In Meister's analysis, it is the human rights worker who ultimately benefits from a stance of melancholic witnessing that contains the other "within himself"; applied to the context of racial reconciliation retreats, the prime beneficiary would be the white student.

In her email, Sybol elaborated her weariness. "I struggle to explain exactly what I mean," she wrote, "but my sense is that white students are still able to evade the meaning, impact, and weight of whiteness in the context [of a retreat]. For example, our experience has often (although not always) been that everyone is all 'peachy keen jelly bean' and lovey-dovey until some 'angry black woman' hits a wall and 'drops the bomb.' Is this fair to those women? The result is that the students spend three or four days dancing around the issue of race, and only for one or maybe two days they really penetrate it."

As facilitators, we can get occasionally frustrated with the slowness of progress or with the extent to which a group is ready to tackle difficult issues with the sincerity it requires. For Sybol, the frustration went further. It was about students of color, and especially black women, bearing most of the emotional and spiritual burden of the process while white students could only "see" their own whiteness through black and brown pain. This kind of deflection, in Sybol's observation, stimulated responses and feelings of white guilt, which, in turn, needed to be assuaged in the group.[23]

There is no denying that the tiptoeing around fraught and dangerous issues of racialized identities, to which students are so accustomed in the larger society, get replicated in such retreats. But how could it be otherwise? The deeply engrained racial discourse in the United States makes open conversations almost impossible, because the field is packed with emotional land mines that will explode as soon as someone steps on them. It takes time to create a semblance of safety—sometimes frustratingly long—before a brave soul dares to make a move. This brave soul is often (but not always) a member of a disenfranchised or disempowered group, not unlike activists in society at large who become seeds and agents of change.

In my response to the latter point, I shared with Sybol my observations gleaned from other facilitation settings. I mentioned that it usually takes one or two courageous people to challenge a group more directly, and these are often people who know the urgency due to their own experiences. "This is neither good nor bad," I wrote. "It just is. It is, on a microlevel, no different from society at large, where it often takes a few people to serve as public catalysts to move things forward—whether it is Martin Luther King Jr., Bryan Stevenson, Rosa Parks, Tony Morrison, or Nelson Mandela. But none of them could function without hundreds of other people contributing to those dynamics of change in smaller and often invisible ways."[24] The same holds true for our retreats, I argued. "You mentioned the 'angry black woman' who shifts the depth (emotional, political, and otherwise) of the conversation. But sometimes we recall in our recollections of those retreats only the most dramatic voices and forget that many people contributed in smaller ways to changing the dynamics."

In a final plea, I reiterated that we had developed a precious opportunity rarely offered to students. "Will it change the larger societal climate? Not immediately. Will it make a difference to those who participate? Yes. Does a program like ours have limits in what it can achieve? Yes. Are their perfect educational alternatives? No."

My final plea did not bring my colleague back to our project. I regretted it. I also understood the sources of her frustration, for I sometimes despair over them as well.

## EXCLUSIONS

Barbara Tint's fifth point of challenge to dialogical encounters refers to the potential difficulty of reentry of participants into society after an intense group process.[25] Transitioning from a safe space, where people learn new ways of relating to each other across differences, back to daily lives is always a challenging moment, even in circumstances where individuals return to relatively stable environments. In my facilitation of groups, we always spend time at the end of a process to make participants aware of those transitions. We ask them, for example, to imagine the moment they return to their families, partners, or homes. We advise them to take their time in processing what they have experienced. We let them know that outsiders often cannot comprehend fully the intensity of their own learning and that communicable insights will emerge only over time. We also suggest they reach out to other participants and consider them allies when they need to talk to someone about their journey. Seeing each other as a support group is often the first step toward creating networks and joint initiatives that can last for years.

Not everyone will take up these offers. Reasons vary widely. Some participants feel resolved about what they experienced, and they integrate it effortlessly into their personal and professional lives. Other participants have a harder time transitioning back into their daily routines, especially those who return to communities under chronic duress. When external conditions remain unchanged or even deteriorate, moments of compassionate listening and empathetic identification that transpired during intergroup encounters can be difficult to integrate. "Empathy is blocked when . . . a conflict stagnates and shows no temporal development, when actions and reactions repeat themselves and when there is no end in sight," writes Shelley Berlowitz, a gender equality advocate and active observer of Palestinian-Israeli encounters.[26] The wider the gap between intimate interactions with one's "enemy"[27] within the protection of an encounter on the one hand and, on the other, the (political, social, economic) insecurities in one's daily environment where adherence to ingroup loyalty is expected or coerced, the more challenging the integration and application of what occurred during reconciliatory processes. This is particularly true for intractable conflicts where the stability of peoples' beliefs and values are "highly dependent on social support" provided by their immediate "daily environment" and where deviance from these norms endangers a person's social standing and well-being.[28]

In my role as facilitator, I encourage people at the end of a workshop to create social media networks, arrange regional meetings, or start joint initiatives. However, I am no longer responsible for and involved in such activities; they are entirely in the hands of former participants, though I am often included in email exchanges or informally informed about events. It is not unusual for tensions to flare up in postworkshop gatherings and social media postings. Most groups who stay in contact with each other through these venues have a fairly high tolerance for heated and belligerent messages, knowing that they all wrestle with integrating what they have learned into their accustomed thinking patterns and community interactions. However, when grievances become venomous or are repeatedly launched as personal attacks, exclusionary mechanisms kick in. These exclusions are not to be confused with ordinary partings of former participants who simply move on in life and pursue other interests. Exclusionary mechanisms, in contrast, are the result of unresolved frustrations, voiced as *ad hominem* attacks or as denunciations of any peace-building activities. Those mechanisms include enforced exclusions or acts of self-exclusion. When a person self-excludes, it is often accompanied by a final flurry of grievances directed at the group; when a person gets excluded, it is usually the result of unremitting personal attacks or one-sided political zealotry, someone who consistently is no longer willing to consider any other point of view.

Kaleed, a Palestinian Muslim from a town in the West Bank, first participated in a student program with Israelis, Palestinians, and Germans. Kaleed did not play a prominent role in this setting, but he came across as a reliable person. Cautiously open to other people's perspectives, he was also eager to convey the Palestinian position of resilience and resistance in the face of the occupation. Most of all, he was curious about the methods we employed to get students to talk, for he had never had any exposure to those approaches. A few years later, he returned as a young man in his early twenties to a multiday intergenerational seminar. He admitted in the opening session that he struggled with the decision to come back. The reason why he returned, he said, had to do with an opportunity to be part of a nonstudent gathering. The more he was drawn into the process over the next few days, the more he seemed to appreciate it. Candid and sincere with himself and others, he began to assert his own position vis-à-vis Israelis but also in relation to a fairly stern Palestinian man who kept asserting his mentoring status over him. Kaleed also questioned the NGO responsible for this gathering and queried my reasons for why and how I facilitated particular sessions. I almost literally saw him grow during those days. At the end of the seminar, he promised to stay committed to the organization; he also announced his wedding plans for the coming year in the West Bank.

Within the next few months, his family suffered a series of humiliating encounters at the hands of the Israeli authorities. As his wedding day approached, Kaleed's emails to the group grew irate. Less and less compromising, he eventually denounced the value of dialogical peace-building and left the group. Undeterred, some of the Israelis stayed informally in touch with him. For his wedding, they collected funds for a gift, which an Israeli woman about his age personally delivered. Kaleed responded in kind. In an email to the group, he wrote:

Yesterday I met with Nurit after almost a year. I had a great time and she will always be one of the gifts that GOD has sent me, a great friend whom I will always be proud of. She also passed your nice wedding gift. I want thank all of you personally for your warm wishes and great gift. It's a lot, thank you all again and again and again.

I heard that you had another meeting a couple of weeks ago. I wish you all the best in your continuous work to bring peace and mutual understanding to the most problematic and unstable area. I send you my wife's regard, and she says thanks for this nice gift.

Although I have left the group, I will never ever lose any of you as best friends. The experiences we have been through together will always take a huge part in my life. You have a close friend here in Palestine who will always be glad to host you. So you will always have a home in Palestine. Finally, may GOD help you all and may God bless you all because what you all are doing is something that needs great and amazing people.

I wish I could end Kaleed's story with this letter. The situation in Israel-Palestine, however, kept deteriorating in cycles of sporadic attacks, killings, and wars.[29] Though Kaleed had left the group, he occasionally expressed his grievances in terse email messages. When the 2014 Israel-Gaza war broke out, he sent two sentences to the group, written as if in haste or having run out of patience: "Another massacre right now at Al Shajaya. 15 martyrs and more than 150 injured . . . this is Israel."[30] Some Israelis responded quickly to the email with calming and empathetic words; others reacted more defensively, pointing out that there are always two sides to each story.

Back-and-forth political bartering and the recycling of accusation and counteraccusations—which in intergroup encounters can be productively disrupted and redirected—flare up more quickly and uncontrollably on social media platforms. I want to share a no-holds-barred email exchange between two participants that eventually led to their removal from the group by the platform administrator.

[Palestinian] Dear all, I have the courage to say that I am sorry, really sorry, for having believed that there is a possibility for achieving peace with this (terrorist) state called Israel. I am sorry for having spent some years of my life as a peace activist. It was all in vain and achieved nothing. The Israelis continue to kill our children and destroy our homes. Shame on Israel. Shame on humanity that sees this and just watches.

[Israeli] When I look at all the history of the conflict here, and the wars that Arabs started against the returning Jews, I do not agree. Did Israel refuse to divide the country into two independent states? Israel, from Ben Gurion to Netanyahu, is willing to do a peace agreement by sharing the land that we both feel so connected to. We really are longing for the end of war and for mutual recognition. But it takes two to tango.

[Palestinian] Israel—go to hell. This is the least to say. From a (former) peace activist.

[Israeli] We are in a war that was forced on us. I just wanted to remind you that you are not the first one that wanted to send Israel to hell. It is a very old slogan that was used by antisemites, and the most famous said it in 1939, and he did send them. I prepare myself for the days after the war: to start building trust from the beginning.

[Palestinian] Yes, we know the accusations and claims—antisemitism, terrorism, and so on. But what do you have to say about the 500 children who were slaughtered in Gaza, the 35 schools, 25 mosques, 2750 houses that were bombed? Shame on Israel.

There is yet another form of exclusion that needs to be mentioned here. This concerns initiatives that wish to bring adversarial groups together in joint interpersonal projects. Yet, even before the encounter gets off the ground, one side gets excluded. In an edited volume on the legacy of the Armenian genocide, for example, a contributing author recounts a creative project that prepared a history hike in Lebanon for Armenian, Turkish, and European students. Midway through the planning process, the facilitation team decided to proceed without the Turkish students because it deemed the "young Armenian participants not ready for it" and not able to "confront their Turkish counterparts from a position of informed strength."[31] The program took place, but the Turkish students had been excluded. To name a different example, at the Martin-Springer Institute in Arizona, we advertised a student leadership program to start conversations between military veteran students and regular (nonveteran) students at Northern Arizona University, with the intent to address the issue of moral injury.[32] We could not, however, garner enough interest among non-veteran students: none signed up, which can be seen as a kind of self-exclusion.

## UNDETERRED

A reader may wonder at this point whether working with groups in conflict within reconciliatory settings is as futile as hamster wheels and imaginary as fighting windmills. Given the frustrations, complications, and resistance mentioned above, is it worth the effort? If microlevel peace-building efforts don't register strongly on macrolevel societal changes, why bother? If they do not solve conflicts quickly, what is the point? Injustices have not disappeared, communities keep being harmed, and traumatic memories continue to haunt us—hence we may as well discontinue those efforts.

It is easy to invalidate intergroup peace-building efforts by pointing to how they neglect to address systemic and structural causes that continue to feed inter- and intracommunal inequities and violence. It is also an unfair criticism. Claiming that reconciliatory work is futile because conflicts still exist is like saying that medical care is pointless because illnesses still exist, teachers are pointless because ignorance still exists, or police efforts are pointless because crime still exists. Just as we have to accept the persistent presence of illness, ignorance, and crime (while countering them with continuous health, education, and protection efforts), conflicts will not disappear. But this does not relieve us from the responsibility to mitigate, change, and reduce them with measures that repair and rebuild broken relations. Working with groups in conflict is one of those measures.

There is no dearth of studies that make constructive suggestions for how to proceed with greater awareness of the challenges mentioned above.[33] The work by social psychologist Daniel Bar-Tal on intractable conflicts must be mentioned here. Intractable conflicts—short of active war, ethnic cleansing, and genocide—are, according to Bar-Tal, among the most difficult scenarios for inserting conflict resolution processes because all sides perceive themselves to be in a no-win situation.[34] Besides the "hard" facts of political, economic, financial, and military conditions, there is, Bar-Tal argues, also a "soft" infrastructure that upholds and feeds the status quo in intractable conflicts. Bar-Tal calls it the "sociopsychological infrastructure," a kind of repertoire of social mechanisms that help people in crisis to "form a stable view" of conflicts they have to endure. Those views are "individually stored" and "frozen" but always "accessible." Hardened over time and continuously validated and reproduced, they are passed on to younger generations through families, education, and social institutions. Among the sociopsychological repertoire that Bar-Tal examines, we find collective memories, collective emotional orientations (such as fear, anger, hatred, and distrust), and a shared "ethos of conflict," the latter providing a cohesive explanation for endured hardships. It also includes the delegitimization of the other and the mobilization of collective victimhood.[35]

I have discussed instances of these elements throughout this book. We have already seen how reconciliatory processes are fed by and impeded by collective memories, by affective identification with large-group identities, the mobilization of collective emotions and competitive victimhood, and mechanisms to delegitimize the other. This repertoire is powerfully entrenched in societies in conflict because it supports people under siege who need to survive adversity and privations. Because this sociopsychological repertoire satisfies people's "basic needs to cope with stress and to successfully withstand the enemy," Bar-Tal writes, it leads to a closing of minds via "stimulat[ing a] tunnel vision, which excludes incongruent information and alternative approaches to the conflict." In such situations, it is very difficult to motivate people to seize opportunities for meeting with their adversary and explore options that do not fall in line with their antagonistic narratives. "If we want to change the relations between the rival groups," Bar-Tal concludes, "it is of vital necessity to change this repertoire."[36] Unsettling empathy, I believe, changes a defensive sociopsychological repertoire. It counters tunnel vision and calls on alternatives to entrenched, harm-inducing conflicts.

In addition to becoming alert to the mechanisms of a fear-based infrastructure, as Bar-Tal suggests, we can invest in positive emotions in the public sphere. Political scientist Neta Crawford, for example, proposes to promote and "institutionalize" empathy in world politics. "Like fear," she writes, "empathy is not only a private experience that waxes and wanes between individuals; empathy, or its lack, may be a feature of the relations between groups and states." And, she adds, "empathy makes friendship possible."[37]

Let us return to Kaleed. Recalling his ambivalent attitudes and shifting responses, we can see in him a young man struggling with impossible demands. Pulled into the sociopsychological repertoire that his community under siege offers him for coping with the chronic stress of uncertainties and fear, he also chose to expose himself to alternatives. He joined, rejoined, and enjoyed intergroup encounters, but he also retreated, rejected, and left them. He kept the group at bay with terse emails, then held out an olive branch. "Although I have left the group," he wrote, "I will never lose any of you as best friends. You have a close friend here in Palestine who will always be glad to host you."

The work with groups in conflict will always be accompanied by empathy failures and empathy errors.[38] The desire for friendship that we intuit in Kaleed's gesture is sometimes all we can hope for. This may sound like an immaterially small motion—but it is nothing to deride. According to sociologist Niza Yanay's musings on justice and political friendship, such friendships are something to behold. She defends friendship as a most precious gift because it defies the logic dictated by ideological demands to national allegiance.

> Friendship crosses the divide between peace and war by choosing life over death, by turning the harm done to the other into the problem of oneself. Of course, those who desire land more than life, who are more afraid of peace than of war, will not seek the friend. . . . In circumstances of conflict, the recognition of dependency is . . . the realization that "*I* cannot tell my full story without *you*," and in order to tell it to you I must account *you* as my friend.[39]

Reconciliatory processes do not require friendships to form, but when they do, it is a gift. Unsettling empathy does not ask us to abandon our community's repertoire that we rely on in situations of conflict, but it shakes us up just enough for the possibility of friendship to manifest itself so that we can tell our stories to each other and thus become accountable to each other.

## NOTES

1. Ashkenazi Jews trace their lineage to (East) European roots and Mizrahi Jews to countries in the Middle East and North Africa. Bedouins in the Negev in southern Israel number over two hundred thousand. Traditionally, they are pastoral nomad tribes of Arab origin and follow Islam.

2. The program was organized and supported by the Martin-Springer Institute at Northern Arizona University and the Martin-Springer Center for Conflict Studies at Ben-Gurion University of the Negev. It was facilitated by Michael Sternberg, Wafa Ebenberi, and Björn Krondorfer. Each student group met prior to the program. The Israeli students were recruited from a course offered at Ben-Gurion University ("Encountering the 'Other' in Conflict Relations"); the American students applied directly to this study-abroad seminar and were required to meet three times for discussion of reading materials prior to departure.

3. After the founding of the State of Israel in 1948, the Negev Bedouins stayed in southern Israel; after 1968, Israel accelerated a policy of resettling them into new townships, generally referred to as recognized villages. Almost half of the Bedouin population of about two hundred thousand refused relocation and stayed in so-called unrecognized villages without running water, electricity, or other essential services (like garbage collection). According to Bedouin and human rights organizations, the resettling of Bedouins is in violation of their historic land rights, a highly contested issue between Bedouin communities and the Israeli government. For two perspectives on opposite sides on this issue, see Yahel Havatzelet, Ruth Kark, and Seth J. Frantzman. "Fabricating Palestinian History: Are the Negev Bedouin an Indigenous People?" (*Middle East Quarterly* [Summer 2012]:3–14); and the 2006 report by the Negev Coexistence Forum for Civil Equality, *The Indigenous Bedouins of the Naqab-Negev Desert in Israel* (submitted to the UN Permanent Forum on Indigenous Issues).

4. Individual relationships across differences continued to flourish in the program, but when it came to American and Israeli group identities, tension remained until the end.

5. The submission of final reflection essays was required only of the American group. Extensive interviews of all participants were conducted by Ben-Gurion University's Martin-Springer Center for Conflict Studies. A long essay was also published in Hebrew by Israeli student Sahar Almog, "Meeting the Other—Bedouin-Jewish Narratives and Complex Relationships with Indigenous Tribes in America" (*Chupchik: Student Union Magazine*, Ben-Gurion University of the Negev, October 2017).

6. See Daniel Bar-Tal and Ilai Alon, "Sociopsychological Approach to Trust (or Distrust)" (2016).

7. More American than Israeli and Bedouin students signed up for this summer program; of the fourteen students, only two were male. The American students understood that to be part of this program meant full participation every day, an understanding that was not equally shared by Israeli students while in Israel. This led to some disruption in the program's coherence. The three facilitators (see note 2 above) pursued the same program goals but had never worked together before.

8. Barbara Tint, "Dialogue, Forgiveness, and Reconciliation" (2010, 276–278). Tint is approaching dialogue work from an "intergroup contact theory" background. Contact theory suggests that when people from different cultures are brought together for a focused time, it will (with the help of "group techniques") "strengthen interpersonal relations and thereby change participants' attitudes and opinions toward one another" (Mohammed Abu-Nimer, *Dialogue, Conflict Resolution, and Change* 1999, 1). These models are rooted in Gordon W. Allport's antiprejudice work of the 1950s, *The Nature of*

*Prejudice* (1954). See also Thomas Pettigrew, "Intergroup Contact Theory" (1998). For an extensive, critical discussion of intergroup contact theory in relation to conflict resolution models, see Abu-Nimer, *Dialogue, Conflict Resolution, and Change* (1999, 1–28), and the edited volume by Miles Hewstone and Rupert Brown, *Contact and Conflict in Intergroup Encounter* (1986).

9. In a short chapter on different expectations in dialogical encounters, Amy Hubbard, based on her participant observations in the 1980s, hypothesizes that majority participants are more interested in "communicating" with the minority through a "conflict resolution frame," while minority participants are more likely to use a "social justice frame" because they like to see "political action" as a result of dialogical efforts ("Understanding Majority and Minority Participation in Interracial and Interethnic Dialogue" 2001, 281–282). Similarly, Shelley Berlowitz observes with regard to Palestinians and Israelis that for the former "the reasons to enter dialogue were strategic," whereas most Israelis "decided to partake in dialogue out of self-reflexive reasons" ("Unequal Equals: How Politics Can Block Empathy" 2016, 42). In their study, "Difficult Dialogs: Majority Group Members' Willingness to Talk about Inequality with Different Minority Groups" (2013), Nida Bikmen and Diane Sunar come to a more nuanced conclusion. They examined whether Turkish university students would be willing to engage issues of power inequality with either Kurdish or Armenian students. They discovered that "ethnic Turk university students were equally willing to have commonality-focused conversations with Kurds and Armenians" but less willing to have power talk with either. However, with Kurdish students (who are also Muslim) they were more willing to address power inequality than with Armenian students, the latter of which were perceived higher in status but not belonging to their religious and cultural in-group. Generally, though, the scores were high for a willingness to talk about power, leading the authors to conclude that "increased contact with ethnic minorities contribute not only to positive majority attitudes but also to endorsement of more equal social relations" (474–475).

10. Zvi Bekerman, "Working towards Peace through Education: The Case of Israeli Jews and Palestinians" (2018, 89–90). Among other similar critiques, Miles Hewstone and Rupert Brown's cautionary remarks can be cited: in "Contact Is Not Enough: An Intergroup Perspective on the 'Contact Hypothesis'" (1986), they evaluate intergroup contact models. Granting that such contact improves relations, they "caution practitioners to be modest in their expectations of such interventions" (42); they also advocate for including a wider social context with its "historical, political and economic divisions" (2).

11. Stephen Sheehi, "Psychoanalysis under Occupation: Nonviolence and Dialogue Initiatives as a Psychic Extension of the Closure System" (2018, 367; emphasis in the original). Sheehi's argument mainly targets psychoanalyst Jessica Benjamin's theory of the "moral third" and "third space." Benjamin's concept offers a possibility for Palestinians and Israelis to create an intersubjective space in which they don't have to uphold their identities: within a third, moral space they are able to abandon the confines of their social identifications as Israelis and Palestinians. See Jessica Benjamin, "Beyond Doer and Done To: An Intersubjective View of Thirdness" (2004).

12. See especially the studies of Thomas Pettigrew, "Intergroup Contact Theory" (1998), and Pettigrew and Linda Tropp, "Does Intergroup Contact Reduce Prejudice? Recent Meta-Analytic Findings" (2000).

13. Julia Chaitin and Shoshana Steinberg recount in detail how empathy was impeded in two separate intergroup encounters where societal mistrust, recriminations, and collective emotions surfaced among individual participants. In one encounter between left-leaning Jewish Israeli and equally left-leaning Christian German students, blame and anger obstructed empathy; in another encounter between Palestinian and Israeli university students, the collective emotion of fear prevented individuals from developing strong empathetic relations ("'You Should Know Better': Expressions of Empathy and Disregard among Victims of Massive Social Trauma" 2008, 212–219).

14. Barbara Tint, "Dialogue, Forgiveness, and Reconciliation" (2010, 277). Dan Bar-On and Fatma Kassem write about their dialogue work with descendants of Holocaust survivors and of perpetrators that "mutual trust" was developed, though the "asymmetry" was not erased. To "maintain these two frames of mind," they observe, "was difficult for group members" ("Storytelling as a Way to Work through Intractable Conflicts" 2004, 292). For the transformative potential of intergroup encounters despite unequal power dynamics, see the life stories of Israelis and Palestinians in Nava Sonnenschein, *The Power of Dialogue between Israelis and Palestinians* (2019). The collected interviews/testimonies were of people who underwent training programs in the School for Peace; see especially Tamar Saguy's introduction to this volume, "Introduction: When Groups Meet—Understanding How Power Dynamics Shape Intergroup Encounters" (2019).

15. Tint, "Dialogue, Forgiveness, and Reconciliation" (2010, 278).

16. Dan Bar-On, "Will the Parties Conciliate or Refuse? The Triangle of Jews, Germans, and Palestinians" (2004, 252). As a psychologist and scholar-practitioner who has facilitated many small groups in conflict settings, Bar-On discusses the limits of intergroup contact, weighing the positives and negatives of such approaches in the face of overwhelming macrolevel challenges. Self-critically, he wonders what "microsettings" can accomplish "if dialogue groups cannot directly be transferred to the macropolitical level." While he concedes that the "learning achieved in the microsetting cannot easily be translated into macroprocesses," he also reminds us that a "macro-analysis [does] not help us work through the deeper processes involved in the refusal to conciliate" (252).

17. The particular insights on high- and low-power groups are gathered from the following sources: on anxiety, resentment, legitimacy, and homogeneity, see Lasana Harris and Susan Fiske, "Diminishing Vertical Distance: Power and Social Status as Barriers to Intergroup Reconciliation" (2008); on empathy deficiency among high-power groups, see Gerben van Kleef et al., "Power, Distress, and Compassion: Turning a Blind Eye to the Suffering of Others" (2008, esp. 1320); on the inability of empathy among victim and low-power groups, Shelley Berlowitz, "Unequal Equals: How Politics Can Block Empathy" (2016, esp. 46–48); Julia Chaitin and Shoshana Steinberg, "'You Should Know Better': Expressions of Empathy and Disregard among Victims of Massive Social Trauma" (2008, esp. 214); Daniel Bar-Tal et al., "A Sense of Self-Perceived Collective Victimhood in Intractable Conflicts" (2009, 252); and Arie Nadler, "Social-Psychological Analysis of Reconciliation" (2002). On the lack of emotional empathy for minorities, Hava Shechter and Gavriel Salomon, "Does Vicarious Experience of Suffering Affect Empathy for an Adversary?" (2005, esp. 136).

18. James Allen, *Without Sanctuary: Lynching Photography in America* (2000). See also my discussion in Chapter 4 on empathy and teaching about "lynching" at the university level.

19. I have since included in my teachings on racialized violence in the United States a unit in which my students discuss the "white experience." I ask them: "What is your white experience?" Initially, this question makes white students quite uncomfortable, but they open up eventually.

20. Stephen Reicher, "Contact, Action and Racialization: Some British Evidence" (1986, 167).

21. On the meaning of this term, see Chapter 2, note 21.

22. Robert Meister, *After Evil: A Politics of Human Rights* (2012, 216, 220; italics in original). For a thick description of power asymmetries as a stumbling block in Israeli-Palestinian dialogue, see Shelley Berlowitz, "Unequal Equal: How Politics Can Block Empathy" (2016). She writes: "Dialogical cooperation had opened a space of mutual humanization in which Jewish-Israelis and Palestinian dialogue partners were able to see each other as equals. . . . But the equality of the dialogue partners was undermined by the increasing political and legal inequality between Jewish-Israelis and Palestinians" (49).

23. Similar concerns have been raised in other contexts. In his reflections on the challenges of Arab-Jewish encounters, Mohammed Abu-Nimer, for instance, quotes Jonathan Kuttab's critique that "when dialogue becomes a substitute for action . . . it assuages the conscience of members of the oppressor group" while for the "oppressed group it becomes a safety valve for venting frustrations" (Abu-Nimer, "Education for Coexistence in Israel: Potential and Challenges" 2001b, 240). Other critics have raised the issue of compliance and co-optation of minority participants in dialogue groups. Regarding some of these concerns, see Amy Hubbard's "Understanding Majority and Minority Participation in Interracial and Interethnic Dialogue" (2001), where she looks at both interracial groups in the United States and interethnic tensions in Palestinian-Jewish groups.

24. Years later, when writing this book, I consulted with Sybol again about this exchange (also to get permission to use her real name). She clarified in an email that for her the list of catalysts were Trayvon Martin, Michael Brown, Eric Garner, Sandra Bland, and Tamir Rice. She stated that the (personal) cost for these activists was incredibly high and that therefore white people needed to "step up and take more responsibility for this work, especially the very painful and exhausting emotional responsibility."

25. On the problem of reentry, see Amy Hubbard, "Understanding Majority and Minority Participation in Interracial and Interethnic Dialogue" (2001). She argues that the "reentry process" is a "central problem for grassroots dialogue" (280). Already in the 1970s, Herbert Kelman and Donald Warwick addressed the role of supportive environments to overcome individual "resistance" to changing attitudes, beliefs, and actions ("Bridging Micro and Macro Approaches to Social Change" 1973, 22–39).

26. Shelley Berlowitz, "Unequal Equal: How Politics Can Block Empathy" (2016, 49).

27. The term "enemy" is used here literally and figuratively. In some cases, groups do perceive each other as actual enemies because they are in the midst of an unresolved conflict; in other cases, groups work through accumulated tensions rooted in historical, religious, racial, or political antagonisms but do not see each other as actual enemies.

28. Herbert C. Kelman and Donald Warwick, "Bridging Micro and Macro Approaches to Social Change" (1973, 26).

29. On the deteriorating political situation and the loss of trust after 2009, see, for example, Yohanan Tzoreff, "Trust and Negotiations: Israel and the Palestinians, 2009–2015" (2016).

30. The Al Shajaya district in Gaza near the border to Israel witnessed intense fighting in 2014, especially when the Israeli military declared it as part of the buffer zone and began to clear it so as to stop Hamas from digging tunnels into Israel.

31. Eugene Sensenig-Dabbous, "The Musa Dagh History Hike: Truth-Telling, Dialogue and Thanatourism" (2016, 233).

32. On moral injury, see note 10, Chapter 3.

33. In a chapter on "Arab-Jewish Encounter Programs: Political Change or Control," Mohammad Abu-Nimer suggests encounter programs be developed that seek political change rather than using them to control the minority. Whereas in the latter case, groups avoid conflict and accept minority-majority asymmetric power relations, the former recognizes the conflict and questions existing power relations (*Dialogue, Conflict Resolution, and Change* 1999, 149–167).

34. Intractable conflicts are "fought over goals viewed as existential, perceived as being of zero sum nature and unsolvable, preoccupy a central position in the lives of the involved societies, [and] require immense investments of material and psychological resources" (Daniel Bar-Tal and Ilai Alon, "Sociopsychological Approach to Trust [or Distrust]" 2016, 317).

35. Daniel Bar-Tal, "Sociopsychological Foundations of Intractable Conflicts" (2007, 1444, 1438). See also Daniel Bar-Tal et al., "A Sense of Self-Perceived Collective Victimhood in Intractable Conflicts" (2009, 252), and Neta Oren and Daniel Bar-Tal, "The

Detrimental Dynamics of Delegitimization in Intractable Conflicts: The Israeli-Palestinian Case" (2007). On the issue of distrust as part of the sociopsychological repertoire of groups, see Daniel Bar-Tal et al., "Lay Psychology of Trust/Distrust and Beyond in the Context of an Intractable Conflict: The Case of Israeli Jews" (2016, esp. 209).

36. Bar-Tal, "Sociopsychological Foundations of Intractable Conflicts" (2007, 1447).

37. Neta Crawford, "Institutionalizing Passion in World Politics: Fear and Empathy" (2014, 549).

38. Making a strong moral-political argument for the increase of empathy in world politics, Neta Crawford concedes that empathy is not foolproof and that "empathic accuracy" must be checked and trained ("Institutionalizing Passion in World Politics" 2014, 543–544).

39. From Niza Yanay's chapter "From Justice to Political Friendship" in her book *The Ideology of Hatred: The Psychic Power of Discourse* (2013, 122; emphasis in original).

# EIGHT

## Stepping into Time and onto Loaded Words

Friendship is a precious gift, especially when it emerges in politically contested situations. Yet the notion of friendship itself can be contested in intergroup encounters. What may be desired by one side might be merely tolerated by the other, and often this difference aligns itself along power asymmetries. In a reverse image of social reality, where boundaries around enclaves of power and privilege are guarded and only selectively permeable, in facilitated encounters it is often the "nonmalevolent beneficiary of privilege"[1] who seeks friendship with the other. With regards to historical trauma, this could be the descendants of a perpetrator society desiring friendship with the (former) victimized communities; with regards to ongoing conflicts, it could be people with access to the benefits of political power who seek friendship with those who are marginalized and disempowered. I have observed these dynamics in groups between Germans and Jews, where, at times, a guilt-driven need to become friends is met on the Jewish side with puzzlement or something akin to benign amusement. I have observed it also in interactions between exiled Serbs and Bosnian Muslims, when the former turn quiet in the presence of the latter, and I have seen it played out in racial reconciliation retreats when minority students try to maintain respectful boundaries against too-eagerly-expressed gestures of camaraderie. Many other examples could be listed here. Not surprisingly, it is also true for Israelis and Palestinians.

Seeking and forming friendships across divides in intergroup encounters is, of course, not a one-way street. Members of less-powerful or minority groups also look for close and meaningful contact. Genuine friendships—beyond identitarian politics and ideological constraints—do emerge, with the effect that a mutual "recognition of dependency" makes people responsible toward each other.[2] Nevertheless, the issue of friend-ship is one of those undercurrents rarely acknowledged in group process-es, even though it is a factor that can motivate or inhibit participation. It is tiptoed around for fear of damaging the emerging bonds of trust. In short, it is a *loaded word.

When working with groups in conflict, I often employ "loaded words." At various points of a process, an exercise with loaded words can intensify interactions or clarify convoluted debates. Among different possibilities, a simple instruction might look like this: every participant is handed a note card and is asked to jot down a topic he or she deems too dangerous or explosive to casually bring up in conversation. Whatever people have in mind, they need to condense it into one or two words, with no explanation provided. Importantly, those cards are always anon-ymous. They are placed face-down on the floor, mixed, then redistrib-uted and read aloud in the group. This is usually followed by an oppor-tunity to briefly respond to and comment on what each participant heard. Are people surprised? Are these the topics everyone expected to emerge? Is it scary or comforting to see them written out? I have sometimes called those cards "land mines"—topics that would explode if you were to step on them. A few years ago, a group gently admonished me about the militaristic metaphor and suggested we replace it with the more neutral "loaded words" idiom. In either case, once the dangerous topics are present and acknowledged, they must be defused.

## ELEPHANT IN THE ROOM

In chapter 1, I introduced a workshop with a group of Israeli and Pales-tinian peace activists. Given the workshop's title, "The Unspoken in the Movement," the group came together for three days in Bethlehem to address internal issues detrimental to their peace-building efforts. They had selected two loaded words: "gender relations" and "friendship." I already described how the loaded issue of gender relations was handled by the group, eventually zooming in on Akeem's story about his child-hood. "Friendship" was the second loaded word tackled by this group.

Perhaps indicative of a general strain in the peace movement, a num-ber of participants in this particular group had a hard time committing fully to the workshop. Though the organizers had clearly conveyed to potential participants that this workshop required their steady pres-ence—and a strong core group complied with the request—on the mar-gins there was constant coming and going. This made it difficult to main-tain experiential and conversational continuity. Though the lack of de-pendability was not a problem unique to this group of peace activists, it slowed the momentum and drained some of the energy of this meeting.

Over the years I have learned that facilitating groups in ongoing conflicts demands the patience and skills to cope with deeply felt ambiguities that participants bring to these encounters. It is part of the "messiness" of working in fragile and contested environments (which I addressed in the previous chapter). Different from interpersonal or group-therapy processes in more stable environments, in which attendance is honored or can be enforced, dependable attendance cannot be counted on when working with people under acute political duress. As facilitator, I have learned to accept this and work around it—despite the disruption it can cause. Individual reasons for a lack of (time) commitment vary, but noncommittal behavior can also be understood as a gesture of defiance, resistance, or self-assertion. In one particular seminar in the West Bank, for example, we had a Palestinian man in his twenties who lay on the floor sleeping or dozing off for most sessions during the first two days. Resting with closed eyes in a corner of our meeting room, he neither left the group nor did he participate. We just accepted his conduct. On the third day, he finally joined our circle and became a key figure in some of the remaining sessions.

In the case of the workshop with peace builders, the situation was different insofar as attendance expectations had been clearly stated in advance. Since the issue of "commitment" was a prime reason for offering this workshop, the loose attendance was perhaps symptomatic of larger frustrations in the peace movement. The constant flux of people was irritating and disruptive of the trust we tried to build up. As the core group wanted to move forward, others held back. It was in this context that the issue of "friendship" emerged.

On the morning of the third day, the group looked at what motivates or inhibits their peace activism. They wondered whether it was permissible to show moments of weakness in the peace movement, or whether, by some unspoken code, they had to always project strength and confidence. When asked what such moments of weakness might look like, the moral emotions of shame and embarrassment floated to the surface. When the group unanimously affirmed that showing weakness would be acceptable, and perhaps even commendable, a few Israeli women courageously and spontaneously sat down in a crouched position on the floor, covered themselves with shawls and blankets, and stayed there in silence. A little later, a Palestinian woman and some men joined them. The heaviness of the image of people covered in "shame" was hard to bear, but we were able to hold it for an extended time.

But tensions mounted, imperceptibly at first, then filling the air so thickly you could slice it with a knife. Those tensions eventually found release in a heated exchange between a Palestinian man and one of the Israeli women in the circle. Half self-reflection, half bitter complaint, the Palestinian man expressed rather forcefully his unease over witnessing this circle of shame. "I cannot carry the emotional weight of these Israeli feelings of shame and guilt," he admitted. "I am trying to acknowledge them as human beings, but I also feel overburdened and misused." His remarks caught one of the Israeli women, still in her vulnerable posture on the floor, off-guard. Their heated exchange escalated to tears and an angry "fuck you."

In the afternoon—after a few lighthearted movement exercises—we returned to the issues raised in the morning. What motivates individual Israelis and Palestinians to engage in joint peace activities? Is it possible to explore those motivations in a safe space? With the morning's impassioned explosion still reverberating, the group did not clamp down emotionally but was ready to leave behind long-winded speeches and mini-lectures in favor of direct communication. I sometimes refer to guarded opening sessions of a facilitated encounter as an *incubation period. It lasts until the moment people get irritated with each other or become impatient with the slow-moving process (because they realize that they could reach more depth). That is when a "birth" finally happens, when people are ready and willing to explore new patterns of communication and address each other directly.[3] In the workshop on "The Unspoken in the Movement," the incubation period ended with the shame circle. What had surfaced in the morning session was the question of what to expect from each other and how to count on each other when in need. Whereas Israelis voiced their desire to develop "authentic relations" with Palestinian peace activists, Palestinians were looking for "reliable partners" among Israelis in their struggle against the occupation. The elephant in the room was finally named: friendship.

We used several sessions to approach the loaded word "friendship." It would be too cumbersome to detail the step-by-step process by which each side found the courage to express their wishes, fears, and hopes. There were some evasions and convoluted verbal exchanges, but the core of their concern always remained in sight. The major difference regarding friendship expectations in joint Palestinian-Israeli peace activities can be summarized easily: whereas Israelis emphasize relational bonds, Palestinians focus on acts of solidarity. This insight in itself was not particularly earth-shattering for either side. Somehow, each side already knew or intuited it. But admitting to each other those divergent perspectives on friendship was hard emotional work, especially since individual members among the group felt that they were already friends. Would they have to realize the unstable grounds on which their friendships rested?

For each side, there were complicating factors. Among the Israelis, most experienced a mental double-bind, with the effect that they danced around the issue of friendship in convoluted ways for quite some time. Their intellectual capacity for keen political analysis told them that asking for friendship of members of an oppressed group would be politically incorrect. It would represent, in their words, a "colonial mindset," in which the more powerful can demand friendship of the less powerful as the price for receiving empathy and solidarity. But this was their head talking, because deep down in their hearts the Israelis desired authentic friendship. Friendship is what they hoped for. Caught within this thorny double-bind cycle, they felt guilty and ashamed about expressing their desire for friendship. "We get ostracized by our own community for engaging in peace activities with Palestinians," an Israeli said. "There is no personal reward in it for us. So if we can't make friends with Palestinians, where do we get support?" Read in this light, the morning's "shame circle" was particularly devastating for Israeli peace activists because they had dared to wallow in a state of vulnerability in front of a mixed group. In return, they did not receive the warm embrace they might have hoped for but a cold shoulder from their Palestinian peers. The Palestinian message was clear: Don't burden us with your unresolved emotions.

Regarding Palestinians, they were largely aware of the fact that Israelis wanted to befriend them. They knew that "friendship" might be the price to pay for finding reliable allies among Israelis. For them, however, the prime motivation to working with Israelis was not relational authenticity but assurance of a common vision in the struggle against injustice. "Friendship, of course, can develop," they conceded, "and when it happens, it is good. But sometimes it is quite confusing because we don't know what is real and what is based on pleasing expectations." For Palestinians, the morning session was emotionally difficult because they knew that they had ignored the agony of ashamedness of a fellow human being. But it was also liberating because they were able to set boundaries around the taxing emotional labor demanded from them as a politically disempowered group.

To what extent, then, are friendships in politically contested environments illusionary? One could argue that friendships become real and blossom only if the political conditions improve; hence, working together to change those conditions is of prime importance. On the other hand, we can ask the uncomfortable question of whether people in the peace camp would still seek friendship if their common struggle against injustice disappeared. If there were no longer a reason to interact—say, because the occupation ended tomorrow—would it still be important to make friends across the aisle? Or would each side simply go home to their own comforts?

There are no good answers to these hypothetical questions. What we were able to do in this workshop, however, was to check in with each group whether they understood each other's perspective. Rather than talking about difference (and getting caught up again in verbal-intellectualized trappings), we used a variation of the living sculpture approach and tapped into resources of our intuitive knowledge. We split into four small groups, two groups of Palestinians, two groups of Israelis. Each group was positioned at a different place in the room. Their task was simple. Within sixty seconds, each group had to spontaneously create a sculpture with their bodies. Within this short time, the two Israeli groups had to form a sculpture about what they understood of the Palestinian perspectives on friendship; similarly, the two Palestinian groups had to form a sculpture about the Israeli perspectives on friendship. Since time was intentionally limited to sixty seconds, none of the four groups had any chance to see what the others were doing.

I started the countdown: sixty . . . fifty-nine . . . fifty-eight . . . fifty-seven . . . To everyone's surprise, the resulting four sculptures were amazingly similar and accurate. The two Israeli sculptures, visualizing what they understood to be the Palestinian perspective, were almost identical. With their bodies, they had created an image of the "elephant in the room," with easily recognizable tusks and a trunk. The Israelis thus acknowledged the extent to which unspoken assumptions about friendship had been a pressing issue for Palestinian peace activists.

The two Palestinian groups also created almost identical sculptures. Each showed three people bound together in close physical contact, connected through variously interlocked arms. The Palestinians thus acknowledged how important intimate connections are for Israeli peace activists.

It was like an epiphany for this mixed group. Despite the taxing labor of admitting and recognizing their differences about friendship—fearing that such candor might undermine their current relations as peace activists—these final sculptures demonstrated how carefully they had absorbed and understood each other's perspectives.

## HOMECOMING

There are always elephants in the room in intergroup encounters. In chapter 6, for example, I described the uncanny, spectral presence of German fathers in a mixed German-Israeli group; their "elephant" became visible only when we invited a ghostly father into our midst. In a different setting—a mentor-training seminar for Palestinians, Germans, and Israelis—another elephant was invited into our midst: an Israeli soldier.

Given that almost all young Israeli men and women serve in the Israel Defense Force (IDF), the presence of military service is deeply embedded in the domestic settings of Israeli families.[4] For Israelis themselves, this reality is so self-evident that it does not require much reflection or discussion. In mixed-group settings, however, it can become a contested reality. Whereas for Israeli families military conscription is part of home life, for Palestinian families IDF soldiers are a threat to home life. Especially among young Palestinians growing up in the West Bank territories, the only Israelis they know are soldiers in uniform controlling their homes, roads, and movements. I have met several young Palestinians in mixed student groups for whom these gatherings were their first opportunity to talk to an Israeli not in uniform.[5] This fact alone can be unsettling. Palestinian participants know that the Israelis they meet have, in almost all cases, served in the military. In Israeli-Palestinian intergroup settings, this is an accepted fact. Sometimes it is raised as an issue though not pursued in depth. Rarely is it explored as an issue of "homecoming."

In this particular Palestinian-German-Israeli mentor-training seminar, it became a topic. When each national group had to identify an obstacle within their own community that, in their view, impeded trust and cross-cultural understanding, the Israeli group named as their obstacle "comfort with the status quo."[6] When it was their turn to explore the meaning of this obstacle to the whole group, the idea emerged to turn it into a scenic play. What if we were to address the "comfort with the status quo" as a question of how military service intersects with Israeli family life? We pulled three chairs into the center, two for parents awaiting the weekend return of their son from military service and one chair for the homecoming soldier-son.[7]

The suggestion to re-create this scene caused irritation and anxiety among the Israeli participants. Even though such homecomings happen in Jewish Israeli families on a routine basis and should not be cause for alarm, the thought of reenacting it in front of German and Palestinian participants was greatly distressing. An ordinary moment in the life of one's own community had the potential to be misinterpreted in the context of historical trauma (Holocaust) and ongoing agonizing events (Nakba, occupation). It was tempting to draw wrong historical parallels: Would Israeli families be perceived as being complicit in the service of national interests, just as ordinary German families had become complicit in the 1930s and 1940s when sons and fathers donned military uniforms? There was also the fear that swift judgment could be pronounced regarding the moral indifference of ordinary Israeli families toward the plight of Palestinians. What seemed like a recurring, mundane family event in a homogeneous context became a highly charged interaction in a heterogeneous context. As soon as we suggested the Israelis reenact such a homecoming for the large group, all of those historical resonances and moral pitfalls occupied our mental landscape. It caused a frantic discussion among the Israeli participants. Were they willing to volunteer for this scene and, if so, who would do it?

Eventually three volunteers agreed to give it a try. There was nothing extraordinary about the normal weekend scene portrayed in a relatively short sequence. The three people (the parents and a son returning for the weekend from military duty) exchanged the usual greetings, asked about each other's well-being, chatted about trivial things, and eventually gathered for dinner. The Israeli woman who had volunteered to play the mother in this scene later wrote: "We tried to re-create what happens when a son comes home for the weekend from his army service and the parents do not ask him what he did when stationed at a checkpoint or in the occupied territories. We found it very difficult to portray what happened, and appeared to be 'at loose ends' when trying to simulate this experience that occurs in thousands of Israeli homes every weekend. This enactment helped us gain insight into the deep problem we have when talking to one another about our experiences as soldiers in order to confront the violence that we and/or our sons and daughters have for years of our lives. 'What did you do this week?' has become a taboo question."

The scene's ordinariness, marked by silences, was more unsettling than if we would have witnessed an improvised play in which the parents and the son had started a political conversation. Intriguingly, the German and Palestinian witnesses of this reenactment were less unsettled than the Israelis themselves. No one used this session to draw parallels to the Holocaust (which is an always-present fear, since it so often gets played out in the public sphere to score rhetorical points). But it raised questions within the Israeli group. They wondered: What is it that we are avoiding? What if we inquired about the whereabouts of our children's military placement? What if we found ourselves in conflict between our moral obligations toward justice and our obligations to our children? The Israeli participants allowed the rest of the group to peek into their kitchens and living rooms during a soldier's homecoming. What remained completely absent in their family talk were Palestinians. There was no mention of them. From those reenacted conversations around the kitchen table, the large group witnessing this scene learned nothing about the reality of Palestinians, as if they lived in a parallel disconnected universe.

The Israeli group had named their own community's obstacle "comfort with the status quo." After their reenactment of a domestic scene, they were left with anything but comfort. Perhaps the most incisive comment during the subsequent conversation about this session was made by a German woman in her thirties who had prior experiences with trilateral German-Israeli-Palestinian encounters. "I have never seen," she said, "the Israelis so lost."

## STEPPING INTO TIME

Stepping onto loaded words is one way of bringing to the fore topics and tensions that need to be addressed when working with groups in conflict. Another approach is to invite participants to step into time—that is, to explore their intellectual and emotional investments in particular historical dates and events. What I mean by "stepping into time" is an approach by which to visualize those investments. This is particularly valuable when facilitating multigenerational groups, since particular historical events do not hold the same symbolic meaning and significance for different generational cohorts. For example, whereas 1945 is a decisive date for Germans born during the Hitler regime, the cultural revolution of 1968 was an important identity marker for the immediate postwar German generation; most German adults in 1989 were awestruck by the fall of the wall and German unification, but this date is less significant to Germans born afterward. If we add to these generational differences various key dates that nations hold dear, we can create a web of intersections and incongruities when it comes to different groups' allegiances to historical events. For instance, whereas the unification of 1989 caused celebration among Germans of a particular age, it triggered fears in Jewish communities; whereas 1948 is remembered as the year of Israel's independence, it is bemoaned by Palestinians as the year of their expulsion. What is someone's defeat and grief might be someone else's triumph and joy.

A few years ago, an association of psychotherapists of German and Jewish descent residing in Germany invited me to lead a workshop for their members in Cologne. Originally founded as an organization to account for the legacy of the Holocaust and Nazism among professional therapists, with a focus on family entanglements, the association has more recently widened its mission to understand "conflicts in the context of politically and individually motivated violence."[8] The association's board proposed to lead a workshop titled "Where Do We Go?" They hoped I could help their members examine options of engagement within a drastically changing political context of populist revolts in Europe and the United States. Eleven people of different ages, with a few people of Jewish background, met over a weekend in a space provided by the University of Cologne.

Given the workshop's title, my facilitation was guided by two conceptual frames: time and movement. "Where Do We Go?" seemed to suggest a historical sequence as well as a direction. I therefore used historical markers to help each participant locate both their political motivations and biographical roots; I also marked spirals on the floor, suggestive of movements outward from a center or inward toward a center. In the descriptions below, I limit myself to the technical aspects of the *timelines we created without providing a full account of the participants' interactions.

Because the meeting took place in early November 2016, we took November 9 as a symbolic (and real) marker of German history, with significance also for Jewish-German relations. I prepared five pieces of paper with different dates and headings written on them:

*Nov. 9, 1923/Hitler's Beer Hall Putsch*          *Nov. 9, 1938/Crystal Night*

*Nov. 9, 1989/Fall of the Wall*          *Nov. 8, 2016/Election of Trump*

*Nov. 9, 2050/?*

On November 9, 1923, Hitler tried unsuccessfully to seize power in Germany. Fifteen years later, on November 9, 1938, he and the Nazi party unleashed a wave of unprecedented violence against the Jewish community in Germany, known as *Kristallnacht* or Night of Broken Glass. On November 9, 1989, the wall separating East and West Germany was torn down, which led to German unification. In November 2016, Donald Trump was elected. I added the 2050 marker to spur our imagination of where we might be, or want to be, in the next generation.

Once those five papers were distributed across the room, participants were asked to stand next to the date/event that most strongly appealed to them—whether for positive or negative reasons. One woman, for example, chose 1989 because she needed to remind herself of a hopeful event in history, especially given recent elections that brought populist autocrats to power. Another person selected the same date, explaining that the *Mauerfall* (fall of the wall) was the most important event in her life, for it also offered new perspectives on her family history hitherto inaccessible behind the Iron Curtain. A younger participant preferred November 2016 because current political issues were most urgent to him, among them hatred of the recent influx of refugees in Germany. Even though none of the eleven participants selected the dates 1923 or 2050, in their conversations they made connections between 1923 and 2016, and they imagined what 2050 might look like and what responsibilities they had to create a future to their liking.

The November 9 session happened early in this workshop to get the group thinking about where they located themselves in political history. It was followed on the next day by a chronological timeline arranged on the floor. Participants were invited to step into the timeline and select a date that they deemed personally significant. Whereas on the previous day we had asked them to locate themselves politically in time, this session aimed at visualizing their biographical roots within collective history. With those two movements (political and biographical positioning), we aimed at deepening everyone's self-understanding regarding their role within an organization interested in combining psychotherapeutic insight with political engagement.

In recognition of the organization's Jewish and German membership, the chronological timeline I designed recalled dates significant to both German and Jewish history. Three lines were laid out on the floor: in the center, a line with significant years; to the left, important events in Jewish history (including Israel); to the right, important events in German history. Given the organization's origin in examining the psychological impacts of war and the Holocaust on families of survivors and perpetrators, this parallelism was intended to encourage participants to remain aware of events outside German national history. The timeline was not meant to be comprehensive but evocative.

The floor map below is a visual illustration of what such a timeline can look like. Depending on who participates in intergroup encounters, a timeline can be enriched with significant world history events or additional national histories. The floor map below, hence, is meant solely as an example.

| | | |
|---|---|---|
| First Zionist Congress | 1897/1871 | German Wilhelmine Empire |
| First Jewish Ghettos in Poland | 1939 | Start of Second World War |
| End of the Holocaust | 1945 | End of Second World War |
| Creation of the State of Israel | 1948/1949 | Creation of West Germany |
| Era of Prime Minister Ben Gurion (nation-building) | 1950s | Era of Chancellor Konrad Adenauer (nation-building) |
| Eichmann Trial in Jerusalem | 1961 | East Germany builds Wall in Berlin |
| Yom Kippur War | 1967/1968 | Student Revolt/Culture War |
| First Palestinian Intifada | 1987/1989 | Fall of the Wall/Unification |
| -------- | 2016 | -------- |

Participants were encouraged to walk up and down the timeline until they found a date/event that spoke to them in terms of their biographical belonging. Subsequently, each participant had a chance to share with the group how a chosen event had affected his or her personal development and (family) biography. One German woman, for example, chose the 1950s, the Konrad Adenauer era, because it was during this decade of nation-building that she first realized the devastating consequences of war trauma in her family. By standing next to a date, people connected physically to historical time as if subtly incorporating time.[9]

A timeline also functions as a snapshot for a group. There might be clusters around certain dates or empty spots at other places. Facilitators can make a group aware of what events are biographically, and hence generationally, strongly present in a particular group, while other historical events are absent in a group's consciousness. Such clusters can tell us something about dominant fears or marginalized dreams in a given group composition. If, for example, a particular generational cohort dominates, they might cluster around a small sample of events. Historically nourished fears, in turn, might determine the solutions they, as a group, might propose, with little patience left for other ideas. The positioning of participants in timelines, in other words, can tell us something about the affective dimension of disagreements over political actions and, as in this particular scenario, an organization's future direction.

This particular group of eleven people was small enough for each person to have a chance to tell us how they saw links between their personal biography and historical events while they were standing where they had placed themselves inside the timeline. When groups are larger, it might get too tiresome to hear from every single person. For large groups, there are other options. For example, after each person finds a place on the timeline, a facilitator can ask a succession of rapid questions (such as, are you comfortable where you stand?) to make people aware of their chosen positions. After such a group snapshot is taken, people can place additional cards on the timeline that contain their name and a few thoughts on their personal connections to a chosen historical event. A timeline thus decorated reflects a group's composition in visual ways that can be selectively probed in small groups.

In 2017, when working with a multigenerational group of Israelis, Germans, and Palestinians, I introduced a different version of a time-line—more interactive in spirit. I had originally planned not to do so, but repeated references to and arguments over historical events had slowed down the group and, at times, unproductively sidetracked it. A Palestin-ian man repeatedly referenced the 1917 Balfour Declaration[10] as the mo-ment when, in his view, "Jewish gangs" and the "Jewish mafia" started to take away Palestinian land. His statements were met with silence or occa-sionally countered with scholarly historical arguments. When he claimed that the two blue stripes framing the Israeli flag represented the Zionist wish to take away all of Palestinian land between the Mediterranean Sea and the Jordan River (the blue stripes), a few Germans protested the inflammatory language. Though this man's polemic (based more on ig-norance than malice) was not my prime reason for introducing timelines, it contributed to the need to visualize people's investment in particular historical events. As scholars of international relations have pointed out, divergent views on historical time, which serve as a basis for claiming certain rights, continue to feed conflicts.[11]

Different from the session in Cologne, where I had prepared cards in advance with significant events, in this trilateral meeting each group had to come up with their own dates they deemed important. I provided each national group with one card, containing a specific date/event: "1948/ Nakba" for Palestinians, "1948/State of Israel" for Israelis, and "1949/ Founding of West Germany's Constitution" for the German group. This, I explained, was their starting point for constructing a timeline of signifi-cant events. Each group received only four additional (blank) cards. I wanted them to discuss among themselves what other dates they considered important in their social and political history between the 1900s and 2020. By limiting it to four additional cards, each group was obliged to prioritize events and make tough decisions, thus preventing them from coming back with a long laundry list of dates. It led to animated discussions among the national groups. When they finally agreed on the four additional cards, I asked them to line them up on the floor in chronological order. Here is what they came back with:

| Palestinians | Israelis | Germans |
|---|---|---|
| ----- | 1897/First Zionist Congress | ----- |
| ----- | 1933–45/Holocaust | 1933/Hitler Seizes Power |
| **1948/Nakba** | **1948/State of Israel** | **1949/German Constitution** |
| 1967/Naksa[12] | 1967/Six-Day War | 1968/Protest Movement |
| 1987/First Intifada | 1995/Rabin Assassination | 1989/Berlin Wall Down |
| 1993/Oslo Agreement | ----- | 2015/Arrival of Refugees |
| 2000/Second Intifada | ----- | ----- |

Much could be said—and was said—in the initial round of feedback when the whole group saw the three different timelines laid out side by side. The bold-printed line in the diagram above shows the date/event cards I had distributed to each group as a starting point. Intriguingly, the contentious issue of the Balfour Declaration that had previously consumed some of the group's energy had disappeared in the Palestinian timeline. Instead, the Palestinians focused very much on the present moment. They did not go back in time before the 1948 Nakba. The Israeli group, not surprisingly, predated 1948 with a card on the Holocaust and with an event symbolizing the initial Zionist stirrings in Europe; as their last card, they chose the assassination of Prime Minister Rabin (rather than, say, the Oslo Peace Accords for which Rabin was killed by an Israeli ultranationalist).[13] That the German group mentioned Hitler but not the Holocaust raised some eyebrows among Israelis; that the German timeline ended with the recent 2015 refugee crisis had much to do with the fact that the majority of the German participants were in their twenties and early thirties and prioritized current concerns.

We continued working with this timeline for two more rounds. In the first round, every participant wrote their birthdate (but not their name) on a color-coded sticky paper (a different color for each national group); they then placed these cards on the correct chronological spot of the timeline. Since the majority of this trilateral group was born after the 1980s, they quickly realized that their birthdate cards on the timeline were visually far removed from the cards containing contentious collective histories. The political conflicts that shaped them and their relations were not based on their own lived experiences but had been passed on to them through their respective families, social and educational networks, and collective identities. To visually see the discrepancies between their lives and inherited memories and histories so clearly presented in the timeline was striking. A few of the participants began to wonder whether these inherited struggles actually disempowered them as a younger generation. Were they actually as free as they assumed they were? Since "groups encode important experiences, especially extensive suffering, in their collective memory, which can maintain a sense of woundedness and past injustice through generations,"[14] it is important for new generations to recognize that they do not have to be held hostage to such frames of collective victimhood. They are permitted to make choices about what burdens of the past they want to accept, reject, integrate, or transform.

Another surprise was a birthdate card that did not follow any linear sense of time. Among the participants was Gilad, a rabbi from a Jewish settlement in the occupied territories who has committed his life to cooperating with Palestinians in finding just solutions for sharing a common land of ancestry. Gilad put his personal birthdate outside of our time frame, to an imagined spot three thousand years ago. He explained that a personal birthdate was meaningless to him and that only his tribal-ancestral birthdate held any importance. He considered himself to be part of a larger stream of collective history. His religious understanding of time was hard to stomach not only for Palestinians but also for more secular-minded people in the group. Nevertheless, his birthdate card presented an intriguing antidote to our modern understanding of the self-importance of individuals.[15]

## ASSERTING A WOMAN'S PLACE

In a last round of working with this timeline, I randomly picked three of the nameless birthdate cards, one of each color. Not knowing who I had picked, I asked who these cards belonged to. Adinah, Dahab, and Silke raised their hands. I invited them to step back into the timeline, next to their cards. The three women were in their twenties and thirties. Once in position, I asked them to adopt a gesture to express their relation to the past, present, and future.

Silke, a German woman, positioned herself in a painful straddle between past and future. Not able to move forward, she could also not hold this uncomfortable position for long. Her gesture seemed an apt depiction of a younger German generation caught between a troubled past and a longing for an unfettered future while assuming a pained position of "responsibility" in the present. It also presented Silke's personal wrestling throughout the workshop, caught in a struggle between her analytical self and emotional self. Desperately clinging to rational models of conflict analysis, her emotions often burst forth in the midst of witnessing and experiencing interpersonal tensions among group members.

Adinah, an Israeli woman, pointed with one hand and finger downward to the past, while the other arm, with wide-open fingers, stretched out toward the future. Somewhat similar to Silke's gesture, Adinah could not hold the position (in the present) without physical pain. What she expressed was a feeling of being mentally torn between past and present. The downward finger might have been both a symbolic anchor in a homeland and a gesture toward the agonies of the past, and the outstretched arm pointed toward hope and possibilities. What Adinah expressed in her balancing act was not atypical for soul-searching Israelis in trilateral settings.

Dahab, a Palestinian woman, removed her sandals, placed one behind herself and one in front of her, then stood with a strong and straightened body on her birthdate card, her head directed toward the future, with no intent of looking back. Dahab wanted to be in the here-and-now. Her sandals indicated a path—where she came from, where she wanted to go. It expressed her desire to leave things behind without turning back and a wish to step into a yet-to-be-known future. It also represented her personal struggle to affirm her place, in her words, as an "independent woman" in Palestinian society, escaping from the clutches of an overbearing father and moving toward a self-determined place.

Similar in age, these three women were generationally connected on the timeline, each of them wrestling with how much the inherited past should determine their own paths forward. In their common quest, Dahab, Silke, and Adinah came up with different answers, molded by their embeddedness in different national, social, cultural, and family histories. In this particular women's constellation, the timeline's historical events did not lead to a heated debate about the legitimacy of a group's historical rights—as is so often the case in dyadic conflict constellations. Rather, the triangular dynamic displayed in three parallel timelines—owned and arranged by each group separately—moved these women to a different place. In the next chapter, we take a closer look at the dynamics of triangulation.

# NOTES

1. I am suggesting the term "nonmalevolent beneficiary of privilege" for those participants who *qua* socioeconomic position in their political environment (religious, ethnic, or national community) have potential or actual access to privilege, yet are receptive to the hardships and suffering of others and are willing to forego some of the benefits of those privileges.

2. Niza Yanay, *The Ideology of Hatred* (2013, 122). How a sought-after human connection in intergroup encounters is expressed may differ depending on one's large-group identification. Nevertheless, people from different backgrounds voice those desires. The differences in expressing one's wish for connection can be illustrated by the statements of two participants from the same mentor-training seminar. A Palestinian man from Nablus put it this way: "It was very good experience for me and made me think a lot about the problems. I try to be positive . . . and we have to find a way to live together. It is hard work to make people see the reality, but at the same time we need to work with all our efforts together. We have to put our fears away and gain more experiences from each other. We should do more talks and dialogue with the other to understand them, so that we can build trust between people." The word "friendship" does not appear here, but the wish for responsible human connection is clearly articulated. A Jewish Israeli woman was more direct about friendship. "The bottom line for me was that, as we all sweated to confront many painful issues, there was a real bond of friendship being forged in its own dimension that seemed to flow alongside, under and through the painful work being done. As a self-selected gathering of people already aspiring to build that bond of friendship, we are not a neutral or average sample; nonetheless, it was very heartening to feel that bond of friendship coming into being."

3. This observation coincides with basic tenets of group psychotherapy. In his comprehensive volume *The Theory and Practice of Group Psychotherapy* (1995), Irvin Yalom distinguishes between three formative stages in group therapy: an "initial stage [of] orientation [and] hesitant participation," followed by a "second stage [of] conflict, dominance [and] rebellion," and concluding with a "third stage" characterized by the "development of cohesiveness" (294–304).

4. On the role and impact of mandatory military service on Israeli men and women, see Danny Kaplan, "The Military as a Second Bar Mitzvah: Combat Service as Initiation to Zionist Masculinity" (2000), and Orna Sasson-Levy, "Research on Gender and the Military in Israel" (2011). Both articles provide more extensive references on this topic.

5. For readers less familiar with the current situation in Israel/Palestine, it could be summarized in the following way. There is a vast difference of experience between Palestinians living in Israel as Israeli citizens (Arab Israelis), Palestinians living in the West Bank, and Palestinians living in the Gaza Strip. Arab Israelis are in daily contact with Israeli Jews; for West Bank Palestinians, contact is more restricted (hence the fact that young people encounter Israelis only as soldiers); and for residents in Gaza, contact with Israeli civilians is rare and nearly impossible after Hamas gained political power.

6. The Palestinian group identified their obstacle as "national aspirations" (see Chapter 3), and the German group named their obstacle "mistrust in being German."

7. It could have been a daughter in uniform, but in this particular reenactment the returning soldier was played by a man.

8. The Study Group on Intergenerational Consequences of the Holocaust, formerly PAKH e.V. http://pakh.de/EN/index.html (accessed January 11, 2019).

9. Relating to the Latin word *corpus* (body).

10. See note 41 in Chapter 1.

11. Rose McDermott, an international relations scholar interested in applying new experimental methods to solving international conflicts, lists the issue of "time horizons" as an area of concern. "The importance of the dynamics underlying relevant

perceived time horizons in international relations," she writes, "should appear self-evident to anyone who has followed the difficulty of resolving internecine conflict between groups that hold divergent views of their historical rights and past sufferings and indignities" ("New Directions for Experimental Work in International Relations" 2011, 514). Her observation certainly applies also to the divergent views on time in the Israel-Palestine conflict.

12. Naksa is the commemoration of the Palestinian people's displacement that followed Israel's victory in the 1967 Six-Day War.

13. Rabin's assassination happened in November 1995 in Tel Aviv at the end of a political rally in support of the Oslo Accords. The ultranationalist assassin Yigal Amir radically opposed Rabin's peace initiative with Palestinians.

14. Ervin Staub and Daniel Bar-Tal, "Genocide, Mass Killing, and Intractable Conflict" (2003, 722). The identification with past collective injuries by new generations who have had no direct experiences with those injuries or indignities is one of the sources that sustain protracted conflicts. In their discussion of people's "self-perceived collective victimhood," Daniel Bar-Tal et al. identify a collective's present preoccupation with "harms done in a distant past" as a strong factor contributing to conflict and competitive victimhood ("A Sense of Self-Perceived Collective Victimhood in Intractable Conflicts" 2009, 236).

15. "It is not unusual," writes international scholar Rose McDermott, "for interested parties to discuss events over a 1,000 years ago as immediate and obviously relevant to current negotiations over territorial boundaries." She mentions particularly Ireland and the Middle East; she also suggests that international relations scholars should use experimental methods to "simulate the momentum of history, memory, and time horizons on processes of bargaining, negotiation, and conflict resolution" ("New Directions for Experimental Work in International Relations" 2011, 514). Such long-held views on history get exacerbated when they blend with religious convictions, especially in fundamentalist movements that anchor the legitimacy over (territorial) rights in divinely willed redemptive or apocalyptic conceptions of history (eschatology).

# NINE

## Triangulating

Throughout this book I have introduced examples from seminars and workshops in which not only two but three or more parties took part, especially with regard to the trilateral gatherings of Israelis, Palestinians, and Germans. In these settings, no one group functioned as a mediator for the two other parties. In other words, these reconciliatory processes were not conceived of as conflict resolution programs that required the services of a neutral third party. Rather, all three or multiple parties were equally involved in those processes.

A "third party" is usually a mediating agent who is not directly involved in a dispute but is instead tasked to reach a settlement between two conflicting sides. People frequently assume that the Germans in the trilateral Israeli-Palestinian-German settings constitute such a third neutral party. This, however, is not the case. The settings within which I am facilitating groups are not defined as "third-party mediations," and they stay below the level of "track II diplomacy," the latter in which non-state actors explore possible problem-solving interventions.[1] The same is true for the multiparty groups that I have (co)facilitated: no group functioned as a neutral mediator in, for example, the majority-minority program on indigeneity for students from Israel and the United States or the racial reconciliation seminars for an ethnically diverse student body.

If not a third-party approach, why inject a group into a contested zone where it is seemingly alien, like Germans in the Middle East or Bedouins in Native American reservations in Arizona? Why take the focus away from those directly affected by a conflict? Why complicate or overburden conflict-resolution or peace-building efforts with perspectives external to a regional conflict? Perhaps the reader has already intuited that it is beneficial to disrupt a dyadic conflict—as in the Palestinian-Israeli case— through the presence of a third group, even when this group does not

195

play the role of mediator. In this chapter I want to address this issue more deliberately and reflect on the specific dynamics that develop when another group gets inserted into a protracted conflict. Instead of introducing techniques of conflict mediation, I suggest that we look at the beneficial impact of *triangulation by involving a third group.

## WE ARE NOT IN A ZOO

When, many years ago, I was first approached by a German led organization to consider facilitating a group of Germans, Israelis, and Palestinians, I initially balked at the proposal. I thought it was a bad idea. I assumed that German participants would automatically slip into the role of mediator, thus keeping at bay their own emotional entanglement in the political history of Israel against the backdrop of the Holocaust. I was worried that individual Germans, despite the remarkable decades-long efforts of postwar German society to come to terms with its history, might end up acting out (rather than working through) their own unresolved issues within the Israeli-Palestinian context. The continuous barrage of impassioned pro-Israel or pro-Palestine sentiments expressed in the public sphere and on social media in Germany is just one indication of the complex and often convoluted psychopolitical identifications of many Germans. "First they imposed war on everyone, now they want to impose peace on everyone," so the mockery of some Israeli skeptics goes, "but one thing we know for sure: it is still the Germans!" Without Germans doing their homework regarding their family histories and politicized identifications, I cannot conceive of Germans as helpful partners.

Because of my work since the 1980s with mixed groups of Jews and Germans (and also German Jews), I am familiar with how strongly second- and third-generation Germans are attached to their ways of intellectualizing and historicizing the legacy of the Holocaust and how fervently they protect themselves against the surfacing of the moral and political emotions of guilt, shame, grief, and resentment.[2] For a particularly striking example, we can briefly listen to Jessica Benjamin, a Jewish American psychoanalyst, who, in a recent book, recalls a meeting with German colleagues many years ago. The meeting had left her shaken and terrified. Benjamin had been invited to supervise a workshop in Germany on "intersubjectivity" (her area of specialty) at the invitation of a German psychoanalytic association. In this workshop, a young German psychoanalyst-in-training shared a protocol with the group in which the issue of Nazi perpetrators in the patient's family history emerged. The male patient's father had been in the SA (Stormtroopers), and his mentally disabled uncle had perished in a psychiatric clinic during the Nazi euthanasia program. This "information," Benjamin recalls, "was communicated without comment and a notable lack of affect, and it was ignored by the workshop participants." As the Jewish American outsider, Benjamin tried to bring this lack of affect and interest to the group's attention. With no success. She describes how the group's resistance increasingly paralyzed and terrified her in her role as a (Jewish) supervisor. The German group kept asking her "theoretical questions about intersubjectivity in the treatment" with no "further mention by anyone of the problem of dealing with the Nazi past of genocide, murder, and violence."[3]

Benjamin's experience illustrates how a mode of intellectualizing can dissociate a group from both their feelings and the moral weight of a country's past. Cutting oneself off from a reckoning with the intimacy of family entanglement in a dictatorial and genocidal regime prevents descendants of a perpetrator society from stepping into a relational process with others. It protects against the unsettling effects of history. Such a group of Germans would be unhelpful in a trilateral meeting with Israelis and Palestinians, for they would, in all likelihood, operate in a mode of analytic distance without rendering themselves vulnerable.

It takes a stepping away from the often invoked but frequently overintellectualized concept of "responsibility" with which German generations are quick to identify. "Responsibility" is the key, they claim, to having learned the lessons from their nation's past. Oliver Fuchs's personal reflections as part of his research project demonstrates vividly how this "responsibility" mantra can obstruct a necessary working-through process. Fuchs, a third-generation German—and in 2015 studying in South Africa—recalls a meeting with a Jewish Holocaust survivor in Cape Town. This meeting triggered his academic interest in studying his peers' relation to German history. For his research he interviewed Germans in their twenties in order to examine how their emotional investment in the past surfaced through discursive patterns in their narratives.

When, earlier, Fuchs had listened to the survivor testimony in Cape Town, he noticed that many of his classmates were quietly crying and visibly touched by her story—except for him. "My own reaction was simply to pass some tissue," he writes. My classmates' "tears were an understandable and appropriate response for witnessing [her] narrative of pain and suffering, except, of course, if one is German." At the time, Fuchs felt that he "had a duty to bear witness" and to endure her pain "without flinching." "Crying," he thought, "would have betrayed my responsibility." Years later, after he had completed his study "German Subjectivity Three Generations after the End of World War Two," he reflected on his earlier "self-protective composure."

> Only in hindsight have I come to understand that, on the day of the encounter with [the survivor], I did not really listen or take in her suffering. I was attending to her words, but her emotional experience, for the most part, did not permeate me. Sitting there stoically was not about an obscure sense of *responsibility*, or doing justice to [her] experience; it was about protecting myself emotionally in the face of a very

real and painful confrontation with the Nazi past. To let myself be
moved in the way my classmates were at that moment would have
been impossible, because of an obliterating fear of letting myself be
touched by the pervasive feeling of shame for the terror and hurt that
Germans—my nation, and probably members of my family—had inflicted upon [her] and millions like her.[4]

Given this candid self-assessment, Oliver Fuchs would have been an
ideal partner in a trilateral meeting.

In actuality, however, there is limited control over who signs up for
attending intergroup encounters. People come from a variety of backgrounds with different levels of experience and differing degrees of prior
exposure to particular conflict constellations. The recollections of Jessica
Benjamin and Oliver Fuchs indicate the range of self-awareness that people might bring to intergroup processes. Those differences have implications for the roles that participants intentionally or subconsciously assume.

When I eventually agreed to the request to lead a trilateral Palestinian-
German-Israeli seminar, I insisted I first meet and work with the German
group separately. This, as it turned out, was crucial since the assembled,
highly motivated Germans were essentially uncertain about their role
and place in a meeting in the Middle East. Time and again I insisted that
they would not be mediators nor observers. The preworkshop was to
assist them in identifying emotional blind spots, questioning cultural assumptions, and disavowing fantasies about becoming rescuers and help-
ers. We explored, for example, how their political ideation—the process
of forming ideas and images—might be related to their upbringing in
families affected by World War II. We also examined how their current
understanding of Israelis and Palestinians might operate as much on the
basis of affect and fantasy as on politically informed judgment.

Ideally, all participants wanting to get involved in reconciliatory processes would do their homework before joining a group. This, of course,
does not always happen. I remember one particular instance when half-
way through a trilateral gathering with Palestinians and Israelis I had to
intervene and challenge two of the attending Germans. Up to this moment neither of them had shared anything personal. They kept themselves closed off, and their reserved behavior was making other people
uncomfortable, especially Israelis and Palestinians. When asked in a
group session about sharing their thoughts and feelings, the two individuals replied that they had not much to contribute and were only there to
observe and learn about the Palestinian-Israeli conflict. Their responses
visibly raised the level of discomfort among other participants, but no
one dared say anything. It was one of those moments when a facilitator's
direct intervention was called for. After more prodding on my part—also
unsuccessfully—I articulated the group's discomfort that I felt was obstructing our process. "We are not in a zoo here," I said. "We are not here

to observe how Palestinians and Israelis act out their conflicts in front of us for the benefit of our knowledge." This intervention was tough to hear for the Germans, but the rest of the group felt relieved. It left the two German participants (and those who sympathized with them) angry. Initially, it pushed them into an even more protective shell. The intervention was a calculated risk on my part as facilitator. Had we avoided the confrontation, it would have stalled the process of trust-building for everyone—and trust, as I have argued throughout this book, requires a willingness to shed protectiveness in favor of some degree of vulnerability.

## TRIANGULATION

In triadic settings, the dynamics of triangulation come into play. It is a concept primarily employed in psychology. I am appropriating this term for my own purposes to understand the ever-shifting dynamics in trilateral encounters. In psychology it is used to diagnose and treat family systems that are marred by dysfunctional communication between three parties. Most commonly it describes a dynamic in which one family member does not communicate directly with another family member because of a conflict and therefore shifts attention to a third family member, thus pulling that third person into a loyalty conflict. When a functioning dyadic system is falling apart and a triangle emerges, people are set up against each other. For example, when communication breaks down between parents, a mother might form a strong bond with a child against her husband, compensating for the broken relationship but also upsetting the child's relationship to the father. Or when a marriage is failing, a third person can be pulled into the triangle through an extramarital affair, which rearranges the dyadic structure with the result of either destroying or restabilizing the marriage.

Whereas some psychological models see triangulation as a necessary step in a child's development (to sever the symbiotic mother-infant relationship), triangulation more often refers to dysfunctional family systems. In family therapy, triangulation is applied to understanding tensions in a dyadic relationship, in which a third person gets involved to either compensate for or alleviate a conflict. "Triangling is an ever-present process . . . in the comfort of dyadic relationships," writes clinical psychologist Peter Titelman. It emerges, or "crystallize[s], when the calm stability of a two-person system is unbalanced by anxiety in the wake of a nodal event" (like marriage, childbirth, death, or divorce).[5]

In my work with groups in conflict, I employ triangulation differently.[6] I conceive of it as a spirited force that can disrupt rigid patterns of interaction between two sides in protracted conflicts. Rather than viewing triangulation as an indication of a dysfunctional system, I see it as a momentum that can unsettle repetitive cycles of accusations and counteraccusations, dislodge mechanisms of competitive victimhood, and mitigate reciprocal delegitimization attempts.[7] For this to function, a "third-party" approach does not work because a mediating party remains outside the conflict itself. In the triangulation dynamics, a third group becomes an integral part of the triangle, not an outsider. Only when all three groups are fully involved in the messiness of interpersonal interactions will the unsettling force of triangulation get activated. With Palestinians and Israelis trapped in the retellings of reciprocal stories of suffering and victimization, the dysfunctional energy in their dyadic relation can be interrupted by shifting alliances in a triangular setting.

In the case of Israeli-German-Palestinian trilateral meetings, Germans are not, and cannot be, a neutral party. When I intervened resolutely in the case of two German participants wanting to stay on the sidelines, I insisted on bringing them into our circle. Their initial refusal to enter into the relational dynamics that a triangular system relies on obstructed the process for the rest of the group: it had triggered the prickly discomfort of being watched like animals in a zoo.

Participants are not left to their own devices in these trilateral processes. The facilitator (or facilitation team) occupies a position external to the group and thus provides guidance, safety, and a frame. Perhaps the best skill facilitators can bring to these triangular dynamics is to be present yet invisible—that is to say, to guide a group according to its needs without ego attachment or attachment to a punctilious obedience to a method. Without such guidance, trilateral groups quickly get ensnared in the dysfunctional patterns of triangulation, not unlike dysfunctional family systems, except with a political edge to it and the weight of collective grievances. Good facilitators do not prevent heated disagreements or explosive situations to play out in particular sessions, but they know how to set limits, redirect a group's attention, and offer alternative patterns of exploration. A group left to its own devices—this, at least, is my experience—gets easily stuck in unproductive and potentially destructive patterns, whereas a facilitator's task is to balance inevitable phases of frustration and stuckness with interventions that move a process forward.

Concretely, how do the benefits of triangulation manifest themselves in trilateral programs? Let us imagine a triangle with Israelis, Germans, and Palestinians in a room prior to any significant interactions. Each group, so to speak, is set up in equal distance to each other in a non-aligned, resting stage. The moment some interaction occurs, the triangle begins to move, with one side edging closer to another, while the third group moves to a position further removed. When, for instance, Palestinians and Israelis enter into a heated exchange about the meaning of 1948 (the founding of the State of Israel versus the Nakba), a thick line of conflict connects them, with only weak links to Germans. In this scenario Germans actively witness something raw that they otherwise might have only read about in newspapers; in response they might align themselves ideationally on either side depending on their political views of the conflict. If we were to switch to a session that would address, for example, the Holocaust as experienced in family histories, a strong line would be established between Israelis and Germans, with Palestinians pushed to the sidelines. In such a constellation, Palestinians are often surprised to witness the role reversal Israelis undergo. Rather than seeing Israelis in the seemingly immovable position of political and military power, they watch close up how (Israeli) Jews slip into the position of a victimized community vis-à-vis the descendants of perpetrators. For a moment the Holocaust ceases to exist as a contested trope of political banter and comes alive, instead, in the intimate motions where loss and grief reside. If, finally, we were to switch to a session that brings together Palestinians and Germans and they speak, for example, about the injustice of dispossessions and loss of homes, they are connected by a thick link, while the sidelined Israelis get anxious.

In none of these scenarios would the group sitting on the sidelines of a temporary dyadic interaction be impartial observers. The opposite is closer to the truth. As active witnesses, the sidelined participants are emotionally involved when watching the interactions between the other two groups unfold, and they respond with rising levels of incredulity, anxiety, and alarm. Too much contact between Israelis and Germans regarding their shared antagonistic history can raise fears among Palestinians about losing the Germans as political allies. Too close an alliance along acts of solidarity between Germans and Palestinians can provoke angst among Israelis about being singled out as Jews and abandoned by the world community. And when Israelis and Palestinians fight tooth and nail one moment but the next moment hug each other as "brothers" and smoke a hookah together, Germans feel excluded, inadequate, and unneeded.

## TURNING MY BACK BECAUSE I TRUST YOU

A year after the 2014 Israel-Gaza war, a group of Israelis, Germans, and Palestinians who knew each other from previous workshops came back together again. At one point in the workshop, the group decided through a process of elimination (stepping on various topic cards until a consensus was found) to explore the topic "collective trauma." Next, we separated the national groups and gave each three note cards with the following task: Write on the first card in one or two words what you perceive as your own collective trauma and on the two remaining cards what you perceive to be the trauma of the other two groups. The German group called their own trauma "collective guilt" and identified "antisemitism" as the Israeli trauma and "Nakba" as the Palestinian trauma. The Palestinians named their own trauma "Nakba" and identified "Holocaust & guilt" for the Germans and "Holocaust & victimization" for the Israelis.

The Israelis referred to their own trauma as "Holocaust & hostile environment" and identified "third-generation conflict" as the trauma for Germans and "Nakba & life under occupation" as the Palestinian trauma.

We spent only a short time in the large group to share observations about those cards. There was clearly much overlap since each group more or less stayed within the parameters of chosen traumas. The similar naming for each other's traumas also reflected the deepening bonds and awareness among the participants in this particular setting. Some clarification was needed, especially the puzzling card "third-generation conflict" that Israelis named for the German trauma. After some attempts at explaining their choice, most Israelis concurred that the phrase kind of missed the target and that, perhaps, they had something in mind closer to the issue of "guilt and responsibility."

In the next rounds, we used these note cards to guide each national group separately through a process of making them aware of the possible implications of identifying those collective traumata. In each case, the other two groups served as active witnesses. In the description below, I will focus on the Israeli group.

To recall: The Jewish Israeli group had identified their own collective trauma as "Holocaust & hostile environment" while naming the trauma for Germans "third-generation conflict" and for Palestinians "Nakba & life under occupation." In a first round of approaching their trauma cards, we placed the Israeli group in the center with everyone else sitting around them listening to their conversation. Since this group of Israeli participants was verbally very eloquent, the conversation was engaging, intelligent, politically correct, and polite. But it lacked some zing, as if the spice was missing that turns a good meal into a memorable meal.

In a second round, we rearranged the space. On one end of the room we seated the German group in a half circle and on the other end the Palestinians, also in a half circle. The Germans and Palestinians became active witnesses of what was about to happen in the center where the Israelis remained. In other words, we placed the Jewish Israeli group right in the middle of the German collective trauma on one side (Holocaust/guilt/third-generation conflict) and the Palestinian collective trauma on the other side (Nakba/life under occupation).

We invited the Israeli participants to get up from their chairs and arrange themselves along the axis between the Palestinians and Germans. We encouraged them to find the distance to either group that seemed personally right to them and then to strike a simple physical pose that expressed something about how they felt in that middle space. Torn between two collective calamities—one in the past, the other in the present—every single Israeli turned his or her attention to the Palestinian group. Most had their back completely turned to the Germans while some stood sideways but with their faces turned in the direction of the Palestinian half circle.

If one assumed that the Holocaust trauma would loom large over Israeli identity, then this constellation was surprising, since this group of Israelis directed their gaze and movement toward the Palestinians and seemed to pay little attention to the trauma of "victimization/Holocaust/ guilt" associated with their relations to Germany. Indeed, the German group was perhaps most surprised by this constellation and felt a little left out. It appeared as if their stories as descendants of a (former) perpetrator society and their wrestling with the moral weight of guilt had become suspended, if not irrelevant.

The Palestinian group, however, was not surprised. They thought it made sense that Israelis would need to confront the realities of living in a divided and contested land today. For them, the German past seemed far away—symbolically condensed in this constellation with German history on the other end of the room and with the bodies of Israelis obstructing their view of the German half circle.

When it was time for the Israeli group to give voice to their spontaneous choices of gesture and placement, we learned that turning their back to the German group was not meant to ignore Germans and the legacy of the Holocaust, as one might have surmised from the constellation. Turning their back to the Germans was not an expression of being disconnected to the European past, they said, but quite to the contrary a gesture of trust toward the German participants. "I felt supported," several Israelis said. "Knowing that Germans are in this room, we feel assured that the Holocaust will be remembered. They take on part of the emotional labor of memory for us, and so we can pay attention to what is happening today." Almost counterintuitively, three of the Israelis proceeded to speak for the first time in this group about their family roots in Europe. They revealed snippets of their family legacy that identified them as children and grandchildren of European Holocaust survivors. Because they perceived the attending German participants as having faced the Holocaust themselves, they were given the emotional space to attend to the urgency of the Palestinian plight. With their backs supported by the German presence, the Israelis could attend to the current situation with Palestinians rather than be consumed by the European past.

Though more could be said about individual gestures and stories that emerged in this scenario, important about this constellation in the context of triangulation is how it visually demonstrated the shaking-up of dyadic patterns. The triangular dynamics unfolded in this setting in such a way that it did not push Germans and Jews back into a constrained dyadic narrative framework that for decades had governed their post-1945 relations. And yet, the Holocaust remained present. The triangularity also loosened the grip of accusatory and counteraccusatory narratives over the legitimacy of analogizing the Holocaust and the Nakba, disrupting the dyadic nature over competing victimization claims between Palestinians and Israelis.[8] Both Holocaust and Nakba were present in the constellation, each in their own space and represented by real people, each of them burdened with stories of grievance and resilience. In the in-between space, the Israeli participants had to navigate and negotiate the presence of both—certainly an unenviable task that did not offer much respite and rest.

With the Israeli attention directed at the Palestinians sitting in a half circle on the other end of the room, one might have expected some elation in the Palestinian group. This, however, was not the case. Instead, they responded with cautious skepticism to the attention they received from Israelis.[9] It was clear that the Palestinian participants—visible through their limp bodily postures and listless facial expressions—remained somewhat unmoved and reticent. This, in turn, left the Israelis unhappy. When one of them inched closer to them, close enough to touch, she was gently but firmly rebuked. Frustration spread among the Israeli participants on account of their inability to connect to Palestinians. They genuinely did not know what was missing but also sensed that, as Israelis, they might not have delved deeply enough into issues of their own social identification.[10] They felt that they had expressed themselves eloquently with plenty of explanations, information, and gestures of solidarity. In this particular constellation, however, they realized that all their explaining did not bridge the emotional gap to the Palestinians.

What was perhaps sensed among Palestinians (and also Israelis) was a lack of more "first hand or at least vicarious familiarity" with the Palestinian experience; too quick a move toward Palestinians led to their defenses going up.[11] Perhaps stirrings of empathy were still buried under the weight of collective history that could not be brushed aside easily. The way the participants negotiated and responded to the time-space coordinates (visualized in this constellation) demonstrated the fluidity and tragic complexity of what is often so swiftly summed up in the phrase "the Israeli-Palestinian conflict," with pundits on all sides claiming to know exactly what needs to be done.

The triangulation dynamic as illustrated above places the Israelis in the middle of two gravitational social fields, the Holocaust and Nakba. It reveals the difficult psychosocial and political situation in which Israelis find themselves. But this is not the whole story. That the Palestinian and German half circles seemed to be stationary and immovable entities was true only for this particular constellation. As social groups and individuals, Germans and Palestinians, too, are in constant movement, stretching and bending backward and forward as they negotiate various commitments to their communities and collective histories.

## REALIZING ITS POTENTIAL

Triangulation dynamics can occur in small instances and grand gestures, and sometimes they do not occur at all. I already mentioned in Chapter 7 the history hike project in Lebanon that was intended to bring together Armenian, Turkish, and European students as equal partners. Midway through the planning process, however, the organizing team decided to exclude the Turkish students, thus forestalling any learning that might have occurred in and through triangular relations. [12]

Triangular dynamics unfold regardless of whether facilitators or groups are aware of them. This happened, for example, in the last four-week summer program I cofacilitated in 2005 for the third generation grappling with the legacy of the Holocaust. [13] Previous programs consisted only of Jewish American and non-Jewish German students and as such remained a dyadic encounter. In 2005, however, we added Polish students. In the facilitation team, we were quite aware of the in-between position of Polish students: they were descendants of a nation victimized by the Nazi occupation but also of a community with their own legacy of antisemitism. At the time, I was not yet familiar with the triangulation concept, and I chalked up some of the complications in this trilateral group as the result of tenacious personalities. Unaware of the full potential of triangular relations when working with groups in conflict, we did not take full advantage of the constantly changing alliances between and among Polish and German students with common European and Christian roots, Jewish and Polish students as victims of Nazism, and Jewish and German students with unacknowledged biases against Poles.

In one minor instance, we were actually on the brink of working with triangular dynamics (without giving it a name). We asked each separate group to create a living sculpture that would best represent their nation's dealing with the past. Proceeding in the usual way, the three groups returned after a short while to show their monuments, and we then probed and analyzed each sculpture. The Polish group showed a monument of three people standing back to back and facing outward, their hands mimicking the three monkeys: hear no evil, see no evil, speak no evil. The Jewish American group presented a circle of people sitting on the floor, their bodies touching each other, looking inward. The German sculpture consisted of disconnected people engaged in their own activities, most of them literal representations of dealing with the past.

We spent time with each sculpture. While sharing observations and associations, the tone of the comments moved imperceptibly from appreciation to criticism. We started with the German sculpture, deciphering each of the characters: one man swept trash under a carpet, and another man turned his back to the past; a woman, further removed from the center, was lost in doing her own things, and another woman on her knees covered her face (a gesture ambiguously placed between mourning and refusing to look). At first, the whole group wondered why the Germans were all isolated and why they did not reach out to talk to and support each other. The group initially expressed compassion for the burden of third-generation Germans, but eventually criticism grew stronger. Polish and Jewish American students asked: Does this German sculpture resist or merely replicate the silence about the past? Do their German peers continue the same tradition of evasion as their forefathers?

The tight-knit Jewish sculpture was first interpreted as an expression of shared grief, and people had empathy for the burden that the Holocaust had left on subsequent generations. Witnessing the close physical and emotional bonds in the Jewish sculpture, German and Polish students seemed also a bit envious. They began to wonder: Could we ever be part of this circle? Would the people in the circle ever turn around and see other people's struggle? Isn't this sculpture a representation of the exclusiveness of Jewish people?

The Polish sculpture was easily understood, and the Jewish and German observers empathized with the difficulty of finding the right words in contemporary Poland to talk about the Holocaust or get access to archival documentation (one of the Polish students had earlier shared how hard it was to get into Polish archives as a critical Holocaust scholar). But then the tone changed: Is this sculpture critical of the nation's dealing with the Nazi occupation and the Holocaust, or is it self-pitying and self-exculpating? Are young Poles not allowed to see, hear, and speak, or do they not make enough of an effort to see, hear, and speak?

Those critical questions left a sour taste among some participants. Appreciative of the compassionate comments they heard first, they felt defensive when critical observations were voiced. The Polish students felt particularly misunderstood—feeding right into a larger cultural stream of post-1945 Polish discourse that demurs at being unfairly judged by the world.[14]

At the time, the facilitation team probed both the students' appreciation and defensiveness. We did so, however, by treating those dynamics as three discreet sets of dyadic conversations—Polish-Jewish, German-Polish, Jewish-German—rather than a web of triangular relations. Had we been aware of the latter dynamics, we could have worked with the fluidity of these relations in more productive and interactive ways and might have been able to cushion some of the distress by offering different perspectives.

Years later, at a mentor-training seminar for Palestinians, Israelis, and Germans, the triangulation dynamics were almost organically adopted. This particular seminar's purpose was to supervise sessions that participants themselves designed and facilitated while, at the same time, moving deeper into new territory of exploring the current situation. The seminar, which was held in Israel, ran along two tracks. Track one consisted of participants forming triads with a member of each national group whose task it was to lead the whole group through a session. Once they had completed their session, another facilitator-in-training triad picked up where the last triad had left the process and so on. The second track consisted of supervisory sessions, which interrupted the content process in order to reflect on and analyze how each trainee-triad operated when leading the whole group. This dual-track approach required the mentors-in-training to switch between participant and facilitator; my role was to be a supervisor for the trainees but also facilitate a few content sessions when the dynamics became dense and convoluted.

In one session, the responsible facilitator triad decided to turn to storytelling. Resourcefully, they added the caveat of creating two circles of active witnessing: a storyteller would choose a single person as listener (intimate active witness) while the whole group was also listening to the story (the outer witnessing circle). It was an ingenious way of preserving the privacy of telling a story from one person to another while the large group eavesdropped on the conversation. A mood of closeness was created that emboldened people to think about incidents in their lives that would touch on issues not easily shared otherwise. The facilitator triad instructed participants to select only one storyteller from each national group, hoping that those chosen would take the risk of sharing something akin to cultural secrets or cultural intimacy.

Sabrina, a German woman in her early twenties, went first. As a child of a German mother and North African Muslim father, she represented the cultural identity of multiethnic Germans.[15] Because her passport included entry stamps from a North African country, she was pulled aside when entering Israel and held overnight at the Tel Aviv airport. At first the authorities threatened to put her on the next flight back to Germany, but after hours of waiting and interrogations she was eventually allowed to enter. Though this experience had rendered Sabrina apprehensive, she remained astoundingly composed and ready to engage.

The topic Sabrina wanted to talk about was how she first learned about the Holocaust. She looked around the room and chose Aaron, an Israeli, as the person to tell the story to. Aaron resided in an Israeli town next to the border to Gaza, intimately familiar with the emotional cost of frequent missile strikes and counterstrikes between Hamas and the Israel army. Sabrina told Aaron about her family's silence regarding the Holocaust; how fellow students made jokes about the Holocaust in high school; that it took until ninth grade, at the age of sixteen, until the Holocaust was first taught in school; how it was taught as dry, objective facts with no assistance provided to process the information emotionally; and that her German family's history relation to the Holocaust remained unknown to her to this day.

Sabeer, who had been engaged in peace networks, went next. As a Palestinian, he was willing to break with imposed norms on how to engage with Israelis. This included his readiness to travel to Poland and

visit the memorial site of the Auschwitz death camp. He chose to tell his
story to an Israeli man. Sabeer recounted how difficult it was to obtain
permission from the Palestinian Authority to travel to Poland. His first
application was rejected, with the explanation that it was not reasonable
for any Palestinian to travel there. When he was eventually allowed to go,
the visit changed his life, because, as Sabeer said, he finally "understood
that fear and trauma drive the current conflict." This is why, he continued, trinational meetings are so important: they connect Germany and
the Holocaust with what is happening in Israel. But something else happened during his visit of Auschwitz, he added, something disturbing that
makes it hard to talk about. Near the ramp, where Jews had arrived in the
infamous cattle cars, Sabeer had overheard an Israeli guide speaking in
Hebrew to a visiting Israeli youth group. The guide sprinkled curse
words in Arabic into his speech. The curse word most frequently used
was *khara* (Arabic for "shit"), but Sabeer could not understand Hebrew
well enough to know what the guide was talking about. He turned to his
Israeli companion and asked for translation help. The youth group
guide's message basically came down to the admonition that "if we [in
Israel] are not careful, the Arabs and Palestinians will do to you the same
*khara* as the Germans." It deeply upset Sabeer to realize how a collective
fear was fostered in Auschwitz and intentionally redirected at Palestinians. "It seems to me that it is not justice or 'love your neighbor' that
drives the peace process," Sabeer concluded, "but fear."[16]

Now it was Aaron's turn to tell his story, the same man who had
listened to Sabrina's account, and he chose Sabeer to be his listener. Aaron wanted to address the 1948 Nakba because, in his view, the Nakba
changed not only Palestinian lives but also Jewish identity. Even Israelis
on the political left, Aaron said, largely ignore the impact of the Nakba on
Jewish Israeli identities. This neglect gets further complicated when
reaching out to other populations in Israel. Teaching at a college in southern Israel that also enrolls many Bedouin students, Aaron realized that
many Bedouin students—who are Israeli citizens and share the Muslim
faith with most Palestinians—do not know about the Nakba. Like Sabeer,
who went to Auschwitz as a Palestinian, Aaron is a risk-taker when it
comes to moving beyond a normative discourse. For Aaron, it is important to challenge the mainstream Israeli discourse about its Arab and
Palestinian population. After a recent military confrontation, when the
Israeli forces killed fifteen people in Gaza, Aaron decided to bring this to
the attention of his college class. He asked his students (Jewish Israelis
and some Bedouins) for a moment of silence for those fifteen people. The
uproar was intense. Students left the classroom and brought their grievances all the way to the upper echelons of the college administration.
Aaron almost lost his job over asking for this moment of silence. For the
remainder of the course, Aaron said, most of his students refused to learn
from him and no longer gave him any credibility. Their identification

with a national narrative was so strong that they were unable to show any sign of empathy for the other side.

The intensifying web spun between the Israeli, Palestinian, and German listeners and storytellers as well as the sensitive nature of the content of the stories developed because the dynamics of triangulation were intentionally employed. A space opened up where risk-taking and vulnerability were rewarded rather than immediately shut down. A Muslim woman of German descent struggling with the legacy of the Holocaust, a Palestinian in Auschwitz understanding Jewish fears and simultaneously getting upset, an Israeli near the Gaza border asking for a moment of empathy for the people killed on the other side—these are no ordinary conversations when working with groups in conflict.

In the subsequent supervisory session, one participant offered the image of fire. "We saw three flames burning in our midst," she said. "For a moment, all other flames had to be extinguished. The storytelling was not really a fishbowl with us listening to what happened in the center. Instead, we created a circle that contained and protected the fire inside." I shared my own observations: "I want everyone to become aware of the fact that the three storytellers and the three listeners in the center demonstrated the basic dynamics of our trilateral group. This is why it was possible for Sabeer to pick up the Auschwitz visit and for Aaron the Nakba theme, or why Sabrina chose to tell Aaron about her experience with the failure of German Holocaust education." I also reminded the group that we always need to remain alert to the forces that pull us back into the master narratives of our large-group identities, luring us into reproducing in our own work the larger social, cultural, and historical patterns. "We have the power to break through those narratives, as we just witnessed, even when sharing those stories is painful, prone to be misunderstood, and sometimes embarrassing when they are revealed in a semipublic setting." In our own storytelling-witnessing scenario, I cautioned, we also fell back and relied on dyadic expectations. For example, a German chose an Israeli to listen to her story about the Holocaust; a Palestinian chose an Israeli to listen to his experiences in Auschwitz; and an Israeli chose a Palestinian to listen to his take on the Nakba and his call for public empathy for Palestinians. In other words, the central player in these three rounds of storytelling was still the Israeli Jew, with the unselfconscious task delegated to him to connect the German/Holocaust past with the Palestinian/Nakba present. Is it possible, I mused, that without the Israelis the Germans might not care as much about Palestinians? If, for example, Sabrina had chosen to tell her story about the Holocaust to a Palestinian rather than Israeli Jewish listener, would it have changed anything? Or if Sabeer had told of his experiences in Auschwitz to a young German, would it have had the same impact? Would the curse word *khara* resonate with a German listener the same as with an Israeli?

"This session," I concluded, "opened many new doors. From here, we can take different directions. Which facilitation team is ready to take us to the next step?"

The multidirectionality at work when the dynamic potency of triangulation unfolds might have something in common with the sanguine expectations Michael Rothberg ascribes to multidirectional memory. When "remembrance and imagination" are embraced as multidirectional forces, Rothberg suggests, "they prove to be difficult to contain in the molds of exclusivist identities." Though always "susceptible . . . to abuse," they more often than not lead to "acts of empathy and solidarity . . . [and are] the very grounds on which people construct and act upon visions of justice."[17] Mining the potential of triangulation when working with groups in conflict defies despair over seemingly irreversible adversarial relations. We can replace gloom and despair with unforeseen and yet-to-be-realized opportunities when we conceive of conflicts as evolving relationships in more fluid social fields. Grounded in remembrance but unbound in our imagination, we can move forward.

## NOTES

1. For different types of conflict resolution processes, see the helpful schematization in Mohammed Abu-Nimer, *Dialogue, Conflict Resolution, and Change* (1999, esp. Chapter 2). He provides a diagram of six different types of conflict intervention methods, from "arbitration" (which is highly dependent on third-party involvement) to a diminishing role of third-party involvement in "arbitration—negotiation—mediation—problem-solving—facilitation—conciliation" (18). Within this scheme, my work with groups in conflict would fit into the last two categories, "facilitation" and "conciliation." See also the discussion of "third party" and "track II diplomacy" in light of restorative justice approaches in Mica Estrada-Hollenbeck, "The Attainment of Justice through Restoration, Not Litigation: The Subjective Road to Reconciliation" (2001). Among others, Estrada-Hollenbeck discusses Herbert Kelman's "Problem Solving Workshops" as a case of track II diplomacy (77–79). Track II diplomacy generally refers to unofficial contacts between non-state actors in order to explore possible solutions to a conflict; those individuals are experts in their fields but do not have any official bargaining power. See, for example, Dalia Dassa Kaye, *Talking to the Enemy: Track Two Diplomacy in the Middle East and South Asia* (2007), and Hussein Agha, Shai Feldman, Ahma Khalidi, and Zeev Schiff, *Track-II Diplomacy: Lessons from the Middle East* (2004).

2. On political emotions, see Sara Ahmed, *The Cultural Politics of Emotion* (2004); Martha Nussbaum, *Political Emotions: Why Love Matters for Justice* (2013); and Johannes Lehmann, "Zorn, Hass, Wut: Zum affektpolitischen Problem der Identität" (2019), where he traces historical forms of resentment that have (re)emerged in Germany's current rise of populism, especially directed at refugees. For some examples of third-generation Germans preferring an intellectual approach to the legacy of the Holocaust, see Krondorfer *Remembrance and Reconciliation* (1995).

3. Jessica Benjamin, *Beyond Doer and Done To: Recognition Theory, Intersubjectivity and the Third* (2018, 65–70). Benjamin describes this scene extensively through the lens of (self) analysis. In a footnote, she also clarifies that this particular encounter was not the predominant response she got in Germany; she positively mentions the group of Jewish and German psychotherapists in Cologne, with whom I had worked on several

occasions (68; see my discussion of a two-hundred-year present in Chapter 2 and timelines in Chapter 8).

4. Fuchs, "German Subjectivity Three Generations after the End of World War Two" (2013, 133–134, 155; emphasis added).

5. Peter Titelman, "The Concept of the Triangle in Bowen Theory" (2008, 20). Ernst Abelin argues for the necessity of infants developing a triangular relationship, in "Die Theorie der frühkindlichen Triangulation" (1986). For family therapy, see Murray Bowen, *Family Therapy in Clinical Practice* (1985). See also Philip Guerin et al., *Working with Relationship Triangles* (1996).

6. While I use triangulation in the context of the larger efforts of trust-building in intergroup encounters, Mari Fitzduff suggests thinking of "triangular relationships" between conflicting groups in service of "building institutional trust" (in contrast to "personal interaction-based trust"). Fitzduff exemplifies this for the case of Northern Ireland, in "Lessons Learned on Trust Building in Northern Ireland" (2016, 42–43).

7. For the detrimental effects of competitive victimhood and of delegitimization, see Neta Oren and Daniel Bar-Tal, "The Detrimental Dynamics of Delegitimization in Intractable Conflicts" (2007), and Bar-Tal et al., "A Sense of Self-Perceived Collective Victimhood in Intractable Conflicts" (2009).

8. On victimization and delegitimization, see Daniel Bar-Tal, Lily Chernyak-Hai, Noa Schori, and Ayelet Gundar, "A Sense of Self-Perceived Collective Victimhood in Intractable Conflicts" (2009), and Neta Oren and Daniel Bar-Tal, "The Detrimental Dynamics of Delegitimization in Intractable Conflicts" (2007).

9. For a broader context, see Meir Litvak and Esther Webman, *From Empathy to Denial: Arab Responses to the Holocaust* (2009).

10. See Avner Dinur's chapter on the clash of identities in collective conflicts, "No Future without a Shared Ethos: Reconciling Palestinian and Israeli Identities" (2018). See also Herbert Kelman's reflections on identity changes, in "The Role of National Identity in Conflict Resolution" (2001). Looking at cost and priorities in protracted conflict zones, Kelman writes: "What made it *possible* to change [certain] priorities was often the discovery that accommodation of the other's identity need not destroy the core of the group's identity, and that a compromise solution to the conflict was therefore negotiable" (195; emphasis in original).

11. See also Hava Shechter and Gavriel Salomon, "Does Vicarious Experience of Suffering Affect Empathy for an Adversary?" (2005, 126).

12. Eugene Sensenig-Dabbous, "The Musa Dagh History Hike: Truth-Telling, Dialogue and Thanatourism" (2016).

13. See note 19 in Chapter 3.

14. On Polish-Jewish relations, see Michael Steinlauf, *Bondage to the Dead: Poland and the Memory of the Holocaust* (1997); Jacek Santorski and Co Agencja Wydawnicza, *Difficult Questions in Polish Jewish Dialogue: How Poles and Jews See Each Other* (2006); Dorota Glowacka and Joanna Zylinska, *Imaginary Neighbors: Mediating Polish-Jewish Relations after the Holocaust* (2007); and Janine Holc, *The Politics of Trauma and Memory Activism: Polish-Jewish Relations Today* (2018).

15. For the views on German history of young Germans of mixed-ethnic and migrant backgrounds, see Viola Georgi, *Entliehene Erinnerungen: Geschichtsbilder junger Migranten in Deutschland* (2003); for the task of Holocaust education in multicultural environments, see Bernd Fechler, Gottfried Kößler, and Till Liebertz-Groß, *"Erziehung nach Auschwitz" in der multikulturellen Gesellschaft* (2000).

16. For critical evaluations of organized Israeli-Jewish youth group visits to Auschwitz, see Jackie Feldman, *Above the Death Pits, Beneath the Flag: Youth Voyages to Poland and the Performance of Israeli National Identity* (2008), and ibid., "'It Is My Brothers Whom I Am Seeking': Israeli Youths' Pilgrimages to Poland of the Shoah" (1995). See also Oren Stier, "Lunch at Majdanek: The March of the Living as Contemporary Pilgrimage of Memory" (1995), and Shira Schnitzer, "The Mistakes of the March: The March of the Living and the Limits of a Holocaust-Based Jewish Identity" (1998). For a critical evaluation concerning German youth groups, see Jonathan Huener, "Antifas-

cist Pilgrimage and Rehabilitation at Auschwitz: The Political Tourism of *Aktion Sühnezeichen* and *Sozialistische Jugend"* (2001).

   17. Michael Rothberg, *Multidirectional Memory* (2009, 19).

# TEN

# The Art of Wit(h)nessing

Active witnessing is an essential component for processes that engender unsettling empathy. In previous chapters, active witnessing has come to our attention in multiple ways. It includes witnessing circles and fish-bowls where groups have the opportunity to eavesdrop on each other's conversations. It also plays a role in the creation and subsequent evalua-tion of living sculptures as well as in the amplification of an anguished voice; in these scenarios we rely on our imaginative sensibilities to attend to another person's doubts, pains, bitterness, contrition, or other affects. Also related to witnessing are the ethical issue of testimonial injustice (when empathetic listening fails) and triangulation dynamics wherein people are simultaneously witnesses and participants. I have also ad-dressed some of the limits of witnessing, such as overwrought, idealized, and vicarious identifications with victim communities; self-referential acts of witnessing within homogeneous groups; and the problematic fig-ure of the "compassionate witness" who is more concerned about making the victim (and himself) feel better than about structural injustice.

Perhaps a good way to distinguish between problematic and construc-tive acts of witnessing is to carefully assess whether they are grounded in passive or active attitudes. Whereas passive witnessing could be de-scribed as wishing to remain in the role of an external observer (and, hence, possibly become complicit in what is being witnessed), active wit-nessing would lead to a moral space where we become responsible for each other. When we become empathetic witnesses, our central reciprocal concern is the well-being of the other as we engage in relational practices of care.[1]

Empathetic witnessing is more than the recording of history. It is a welcoming of personal testimonies for the sake of enriching political analysis and historical research.[2] It practices attentive listening that does not instrumentalize the other but unsettles us. Empathetic witnessing is also an imaginative act that comes into play in the literary, visual, and performing arts.[3] It is to the latter issue that this chapter turns. I want to introduce the idea of witnessing through the arts as an act of *wit(h)nessing—as a kind of reciprocal and relational commitment to the other in which unsettling empathy is at home. Though we might want to chalk up "wit(h)nessing" as clever wordplay, it is meant to emphasize that witnessing must be "with" someone if it is to assume the relational quality that unsetting empathy requires. I trace this kind of wit(h)nessing in an artistic collaboration where people from different sides of a trau-matic past or ongoing conflict create something new together. The prod-uct of such a collaborative creation—whether a painting, sculpture, poem, or dance—becomes itself a witness of the dialogical engagement out of which it was born; and that product, in turn, invites an audience for yet another round of interaction.[4]

The living sculpture improvisations I have introduced in previous chapters are, arguably, akin to a deliberately created artistic object. In these improvisations, groups in conflict present a physical monument with and through their bodies to visualize a particular situation as part of their encounter. Certainly, these sculptures are visual representations of what people are ready to express nonverbally in a given conflict setting. The beauty of these sculptures rests in their temporary nature as a crea-tive expression. While these living sculptures can be photographed for the sake of documentation or memory, such visual evidence has little lasting effect or intrinsic aesthetic and artistic value. Living sculptures make sense in the environment in which they are created but remain largely inaccessible to those outside the particular setting of an intercul-tural encounter.

In this chapter, I do not focus on the creativity that emerges in reconci-liatory group processes but on an artistic collaboration with artist Karen Baldner. Together, Karen and I created objects that captured our work-ing-through process regarding our family and collective histories; our art objects were intended for public viewing and engagement.

## SECONDARY WITNESSING

Karen Baldner and I could be called *secondary witnesses, representing different sides of the cataclysmic events of the mid-twentieth century in Europe. Karen is a descendant of a persecuted Jewish German family with assimilated roots in Berlin; I am a descendant of an ethnic German family, with roots stretching from Transylvania to Moravia and East Prussia. Whereas Karen's extended family struggled against the ever-tightening restrictions, dispossession, and persecution of Nazi antisemitic policies in order to survive, members of my extended family negotiated degrees of complicity with a regime that eventually upended their own lives, losing their homes in the East as refugees and expellees at the end of the war. Karen and I are direct descendants of families affected by the Holocaust and World War II, but we also chose to become secondary witnesses. Literary theorist Geoffrey Hartman, who wondered whether the "term witness [can be] applied to others than the eyewitnesses," suggested that the term "secondary witness" can be extended to those in the "next generation . . . who previously would have been called, quite simply, intellectuals, scholars, or artists."

> The difference justifying the change in terms centers on what it means to transmit Holocaust history in the form of memory—a memory that seeks a memory, because it has recognized in itself a personal core that feels empty when in close proximity to a generation struggling with the burden of a great if catastrophic event. The blessing of having been born after that event does not of itself bring relief.[5]

In a similar vein, Froma Zeitlin, a classics scholar, has suggested the term "vicarious witness" to distinguish Holocaust testimonies of those who experienced the events directly (memoirs, diaries, chronicles, photographs, etc.) from those who "record, recall, re-vision and reenact a wide range of responses to that cataclysmic event." Whereas Holocaust testimonials "inhabit a haunted terrain of traumatized memory," she writes, the vicarious witness is someone who "cross[es] the threshold into forbidden zones." In these zones new strategies evolve to cope with the disaster, which "register the increasing distance of our age from what we still feel compelled to confront and remember."[6] To approach memories of a traumatized landscape through the arts as a post-Shoah and postwar generation implies to assume the role of vicarious witness.

The contemporary figure of the witness, as some critics have pointed out, is also a problematic figure. Being a witness could become a way of aestheticizing the tragedies of others. With the proliferation of witnesses as producers and consumers of artistic representations of calamities, it is tempting to claim for oneself a stance of moral witnessing while actually remaining at a safe distance. French anthropologist Didier Fassin, for example, worries about the political implication of "the multiplication of witness figures, from observer to survivor, from involved party to guarantor of the truth."[7] My artist friend Karen and I were aware of these (ethical) hazards when we started working together. As direct descendants by birth, we made, as adults, a deliberate choice to also become secondary or vicarious witnesses. Being a descendant implies an involuntary inheritance; becoming a secondary witness requires an intentional and reflective embrace of coping with a troubling past. As two people artistically re-visioning the memories and materials passed on to us, Karen and I tried to come to terms with our relationship in light of a traumatic past.[8]

Starting in 2002, Karen Baldner and I have worked together on creating objects about our German and Jewish family histories. We transformed cultural messages we had received from our familial and social networks into contemporary material representations. Karen and I, as descendants of a persecuted Jewish German family and a nonpersecuted German family, respectively, ventured into the haunted spaces left by the legacy of the Holocaust and World War II. We understood early on that rendering ourselves vulnerable in the face of the other is a promising way to create dialogue that would remain true to our quest of accounting for the past without having the past determine our friendship in the present. We collected, assembled, and arranged scraps of memory in response to revealing discomfiting details of family lore and history. A landscape of ruptured lives eventually began to unfold in front of our eyes, and each of us looked at this materialized vista through the lens of our cultural, gendered, and familial dispositions. Because of our differences, and because the geographical distance between our homes limited our face-to-face encounters, we went about our collaboration slowly. Over time, we created a respectable body of work that has received a modicum of public recognition through exhibitions at galleries and museums.[9]

Our body of work includes installations with typewriters and corroded metal-framed panels. Most of our objects, however, involve handmade paper and imprinted words: lithographs, prints, and artist books.[10] We transformed personal conversations about the fragility of traumatic memory into material objects available for public viewing; hence, we have sometimes called our art pieces *material witnesses. In quite literal ways, we mixed our dialogue into the wet pulp for papermaking. Once pressed and dried, the pulp became the parchment onto which we recorded voices from a fragmented past. Upon further cutting, arranging, layering, printing, lithographing, and framing, the parchment turned into a palimpsest of collected, faded, erased, and recombined memories. The used materials merged with the metaphoric, the personal with the historical, and the traumatic with the imagined. Familial idiosyncrasies merged with public remembrances. Metonymically, the pulp we used became our inherited legacy, paper parchment resembled our skin, and palimpsest-like installations mirrored anxieties that had been inscribed into the biographies and bodies of our families and ourselves.

Karen, who is a visual artist by profession, grew up in post-Shoah Germany and today resides in Bloomington, Indiana. In the tradition of bookmaking, Karen knows how to turn pulp into paper, how to print and etch, and how to wrap book covers in fine leather and plain felt. In contrast to me, she has the artist's patience to cut, fold, sew, glue, stitch, and press. Familiar with the art history of books and with binding techniques, she knows how to prepare the surface of paper, how to turn iron into rust, and how to scratch and corrode mirrors—all materials we used in our work. Karen also knows about lost homes and about the loss of trust and innocence. In Germany's interwar period, her maternal grand-parents owned the German Fischer Verlag, at the time one of the largest literary publishing houses in Germany. As assimilated Berlin Jews, they were an integral part of Germany's cultural life before Hitler's rise to power. Among others, they published Rainer Maria Rilke, Thomas Mann, Arthur Schnitzler, Franz Werfel, Hugo von Hofmannsthal, Hermann Hesse, and Alfred Döblin. In 1935, they managed to rescue part of their publishing house from the Nazi encroachment by resettling in Vienna. In 1938, they had to abandon their Austrian apartment overnight and es-cape to Stockholm. When Sweden became an inhospitable place, they fled again, this time to Moscow and from there with the Trans-Siberian Express to Wladiwostok, to Japan, to Santa Monica, to Connecticut.

What I brought to our project was my academic training, my love for writing and reading, my experience with facilitating intercultural en-counters, my imagination, and my joy in the creative process. I had no training required for book binding, papermaking, or printing, and I gen-erally have low tolerance for solving the technical hitches in the artistic process. But I thrive when opportunities free me to think and act creative-ly.

I met Karen accidentally in 1992. With a book on Holocaust art tucked under her arm, she exited the library of the college where we both were teaching. I stopped her, and we started a conversation—tentatively, hesi-tantly, cautiously. At the time, Karen did not want to talk about her grandparents. Her family biography seemed of little interest to her American environment. Her maternal grandparents, unlike most Jewish refugees, had decided to return to Germany after 1945 to gather and rebuild what was left of their publishing enterprise. Toward the end of their active and embattled lives, they retired and retreated to Italy. Their wounds of betrayal never healed. Both grandmother and grandfather wrote extensive autobiographies, testifying to their love of German cul-ture as well as to their lingering suspicion toward a nation that they had once called home.[11] In Karen's eyes, I was a descendant of those who, by collective belonging, had expelled and then alienated her grandparents from their *Heimat* (home nation). While I was inquisitive about Karen's family history, she was reticent in her responses. It took almost ten more years before we decided to embark on our collaborative art project.

Born in 1952 and 1959, respectively, Karen and I grew up in a world ruptured by the Holocaust and the war. In our childhood years, both of us had actually lived in the same city, in Frankfurt. We knew that the effects of a historical trauma make impossible any unencumbered, inno-cent meeting. To negotiate the sensitive nature of our encounters, we anchored our dialogue in the materiality of artistic objects. We unpeeled layers of family memories and cultural histories, then reassembled them and eventually displayed them publicly. Our objects were infused with tangible and touchable personal memories. Mirroring partial and incomplete truths, our material witnesses mediated, facilitated, and deepened our heart-to-heart conversations. Once placed into public environments, they were seen and touched by others, inviting audiences into the privacy of our haunted space.

Our art objects told nonlinear stories of our families of origin and of the accumulated layers of emotional and political baggage of generations: fragments of memories of conquest and exile, of forced flights and voluntary migration, of refugees and immigrants, of assimilation and defeat, of lost childhoods and interrupted lives, of new beginnings and unfinished business, of bodies violated and restored, of men and women, of Jews and Germans, of Karen and me. Unearthing old longings, we revived worn stories. We discovered anew the intimate other in our families. Often catching a glimpse of shadows only, we greeted the dead sitting at our tables. We deciphered handwritten testimonies on forgotten postcards, diaries, and letters that had been handed down to us. We recalled family utterances about Jews and about Germans in our respective families that left us with a visceral discomfort in the act of summoning them. We recalled resentment and love expressed in the familiarity and fragility of kinship. We mixed the contradictory richness of family lore into the wet pulp like precious spices and embedded it in sheets of paper like traces of fragrance.

Our objects included visual and verbal quotes from our family archives, sometimes with the approval of loved ones, at other times against their reticence. In the process, Karen and I became transparent to each other: beyond the moral emotions of shame, guilt, resentment, and recriminations. These feelings never completely evaporated, but they stopped dictating our aesthetic exploration. We juxtaposed memories like a palimpsest reaching back to the injuries of the past while pointing to the possibilities of the future.

Some of our "material witnesses" were crude iron frames that surrounded fragile, intimate revelations transposed on Plexiglas panels. Personal and collective memories were glued or etched on various surfaces, more as secret codes than historical explanations. Like wooden wings on a traditional triptych, these transparent panels swung open, squeaking in their rusted metal hinges and making visible family secrets scribbled onto their surface. We also created paper cast models of our hands, pinned them against a wall, with strings of handmade paper flowing out of the fingertips—the blood and ink of our lives. As if adding commentary to Talmudic pages, our marginalia examined past choices made by our families and communities. Emblazoned with words and quotes, these strings entangled and intertwined; they not only gave testimony to our previous conversations but also performed their own visual dialogue.

## AT-HOMENESS

Books are rooted in the German and the Jewish traditions, but they are also personally important to Karen and me. They were the livelihood of Karen's grandparents, and they are part of my livelihood as a scholar. Karen always liked to make pages from pulp; I always liked to put words onto those pages. She liked to bind books; I liked to write them. Books contain worlds: intimate notes and dogmatic declarations, prayers and business records, stories and prohibitions, memories and visions. They contain destructive ideologies and give testimony to suffering. You can close worlds by closing books. You can burn books. You can lock them away. You can enshrine them. You can hide messages in them or adorn them with marginal notes. You can erase words. You can turn pages into mirrors so that you may encounter yourself. Karen and I experimented with such possibilities, exploring the quality of different materials and searching for the style that befit best the stories we wanted to tell.

In homage to a particularly German binding style, we created medieval girdle books. These are pocket-size books that can be carried suspended from a waist belt. They are intimate and inconspicuous but add weight to the body. They are a little piece of "home" that people can take along wherever they go. We called our first girdle book *Heimat* (home/homeland). It was constructed from handmade paper, some the color of earth, others the color of ashes. We embedded in the paper scraps of European maps, and we hand-printed black letters on their surfaces. Lithographed negatives of family snapshots gilded dark surfaces, and strings of bright yellow, red, and black wire thread poured out of *Heimat*, uncontainable by the cover. The pages recalled conflicting bits of memories, citations, and ideas unfolding like a stream of consciousness. *Heimat* documented our uncertainties about our German homes of origin—an uneasiness that was echoed in the printed title on the leather cover. Referencing the German painter Albrecht Dürer, we printed his first name's signature "A" upside down in the word "HEIM $\forall$ T" on the cover. This inconspicuous distortion also alluded to the upside-down "B" in the phrase "ARBEIT MACHT FREI" [Work Liberates] of the infamous entrance gate to Auschwitz.

*Heimat* was our attempt to visualize the uneasiness that the term "Heimat/home" evokes in Germany. Rather than anchored in the comfort of lasting traditions and geography, our family stories were saturated with experiences of uprootedness: stories of exile, flight, broken trust, hiding, assimilation, war, expulsion, and emigration. The loss of home—and its companion, a nostalgic yearning for home—throbbed like a heartbeat under the surface of the present. Such loss cannot be recovered, but it unsettles the present, oscillating between resentment and bereavement, public regrets and private tears. "Home is memory of irretrievable childhood," writes postwar German novelist Bernhard Schlink. "It is a scent,

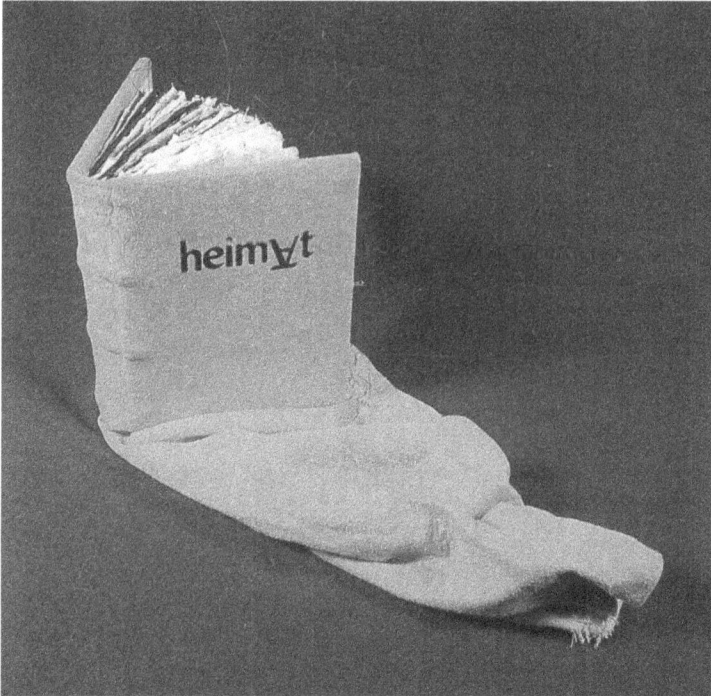

**Figure 10.1.   *Heimat* (2005). Baldner and Krondorfer. Girdle book. Various print
on handmade paper (5" x 4" x 1").**

the most fleeting of sensations."[12] Schlink's view is filled with poetic
sentimentalism. It is the sweet pain of nostalgic yearning not marred by
the bitterness of those who have been forcibly expelled as noncitizens.
His musings are quite different from the views of Jean Amery, a Holocaust survivor. "One must have a home in order not to need it," he
writes. "Traditional homesickness" is nothing but "comforting self-pity."
Like other survivors, Amery had to realize that the country (Germany) he
had once called home "had never been ours." What was left, Amery
laments, is the hurt that arises from a "combination of hatred for our
homeland and self-hatred."[13] Whereas I could easily be swayed by
Schlink's sentimentalism, Karen felt attached to Amery's disenchanting
realism. In the beginning of our project, Karen never referred to Germany
as her home and she would rarely speak German with me—as if she had
cut off any ties to the country of her childhood, a place she perceived as
unwelcoming.

For Karen, home was something that other people possessed, but not
her. Her assimilated German Jewish grandparents had been forced out of
Berlin. They lost their private home and their publishing house, their

citizenship and their trust. Karen, who was born to one of their daughters, did not experience the expulsion personally, but she grew up with a loss that had become her family's *unheimlicher* companion—the uncanny presence of not-at-homeness.[14]

Uncannily, the ideology of racial hatred Karen's parents and grandparents had experienced recurred as a physical assault in her own life. The inherited anguish of her family's severed national roots returned in the form of a bullet that sliced the flesh below Karen's rib cage and struck the wooden floor of her American home. The scars have remained visible, both in her body and in her house. The assailant—her then-husband—killed himself after the attack. Instantly, her house and her body had become unstable, violated places. Just as Karen's ancestors' at-homeness had been plundered and ransacked, her American home had been desecrated and her skin ripped open. The experience of many Jews collided with the experience of many women. Expelled from the metaphoric womb of home and assaulted by an intimate male other, Karen began to draw her flayed body in charcoal on torn paper: lifeless skin that lacked skeletal and muscular support; a limp integument devoid of any belonging.

Insofar as people generally feel at home in their bodies, skin demarcates the boundaries of home, the boundary between me and the other. Skin repels and absorbs, invites and rejects, tickles and burns, protects and gets torn. It is a permeable membrane that facilitates the exchange between inside and outside. Skin channels sensuality, yearned for at times, unwelcome at others. If trespassed and intruded on, that which ought to be truly ours turns into an alienating place. Instead of providing comfort, pleasure, and safety, the body-as-home turns into a storage room filled with anxiety. That Karen and I relied on handmade paper in many of our objects had to do with its quality that mirrors the characteristics of skin.

Years later, Karen became the victim of yet another assault, this time by a man unknown to her. He broke into her house and raged against her body. De-skinned. Flayed. Raw. Naked. In response, Karen drew bodies unprotected on ripped paper in order to restore herself—to restore what seemed like a chain of violations: from her maternal grandparents' flight from Berlin and her paternal grandfather's imprisonment in a Nazi forced labor camp to her ravaged American home and body.

When I met Karen for the first time as she exited the library—a book on Holocaust art tucked under her arm—the assaults were in the past, but the road to recovery was not yet completed. I invited her to meet and talk about our different backgrounds. But she declined. I had no idea, back then, of Karen's shattered sense of safety. My own body had never experienced the kind of violations she survived. To enter into the fragile place of wounded memories and explore accumulated layers of mistrust between Jews and Germans frightened her. Only many years later would Karen tell me about the sexual assault.

## WIT(H)NESSING

Years passed before we embarked on our collaborative project. We stayed in contact through email, occasional phone conversations, and rare visits. During this period, Karen's art focused on the female body to express the loss of physical integrity, while my scholarship shifted to questions on masculinity and religion. While I completed a book on the intersection of the religious imagination and the male body, Karen completed a series of drawings that rendered the body of the other—male and Christian—wounded and vulnerable. Her drawings seemed a perfect fit for the cover of my book, and so began our first collaboration. [15]

Naked and exposed, her drawings of Christ-like male bodies stretched across torn parchment in the pose of crucifixion, radiating pain and ecstasy. An eerie mood of violation and sensuality exuded from these broken bodies. Karen writes: "My new body of work followed on the heels of a cycle of drawings that looked at my own wounded body. In an attempt to widen my circle from my own gendered female wound, it made most sense to me to look at the wounded male body through the lens of an iconic body, such as the Christ figure." It was the serendipitous merging of her artistic and my scholarly explorations of male bodily vulnerability that finally started our dialogue. Our parallel interests in the artistic and historical renditions of the male and female body—pursued through distinct professional venues—influenced how we began exploring our Jewish and German identities. Sensitized to the vulnerability of gendered bodies, we queried our Jewish and German acculturated bodies. How did history write itself into and onto our skins? Were our bodies "memory texts"? Would we be able to decipher the codes of communal belonging chiseled into our very being? It took the perspective of the other to realize how much we were sculpted by the cultural ethos of our families and communities.

When Karen was ready to start a more sustained conversation, the medium of art as a third space became essential. A *third space, in the understanding of psychoanalyst Jessica Benjamin, is not a concrete space or thing that "creates another point of reference outside the dyad" but a "quality or experience of intersubjective relatedness." This relational and creative quality of thirdness accurately describes what Karen and I experienced through the medium of art. "In the process of creating thirdness," Benjamin writes, "we develop the intersubjective capacities for . . . co-creation." For Karen and me, it was a surrendering to a process out of which art emerged. Inasmuch as "surrender refers us to recognition,"

Benjamin states, thirdness is a "letting go of the self, and thus also implies the ability to take in the other's point of view or reality."[16]

Karen's readiness to embrace the relational possibility of "thirdness" coincided with an urgency she had never felt before to understand her family origins. With her grandparents dying (and having already lost both her mother and her brother at a younger age), Karen felt called to become the visual scribe for her family's legacy. She gently urged her reluctant father to talk about his survival during the war years in Berlin. In the terminology of Nazism, her father had been classified a *Halbjude*, a half Jew. His mother, from a renowned Jewish family, owners of a German department store chain, had married Max, a non-Jewish classical musician. Karen also realized that her own victimization was somehow linked to the ambience of victimhood in her childhood home. She writes: "My own wounded body fit right in with the familiar wounded 'family body.' It is this awareness that brought me to seriously immerse myself in my family history." Her tormented female body became entwined with the anguish of her Jewish German family origins. To that effect, she identified increasingly as a second-generation artist.

Karen writes:

> Somehow, through all the emotional haze of growing up in a trauma-infused home I wished nothing more than to be heard by another German, to tell the perpetrator about the outrage that I felt beneath the lines of my families' persecution story. When I revisited Björn's offer for an encounter, it was at a point when, similar to the rape healing, I was ready to integrate my identity as a Jew and a German into a larger post-Shoah context. I also gained confidence in the language of collaborating. Meanwhile, my understanding of Shoah history grew as I became more steeped in family history and identified as a member of the second generation after the Shoah. What attracted me to Björn was his reconciliation work, his personalized and subjective involvement with history, and ultimately his willingness to be vulnerable. I felt a strong need to go beyond verbal dialogue because it invariably felt like it allowed for escaping responsibility. The creative process, however, always leaves traces that make the creators accountable. In our collaboration, we had the courage to leave such traces.

When Karen asked me to reignite our dialogue beyond occasional conversations, I was hesitant. Having worked for many years on issues of post-Shoah relations, both in facilitated encounters and in my research, I was unsure of whether I wanted to enter yet another round of intensely personal exchanges. In my own search for family history, I had earlier reached a pivotal point when discovering a perplexing aspect of my father's life: at age seventeen, he had been stationed in a military unit in close proximity to the Jewish slave labor camp of Blechhammer. When Karen asked me to return to our family biographies, I was not ready to return to those stories.

This was the situation when Karen and I began our collaborative journey: she reached out at a moment when I was about to withdraw from soul-searching with respect to Jewish-German dialogue. The allure of collaborating through the arts, however, won out, and I said yes.

For five days, we retreated to a studio in Manhattan. During these days, we mostly talked, interrupted only by simple drawing exercises. We told each other our family histories in frank and detailed openness. We sketched our family trees on poster-size papers and pinned them to the wall. We added names and dates, drew arrows between family members, appended our emotional relations to them, and identified cultural topoi replicated in familial experiences. Without judgment, we listened to each other's memories and stories. Karen allowed herself to see my father as a teenager—beyond the *Wehrmacht* uniform he donned in 1943. She teared up when I showed her a postcard I had retrieved from the family archive. It had been written by my grandmother to my mother in January 1945, when my grandmother had stayed behind as the last person of the family at her home near Königsberg/Kaliningrad in East Prussia. Soviet forces had already encircled this region, and my grandmother did not expect to survive. To her seventeen-year-old daughter (my mother), whom she had sent off to find her own way westward, she penned the following words: "Facing the inevitable separation, I greet and I kiss you one last time. I submit to the inevitable and pray for your future destiny. Hour by hour, the situation grows worse, rescue is hopeless. In eternal love your loving mother."

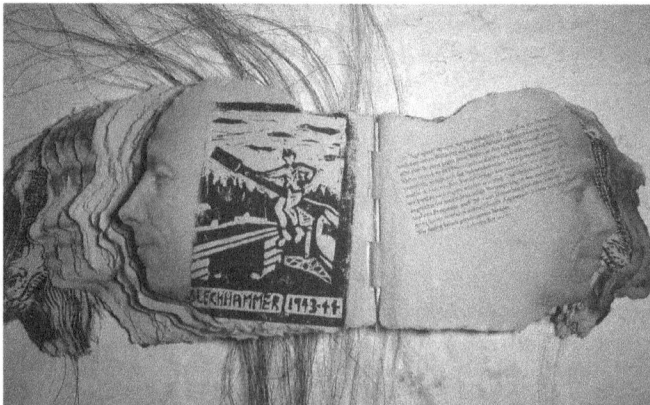

Figure 10.2. *pushmepullyou* (2007). Baldner and Krondorfer. Piano hinge binding with horse hair, linoleum cut, text transfer, digital print on handmade paper, unique book (7" x 11"x 1/4"). First exhibited in the show *Sündenbock* (scapegoat), Neue Synagoge, Berlin, 2007. Each individually designed page contains recollections of our cultural and familial legacies.

Both my mother and grandmother survived the chaotic flight in the winter of 1945—but they did not know this when my grandmother sent these words, which she must have believed to be her last testament. Karen remembers: "There were moments when I felt really touched, sometimes in tears, but happy tears. For example, when you read to me from materials that must have been difficult for you; yet you read them to me word for word." I felt similarly touched when Karen shared documents of her family archive. Her father, hitherto reticent to bring up the past, had handed her a journal of the war years in Berlin. I was honored to read parts of these handwritten pages in Karen's home in Bloomington during one of our many follow-up meetings.

In a small installation called "Obituaries/Nachrufe," we arranged family documents about our grandfathers, who had died before we were born. Presented as fragments of our unknown grandfathers, "Obituaries/ Nachrufe" had the feel of *objets trouvé*: haphazardly retrieved scraps from family archives, collected at the mercy of coincidence and caprice, and displayed as a mosaic of war mementos. My unknown maternal grandfather had been a *Wehrmacht* officer; he died of stomach cancer in 1941. As a young man he had fought in World War I and served in the army twenty years later in World War II. Karen's unknown paternal grandfather, Max, a musician, had married into a Jewish German family. He died in 1946 from the effects of his imprisonment in the forced labor camp of Leuna. He and his Jewish wife and children lived in what the Nazis called a mixed marriage. During the war, the family had found temporary refuge at the Silesian estate of Yorck von Wartenburg.[17] When von Wartenburg got involved in the failed July 20 plot to assassinate Hitler, the family returned to Berlin. Refusing to get a divorce from his Jewish wife, Max was sent to the Leuna concentration camp. He never recovered from his deteriorated health and died one year after liberation.

We told the story of the personalities of "the grandfathers we never knew" through obituary materials affixed, glued, and etched on and between Plexiglas panels. Snippets of letters of consolation from former comrades, public eulogies of friends, and various symbolic materials (fabric, hair, straw, sand) alluded to their personalities and deaths. Hinged to a center piece, the multiple Plexiglass panels could be manually opened and closed, layered on top of each other in different ways. Visitors could thus combine the panels at random, with two different sides of German society becoming transparent in surprising synchronicity, juxtaposition, and nonlinear chronology.

Another material witness was our typewriter installation. A set of three typewriters was arranged waist-high above the floor, as if floating in air. Three different stories emerged, one from each typewriter: one written by Karen, one by me, and one written together. Paper cast models of our hands, cut at the wrist, hovered over each typewriter like a spectral presence. Scraps of paper, rising from a messy heap of fabric, hairs, and strings on the floor, were fed into the typewriters, like memories winding their way upward, dangling freely in the air, inchoate, often illegible. Those loose memory strings came attached when pressed into the mechanics of the typewriter. There, bent to the rules of technology and grammar, the strings began to tell a story. "When I was a child, JUDE was a word that triggered extreme discomfort . . . " So began my typewriter. Karen's "Jewish" hands floating in midair typed: "I grew up among you but how could I call myself one of you . . . "

At times, our friendship seemed to evolve *because* of our Jewish and German identities; at other times, our collaboration moved us *beyond* this legacy. Our dialogue was not limited to an *ars memoria* but also expressed bonds of affection. We were not prisoners of the unresolved lives of our

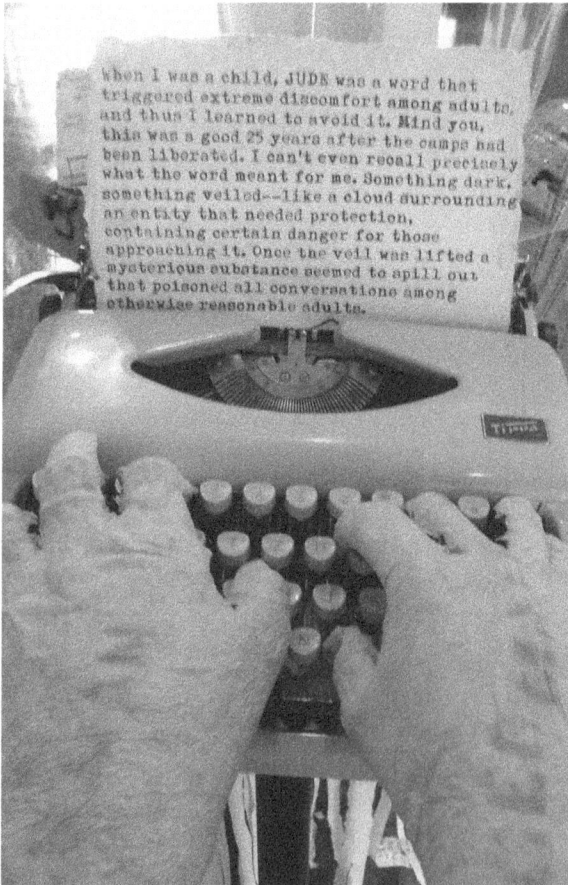

**Figure 10.3.** *with-drawing the line: Triptych* (2008). Baldner and Krondorfer. Installation with typewriters, handmade paper, fabric (approx. 50" x 50").

**Figure 10.4.** *with-drawing the line: Triptych* **(2008). Baldner and Krondorfer. Installation with typewriters, handmade paper, fabric (approx. 50" x 50").**

families of origin; we also lived auspiciously in the presence of our families of choice. Years later, I took my daughters to Karen's studio, where they learned bookmaking and printing from her during a summer art camp. And when either Karen or I went through a life crisis, we were able to offer each other long-distance support.

One of these moments of crisis coincided with a new idea about producing another artist book, this time not about *Heimat* but about *Wit(h)nessing*. To alleviate my distress, Karen wrote in a letter: "Since your life crisis began I have felt out of sync with our tenacious ideas for this book. Instead, what emerges for me is how much I like our title, *Wit(h)ness*. And how drawn I feel to the bottom line of what our project has always meant to me: that it is about us today, against the backdrop of the Shoah, and ultimately about two people who are sharing in each other's lives. I am wondering if we could make the book about what is happening to us right now. Our work has always been a kind of witnessing process and certainly a 'withness.' My point here is that there is a subtext: the need to move away from the Shoah and the struggle to find a shape for this urge. You may remember that I felt attracted to using your article on 'Forgetting'[18] as a springboard for our book last summer. There are profound life processes at work for each of us and we are actually

witnessing them to each other. The title 'wit(h)ness' is beautifully serendipitous and beckoning."

We created our first exemplar of *Wit(h)ness,* which queried the value
of remembering and forgetting. Bound in felt fabric, we chose again the
medieval girdle book format (later, we produced a numbered edition of
this work). Each of the white pages was embossed with uncolored letters.
Sunken into the texture of handmade cotton paper, our words left tangible evidence of the intangible. The few select phrases, at times almost
invisible like a spectral presence, were traceable with either fingers or
eyes. Each phrase was a response to what the other person wrote, but we
did not line them up chronologically. The words were meant to be evocative, not narrative: "remembrance is betrayal of the totality of memory";
"with hold"; "risking"; "undo what others failed to do"; "at home in a
place saturated with pain." On other pages, the negative space left by the
hollowed-out letters read, "white memory" or "folding noisy ghosts into
my life." Wit(h)nessing to each other, we circumambulated the *terra in-
cognita* of a trauma-laden, guilt-ridden, elusive past: the imprint of fading
postmemory, the white lies of remembrance, the white fire of etched
forgetfulness.[19]

At the time of creating and completing our wit(h)nessing project, we
did not know that another artist, also of the second generation, had already played around the neologism of "wit(h)nessing" in essays accompanying her work. The belated discovery of an unintended affinity with
another artist was, in its own ways, *unheimlich* (uncanny). The Israeli
artist Bracha Ettinger, daughter of a Holocaust survivor, had used the
same term in her oeuvre of artistic and theoretical testimony to the inef-
fable trauma of her parents' survival. Ettinger, who is also a feminist
theorist and psychoanalyst, employed the term to account for the ethical
act of bearing witness as a shared experience with others. Building upon
Levina's philosophy, her erased and reworked documentary photographs of the Holocaust aimed—in the words of one of her interpreters—
at the "intersubjective zone of closeness and togetherness, in which fractured subjects continuously engage."[20] Like our *Wit(h)nessing* girdle
book, in which white-on-white words testified to the ephemeral presence
of forgetting and remembering, Ettinger asserts that the task of an artist is
to release the "unforgettable memory of oblivion."[21] Humanities scholar
Dorota Glowacka writes about Ettinger's artistic-philosophical work:
"The connectivity occurs in the movement toward the threshold of the
visible, opening up the possibility of 'com-passionate wit(h)nessing.'" A
space "of bearing witness . . . opens up when the gaze is traumatized"
and when it is "shared and experienced together with others." It was not
until Karen and I had completed the first exemplar of *Wit(h)ness* that my
colleague Glowacka made me aware of the overlap and semblance. Despite the very different style and materials of Ettinger's art, the intellectual affinity was undeniable. "For Ettinger," Glowacka writes, "the skin-

parchment is first and foremost the site of contact, vulnerability and sharing; of sensuousness and touch."[22] Karen and I relied so heavily on handmade paper—our skin parchment—because of its expressive, vulnerable quality. Wit(h)nessing was—in an eerie parallel to Ettinger's ideas—our way to express through the arts the capacity of empathy to bring together affect and critical awareness. It is an "empathy," art theorist Jill Bennett writes, "grounded not in affinity . . . but on a *feeling for* another that entails an encounter with something irreducible and different, often inaccessible."[23]

## MATERIAL WITNESS

Our choice of material—handmade paper, fabric, leather, horsehair, felt, Plexiglas, plastic, twine, colored wire threads, mirrors, rusted steel—had to do with how it felt to touch it and also its evocative power. We wanted to blend contemporary sensibilities with cultural histories. At times, we used coarse materials, like steel, in deliberate contrast to the fragility of parchment paper. In "Who Am I in Your Presence/Wer bin ich in deiner Gegenwart," our first art object, we placed a scratched mirror into a crude, rusted steel frame with Plexiglas panels attached to hinges on each side. The movable panels outlined the profile of each of our faces. Surfacing from behind the scratched mirror, a map of Europe revealed locations of lost and abandoned homes related to our family histories.

Karen and I frequently worked with maps. We collected old atlases from which we removed pages with maps of Europe. On these cut-outs, we marked the birthplaces of parents, grandparents, and great-grandparents. Mapping those places, we discovered, to our surprise, how often the geographies of our families overlapped. Connecting the dots, we traced the migration patterns of our Jewish and German ancestors, leaving crisscrossing lines on the European landscape like a spider web. Despite the many losses of homes—from Transylvania to East Prussia, from Moravia to Berlin—we sensed something like *Heimat* when immersing ourselves in geographies. The pockmarked landscape became a staging ground for our postmemories. We traced the silhouettes of our faces as if tracing topographical patterns and layered them on top of maps attached to transparent Plexiglass panels, framed by the unforgiven steel of a violent past.

The choice of materials occasionally challenged our different sense of aesthetics. Those likes and dislikes, we discovered, had gender implications. "Some materials are beyond my physical realm as a woman, a short woman for that," Karen states.

> I would not gravitate toward rusted steel, mirrors, even wood and Plexiglass, let alone a combination of these. Not to mention packing, crating, and shipping such materials all over the country and abroad. I

*Chapter 10*

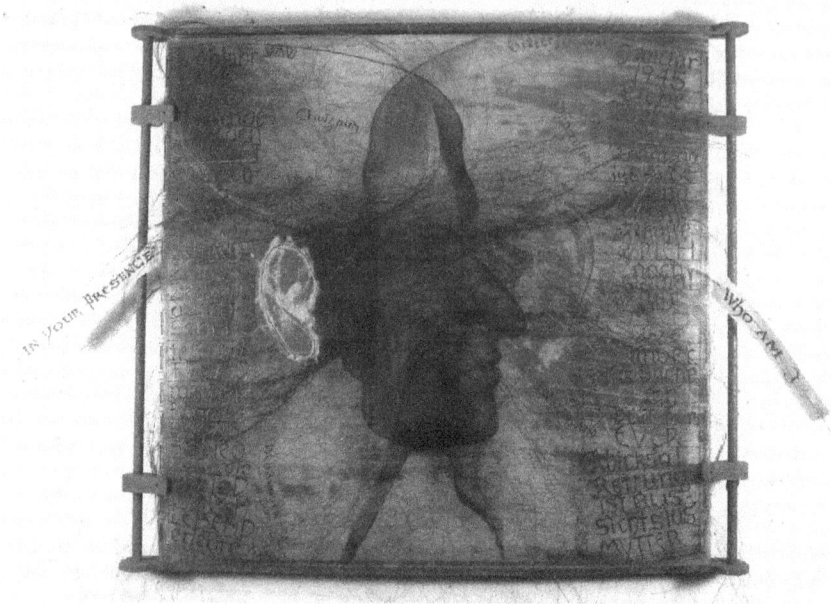

**Figure 10.5.** *Who Am I in Your Presence / Wer Bin Ich in Deiner Gegenwart* (2004). Baldner and Krondorfer. Wall-mounted, iron-framed, Plexiglas panels (20" x 72" x 20").

had to force myself to familiarize myself with lifting, cutting, welding, and sandblasting metal. I had to learn about table saws, varieties of blades, specialty glues. I had to befriend the workshops that dealt with metal fabrication and solicit help from a world that I found was mostly dominated by men. In the end I was grateful for having learned a lot about a new language of materials and the particular synergy of matter that has become our signature vocabulary. Because of our joint work I have become more sensitized to the material choices in my own work as being feminine. I have sometimes felt myself internally chuckling when Björn came up with something I would never think about. His choices felt particularly masculine, which I enjoyed as they would surprise me. I guess I didn't want to admit my delight as I was afraid it would make him—creatively—self-conscious. His idea about steel frames is a case in point. I really liked the idea, but steel continues to be foreign to me. In the end it is part of the process of listening to each other.

Karen once asked me whether papermaking seemed foreign to me, as a man. It did not. Getting my hands wet in the pulp had been a way of actively partaking in the act of creation. Lacking the skills and technical know-how, I was otherwise largely sidelined in the actual labor with the material aspects of our work. If anything felt like a challenge to my masculine identity, it was the humbling realization of my inadequate technical skills.

Our use of particular materials drew inspiration from other artists. Although Karen and I refrained from making deliberate references to other second-generation artists, our dialogue over several years took place within contemporary aesthetic sensibilities. Our "material witnesses" were no islands, we discovered, when, for example, we learned of Bracha Ettinger's work. We were also inspired by the monumental oeuvre of the visual maestros of German *Vergangenheitsbewältigung* (coming to terms with the past) like Joseph Beuys, Gerhard Richter, and Anselm Kiefer.[24] Karen and I created our installations, like the floating typewriter triptych, on a far humbler scale, and other works contained echoes of people like Jean Amery, Paul Celan, Shimon Attie, Christian Boltanski, Ruth Liberman, Kara Walker, and Rachel Whiteread—each of them struggling in their own ways with the presence of absence.[25]

The visual language we learned to speak via our "material witnesses" eventually changed something else in our wit(h)nessing encounter. For a long time, Karen found it difficult to speak German with me, even though this is the language she learned in her childhood and in school. I had once confided to her that I felt a familiarity between us because of our common German roots, but she balked at the idea and insisted on difference, not sameness. Her response puzzled me, for I truly felt that— around her, while surrounded by Americans—I was in the presence of a fellow German, who, like me, happened to live in the United States. Karen wrote in a response letter,

> My relatives were ever vigilant towards the "German other," paranoid about being lashed out against, prepared to be victimized yet again, scrutinizing almost everyone around us. When you led me into German colloquialisms (and I allowed myself to be led into them) I simultaneously hated and enjoyed the language. In one of the pages of our *Heimat* book, I wrote that you are re-teaching me the German language, and you answered that my admission is painfully embarrassing to you. Yet, for me a huge hurdle was crossed in this interaction.

We changed over time. Karen allowed herself to indulge in longings for German culture while I adopted U.S. citizenship. We became comfortable conversing in German and English indiscriminately, often switching languages in midsentence. But we agonized over the use of language in our art. What language should we speak? Since blending image and text was important to our work, we ended up injecting and inserting words in our German mother tongue and adopted English language. At the risk of estranging an audience unfamiliar with German, the added layers of foreign words looked like the patina of old photographs. Ultimately, our material witnesses—the traces of our *ars memoria*—were meant for transformation, not documentation.

## INTERSTICES OF TIME

Our separate memories, which morphed into visually unified pieces, remain open to interpretation and inspiration. In our art we blended what philosopher Avishai Margalit isolates as two distinct modes of memory: a "common memory [that] aggregates the memories of all those people who remember a certain episode," and a "shared memory [that] integrates different perspectives" and "requires communication." A shared memory does not erase differences but engages them creatively.[26] It keeps differences in the unsettling place of empathic witnessing where they don't merge into an indistinguishable whole but hold an edgy but creative tension of irreducibility.

Karen and I had taken the risk of listening to each other and moving beyond inherited roles of descendants of victims and perpetrators. There was no longer a fixed and predetermined position from which to speak. When our completed "material witnesses" stared back at us like mirrors, they prompted us to wonder whether we had accomplished the level of honesty and integrity we were striving for. We do not know for certain. But we did the best we could.

When a storm blows from a topography of hungry ghosts, it pushes us forward into a landscape of inquisitive spirits. The dead might be sitting at our table, but we do not have to continue eating from the same anxious memories. Acts of bearing wit(h)ness happen in the interstices of time where yesterday's harms and injustices are accounted for and where tomorrow will become what we imagine it to be. In the meantime, our wit(h)nessing in the here-and-now invites us to exchange cultural secrets; it welcomes personal memories, encourages vulnerabilities, and embraces today as an opportunity to make choices.

## NOTES

1. In general terms, a witness can be a third-party observer of a conflict not his own, or a person who lived through an ordeal and testifies to it afterward; see Didier Fassin, "The Humanitarian Politics of Testimony" (2008, 535). In the case of an external observer, the act of witnessing is mediated (and perhaps more passive), while in the latter case the act of testifying to one's own ordeal is based on one's actual experience (and hence more active). When I speak of "empathetic witnesses," the active-passive distinction I am drawing is broader and presumes making choices. For example, a witness as a third-party observer can decide to maintain his passive distance to an event or to get actively involved; in the latter case, a door is opened to the possibility of unsettling empathy. Regarding empathetic witnessing, see also Susannah Radstone's cautionary remarks in "Social Bonds and Psychical Order: Testimonies" (2001). Radstone suggests looking at the "darker side" of witnessing since the "position of witness . . . can exceed an empathic identification with victimhood to include identifications with other positions," such as "perpetration." She proposes a positioning of

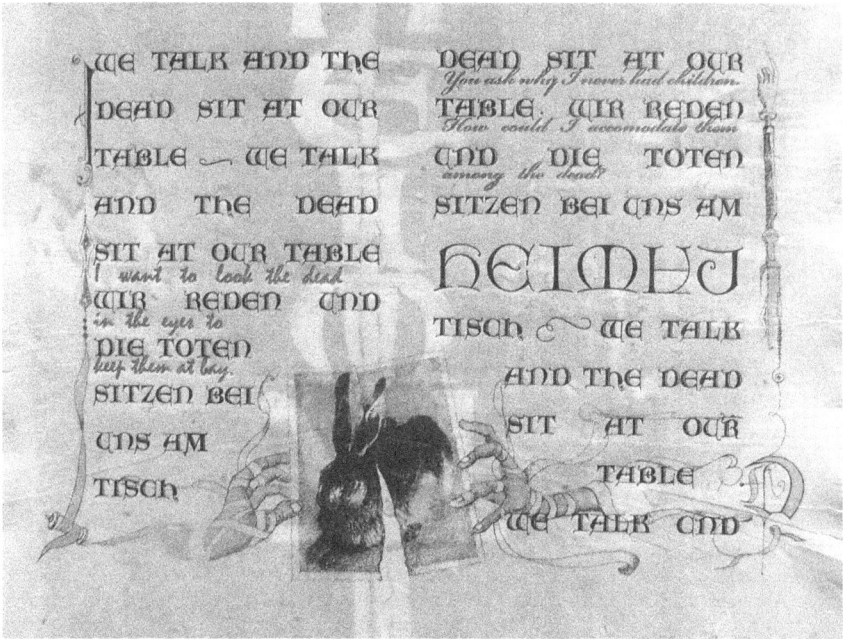

**Figure 10.6.** *Ghosts* (2010). Baldner and Krondorfer (40" x 18" x 24"). Mixed media print in handmade paper with text stencil. Edition.

witnessing in the "grey zone" that "works against the grain of canonical testimonial work" (61, 75).

2. Annette Wieviorka, *The Era of Witness* (2006). For a discussion of Wieviorka's place in the changing landscape of Holocaust testimonials, see Dorota Glowacka, *Disappearing Traces: Holocaust Testimonial, Ethics, and Aesthetics* (2012).

3. See Jill Bennett, *Empathic Vision: Affect, Trauma, and Contemporary Art* (2005).

4. I have been involved in different kinds of artistic collaboration. This includes the performing arts in The Jewish-German Dance Theatre (1985–1989; see Introduction) and smaller projects like designing an image and poetry projection accompanying a performance of Donald McCullough's "Holocaust Cantata" by a college's chamber singers. I could also mention the collaboratively curated exhibit "Echoes of Loss: Artistic Responses to Trauma" (2018) with art historian Tara Kohn. Though we did not create art ourselves, we together envisioned, planned, and installed this exhibit on trauma with international artists; see Krondorfer and Kohn, *Echoes of Loss* (2018). In this chapter, I focus on the collaborative work with artist Karen Baldner.

5. Geoffrey Hartman, "The Humanities of Testimony" (2006, 258). The term "secondary witness" has primarily been used in the literature to discuss the effects of Holocaust memory on those born after the Holocaust; see Dominick LaCapra, *History and Memory* (1998, 40–42, 135–136). In some writings, the terms "second-generation witness" and "secondary witness" are conflated (see, for example, Michael Bernhard-Donals's imprecise use of "secondary witness," "second-generation witness," and "second-hand witness," all listed in the index of *Forgetful Memory* 2009). Strictly speaking, the children of Holocaust survivors are the second generation, whereas secondary witnesses do not need to have familial relation to the Holocaust or belong to a particular generation. The term "secondary witness" is, of course, not limited to the Holocaust and can refer to other historical traumas.

6. Froma Zeitlin, "The Vicarious Witness: Belated Memory and Authorial Presence in Recent Holocaust Literature" (1998, 5).

7. Didier Fassin, "The Humanitarian Politics of Testimony" (2008, 552). "The witness," Fassin writes, "has become a key political figure of our time," which can lead to "the polysemy and instability of the configuration of testimony" (552–553). Amos Goldberg voices criticism regarding the consumption of "Holocaust images [for] melodramatic pleasure" and contends that "the excessive voices of witnesses" have replaced the "ethical revolutionary functions" of a Holocaust witness with "an aesthetic one" ("The Cultural Construction of the Holocaust Witness as a Melodramatic Hero" 2016b, 270). For other critical views on secondary witnessing, see Gary Weissman, *Fantasies of Witnessing* (2004), and Ruth Franklin, *A Thousand Darknesses: Lies and Truth in Holocaust Fiction* (2011).

8. In line with Geoffrey Hartman's understanding, "secondary witnesses" deliberately adopt an empathetic relationship to a traumatic history not their own—as intellectuals or through the literary, visual, and musical arts. See Hartman, "The Humanities of Testimony" (2006). Also Jill Bennett, *Empathic Vision: Affect, Trauma, and Contemporary Art* (2005); Ernst Van Alphen, *Caught by History: Holocaust Effects in Contemporary Art, Literature and Theory* (1997); Dora Apel, *Memory Effects: The Holocaust and the Art of Secondary Witnessing* (2002); and Amy Wlodarski, *Musical Witness and Holocaust Representation* (2015).

9. Since 2004, our work has been exhibited in solo and group shows in numerous venues, including *The Jewish/German Dialogue Project* (JCC Indianapolis, 2014–2015); *Wounded Landscapes* (Northern Arizona University Art Museum, 2014); *Dialogue through the Arts* (Julio Fine Arts Gallery, Baltimore, Maryland, 2012); *Trifold* (Williamsburg Art & Historical Center, Brooklyn, NY, 2010); *remembering* (Herron School of Art & Design, Indianapolis, 2010); *Bookish* (Harrison Center for the Arts, Indianapolis, 2009); *Witnesses* (Center for Book Arts, New York, 2008); *Sündenbock* (Meshulash Exhibit, Neue Synagoge, Berlin, 2007); *book bodies* (Indy Art Museum, IN, 2007); *Conflict/Peace* (Columbia Art Center, MD, 2007); *Annual National Affiliate Show* (Soho 20 Chelsea, New York City, 2010, 2006, 2005); *Homeland/Heimaten* (DAI, Heidelberg, Germany, 2004); and *Monologues/Dialogues* (Arthur M. Glick Jewish Community Center Gallery, Indianapolis, Indiana, 2004). At the opening of our solo exhibit *pushmepullyou* at Mathers Museum (Indiana University, Bloomington, Indiana, 2008), a symposium of scholars discussed our work. It included art historian Lisa Saltzman as keynote speaker, followed by a panel with Susan Gubar, Alvin Rosenfeld, Edward Linenthal, and David Thelen.

10. Our work can be seen on Baldner's website, http://karenbaldner.com/the-jewishgerman-dialogue-project.html.

11. Gottfried Berman-Fischer, *Bedroht—Bewahrt: Weg eines Verlegers* (1971), and Brigitte B. Fischer, *Sie schrieben mir, oder was aus meinem Poesiealbum wurde* (1981).

12. Bernhard Schlink, *Heimat als Utopie* (2000, 25).

13. See Jean Amery's chapter, "How Much Home Does a Person Need?" in *At the Mind's Limits* (1980, 46, 50–51).

14. As has often been pointed out, the German word for "uncanny," un*heim*lich, contains the word "Heimat/home."

15. See the cover of Krondorfer's *Men's Bodies, Men's Gods: Male Identities in a (Post-) Christian Culture* (1996).

16. Jessica Benjamin, *Beyond Doer and Done To: Recognition Theory, Intersubjectivity and the Third* (2018, 23–24).

17. Yorck von Wartenburg was part of the inner circle of the July 20, 1944, plot to assassinate Hitler. He was a lawyer who served in the Nazi German government in Berlin but refused to join the NSDAP (Nazi Party). During World War II, he served in the Armed Forces High Command in Berlin and later joined the resistance of the Kreisau Circle. After the failed plot, he was arrested and executed in August 1944 in Berlin-Plötzensee.

18. Krondorfer, "Is Forgetting Reprehensible? Holocaust Remembrance and the Task of Oblivion" (2008a).

19. In the Jewish tradition, we find the saying that the Torah was written in "black fire upon white fire." Various interpretations of this enigmatic saying have been suggested, including that black fire forms the letters and words (the content), whereas white fire is the empty negative space between letters.

20. Dorota Glowacka, *Disappearing Traces: Holocaust Testimonial, Ethics, and Aesthetics* (2012, 184).

21. Bracha Ettinger, "Trauma and Beauty: Trans-Subjectivity in Art" (1999, 18), and ibid., "Wit(h)nessing Trauma and the Matrixial Gaze" (2001).

22. Glowacka, *Disappearing Traces* (2012, 187, 191).

23. Jill Bennett, *Empathic Vision* (2005, 10; emphasis in original).

24. On postwar German painting, see Lisa Saltzman, *Anselm Kiefer and Art after Auschwitz* (1999), and Matthew Biro, "Representation and Event: Anselm Kiefer, Joseph Beuys, and the Memory of the Holocaust" (2003). Also Astrid Schmetterling, "Archival Obsessions: Arnold Dreyblatt's Memory Work" (2007).

25. On poetic voices, see, for example, Susan Gubar, *Poetry after Auschwitz: Remembering What One Never Knows* (2003); on visual and conceptual artists, see Lisa Saltzman, *Making Memory Matter: Strategies of Remembrance in Contemporary Art* (2006); Dora Apel, *Memory Effects: The Holocaust and the Art of Secondary Witnessing* (2002); Stephen Feinstein, *Absence/Presence: The Artistic Memory of the Holocaust and Genocide* (1999); and Leslie Morris, "Berlin Elegies: Absence, Postmemory, and Art after Auschwitz" (2003).

26. Avishai Margalit, *The Ethics of Memory* (2002, 51). In contrast to Margalit, for whom a shared memory "calibrates the different perspectives . . . into one version" (51), I locate the importance of a shared memory in its dependence on communication, which requires continuous negotiations over the meaning of differences.

# Epilogue

Asking for the full potential of unsettling empathy to evolve and unfold in the agonizing spaces of adversarial relations is the opposite of filling those spaces with empty speech that is devoid of and divorced from the affective content of conflict. Unsettling empathy is as much an ethical vision as a practical path. It does not deny the realities of hatreds, but it imagines alternative pathways forward. We need to remind ourselves that hatred is no more real than empathy since hatreds are a manufactured reality. The difference is that hatreds are harmful and lethal, while empathy is repairing and life-affirming. Empathy can fail and err, and there will always be situations in which forms of compassion are inadequate and ineffective. But the same holds true for resorting to violence and hatred, since they fail to achieve their stated goals just as often, except that violence and hatred always leave a trail of tears, broken bones, and broken dreams. The choice is ours.

Intergroup encounters are like seeds for probing and inhabiting alternatives beyond *realpolitik*. An observer of reconciliatory processes put it this way: "One can, of course, question the relevance of such small-scale encounters and ask what difference a drop of well-meaning knowledge can make to an ocean of ignorance with a propensity to violence." But, he continues, this "question is just as difficult to dismiss as the trust-building intimacy [of intergroup encounters], which is an obvious contradiction of the public sphere, especially with fundamentally hostile groups."[1] There are no miracles in reconciliatory processes. What unsettling empathy offers is an ethical posture that confronts and engages the realities of harm and injustice while refusing to be determined by them. A growing number of scholars of international relations no longer shies away from claiming the importance of (moral) emotions in politics, suggesting, like Neta Crawford, that "empathy is essential for the development of deep, deliberate democracy."[2] In current times, we find ourselves at the precarious brink of abolishing politics understood as a commitment to regulate the well-being of all. A *realpolitik* devoid of any empathy would be a bleak future. This book argues for a different path.

Sometimes the transformative potential of unsettling empathy reveals itself only in small signs, such as the exchange of a brief gesture between a Palestinian young man from Ramallah, who had been spouting angry and politicized phrases for much of the time during an intercultural meeting, and an orthodox young woman from the suburbs of Tel Aviv, who had never met Palestinians before on a personal level. As these two young people were standing in line for lunch, they exchanged a friendly poke with their elbows and smiled at each other. If success were measured by standards of grand political solutions alone, such an exchange would be disappointing. What this little gesture captures, however, is an opening in a seemingly intractable situation. The little poke with the elbow (with no further words exchanged) was all that these two people were able to muster at that time. Amid cultivated mistrust and political hatred it signaled the possibility of a different symbolic order.

We have to seek out opportunities where we can cultivate different symbolic orders and practice caring responsiveness. Unsettling empathy is part of our responsiveness toward each other. To the degree that injustices, inequities, and injuries are unequally distributed, the posture of unsettling empathy makes, at times, firmer moral and political demands on people in positions of privilege and on nonmalevolent beneficiaries of past and present injustices. But unsettling empathy is not a unilateral movement; it is a recognition of our shared responsiveness to each other.

Walking a path of unsettling empathy does not promise salvation but embraces possibilities. It is grounded in the choice of engaging with the respective other with an openness that is marked but not controlled by the past; it is embedded in but not preordained by present conditions. Unsettling empathy cannot be commanded or enforced. What we can do, however, is create the right environments—those tender, anguished, and painstaking working-through processes—in which empathy unsettles us into responsibility toward each other.

## NOTES

1. Wolf Schmidt, "Peace Making by Storytelling" (2000, 16).
2. Neta Crawford, "Institutionalizing Passion in World Politics: Fear and Empathy" (2014, 549). See also Emma Hutchinson and Roland Bleiker, "Theorizing Emotions in World Politics" (2014), and Rose McDermott, "The Body Doesn't Lie: A Somatic Approach to the Study of Emotions in World Politics" (2014), and ibid., "New Directions for Experimental Work in International Relations" (2011, 514–515).

# Glossary

The glossary contains terms I deem essential when working with groups in conflict. The short descriptions below reflect how I employ them in this book. The list is divided into *Frames*, *Dynamics*, and *Approaches*, with terms listed in alphabetical order. References to other terms within the glossary are *italicized*.

## FRAMES

**cultural trauma**: I introduce cultural trauma to distinguish it from *historical trauma* and medical trauma. Cultural trauma theorists emphasize that it is the social environment that largely determines whether an event is experienced as traumatic. In protracted conflicts, the cause of trauma is not a sudden, blunt force threatening to disintegrate a person but collective and structural forms of violence. With regard to working with groups in conflict, in cultural trauma settings there is a less-developed ability to understand the situation through trauma for the people affected. Communities under chronic duress might not recognize their conditions as traumatic because not enough time may have passed between event and memory that the affected people can read it as such, or because a conflict has been going on for so long that it has taken on an air of normalcy, with the result that communities might underestimate the extent to which they have been shattered and fragmented.

**empathy**: Empathy is our imaginative ability to understand the experience of someone other than ourselves by entering into a relational process that is both affective and cognitive. It is an other-oriented perspective. Although rooted, located, and activated in the self, empathy is not about the self but about the other. See also *unsettling empathy*.

**historical trauma**: Historical trauma refers to events in the past that have left people, communities, or societies traumatized by the severity of harm inflicted on them. With regards to working with groups in conflict, the temporal distance to the past serves as a buffer that allows the conflicting parties to approach agonistic memories with greater emotional and political openness. In settings where historical trauma is the primary source of contentious social relations (in contrast to *cultural trauma* where conflicts are ongoing), there is generally a stronger willingness to set into motion efforts of restoration and repair. Nevertheless, the impact of his-

239

torical trauma reverberates across multiple generations (see *transmitted trauma*).

**memory objects**: Objects can be carriers of memory that have symbolic and real significance for social groups and across generations. Memory objects have a testimonial and numinous quality: they are preserved not for their material value or aesthetic beauty but because they hold an intangible and intrinsic value to a person, family, or community. They are artifacts that evoke reverence and awe, loss and hope. They hold emotional weight for those who own them. They are imbued with generational obligations (see *acts of obligation*) and are often passed on in families or find their way into museums or the public sphere.

**memory work**: Memory work—as opposed to memory itself, which can simply be the consumption and regurgitation of things in the past—refers to an active process of *working through* the past. Whereas memory remains largely uninterrogated, memory work is a deliberate and active process. Put differently, memory in and of itself is not a moral good, whereas memory work is cognizant of the interplay between the (traumatic) content of memories, the narrative form it takes to get communicated, and the sociopolitical context within which it gets a hearing. In short, it is a form of both critical and empathetic inquiry.

**reconciliatory processes**: I speak of reconciliatory processes (or practices) to indicate the open-endedness of such work. Reconciliation is the possibility to counteract the damage done to communities that have been literally and symbolically disfigured by widespread injustices and violence-induced harm. Processes that initiate reconciliatory possibilities are not prescriptive of a particular goal; rather, they embrace an active dynamic that propels former adversaries into newly defined relationships. Reconciliatory processes transcend the limitation of self-interested action by moving toward an other-directed care.

**social reconciliation**: Social reconciliation seeks to overcome adversity between and within communities by prioritizing human relationships over structural concerns (in contrast to political reconciliation, which prioritizes issues of structural interdependence over interpersonal relationships). Social reconciliation is frequently practiced on grassroots and communal levels, like intergroup dialogues and intercultural encounters. The incentive for participants is emotional release, *trust-building*, human connectedness, *acknowledgment*, and the ability to imagine alternatives to current conflicts and political stalemates.

**transmitted trauma**: Historical and cultural trauma theorists have recently been joined by epigenetic scientists to assume that trauma can be transmitted to other generations. I differentiate between intergenerational and transgenerational transmission, out of which different obligations and *generational delegations* might emerge. "Intergenerational" refers to traumatic patterns and memories transmitted within a family system, while "transgenerational" refers to traumatic patterns and memories transmitted across unified social identities, independent of personal family histories.

**unsettling empathy**: Based on the definition of *empathy* as an other-oriented perspective, unsettling empathy is an ethical posture toward the other that unsettles our assumptions about the world and that compels us to fully validate the existence of others as others and not as we wish them to be. It requires two elements: a willingness to be challenged by the other and the ability to embrace this challenge and turn it into a positive disposition.

## DYNAMICS

**acknowledgment**: People and communities want their suffering to be acknowledged, whether in the form of public recognition from official bodies or in interpersonal encounters. As a moral activity, acknowledgment gives voice and agency back to people who have been harmed and victimized. Acknowledgment is a crucial step toward restoring damaged relationships.

**acts of obligation**: This term raises awareness of the power of loyalty that people feel toward their families, communities, and nations, especially when they get challenged in intergroup encounters. When a sense of social belonging is questioned or threatened, people tend to demonstrate loyalty to family and community through acts of obligation. These can take the form of public acts (such as honoring a religious convention in the presence of others, even though it is of little importance otherwise) or impulsive acting out, especially when a discrepancy is felt between, on the one hand, emerging bonds of friendship with the other and, on the other, an allegiance to one's own community's messages of mistrust and animosity. Acts of obligation can be triggered in intercultural encounters due to subliminal *general delegations* of unfinished tasks.

**chosen trauma**: A chosen trauma (introduced by Vamik Volkan) refers to those historical events that a group collectively remembers as a time of having suffered extreme loss or national humiliation at the hands of an enemy. No group chooses to be victimized, but collectives (people under duress, communities under assault, defeated nations, etc.) come to agree on a tragic or harmful event in their past, which they grant the foundational status of a trauma. When working with groups in conflict, facilitators need to be aware that chosen traumas secure group cohesion; are dwelled upon in the spheres of politics, culture, and family; and can be passed on generationally (see *transmitted trauma*). Because chosen traumas are accepted as a reference point for understanding oneself within a collective, they can become stumbling blocks in *reconciliatory processes*.

**cultural intimacy**: Cultural intimacy refers to those moments when a group renders itself vulnerable in the presence of the other at the risk of being misinterpreted. It is a willingness not to self-censor social uncertainties or cultural embarrassments. The term is related to *cultural secrets* but differs from it in that it refers to moments of unguarded behavior rather than an unveiling of social rules that are usually hidden from view to outsiders.

**cultural secrets**: The sharing of cultural secrets in conflicted groups contributes to *trust-building*. Cultural secrets refer to interactions and agreements within a social group that remain hidden to outsiders unless they are let into a "secret." Groups in conflict are characterized by defensiveness and mistrust, frequently leading to repetitive references to *master narratives* or competitive retellings of injuries, memories, and injustices. To break these cycles, sharing cultural secrets allows people to eavesdrop on another group's internal uncertainties and contradictions; it helps in defying projections and counterprojections; it is related to *cultural intimacy*.

**generational delegation**: When a generation fails to resolve certain issues, it can delegate them to the next generation with the expectation that the new generation assumes the tasks and duties that come with those burdens. A generational delegation can thus turn into *acts of obligation* for subsequent generations. In intergroup encounters, generational delegations can become a source of conflict when people identified with events from the past not directly their own feel obliged to defend the validity of messages received from previous generations.

**haunting presence**: Occasionally, intensified *memory work* can move beyond the ordinary experience of linear time in the form of a haunting presence. A haunting presence describes the intrusion of traumatic memories or of memories that are unwelcome and unresolved. While "haunting" in psychosocial terms usually references psychoanalytic and therapeutic frames, a haunting presence can also refer to recalcitrant memories and buried histories in social and collective groups. A haunting presence can manifest itself as a "ghost" in intergroup encounters. These ghostly figurations make tangible unresolved memories and histories, and they can transmigrate across generations until they eventually fade away when an unresolved past is *worked through* individually and collectively. See also *mimetic enactment*.

**idealized identification**: This term relates to the possibility of compassion for another person by identifying with people different from oneself, usually in the context of real or imagined *power asymmetries*. In situations of sustained social conflict, idealized identification can go two ways: victimized or colonized people can idealize their aggressors and oppressors, or people in power and descendants of perpetrators can idealize victims. Especially for descendants of wrongdoers, it is tempting to not want to carry the weight of their ancestors' guilt and, instead, to identify with those who have been victimized. Idealized identification (like *vicarious identification*) blurs boundaries by trying to become the other, as opposed to *unsettling empathy* where boundaries are respected between self and other.

**large-group identification**: This term refers to the power that large-group identities exert on individuals. Whereas the term "identity" assumes a stable component of someone's social makeup, "identification" presumes that people are actively involved in constructing and maintaining their social and political identities. Whereas large-group identities provide social cohesion and a sense of belonging, the term "large-group identification" assigns agency and hence also responsibility to people. When working with groups in conflict, people need to be made aware of the extent to which they choose to embrace or distance themselves from collective identities.

**master narrative**: A master narrative is a story in and through which a collective (social, religious, national) recognizes and understands itself. A master narrative offers coherence to varied experiences of individual members belonging to a larger social group. Group cohesion and master narratives are tightly interwoven, which accounts for the fact that a master narrative can accommodate a wide-ranging multiplicity of individualized stories. What would otherwise remain a conglomeration of discreet and fragmented experiences, a master narrative presses into patterns, thus providing legitimacy to large-group experiences from which people derive truth and fundamental certainties about themselves. Because master narratives remove complexity and ambiguity from real-life experiences, when working with groups in conflict it is important to make people aware of the complexities in their own lives when sharing stories with each other (see also *storytelling*).

**mirroring effect**: This term refers to a dynamic that obstructs the emergence of *unsettling empathy*. A mirroring effect comes into play when people in intergroup encounters mistake their sharing of stories (of suffering) with genuine conversation. They (mis)use the other group as passive recipients for their perspectives—as a mirror, so to speak—and they expect the other to absorb and agree with their views. In such a unidirectional flow of sharing, a person or group replicates a self-contained rather than other-directed narrative, wherein a personal story remains caught in the trappings of a *master narrative*. This form of *storytelling* tends to remain caught in its own mirror image of the past, more invested in validating and legitimizing the in-group account of one's injurious past rather than seeking new relational possibilities and alternative pathways in the presence of the other.

**moral emotions**: When responding to or making sense of human-made disasters, people react emotionally. Such emotionality is—when it is not blocked by layers of mental and intellectual protectiveness—a natural sign to respond to people in distress. The term "moral emotion" further qualifies those instinctive responses insofar as it looks at a set of emotions that implicate a person morally. Moral emotions include embarrassment, guilt, shame, anger, disgust, and contempt, but also gratitude and pride. Moral emotions that emerge in intergroup encounters are difficult to process because they resonate deeply in people and render them *vulnerable*. Working constructively with moral emotions requires *safe spaces*.

**power asymmetry**: When working with groups in conflict, rarely do we encounter a situation where the conflicting parties are equal regarding their external conditions. Imbalances of political, economic, educational, or military power need to be recognized as a problem of power asymmetries. Critics of grassroots dialogue groups and *reconciliatory processes* argue that power asymmetries invalidate the effectiveness of microlevel *trust-building* and peace-building initiatives. Though such a metacritique is not without merits, most communities in distress are in conflict because of existing imbalances of power and privilege and because they experience inequities and injustices. It is within such unequal situations where working with groups in conflict often takes place and where acquiring a posture of *unsettling empathy* leads to a softening of entrenched positions. In other words, facilitating groups in conflict is almost by definition a commitment to *working through* the messiness of existing power imbalances.

**safe space**: When working with groups in conflict, the provision of safe spaces is essential. Safe spaces create opportunities to leave aside—at least temporarily—the visible and invisible chains that tie individuals to collective identities. It allows people to gain new perspectives by defusing *large-group identifications* and by loosening the affective ties to one's own *master narratives* and *chosen traumas*. The protective environment that needs to be provided in order for *unsettling empathy* to occur has to be an intentional space not determined by rules that communities impose on themselves. See also *third space*.

**secondary witness**: A secondary witness is not an eyewitness of an event but somebody who is or feels deeply connected to a cataclysmic event. It refers to people who choose to wrestle deeply with the implications of such events, often as artists, scholars, and intellectuals. Secondary witnessing might be performed by direct or affiliated descendants (see *transmitted trauma*), but it is always a choice (see also *wit(h)nessing*). Being a direct descendant (often called second or third generation) implies an involuntary inheritance, while becoming a secondary witness requires an intentional and reflective embrace of coping with a troubling past. The term "vicarious witness" largely overlaps with this description.

**testimonial injustice**: Testimonial injustice occurs when the voices of individuals and communities who have been harmed and victimized are not *acknowledged*. Such nonacknowledgment can occur in the form of being ignored, belittled, doubted, dismissed, discredited, legally challenged, and so forth. It can take the form of outright denial and malicious dismissal of victim perspectives, though this does not happen often in *reconciliatory processes*. More often, the testimonial injustice surfacing in intergroup encounters expresses itself in gestures of disregard and inattentiveness.

**third space**: A third space is a particular rendition of *safe spaces* in which people come together to explore their intersubjective relations and create something new together. It refers to Jessica Benjamin's concept of "thirdness," which describes less a tangible thing than a quality of experience. It engenders a relational and creative space for people in conflict.

**triangulation**: I appropriate this psychological term for the purpose of understanding the ever-shifting dynamics in trilateral group encounters. In psychology, triangulation refers to diagnosing and treating family systems that are marred by dysfunctional communication between three parties. In my work, I conceive of it as a dynamic that can disrupt rigid patterns of interaction between two sides in protracted conflicts. Rather than viewing triangulation as an indication of a dysfunctional system, I see it as a force that can unsettle repetitive cycles of accusations and counteraccusations, dislodge mechanisms of competitive victimhood, and mitigate reciprocal delegitimization attempts. In triangulation dynamics, there is no third-party mediator or observer; instead, all groups are fully involved in the thickness of interaction.

**trust-building**: Trust, one of the more fragile aspects of human relations, can easily be broken; once lost, it is hard to regain. To (re)build trust between current and former adversaries is of prime importance for processes of *social reconciliation*. On a fundamental level, reconciliation efforts aim at overcoming distrust and animosity and at (re)establishing trust in the wake of harm, tension, and alienation. Many approaches described in this book relate to transforming mistrust to trust. Without a modicum of trust, people under duress are thwarted from *risk-taking*, which is an essential step toward developing *unsettling empathy*.

**vicarious identification**: The term refers to people's desire to identify with a legacy that they themselves did not experience directly. Vicarious identification is an important element when working with groups in conflict because it opens up the possibility for understanding the perspective of someone other than oneself. It is a step toward *unsettling empathy* but falls short of it because vicarious identification blurs boundaries, whereas *empathy* respects boundaries. The term relates to *idealized identification*.

**wit(h)nessing**: The act of wit(h)nessing is a reciprocal and relational commitment to the other in which *unsettling empathy* is at home. The term emphasizes that witnessing must be "with" someone if it is to assume the relational quality that *empathy* requires (see also *secondary witness*). I apply this term to (artistic) collaborations where people from different sides of a traumatic past or ongoing conflict create something new together. It can also be described as an ethical act of bearing witness as a shared experience with others.

**working through**: The distinction between "working through" and "acting out" is essential when working with groups in conflict. Whereas an acting-out is an uninterrogated and sometimes impulsive reliving of the past in the present, a working-through is a practice in the present in which the past is brought into critical articulation. It includes the examination of the effects of history as well as attentiveness to political and *moral emotions* that accompany adversarial relations.

## APPROACHES

**amplification**: Amplification is a technique in which muted messages or emotions in an intergroup encounter are augmented in order to become heard and visible. Amplification can happen in various ways, such as lending one's voice to another person who is temporarily overwhelmed by painful memories or conflicting emotions, intensifying and repeating a particular physical gesture, or doubling/mirroring a person's particular demeanor. It is never meant to embarrass people but to help them realize a hidden code or message, to reconnect them to their feelings, or release them from mental and emotional paralysis.

**de-rolling**: This is an exercise that assists people to ground themselves in the here-and-now of who they are after they have taken risks (*risk-taking*) and rendered themselves *vulnerable* within a group setting. Participants who have volunteered for a particularly sensitive role-play or *mimetic enactment* or have (inadvertently) displayed unguarded emotions need to be released from these places of potential social embarrassment. I frequently employ de-rolling in a physical sense. For example, I might ask people to roll, literally, on the floor from one end of the room to the other (leaving something behind at the other end). Sometimes, the physicality of a movement is more effective than a verbal "permission" to step out of one's adopted role. See also *nonverbal communication*.

**direct intervention**: This is a means at the disposal of facilitators when groups begin to spin out of control in potentially detrimental ways. It describes situations when a more resolute intervention by facilitators is necessary. Direct interventions appear in many forms, such as stopping a process, stepping in when an individual needs protection, or articulating a discomfiting, hazardous, or embarrassing aspect (the elephant in the room) that none of the participants is willing to bring up publicly. Direct interventions are a calculated risk because they can frustrate or anger some group members, while they benefit the group process as a whole.

**direct statements**: To move groups from a cautious *incubation period* to a more *risk-taking* active process, a facilitator needs to get participants to respond to each other more directly. It is important for groups in conflict to move from making general statements to engaging each other with direct statements. Rather than speaking about "them," participants are encouraged to speak to each other directly. Rather than asking, for example, why "Germans" believe such and such or why "Mexican Americans" feel this or that way, a group needs to acquire sufficient trust to call on "Hildegard" or "Morissa" directly.

**fishbowl**: This is a technique in which a smaller number of people sits in an inner circle to talk about a given topic while a surrounding larger group eavesdrops on their conversation. The fishbowl exercise is particularly effective in large groups where discussions tend to lose focus. The fishbowls I conduct usually include a tap-in, tap-out option. If a person wants to join the conversation, he or she can tap a person in the circle on the shoulder and take this person's seat.

**incubation period**: We know from principles of group psychotherapy that groups pass through different formative stages, wherein the initial stage is characterized by hesitant participation. I call it the incubation period, in which people are generally guarded or fall back on habitual forms of communication such as giving mini-lectures instead of making *direct statements*. An incubation period usually lasts until people get irritated with each other or become impatient with the slow-moving process. An attentive facilitator will seize such a moment and move people to a place where they are ready and willing to explore new patterns of communication.

**living sculpture**: Living sculptures are a means of scenic improvisation in which *large-group identifications* are made visible through theme-centered and embodied presentations of a "monument." Living sculptures are an effective method of *nonverbal communication* to connect people to their deeply held assumptions and to make them realize discrepancies between cognitive and affective levels of knowing. In small groups, participants prepare a sculpture with their own bodies related to a given theme. Groups can think of these sculptures as monuments displayed in a public square. Preparation time is limited so as to preserve the improvisational spirit of this exercise. The living sculpture is eventually presented to the whole group, followed by a careful analytic probing of these sculptures by means of *amplification*, mirroring, replacement, intensification, vocalization of feelings, sound, or gestural adjustments.

**loaded words**: I often employ loaded words at various points of a *reconciliatory process*. Loaded words can intensify interactions or clarify convoluted debates. Here is one version of how it can be done: Every participant is handed a note card and asked to jot down a topic he or she deems too dangerous or explosive to casually bring up in conversation. Whatever they have in mind, they need to condense it to one or two words, with no explanation provided. These anonymous cards are placed face-down on the floor, mixed, then redistributed and read aloud in the group. This is usually followed by an opportunity to respond to and comment on what each participant heard. Eventually, a group may choose (see *topic selection*) to *work through* one or two of these "loaded word" cards.

**material witness**: Material witnesses are tangible objects that are the result of creative collaborations of people who find themselves in past and present adversarial relations. These objects are the product of processes that unfold in a *third space*. What makes material witnesses so effective is that a conflict becomes materialized. As a finished object it can stand on its own—independent of its creators. This materialized object is witness to the process of production and thus offers feedback or commentary to those who created it, possibly engendering further conversations. It also stands as a witness to a conflict now available for public viewing and engagement.

**mimetic enactment**: By mimetic enactment I refer to an intensified, intimate role-play in which a person embodies the persona of someone else, usually someone well known to the person, like a family member. Mimetically embodying someone else requires a level of imaginative investment that reaches beyond regular play-acting. It is an emptying out of one's own personality and allowing someone else's personality to temporarily inhabit one's body. See also *haunting presence*.

**nonverbal communication**: In my work with groups in conflict, I always use forms of communication that reach beyond dialogue, discussion, and conversation. Nonverbal communication includes creative, body-centered, and physical components such as *living sculptures*, role-play, movement, improvisations, constellations, or contemplative sessions. Since I want participants to challenge themselves and others on cognitive and affective levels, these nonverbal components are a core element of my facilitation. Nonverbal communication reaches behind and underneath the comforting familiarity of political banter and *master narratives*. It is a mode of exploration that challenges, changes, and transforms relationships.

**open forum**: An open forum refers to an unstructured, nonthematic talking session among participants. I usually offer several open forums during a workshop. Sitting in a circle, people can bring up any topic or issue they deem relevant at that moment. Different from a *reflection circle*, an open forum does not focus on a particular theme. There are various ways to conduct these forums: one can go around in a circle and give everyone a chance to say something before opening it up to a free-floating conversation; one can also encourage every person to speak—though not in any particular order—before zooming in on whatever caught the group's attention; or no structure is provided at all so that a group learns how to self-regulate.

**reflection circle**: Similar to an *open forum*, a reflection circle gives participants an opportunity to share something with the whole group. A reflection circle, however, is more directed. Participants are not allowed to respond to whatever other people share (thoughts, opinions, dreams, memories, feelings, etc.). A reflection circle usually happens during a day's opening or closing session.

**risk-taking**: If participants are unwilling to step outside of inherited and rehearsed conventions, intergroup encounters are bound to iterations rather than change. The willingness to take risks is an essential component of *unsettling empathy; nonverbal forms of communication* often pave the way to do so. Risk-taking and *trust-building* depend on each other. Taking risks can consist of letting go of part of one's emotional investment in *master narratives* or a readiness to share *cultural secrets* and moments of *cultural intimacy* with one's "enemies." For others, risk-taking might entail imagining oneself free of generational obligations or simply listening attentively to people whom one has shunned before.

**shared language**: Group processes in the mode of *social reconciliation* aim at changing patterns of communication away from habitual discourse and defensive postures of lecturing. As groups inch closer together, they develop a common vocabulary and rely on a shared reference system that, imperceptibly, bonds its members. The shared language that evolves in a particular setting would make little sense to outsiders; it also stands in contrast to public debates or external political contestations.

**storytelling**: Storytelling is part of the repertoire of *social reconciliation*. It relies heavily on personal honesty and interpersonal trustworthiness. Intergroup encounters that include reciprocal storytelling as an important component frequently opt for some degree of confidentiality. The incentive for participants is *acknowledgment* and human connectedness. Because of the persuasive and unifying force of cultural and national *master narratives*, facilitators must use caution when using individual storytelling when working with groups in conflict. As important as they are, individual stories cannot easily defy the mold within which they are cast by dominant narrative frames. In this sense, individual storytelling in situations of conflict is rarely innocent.

**symbolic object**: When working with groups in conflict, I am a minimalist when it comes to technology and materials. What I frequently use, though, are simple objects that are symbolically dense, polyvalent, and evocative, such as a simple key or a cardboard box. These objects (including *memory objects*) appear and reappear as a guide at various moments in the workshop. They have enough evocative power to function as a focal point or projection screen without dominating the process.

**timelines**: In this exercise groups create a visual presentation of historical events, usually as patterns on the floor with cards that contain dates/events. People relate to these dates/events by stepping onto these cards. By "stepping into time," they explore their intellectual and emotional investments in particular historical moments. This approach is valuable when facilitating multigenerational groups since specific historical events do not hold the same symbolic meaning for different generational cohorts. Timelines provide snapshots of a group's composition and their affective investments in history. They also offer opportunities for individuals to locate themselves biographically in political and national histories. When working with groups in conflict, timelines visually represent different understandings of time horizons.

**topic selection**: In open-ended processes, there is always the question of who sets the agenda and who chooses a particular topic to be addressed. If groups are given a lot of autonomy, it may take people hours of heated discussion before they agree on a topic. Or a facilitator (or facilitation team) predetermines and announces a topic to be addressed. The approach I use—and which I call "topic selection"—is an efficient way to give agency to the group about their topic choice. All participants are asked to write down on a large index card one (and only one!) topic that is most urgent at this moment. To preserve anonymity, each card is placed face-down on the floor, shuffled, and then spread across the floor. The cards are then turned over so that anyone can read them and discover the diversity of topics without being able to identify who has written them. To select among these topics, everyone walks around the index cards on the floor and, when ready, steps on a card of his or her choice. Several people can step on the same card. Any card with only a few votes will be removed. People whose card of choice is taken away join one of the remaining groups. When this is repeated three or four times, a clear majority for a specific topic card is usually found in less than ten minutes. It is a simple but effective way of making the group responsible for its choices. See also *loaded words*.

**two-hundred-year present**: Inspired by Elise Boulding's idea of a "two-hundred-year present," we can create family constellations that demonstrate a generational chain of physical touch. Although it seems, at first, that no individual life span can reach a two-hundred-year present of physical touch, it begins to make sense when we consider the birthdays of those who have touched us when we were born (grandparents) and those who we will touch before we die (grandchildren). The mechanics to set up a generational chain are simple: A volunteer agrees to show her family history, and she will stand in the center of a line representing herself at the current stage of life. As protagonist, she invites four additional people, each representing a parent and a grandparent, to stand on one side of her, and a child and grandchild to stand on the other side. A generational constellation thus becomes visible. As in the case of *living sculptures*, the *working-through* phase happens after the constellation is created. The family timeline will become the subject of careful analytic probing by the various means available to facilitators: *amplification*, mirroring, intensification, and so on.

**vulnerability**: To render oneself vulnerable is, like *risk-taking*, a vital component in processes geared toward *social reconciliation*. To take a step into vulnerability—to let go of protectiveness and defensiveness—is not easy for many people and is often determined by additional factors such as gender, professional status, or minority-majority relations. Without some degree of vulnerability, it would be difficult for *unsettling empathy* to transpire.

**witnessing circle**: Different from *open forums, reflection circles*, and *fishbowls*, a witnessing circle is a spatial constellation in which select members of one group enter into a conversation while members of the other group become attentive listeners. The listeners are the active witnesses of what transpires in the inner circle, and they will later have a chance to share their observations and interact with the inner circle.

# Bibliography

Aarons, Victoria, and Alan L. Berger. 2016. *Third-Generation Holocaust Narratives: Memory in Memoir and Fiction*. Lanham, MD: Lexington Books.

Abelin, Ernst. 1986. "Die Theorie der frühkindlichen Triangulation: Von der Psychologie zur Psychoanalyse." In *Das Vaterbild in Kontinuität und Wandlung*, ed. Jochen Stork. Stuttgart: Fromann-Holzboog. Pp. 45–72.

Abraham, Nicolas. 1994. "Notes on the Phantom: A Complement to Freud's Metapsychology." In *The Shell and the Kernel: Renewals of Psychoanalysis*, eds. Nicolas Abraham and Maria Torok, trans. Nicholas Rand. Chicago: University of Chicago Press. Pp. 171–176.

Abu-Lughod, Lila. 2007. "Return to Half-Ruins: Memory, Postmemory, and Living History in Palestine." In *Nakba: Palestine, 1948, and the Claims of Memory*, ed. Lila Abu-Lughod and Ahmad Sa'di. New York: Columbia University Press. Pp. 77–104.

Abu-Lughod, Lila, and Ahmad Sa'di. 2007. "Introduction: The Claims of Memory." In *Nakba: Palestine, 1948, and the Claims of Memory*. Lila Abu-Lughod and Ahmad Sa'di. New York: Columbia University Press. Pp. 1–24.

Abu-Nimer, Mohammed. 1999. *Dialogue, Conflict Resolution, and Change: Arab-Jewish Encounters in Israel*. New York: SUNY Press.

———. (ed.). 2001a. *Reconciliation, Justice, and Coexistence: Theory & Practice*. Lanham, MD: Lexington Books.

———. 2001b. "Education for Coexistence in Israel: Potential and Challenges." In *Reconciliation, Justice, and Coexistence: Theory & Practice*, ed. Mohammed Abu-Nimer. Lanham, MD: Lexington Books. Pp. 235–254.

Agha, Hussein, Shai Feldman, Ahma Khalidi, and Zeev Schiff. 2004. *Track-II Diplomacy: Lessons from the Middle East*. Cambridge, MA: Belfer Center Studies in International Security (Harvard University).

Ahmed, Sara. 2004. *The Cultural Politics of Emotion*. New York: Routledge.

Alexander, Jeffrey. 2004. "Toward a Theory of Cultural Trauma." In *Cultural Trauma and Collective Identity*, eds. Jeffrey Alexander, Ron Eyerman, Bernard Giesen, Neil J. Smelser, and Piotr Sztompka. Berkeley: University of California Press. Pp. 1–30.

———. 2012. *Trauma: A Social Theory*. Cambridge, UK: Polity Press.

Alger, Jonathan, and Mark Piper. 2019. "Administration, Faculty, and the Hard Free-Speech Questions." *Academe: Magazine of the American Association of University Professors* 105/1 (Winter): 14–19.

Allen, James. 2000. *Without Sanctuary: Lynching Photography in America*. Santa Fe, NM: Twin Palms.

Allport, Gordon W. 1954. *The Nature of Prejudice*. Cambridge, MA: Addison-Wesley.

Alon, Ilai, and Daniel Bar-Tal (eds.). 2016. *The Role of Trust in Conflict Resolution: The Israeli-Palestinian Case and Beyond*. Cham, Switzerland: Springer International.

Al Ramiah, Ananthi, and Miles Hewstone. 2013. "Intergroup Contact as a Tool of Reducing, Resolving, and Preventing Conflict: Evidence, Limitations, and Potential." *American Psychologist* 68/7 (October): 527–542.

Améry, Jean. 1980. *At the Mind's Limits: Contemplations by a Survivor on Auschwitz and Its Realities*. Trans. Sidney and Stella Rosenfeld. Bloomington: Indiana University Press.

Amir, Dana. 2017. "Traumatic Miss and the Work of Mourning." *fort da* 23/2: 7–16.

Amstutz, Mark. 2005. *The Healing of Nations: The Promise and Limits of Political Forgiveness*. Lanham, MD: Rowman & Littlefield.

Andermahr, Sonya. 2015. "Decolonizing Trauma Studies: Trauma and Postcolonialism—Introduction." *Humanities* 4: 500–505.

Apel, Dora. 2002. *Memory Effects: The Holocaust and the Art of Secondary Witnessing.* New Brunswick, NJ: Rutgers University Press.

Apel, Dora, and Shawn Michelle Smith. 2008. *Lynching Photographs.* Oakland: University of California Press.

Arendt, Hannah. 1989. *The Human Condition.* Chicago: University of Chicago Press.

Aschheim, Steven. 2012. "The (Ambiguous) Political Economy of Empathy." In *At the Edges of Liberalism: Junctions of European, German, and Jewish History,* ed. Steven Aschheim. New York: Palgrave Macmillan. Pp. 133–142.

Assman, Aleida. 2011. *Cultural Memory and Western Civilization: Function, Media, Archives.* Trans. David Henry Wilson. Cambridge, UK: Cambridge University Press.

———. 2016. "Looking Away in Nazi Germany." In *Empathy and Its Limits,* eds. Aleida Assman and Ines Detmers. New York: Palgrave Macmillan. Pp. 128–149.

Assman, Aleida, and Ines Detmers. 2016. "Introduction." In *Empathy and Its Limits,* eds. Aleida Assman and Ines Detmers. New York: Palgrave Macmillan. Pp. 1–17.

Assman, Jan. 2011a. *Cultural Memory and Early Civilization: Writing, Remembrance, and Political Imagination.* Trans. David Henry Wilson. Cambridge, UK: Cambridge University Press.

———. 2011b. "Communicative and Cultural Memory." In *Cultural Memories: The Geographical Point of View,* eds. Peter Meusburger, Michael Heffernan, and Edgar Wunder. Dordrecht and Heidelberg: Springer. Pp. 15–28.

Auerbach, Yehudith. 2004. "The Role of Forgiveness in Reconciliation." In *From Conflict Resolution to Reconciliation,* ed. Yaacov Bar-Siman-Tov. New York: Oxford University Press. Pp. 149–175.

Augé, Marc. 2004. *Oblivion.* Trans. Marjolijn de Jager, with a Foreword by James E. Young. Minneapolis: University of Minnesota Press.

Baconi, Tareq. 2018. *Hamas Contained: The Rise and Pacification of Palestinian Resistance.* Stanford, CA: Stanford University Press.

Baeck, Leo. 1958. *Judaism and Christianity.* Philadelphia: Jewish Publication Society.

Barglow, Raymond. 1999. "The Angel of History: Walter Benjamin's Vision of Hope and Despair." *Tikkun Magazine* 14/1 (January/February): 50–55.

Bar-On, Dan. 1989. *Legacy of Silence: Encounters with Children of the Third Reich.* Cambridge, MA: Harvard University Press.

———. (ed.). 2000. *Bridging the Gap: Storytelling as a Way to Work through Political and Collective Hostilities.* Hamburg: Körber-Stiftung.

———. 2004. "Will the Parties Conciliate or Refuse? The Triangle of Jews, Germans, and Palestinians." In *From Conflict Resolution to Reconciliation,* ed. Yaacov Bar-Siman-Tov. New York: Oxford University Press. Pp. 239–253.

Bar-On, Dan, and Fatma Kassem. 2004. "Storytelling as a Way to Work through Intractable Conflicts: The German-Jewish Experience and Its Relevance to the Palestinian-Israeli Context." *Journal of Social Issues* 60/2: 289–306.

Bar-On, Mordechai. 2006. "Conflicting Narratives or Narratives of Conflict: Can the Zionist and Palestinian Narratives of the 1948 War Be Bridged?" In *Israeli and Palestinian Narratives of Conflict: History's Double Helix,* ed. Robert Rotberg. Bloomington: Indiana University Press. Pp. 142–173.

Baron-Cohen, Simon. 2011. *The Science of Evil: On Empathy and the Origins of Cruelty.* New York: Basic Books.

Bar-Tal, Daniel. 2007. "Sociopsychological Foundations of Intractable Conflicts." *American Behavioral Scientist* 50/11 (July): 1430–1453.

Bar-Tal, Daniel, and Dilka Antebi. 1992. "Siege Mentality in Israel." *International Journal of Intercultural Relations* 16/3 (June): 251–275.

Bar-Tal, Daniel, Lily Chernyak-Hai, Noa Schori, and Ayelet Gundar. 2009. "A Sense of Self-Perceived Collective Victimhood in Intractable Conflicts." *International Review of the Red Cross* 91/874 (June): 229–258.

Bar-Tal, Daniel, and Ilai Alon. 2016. "Sociopsychological Approach to Trust (or Distrust): Concluding Comments." In *The Role of Trust in Conflict Resolution: The Israeli-Palestinian Case and Beyond*, eds. Ilai Alon and Daniel Bar-Tal. Cham, Switzerland: Springer International. Pp. 311–334.

Bar-Tal, Daniel, Amiram Raviv, Paz Shapira, and Dennis Kahn. 2016. "Lay Psychology of Trust/Distrust and Beyond in the Context of an Intractable Conflict: The Case of Israeli Jews." In *The Role of Trust in Conflict Resolution: The Israeli-Palestinian Case and Beyond*, eds. Ilai Alon and Daniel Bar-Tal. Cham, Switzerland: Springer International. Pp. 197–213.

Bartov, Omer. 2019. "National Narratives of Suffering and Victimhood: Methods and Ethics of Telling the Past as Personal Political History." In *The Holocaust and the Nakba: A New Grammar of Trauma and History*, eds. Bashir Bashir and Amos Goldberg. New York: Columbia University Press. Pp. 187–205.

Bashir, Bashir, and Amos Goldberg. 2014. "Deliberating the Holocaust and the Nakba: Disruptive Empathy and Binationalism in Israel/Palestine." *Journal of Genocide Research* 16/1: 77–99.

———. (eds.). 2019. *The Holocaust and the Nakba: A New Grammar of Trauma and History*. New York: Columbia University Press.

Batson, Daniel C. 2009. "These Things Called Empathy: Eight Related but Distinct Phenomena." In *The Social Neuroscience of Empathy*, eds. Jean Decety and William Ickes. Cambridge, MA: MIT Press. Pp. 3–15.

Batson, Daniel C., and Adam Powell. 2003. "Altruism and Social Behavior." *Handbook of Psychology*, ed. Irving Weiner. Hoboken, NJ: Wiley & Sons. Pp. 463–484.

Beelitz, Thomas. 2013. "Pastoralpsychologisches Arbeiten im Land der Täter: Ein Zwischenbericht." *Wege zum Menschen* 65/3: 3–18.

Bekerman, Zvi. 2018. "Working towards Peace through Education: The Case of Israeli Jews and Palestinians." *Asian Journal of Peacebuilding* 6/1: 75–98.

Benjamin, Jessica. 2004. "Beyond Does and Done To: An Intersubjective View of Thirdness." *The Psychoanalytic Quarterly* 73/1: 5–46.

———. 2018. *Beyond Doer and Done To: Recognition Theory, Intersubjectivity and the Third*. London: Routledge.

Benjamin, Walter. 1969. "Theses on the Philosophy of History." In *Illuminations: Essays and Reflections*, ed. Hannah Arendt, trans. Harry Zohn. New York: Schocken Books. Pp. 196–209.

Bennett, Jill. 2005. *Empathic Vision: Affect, Trauma, and Contemporary Art*. Stanford, CA: Stanford University Press.

Berens, Claudia (ed.). 1996. *"Coming Home" from Trauma: The Next Generation, Muteness, and the Search for a Voice*. Hamburg: Hamburger Institut für Sozialforschung.

Berg, Nicolas. 2003. *Der Holocaust und die westdeutschen Historiker: Erforschung und Erinnerung*. Göttingen: Wallstein.

Berger, Alan, and Naomi Berger (eds.). 2001. *Second Generation Voices: Reflections by Children of Holocaust Survivors and Perpetrators*. Syracuse, NY: Syracuse University Press.

Bergmann, Martin, and Milton Jucovy (eds.). 1990. *Generations of the Holocaust*. New York: Columbia University Press.

Berlant, Lauren. 1999. "The Subject of True Feeling: Pain, Privacy, and Politics." In *Cultural Pluralism, Identity Politics, and the Law*, eds. Austin Sarat and Thomas Kearns. Ann Arbor: University of Michigan Press. Pp. 49–84.

Berliner, David. 2005. "The Abuses of Memory: Reflections on the Memory Boom in Anthropology." *Anthropological Quarterly* 78/1: 197–211.

Berlowitz, Shelley. 2016. "Unequal Equals: How Politics Can Block Empathy." In *Empathy and Its Limits*, eds. Aleida Assman and Ines Detmers. New York: Palgrave Macmillan. Pp. 38–51.

Berman-Fischer, Gottfried. 1971. *Bedroht – Bewahrt: Weg eines Verlegers*. Frankfurt: Fischer.

Bernhard-Donals, Michael. 2009. *Forgetful Memory: Representation and Remembrance in the Wake of the Holocaust*. Albany, NY: SUNY Press.

Bikmen, Nida, and Diane Sunar. 2013. "Difficult Dialogs: Majority Group Members' Willingness to Talk about Inequality with Different Minority Groups." *International Journal of Intercultural Relations* 37: 467–476.

Biro, Matthew. 2003. "Representation and Event: Anselm Kiefer, Joseph Beuys, and the Memory of the Holocaust." *The Yale Journal of Criticism* 16/1: 113–146.

Boulding, Elise. 1990. *Building a Global Civic Culture*. Syracuse, NY: Syracuse University Press.

Bowen, Murray. 1985. *Family Therapy in Clinical Practice*. New York: Jason Aronson.

Boyle, Deirde. 2009. "Traumatic Memory and Reenactment in Rithy Panh's *S-21: The Khmer Rouge Killing Machine 99*." *Framework: The Journal of Cinema and Media* 50/1–2 (Spring & Fall): 95–106.

Boys, Mary C. (ed.). 2005. *Seeing Judaism Anew: Christianity's Sacred Obligation*. Lanham, MD: Sheed & Ward.

Bradley, Ernestine. 2005. *The Way Home: A German Childhood, an American Life*. New York: Pantheon Books.

Braiterman, Zachary. 1998. *(God) After Auschwitz: Tradition and Change in Post-Holocaust Jewish Thought*. Princeton, NJ: Princeton University Press.

Braithwaite, John. 2014. "Traditional Justice." In *Restorative Justice, Reconciliation, and Peacebuilding*, eds. Jennifer Llewellyn and Daniel Philpott. New York: Oxford University Press. Pp. 214–239.

Breithaupt, Fritz. 2012. "A Three-Person Model of Empathy." *Emotion Review* 4/3 (January): 84–91.

———. 2016. "Empathy for Empathy's Sake: Aesthetics and Everyday Empathic Sadism." In *Empathy and Its Limits*, eds. Aleida Assman and Ines Detmers. New York: Palgrave Macmillan. Pp. 151–165.

Brown, Rupert, and John Turner. 1981. "Interpersonal and Intergroup Behavior." In *Intergroup Behaviour*, eds. John Turner and Howard Giles. Oxford: Basil Blackwell. Pp. 33–65.

Brudholm, Thomas. 2008. *Resentment's Virtue: Jean Amery and the Refusal to Forgive*. Philadelphia: Temple University Press.

Brunner, Claudia, and Uwe von Seltmann. 2004. *Schweigen die Täter, reden die Enkel*. Frankfurt: Büchergilde Gutenberg.

Bubandt, Nils, and Rane Willerslev. 2015. "The Dark Side of Empathy: Mimesis, Deception, and the Magic of Alterity." *Comparative Studies in Society and History* 57/1: 5–34.

Bukiet, Melvin Jules (ed.). 2002. *Nothing Makes You Free: Writing by Descendants of Jewish Holocaust Survivors*. New York: W. W. Norton.

Burg, Avraham. 2008. *The Holocaust Is Over: We Must Rise from Its Ashes*. New York: Palgrave Macmillan.

Carbonell, Bettina Messias. 2012. "The Afterlife of Lynching: Exhibitions and the Re-Composition of Human Suffering." In *Museum Studies: An Anthology of Contexts* (2nd ed.), ed. Bettina Messias Carbonell. Malden, MA: Blackwell. Pp. 347–356.

Caruth, Cathy. 1996. *Unclaimed Experience: Trauma, Narrative, and History*. Baltimore: Johns Hopkins University Press.

Chacour, Elias. 2013 (first published 1984). *Blood Brothers: The Dramatic Story of a Palestinian Christian Working for Peace in Israel*. Grand Rapids, MI: Baker Books.

Chaitin, Julia. 2011. *Peace-Building in Israel and Palestine: Social Psychology and Grassroots Initiatives*. New York: Palgrave Macmillan.

Chaitin, Julia, and Shoshana Steinberg. 2008. "'You Should Know Better': Expressions of Empathy and Disregard among Victims of Massive Social Trauma." *Journal of Aggression, Maltreatment & Trauma* 17/2: 197–226.

———. 2014. "'I Can Almost Remember It Now': Between Personal and Collective Memories of Massive Social Trauma." *Journal of Adult Development* 21/1 (March): 30–42.

Chakravarti, Sonali. 2014. *Sing the Rage: Listening to Anger after Mass Violence*. Chicago: University of Chicago Press.

Chandler, David. 2003. "Coming to Terms with the Terror and History of Pol Pot's Cambodia (1975–79)." In *Dilemmas of Reconciliation: Cases and Concepts*, eds. Carol Prager and Trudy Govier. Waterloo, ON: Wilfrid Laurier University Press. Pp. 307–326.

Cherish, Barbara. 2011. *The Auschwitz Kommandant: A Daughter's Search for the Father She Never Knew*. Stroud, UK: The History Press.

Clooney, Frank. 2001. "Food, the Guest and the *Taittiriya Upanishad*: Hospitality in the Hindu Traditions." In *Hosting the Stranger: Between Religions*, eds. Richard Kearney and James Taylor. New York: Continuum. Pp. 139–145.

Cobban, Helena. 2007. *Amnesty after Atrocity? Healing Nations after Genocide and War Crimes*. Boulder, CO: Paradigm.

Cohen, Raymond. 2004. "Apology and Reconciliation in International Relations." In *From Conflict Resolution to Reconciliation*, ed. Yaacov Bar-Siman-Tov. New York: Oxford University Press. Pp. 177–195.

Confino, Alon. 2012. *Foundational Pasts: The Holocaust as Historical Understanding*. New York: Cambridge University Press.

Conrad, Keziah. 2014. "Dwelling in the Place of Devastation: Transcendence and the Everyday in Recovery from Trauma." *Anthropological Theory* 14/1: 74–91.

Coplan, Amy. 2011. "Understanding Empathy: Its Features and Effects." In *Empathy: Philosophical and Psychological Perspectives*, eds. Amy Coplan and Peter Goldie. New York: Oxford University Press. Pp. 3–18.

Coplan, Amy, and Peter Goldie (eds.). 2011. *Empathy: Philosophical and Psychological Perspectives*. New York: Oxford University Press.

Corkalo, Dinka, Dean Adjdukovic, Harvey Weinstein, Eric Stover, Dinja Djipa, and Miklos Biro. 2004. "Neighbors Again? Intercommunal Relations after Ethnic Cleansing." In *My Neighbor, My Enemy: Justice and Community in the Aftermath of Mass Atrocity*, eds., Eric Stover and Harvey Weinstein. Cambridge, UK: Cambridge University Press. Pp. 143–161.

Cornille, Catherine. 2001. "Interreligious Hospitality and Its Limits." In *Hosting the Stranger: Between Religions*, eds. Richard Kearney and James Taylor. New York: Continuum. Pp. 35–43.

———. 2008. *The Impossibility of Interreligious Dialogue*. New York: Herder & Herder.

Cornille, Catherine, and Christopher Conway (eds.). 2010. *Interreligious Hermeneutics*. Eugene, OR: Wipf & Stock.

Craps, Stef. 2013. *Postcolonial Witnessing: Trauma Out of Bounds*. New York: Palgrave Macmillan.

Crawford, Neta. 2014. "Institutionalizing Passion in World Politics: Fear and Empathy." *International Theory* 6/3: 535–557.

Cunningham, Philip, Norbert Hofmann, and Joseph Sievers (eds.). 2007. *The Catholic Church and the Jewish People*. New York: Fordham University Press.

Danieli, Yael. 1988. "Confronting the Unimaginable: Psychotherapists' Reactions to Victims of the Holocaust." In *Human Adaptation to Extreme Stress*, eds. John P. Wilson, Zev Harel, and Boaz Kahana. New York: Plenum. Pp. 219–238.

———. (ed). 1998. *International Handbook of Multigenerational Legacies of Trauma*. New York: Kluwer Academic/Plenum.

Danieli, Yael, Fran Norris, and Brian Engdahl. 2017. "A Question of Who, Not If: Psychological Disorders in Children of Holocaust Survivors." *Psychological Trauma: Theory, Research, Practice, and Policy* 9: 98–106.

David, Lea. 2017. "Against Standardization of Memory." *Human Rights Quarterly* 39: 296–318.

Davis, Mark H. 2018. *Empathy: A Social Psychological Approach*. New York: Routledge.

Dean, Carolyn. 2004. *The Fragility of Empathy after the Holocaust*. Ithaca, NY: Cornell University Press.

Degruy, Joy. 2005. *Post Traumatic Slave Syndrome: America's Legacy of Enduring Injury and Healing*. Milwaukie, OR: Uptone Press.

De Gruchy, John. 2002. *Reconciliation: Restoring Justice*. Minneapolis: Fortress.

Denham, Aaron. 2008. "Rethinking Historical Trauma: Narratives of Resilience." *Transcultural Psychiatry* 45/3: 391–414.

Derrida, Jacques. 2001. "To Forgive: The Unforgivable and the Imprescriptible." In *Questioning God*, eds. John D. Caputo, Mark Dolley, and Michael Scanlon. Bloomington: Indiana University Press. Pp. 21–51.

De Vries, Hent, and Nils Schott (eds.). 2015. *Love and Forgiveness for a More Just World*. New York: Columbia University Press.

Dietrich, Donald. 1995. *God and Humanity after Auschwitz: Jewish-Christian Relations and Sanctioned Murder*. New Brunswick, NJ: Transaction.

Dinur, Avner. 2018. "No Future without a Shared Ethos: Reconciling Palestinian and Israeli Identities." In *Reconciliation in Global Context: Why It Is Needed and How It Works*, ed. Björn Krondorfer. Albany, NY: SUNY Press. Pp. 151–178.

Ebbinghaus, Angelika (ed.). 1996. *Opfer und Täterinnen: Frauenbiographien des Nationalsozialismus*. Hamburg: Fischer.

Edkins, Jenny. 2003. *Trauma and the Memory of Politics*. Cambridge, UK: Cambridge University Press.

———. 2006. "Remembering Relationality: Trauma Time and Politics." In *Memory, Trauma, and World Politics: Reflections on the Relationship between Past and Present*, ed. Duncan Bell. New York: Palgrave Macmillan. Pp. 95–115.

Edwards, Bruce. 1998. "History, Myth, and Mind." *Mind and Human Interaction* 9: 1–4.

Einhorn, Erin. 2008. *The Pages In Between: A Holocaust Legacy of Two Families, One Home*. New York: Touchstone Book.

Eisen, Robert. 2011. *The Peace and Violence of Judaism: From the Bible to Modern Zionism*. Oxford: Oxford University Press.

Emerick, Barrett. 2016. "Empathy and a Life of Moral Endeavor." *Hypatia* 31/1: 171–186.

Epstein, Helen. 1988. *Children of the Holocaust: Conversations with Sons and Daughters of Children of Survivors*. New York: Penguin.

———. 1997. *Where She Came From: A Daughter's Search for Her Mother's History*. Boston: Little, Brown.

Estrada-Hollenbeck, Mica. 2001. "The Attainment of Justice through Restoration, Not Litigation: The Subjective Road to Reconciliation." In *Reconciliation, Justice, and Coexistence: Theory & Practice*, ed. Mohammed Abu-Nimer. Lanham, MD: Lexington Books. Pp. 65–85.

Ettinger, Bracha. 1999. "Trauma and Beauty: Trans-Subjectivity in Art." *Paradoxa* 3: 15–23.

———. 2001. "'Wit(h)nessing Trauma and the Matrixial Gaze': From Phantasm to Trauma, from Phallic Structure to Matrixial Sphere." *Parallax* 7/4: 89–114.

Eyerman, Ron. 2001. *Cultural Trauma: Slavery and the Formation of African American Identity*. Cambridge, UK: Cambridge University Press.

Fanon, Frantz. 1967. *Black Skins, White Masks*. Trans. Charles Lam Markmann. New York: Grove Press.

Fassin, Didier. 2008. "The Humanitarian Politics of Testimony: Subjectification through Trauma in the Israeli-Palestinian Conflict." *Cultural Anthropology* 23/3: 531–588.

Fassin, Didier, and Richard Rechtman. 2009. *The Empire of Trauma: An Inquiry into the Condition of Victimhood*. Trans. Rachel Gomme. Princeton, NJ: Princeton University Press.

Fattah, Khaled, and K. M. Fierke. 2009. "A Clash of Emotions: The Politics of Humiliation and Political Violence in the Middle East." *European Journal of International Relations* 15/1: 67–93.

Faye, Esther. 2003. "Being Jewish after Auschwitz: Writing Modernity's Shame." *Australian Feminist Studies* 18/42: 245–259.

Fechler, Bernd, Gottfried Kößler, and Till Liebertz-Groß (eds.). 2000. *'Erziehung nach Auschwitz' in der multikulturellen Gesellschaft: Pädagogische und soziologische Annäherungen.* Weinheim and München: Juventa.

Feinstein, Stephen (ed.). 1999. *Absence/Presence: The Artistic Memory of the Holocaust and Genocide.* Exhibition catalogue, ed. and curated by Stephen Feinstein. Minneapolis: Katherina E. Nash Gallery, University of Minnesota.

Feldman, Jackie. 1995. "'It Is My Brothers Whom I Am Seeking': Israeli Youths' Pilgrimages to Poland of the Shoah." *Jewish Folklore and Ethnology Review* 17/1-2: 33–37.
———. 2008. *Above the Death Pits, Beneath the Flag: Youth Voyages to Poland and the Performance of Israeli National Identity.* New York: Berghahn.

Felman, Shoshana, and Dori Laub (eds.). 1992. *Testimony: Crises of Witnessing in Literature, Psychoanalysis, and History.* New York: Routledge.

Felstiner, John. 1986. "Paul Celan's Todesfuge." *Holocaust and Genocide Studies* 1/2: 249–264.

Ferguson, Heather. 2016. "Ghostly Intrusions: Unformulated Trauma and Its Transformation in the Therapeutic Dyad." In *Ghosts in the Consulting Room: Echoes of Trauma in Psychoanalysis*, eds. Adrienne Harris, Margery Kalb, and Susan Klebanoff. New York: Routledge. Pp. 36–51.

Ferreday, Debra, and Adi Kuntsman. 2011. "Haunted Futurities." *borderlands e-journal* 10/2: 1–14 (www.borderlands.net.au) accessed March 14, 2019.

Feshbach, Norma Deitch, and Seymour Feshbach. 2009. "Empathy and Education." In *The Social Neuroscience of Empathy*, eds. Jean Decity and William Ickes. Cambridge, MA: MIT Press. Pp. 87–90.

Fine, Ellen. 1988. "The Absent Memory: The Act of Writing in Post-Holocaust French Literature." In *Writing and the Holocaust*, ed. Berel Lang. New York: Holmes & Meier. Pp. 41–57.

Fischer, Brigitte B. 1981. *Sie schrieben mir, oder was aus meinem Poesiealbum wurde.* Munich: dtv.

Fischer, Nina. 2015. *Memory Work: The Second Generation.* New York: Palgrave Macmillan.

Fitzduff, Mari. 2016. "Lessons Learned on Trust Building in Northern Ireland." In *The Role of Trust in Conflict Resolution: The Israeli-Palestinian Case and Beyond*, eds. Ilai Alon and Daniel Bar-Tal. Cham, Switzerland: Springer International. Pp. 41–58.

Franklin, Ruth. 2011. *A Thousand Darknesses: Lies and Truth in Holocaust Fiction.* Oxford: Oxford University Press.

Frei, Norbert. 1999. *Vergangenheitspolitik: Die Anfänge der Bundesrepublik und die NS-Vergangenheit.* Munich: dtv.

Freud, Sigmund. 1914/1974. "Remembering, Repeating, and Working-Through." In *The Standard Edition of the Complete Psychological Works of Sigmund Freud.* London: Hogarth. Pp. 12: 145–156.
———. 1919/1974. "The Uncanny." In *The Standard Edition of the Complete Psychological Works of Sigmund Freud.* London: Hogarth. Pp. 217–252.

Fricker, Miranda. 2007. *Epistemic Injustice: Power and the Ethics of Knowing.* New York: Oxford University Press.

Frosh, Stephen. 2013. *Hauntings: Psychoanalysis and Ghostly Transmissions.* New York: Palgrave Macmillan.

Fuchs, Oliver (with Lou-Marie Krüger and Pumla Gogodo-Madikizela). 2013. "An Exploration of German Subjectivity: Three Generations after the End of World War Two." *The Humanistic Psychologist* 41: 133–158.

Gabriel, Barbara. 2004. "The Unbearable Strangeness of Being: Edgar Reitz's *Heimat* and the Ethics of Unheimlich." In *Postmodernism and the Ethical Subject*, eds. Barbara Gabriel and Suzan Ilcan. Montreal: McGill-Queen's University Press. Pp. 149–202.

Gahleitner, Silke, Marie-Luise Kindler, Luise Krebs, and Iris Wachsmuth (eds.). 2013. *Das ist einfach unsere Geschichte: Im Dialog mit der zweiten Generation nach dem Nationalsozialismus.* Gießen: Psychosozial-Verlag.

Gastfriend, Edward. 2000. *My Father's Testament: Memoir of a Jewish Teenager, 1938–1945.* Ed. with an Afterword by Björn Krondorfer. Philadelphia: Temple University Press.

Geary, Patrick. 1994. *Phantoms of Remembrance: Memory and Oblivion at the End of the First Millennium.* Princeton, NJ: Princeton University Press.

Geiger, Daniel. 2008. "The Dark Side of Narratives: Challenging the Epistemological Nature of Narrative Knowledge." *International Journal of Management Concepts and Philosophy* 3/1: 66–81.

Georgi, Viola. 2003. *Entliehene Erinnerungen: Geschichtsbilder junger Migranten in Deutschland.* Hamburg: Hamburger Edition.

Glowacka, Dorota. 2012. *Disappearing Traces: Holocaust Testimonial, Ethics, and Aesthetics.* Seattle: University of Washington Press.

Glowacka, Dorota, and Joanna Zylinska (eds.). 2007. *Imaginary Neighbors: Mediating Polish-Jewish Relations after the Holocaust.* Lincoln: University of Nebraska Press.

Gobodo-Madikizela, Pumla. 2004. *A Human Being Died That Night: A South African Woman Confronts the Legacy of Apartheid.* Boston: Houghton Mifflin Company.

———. 2008. "Transforming Trauma in the Aftermath of Gross Human Rights Abuses: Making Public Spaces Intimate." In *Social Psychology of Intergroup Reconciliation: From Violent Conflict to Peaceful Co-Existence*, eds. Arie Nadler, Thomas Malloy, and Jeffrey Fisher. London: Oxford. Pp. 57–76.

———. 2012. "Remembering the Past: Nostalgia, Traumatic Memory, and the Legacy of Apartheid." *Peace and Conflict: Journal of Peace Psychology* 18/3: 252–267.

———. 2015. "Psychological Repair: The Intersubjective Dialogue of Remorse and Forgiveness in the Aftermath of Gross Human Rights Violations." *Journal of the American Psychoanalytic Association (JAPA)* 63/6 (December): 1085–1123.

Gökçiğdem, Elif (ed.). 2016. *Fostering Empathy through Museums.* Lanham, MD: Rowman & Littlefield.

———. (ed.). 2019. *Designing for Empathy: Perspectives on the Museum Experience.* Lanham, MD: Rowman & Littlefield.

Goldberg, Amos. 2015. "Narrative, Testimony, and Trauma: The Nakba and the Holocaust in Elias Khoury's *Gate of the Sun*." *Interventions: International Journal of Postcolonial Studies* 18/3: 1–24.

———. 2016a. "Empathy, Ethics, and Politics in Holocaust Historiography." In *Empathy and Its Limits*, eds. Aleida Assman and Ines Detmers. New York: Palgrave Macmillan. Pp. 52–76.

———. 2016b. "The Cultural Construction of the Holocaust Witness as a Melodramatic Hero." In *Melodrama after the Tears: New Perspectives on the Politics of Victimhood*, eds. Scott Loren and Jörg Metelmann. Amsterdam: Amsterdam University Press. Pp. 263–280.

Gonzales-Day, Ken. 2006. *Lynching in the West: 1850–1935.* Durham, NC: Duke University Press.

Gordon, Avery. 1997. *Ghostly Matters: Haunting and the Sociological Imagination.* Minneapolis: University of Minnesota Press.

———. 2011. "Some Thoughts on Haunting and Futurity." *borderlands e-journal* 10/2: 1–21 (www.borderlands.net.au) accessed March 14, 2019.

Gordon, Mordechai. 2015. "Between Remembering and Forgetting." *Studies in Philosophy & Education* 34: 489–503.

Görg, Manfred, and Michael Langer (eds.). 1997. *Als Gott weinte: Theologie nach Auschwitz.* Regensburg: Friedrich Pustet.

Goulding, Cathlin. 2017. "Living with Ghosts, Living Otherwise: Pedagogies of Haunting in Post-Genocide Cambodia." In *(Re)Constructing Memory: Education, Identity, and Conflict*, eds. Michelle Bellino and James Williams. Rotterdam: Sense. Pp. 241–268.

Govier, Trudy. 2002. *Forgiveness and Revenge.* New York: Routledge.

———. 2003. "What Is Acknowledgement and Why Is It Important?" In *Dilemmas of Reconciliation: Cases and Concepts*, eds. Carol Prager and Trudy Govier. Waterloo, ON: Wilfrid Laurier University Press. Pp. 65–89.

Govier, Trudy, and Wilhelm Verwoerd. 2002a. "Trust and the Problem of National Reconciliation." *Philosophy of the Social Sciences* 32/2 (June): 178–205.

———. 2002b. "The Promise and Pitfalls of Apology." *Journal of Social Philosophy* 33 (Spring): 67–82.

Grand, Sue. 2000. *The Reproduction of Evil: A Clinical and Cultural Perspective*. Hillsdale, NJ: The Analytic Press.

Grimwood, Marita. 2007. *Holocaust Literature of the Second Generation*. New York: Palgrave Macmillan.

Grob, Leonard. 2008. "'Forgetting' the Holocaust: Ethical Dimensions of the Israeli-Palestinian Conflict." In *Anguished Hope: Holocaust Scholars Confront the Palestinian-Israeli Conflict*, eds. Leonard Grob and John K. Roth. Grand Rapids, MI: Eerdmans. Pp. 94–106.

Grubrich-Simitis, Ilse. 1984. "Vom Konkretismus zur Metaphorik: Gedanken zur psychoanalytischen Arbeit mit Nachkommen der Holocaust-Generation." *Psyche: Zeitschrift für Psychoanlyse und ihre Anwendungen* XXXVIII/1 (January): 1–28.

Grünberg, Kurt. 2000. "Zur Tradierung des Traumas der nationalsozialistischen Judenvernichtung." *Psyche: Zeitschrift für Psychoanlyse und ihre Anwendungen* LIV, 9/10 (September/October): 1002–1037.

Gubar, Susan. 2003. *Poetry after Auschwitz: Remembering What One Never Knows*. Bloomington: Indiana University Press.

Gubkin, Liora. 2007. *You Shall Tell Your Children: Holocaust Memory in American Passover Rituals*. New Brunswick, NJ: Rutgers University Press.

Gudmundsdottir, Gunnthorunn. 2017. *Representation of Forgetting in Life and Writing Fiction*. New York: Palgrave Macmillan.

Guerin, Philip, Thomas Fogarty, Leo Fay, and Judith Gilbert Kautto. 1996. *Working with Relationship Triangles*. New York: Guilford Press.

Haidt, Jonathan. 2003. "The Moral Emotions." In *Handbook of Affective Sciences*, eds. Richard Davidson, Klaus Scherer, and Hill Goldsmith. Oxford: Oxford University Press. Pp. 852–870.

Halbwachs, Maurice. 1992. *On Collective Memory*. Trans. Lewis Coeser. Chicago: University of Chicago Press.

Hall, Ian. 2008. "Avenging Evil: A Reconsideration." In *Confronting Evil in International Relations: Ethical Responses to Problems of Moral Agency*, ed. Renée Jeffrey. New York: Palgrave Macmillan. Pp. 151–178.

Halpern, Jodi, and Harvey M. Weinstein. 2004. "Rehumanizing the Other: Empathy and Reconciliation." *Human Rights Quarterly* 26: 561–583.

Hamber, Brandon. 2009. *Transforming Societies after Political Violence: Truth, Reconciliation, and Mental Health*. Cham/Heidelberg/New York: Springer.

Hamber, Brandon, and Elizabeth Gallagher (eds.). 2014. *Psychosocial Perspectives on Peacebuilding*. Cham/Heidelberg/New York: Springer.

Hammerich, Beata, Johannes Pfäfflin, Peter Pogany-Wnendt, Erda Siebert, and Bernd Sonntag. 2009. "A Reflection on the Dialogue Process between Second Generation Descendants of Perpetrators and of Holocaust Survivors in Germany." In *Memory, Narrative and Forgiveness: Perspectives on the Unfinished Journeys of the Past*, eds. Pumla Gobodo-Madikizela and Chris N. Van der Merwe. Newscastle, UK: Cambridge Scholars. Pp. 27–46.

Hardin, Russell. 2002. *Trust and Trustworthiness*. New York: Russell Sage.

Harris, Adrienne, Margery Kalb, and Susan Klebanoff. 2016. *Ghosts in the Consulting Room: Echoes of Trauma in Psychoanalysis*. New York: Routledge.

Harris, Lasana, and Susan Fiske. 2008. "Diminishing Vertical Distance: Power and Social Status as Barriers to Intergroup Reconciliation." In *The Social Psychology of Intergroup Reconciliation*, eds. Arie Nadler, Thomas Malloy, and Jeffrey Fisher. New York: Oxford University Press. Pp. 301–317.

Hartman, Geoffrey. 2006. "The Humanities of Testimony: An Introduction." *Poetics Today* 27/2 (June): 249–260.

Harvey, Elizabeth. 2003. *Women and the Nazi East: Agents and Witnesses of Germanization*. New Haven, CT: Yale University Press.

Harvey, Jean. 2007. "Moral Solidarity and Empathetic Understanding: The Moral Value and Scope of the Relationship." *Journal of Social Philosophy* 38/1: 22–37.

Hass, Aaron. 1995. *The Aftermath: Living with the Holocaust*. New York: Cambridge University Press.

Hatzfeld, Jean. 2009. *The Antelope's Strategy: Living in Rwanda after the Genocide*. Trans. Linda Coverdale. New York: Farrar, Straus and Giroux.

Havatzelet, Yahel, Ruth Kark, and Seth J. Frantzman. 2012. "Fabricating Palestinian History: Are the Negev Bedouin an Indigenous People?" *Middle East Quarterly* (Summer 2012): 3–14.

Hayner, Priscilla. 2002. *Unspeakable Truths: Facing the Challenge of Truth Commissions*. New York: Routledge.

Hedges, Chris. 2003. *War Is a Force that Gives Us Meaning*. New York: Anchor Books.

Herman, Judith Lewis. 1992. *Trauma and Recovery: The Aftermath of Violence—From Domestic Abuse to Political Terror*. New York: Basic.

Herzfeld, Michael. 2016. *Cultural Intimacy: Social Poetics and the Real Life of States, Societies and Institutions* (3rd edition). New York: Routledge.

Hewstone, Miles, and Rupert Brown (eds.). 1986a. *Contact and Conflict in Intergroup Encounters*. Oxford: Basil Blackwell.

Hewstone, Miles, and Rupert Brown. 1986b. "Contact Is Not Enough: An Intergroup Perspective on the 'Contact Hypothesis.'" In *Contact and Conflict in Intergroup Encounters*, eds. Miles Hewstone and Rupert Brown. Oxford: Basil Blackwell. Pp. 1–44.

Hewstone, Miles, and Ed Cairns. 2001. "Social Psychology and Intergroup Conflict." In *Ethnopolitical Warfare: Causes, Consequences, and Possible Solutions*, eds. Daniel Chiron and Martin Seligman. Washington, DC: American Psychological Association. Pp. 319–342.

Himmler, Katrin. 2005. *Die Brüder Himmler: Eine deutsche Familiengeschichte*. Frankfurt: Fischer.

Hirsch, Marianne. 1997. *Family Frames: Photography, Narrative, and Postmemory*. Cambridge, UK: Cambridge University Press.

———. 1998. "Past Lives: Postmemories in Exile." In *Exile and Creativity*, ed. Susan Rubin Suleiman. Durham, NC: Duke University Press. Pp. 418–446.

———. 2012. *The Generation of Postmemory: Writing and Visual Culture after the Holocaust*. New York: Columbia University Press.

Hoffman, Eva. 2002. *After Such Knowledge: Memory, History, and the Legacy of the Holocaust*. New York: Public Affairs.

Holc, Janine. 2018. *The Politics of Trauma and Memory Activism: Polish-Jewish Relations Today*. Cham, Switzerland: Palgrave Macmillan.

Hubbard, Amy. 2001. "Understanding Majority and Minority Participation in Interracial and Interethnic Dialogue." In *Reconciliation, Justice, and Coexistence: Theory & Practice*, ed. Mohammed Abu-Nimer. Lanham, MD: Lexington Books. Pp. 275–289.

Huener, Jonathan. 2001. "Antifascist Pilgrimage and Rehabilitation at Auschwitz: The Political Tourism of *Aktion Sühnezeichen* and *Sozialistische Jugend*." *German Studies Review* XXIV/3 (October): 513–532.

Humphries, Isabelle, and Laleh Khalili. 2007. "Gender and Nakba Memory." In *Nakba: Palestine, 1948, and the Claims of Memory*, eds. Lila Abu-Lughod and Ahmad Sa'di. New York: Columbia University Press. Pp. 207–227.

Hunt, Lynn. 2007. *Inventing Human Rights: A History*. New York, London: W. W. Norton.

Hutchinson, Emma, and Roland Bleiker. 2014. "Theorizing Emotions in World Politics." *International Theory* 6/3 (November): 491–514.

Huyssen, Andreas. 2003. *Present Pasts: Urban Palimpsests and the Politics of Memory*. Stanford, CA: Stanford University Press.

Igreja, Victor, Beatrice Dias-Lambranca, and Annemiek Richters. 2008. "Gamba Spirits, Gender Relations, and Healing in Post-Civil War Gorongosa, Mozambique." *Journal of the Royal Anthropological Institute* 14: 353–371.

Igreja, Victor, Beatrice Dias-Lambranca, Douglas Hershey, Limore Racin, Annemiek Richters, and Ria Reis. 2010. "The Epidemiology of Spirit Possession in the Aftermath of Mass Political Violence in Mozambique." *Social Science & Medicine* 71: 592–599.

Irwin-Zarecka, Iwona. 1994. *Frames of Remembrance: The Dynamics of Collective Memory.* New Brunswick, NJ: Transaction.

Jamal, Amal. 2016. "Trust, Ethics, and Intentionality in Conflict Transformation and Reconciliation." In *The Role of Trust in Conflict Resolution: The Israeli-Palestinian Case and Beyond,* eds. Ilai Alon and Daniel Bar-Tal. Cham, Switzerland: Springer International. Pp. 215–239.

Jawad, Saleh Abdel. 2006. "The Arab and Palestinian Narratives of the 1948 War." In *Israeli and Palestinian Narratives of Conflict: History's Double Helix,* ed. Robert Rotberg. Bloomington: Indiana University Press. Pp. 72–114.

Jayyusi, Lena. 2007. "Iterability, Cumulativity, and Presence: The Relational Figures of Palestinian Memory." In *Nakba: Palestine, 1948, and the Claims of Memory,* eds. Lila Abu-Lughod and Ahmad Sa'di. New York: Columbia University Press. Pp. 107–133.

Jankélévtich, Vladimir. 2005. *Forgiveness.* Trans. Andrew Kelley. Chicago: University of Chicago Press.

Jeffrey, Renée (ed.). 2008. *Confronting Evil in International Relations: Ethical Responses to Problems of Moral Agency.* New York: Palgrave Macmillan.

Kakar, Sudhir. 1996. *The Colors of Violence: Cultural Identities, Religion, and Conflict.* Chicago: University of Chicago Press.

Kaldor, Mary. 2012. *New and Old Wars: Organized Violence in a Global Era* (3rd ed.). Cambridge, UK: Polity Press.

Kamali, Mohammad Hashim. 2002. *The Dignity of Man: An Islamic Perspective.* Kuala Lumpur: Islamic Text Society.

Kansteiner, Wulf. 2004. "Genealogy of a Category Mistake: A Critical Intellectual History of the Cultural Trauma Metaphor." *Rethinking History* 8/2 (June): 193–221.

Kansteiner, Wulf, and Harald Weilnböck. 2008. "Against the Concept of Cultural Trauma (or How I Learned to Love the Suffering of Others without the Help of Psychotherapy)." In *Cultural Memory Studies: An International and Interdisciplinary Handbook,* eds. Astrid Erll and Ansgar Nünning. Berlin/New York: Walter de Gruyter. Pp. 229–240.

Kaplan, E. Ann. 2005. *Trauma Culture: The Politics of Terror and Loss in Media and Literature.* New Brunswick, NJ: Rutgers University Press.

Kaplan, Danny. 2000. "The Military as a Second Bar Mitzvah: Combat Service as Initiation to Zionist Masculinity." In *Imagined Masculinities: Male Identity and Culture in the Modern Middle East,* eds. Mai Ghoussoub and Emma Sinclair-Webb. London: Saqi Books. Pp. 127–144.

Kassem, Fatma. 2000. "A Step to Make My Dream Come True." In *Bridging the Gap: Storytelling as a Way to Work through Political and Collective Hostilities,* ed. Dan Bar-On. Hamburg: Körber-Stiftung. Pp. 95–100.

Katriel, Tamar. 2011. "Showing and Telling: Photography Exhibitions in Israeli Discourses of Dissent." In *Curating Difficult Knowledge: Violent Pasts in Public Places,* eds. Erica Lerner, Cynthia Milton, and Monica Eileen Patterson. New York: Palgrave Macmillan. Pp. 109–127.

Kattago, Siobhan. 2001. *Ambiguous Memory: The Nazi Past and German National Identity.* Westport, CT: Praeger.

Kaye, Dalia Dassa. 2007. *Talking to the Enemy: Track Two Diplomacy in the Middle East and South Asia.* Santa Monica, CA: Rand Corporation.

Keating, Tom. 2003. "What Can Others Do? Foreign Governments and the Politics of Peacebuilding." In *Dilemmas of Reconciliation: Cases and Concepts*, eds. Carol Prager and Trudy Govier. Waterloo, ON: Wilfrid Laurier University Press. Pp. 169–196.

Keen, Suzanne. 2006. "A Theory of Narrative Empathy." *Narrative* 14/3 (October): 207–236.

Keeping, Janet. 2003. "National Reconciliation in Russia." In *Dilemmas of Reconciliation: Cases and Concepts*, eds. Carol Prager and Trudy Govier. Waterloo, ON: Wilfrid Laurier University Press. Pp. 327–342.

Keil, Martha, and Philipp Mettauer (eds.). 2016. *Drei Generationen: Shoah and National-sozialismus im Familiengedächtnis*. Innsbruck: Studienverlag.

Kellermann, Natan. 2013. "Epigenetic Transmission of Holocaust Trauma: Can Nightmares Be Inherited?" *The Israel Journal of Psychiatry and Related Sciences* 50/1: 33–39.

Kelman, Herbert C. 2001. "The Role of National Identity in Conflict Resolution: Experiences from Israeli-Palestinian Problem-Solving Workshops." In *Social Identity, Intergroup Conflict, and Conflict Resolution*, eds. Richard Ashmore, Lee Jussim, and David Wilder. New York: Oxford University Press. Pp. 187–212.

———. 2004. "Reconciliation as Identity Change: A Social Psychological Perspective." In *From Conflict Resolution to Reconciliation*, ed. Yaacov Bar-Siman-Tov. New York: Oxford University Press. Pp. 111–124.

———. 2005. "Building Trust among Enemies: The Central Challenge for International Conflict Resolution." *International Journal of Intercultural Relations* 29: 639–650.

———. 2008. "Reconciliation from a Social-Psychological Perspective." In *The Social Psychology of Intergroup Reconciliation*, eds. Arie Nadler, Thomas Malloy, and Jeffrey Fisher. New York: Oxford University Press. Pp. 15–32.

Kelman, Herbert C., and Donald Warwick. 1973. "Bridging Micro and Macro Approaches to Social Change: A Social-Psychological Perspective." In *Process and Phenomenon of Social Change*, ed. Gerald Zaltman. New York: Wiley-Interscience. Pp. 13–59.

Kessler, Edward. 2010. *Introduction to Jewish-Christian Relations*. Cambridge, UK: Cambridge University Press.

Keßler, Hildrun. 1996. *Bibliodrama und Leiblichkeit: Leibhafte Textauslegungen im theologischen und therapeutischen Diskurs*. Stuttgart: Kohlhammer.

Khalidi, Rashid. 1997. *Palestinian Identity: The Construction of Modern National Consciousness*. New York: Columbia University Press.

Kidron, Carol. 2018. "Resurrecting Discontinued Bonds: A Comparative Study of Israeli Holocaust and Cambodian Genocide Trauma Descendant Relations with the Genocide Dead." *Ethos* 46/2: 230–253.

Kirstein-Keshet, Yehudit. 2011. "Of Ghosts and Dybbuks: The Haunting of the Israeli Imagination." *borderlands e-journal* 10/2: 1–19 (www.borderlands.net.au) accessed March 14, 2019.

Kiss, Elizabeth. 2000. "Moral Ambition within and beyond Political Constraint: Reflections on Restorative Justice." In *Truth v. Justice: The Morality of Truth Commissions*, eds. Robert Rotberg and Dennis Thompson. Princeton, NJ: Princeton University Press. Pp. 68–98.

Klein, Melanie. 1975. *Love, Guilt, and Reparation and Other Works, 1921–1945*. New York: Free Press.

Koopman, Emy. 2010. "Reading the Suffering of Others: The Ethical Possibilities of 'Empathic Unsettlement.'" *Journal of Literary Theory* 4/2: 235–252.

Kramer, Roderick, and Peter Carnevale. 2001. "Trust and Intergroup Negotiations." In *Blackwell Handbook of Social Psychology: Intergroup Processes*, eds. Rupert Brown and Sam Gaertner. Oxford: Blackwell. Pp. 431–450.

Krell, Marc. 2003. *Intersecting Pathways: Modern Jewish Theologians in Conversation with Christianity*. New York: Oxford University Press.

Kritz, Neil (ed.). 1995. *Transitional Justice: How Emerging Democracies Reckon with Former Regimes*. Washington, DC: United States Institute for Peace Press.

Krog, Antje. 1998. *Country of My Skull: Guilt, Sorrow, and the Limits of Forgiveness in the New South Africa*. New York: Three Rivers Press.

Krondorfer, Björn (ed.). 1992. *Body and Bible: Interpreting and Experiencing Biblical Narratives*. Philadelphia: Trinity Press International. [2008 Korean translation, with a new Preface, trans. Hun Young Hwang and Sae Joon Kim. Seoul: Chang-Ji Co].

———. 1995. *Remembrance and Reconciliation: Encounters between Young Jews and Germans*. New Haven, CT: Yale University Press.

———. (ed.). 1996. *Men's Bodies, Men's Gods: Male Identities in a (Post-) Christian Culture*. New York: New York University Press.

———. 2002. "Eine Reise gegen das Schweigen." In *Das Vermächtnis annehmen: Kulturelle und biographische Zugänge zum Holocaust: Beiträge aus den USA und Deutschland*, eds. Brigitta Huhnke and Björn Krondorfer. Giessen: Psychosozial Verlag. Pp. 315–344.

———. 2006. "Nationalsozialismus und Holocaust in Autobiographien protestantischer Theologen." In *Mit Blick auf die Täter: Fragen an die deutsche Theologie nach 1945*, Björn Krondorfer, Katharina von Kellenbach, and Norbert Reck. Gütersloh: Gütersloher Verlag. Pp. 23–170.

———. 2008a. "Is Forgetting Reprehensible? Holocaust Remembrance and the Task of Oblivion." *Journal of Religious Ethics* 36/2 (June): 233–267.

———. 2008b. "Werkstatt-Bericht: Bibliodrama und Sutradrama: Buddhistische und christliche Senfkörner." *Textraum: Bibliodrama Information* 15/28 (April): 44–47.

———. 2010. "Interkulturelle Begegnungsprogramme zum Holocaust: Familienbiographie und kreative Erinnerungsarbeit." In *Elemente einer zeitgemässen politischen Bildung*, eds. Christian Geißler and Bernd Overwien. Münster: Lit Verlag. Pp. 253–269.

———. 2012. "Beyond Uniqueness: Holocaust and Transitional Justice." In *Doppelte Vergangenheitsbewältigung und die Singularität des Holocaust*, ed. Lucia Scherzberg. Saarbrücken: universaar. Pp. 277–316.

———. 2013a. "Interkulturelle Erinnerungsarbeit als offener Prozess." In *Handbuch Nationalsozialismus und Holocaust: Historisch-Politisches Lernen in Schule, außerschulische Bildung und Lehrerbildung*, eds. Hanns-Fred Rathenow, Birgit Wenzel, and Norbert Weber. Schwalbach: Wochenschau Verlag. Pp. 481–497.

———. 2013b. "From Pulp to Palimpsest: Witnessing and Re-Imagining through the Arts" (with Karen Baldner). In *Different Horrors, Same Hell: Gender and the Holocaust*, eds. Myrna Goldenberg and Amy H. Shapiro. Seattle: University of Washington Press. Pp. 132–162.

———. 2015. "Notes from a Field of Conflict: Trilateral Dialogical Engagement in Israel/Palestine." *Journal of Ecumenical Studies* 50/1: 153–158.

———. 2016. "Unsettling Empathy: Intercultural Dialogue in the Aftermath of Historical and Cultural Trauma." In *Breaking Intergenerational Cycles of Repetition: A Global Dialogue on Historical Trauma and Memory*, ed. Pumla Gobodo-Madikizela. Opladen: Barbara Budrich. Pp. 90–112.

———. 2017. "Torture." In *Losing Trust in the World: Holocaust Scholars Confront Torture*, eds. Leonard Grob and John Roth. Seattle/London: University of Washington Press. Pp. 23–41.

———. (ed.). 2018. *Reconciliation in Global Context: Why It Is Needed and How It Works*. Albany, NY: SUNY Press.

Krondorfer, Björn, and Ovidiu Creanga. 2020. *The Holocaust and Masculinities: Critical Inquiries into the Presence and Absence of Men*. Albany, NY: SUNY Press.

Krondorfer, Björn, and Tara Kohn. 2018. *Echoes of Loss: Artistic Responses to Trauma*. Catalogue & Essay. Flagstaff, AZ: Flagstaff Arts Council.

Kuhn, Annette. 1995. *Family Secrets: Acts of Memory and Imagination*. London: Verso.

Kuntz, Andreas. 1991. "Objektbestimmte Ritualisierungen: Zur Funktion von Erinnerungsobjekten bei der Bildung familiarer Geschichtstheorien." In *Erinnern und Vergessen: Vorträge des 27. Deutschen Volkskundekongresses Göttingen 1989*, eds. Brigitte Bönisch-Brednich, Rolf Brednich, and Helge Gerndt. Göttingen: Volker Schmerse. Pp. 219–234.

LaCapra, Dominick. 1998. *History and Memory after Auschwitz*. Ithaca, NY: Cornell University Press.

———. 2001. *Writing History, Writing Trauma*. Baltimore: Johns Hopkins University Press.

Lambek, Michael. 1996. "The Past Imperfect: Remembering as Moral Practice." In *Tense Past: Cultural Essays in Trauma and Memory*, eds. Paul Antze and Michael Lambek. New York: Routledge. Pp. 235–254.

Lambek, Michael, and Paul Antze. 1996. "Introduction: Forecasting Memory." In *Tense Past: Cultural Essays in Trauma and Memory*, eds. Paul Antze and Michael Lambek. New York: Routledge. Pp. xi–xxxviii.

Landsberg, Alison. 2004. *Prosthetic Memory: The Transformation of American Remembrance in the Age of Mass Culture*. New York: Columbia University Press.

Laqueur, Walter. 2006. *The Changing Face of Antisemitism: From Ancient Times to the Present Day*. New York: Oxford University Press.

Lederach, John Paul. 1997. *Building Peace: Sustainable Reconciliation in Divided Societies*. Washington, DC: United States Institute of Peace.

———. 2005. *The Moral Imagination: The Art and Soul of Building Peace*. New York: Oxford University Press.

Leesem, Peter, and Jason Crouthamel (eds.). 2016. *Traumatic Memories of the Second World War and After*. New York: Palgrave Macmillan.

Leffler, Elliot. 2016. "Rechoreographing Intercultural Encounters: The Power and Limits of Dramatic Play in Segregated Communities." *Research in Drama Education: The Journal of Applied Theatre and Performance* 21/2: 139–153.

Lehmann, Johannes. 2019. "Zorn, Hass, Wut: Zum affektpolitischen Problem der Identität." In *Hass/Literatur: Literatur- und kulturwissenschaftliche Beiträge zu einer Theorie- und Diskursgeschichte*, eds. Jürgen Brokoff and Robert Walter-Jochum. Bielefeld: Transcript. Pp. 139–166.

Lerner, Paul. 2003. *Hysterical Men: War, Psychiatry, and the Politics of Trauma in Germany, 1890–1930*. Ithaca, NY: Cornell University Press.

Levine, Peter. 2015. *Trauma and Memory: Brain and Body in a Search for the Living Past: A Practical Guide for Understanding and Working with Traumatic Memory*. Berkeley, CA: North Atlantic Books.

Leys, Ruth. 2000. *Trauma: A Genealogy*. Chicago: University of Chicago Press.

Litvak, Meir (ed.). 2009. *Palestinian Collective Memory and National Identity*. New York: Palgrave Macmillan.

Litvak, Meir, and Esther Webman. 2009. *From Empathy to Denial: Arab Responses to the Holocaust*. New York: Columbia University Press.

Llewellyn, Jennifer, and Daniel Philpott (eds.). 2014a. *Restorative Justice, Reconciliation, and Peacebuilding*. New York: Oxford University Press.

———. 2014b. "Restorative Justice and Reconciliation: Twin Frameworks for Peacebuilding." In *Restorative Justice, Reconciliation, and Peacebuilding*, eds. Jennifer Llewellyn and Daniel Philpott. New York: Oxford University Press. Pp. 14–36.

Loren, Scott. 2016. "Tears of Testimony: Glenn Beck and the Conservative Moral Occult." In *Melodrama after the Tears: New Perspectives on the Politics of Victimhood*, eds. Scott Loren and Jörg Metelmann. Amsterdam: Amsterdam University Press. Pp. 247–260.

Lower, Wendy. 2013. *Hitler's Furies: German Women in the Nazi Killing Fields*. Boston: Houghton Mifflin Harcourt.

MacNair, Rachel M. 2002. *Perpetration-Induced Traumatic Stress: The Psychological Consequences of Killing*. Westport, CT: Praeger.

Maier, Charles. 1988. *The Unmasterable Past: History, Holocaust, and German National Identity*. Cambridge, MA: Harvard University Press.

Maines, Rachel P., and James J. Glynn. 1993. "Numinous Objects." *The Public Historian* 15/1 (Winter): 8–25.

Margalit, Avishai. 2002. *The Ethics of Memory*. Cambridge, MA: Harvard University Press.

Martin, Gerhard Marcel. 1995. *Sachbuch Bibliodrama: Praxis und Theorie*. Stuttgart: Kohlhammer.

Mason, Albert. 2015. "Beyond Right and Wrong: An Exploration of Justice and Forgiveness." In *Love and Forgiveness for a More Just World*, eds. Hent de Vries and Nils Schott. New York: Columbia University Press. Pp. 128–140.

Matuštík, Martin Beck. 2015. *Out of Silence: Repair across Generations*. Phoenix, AZ: New Critical Theory.

McDermott, Rose. 2011. "New Directions for Experimental Work in International Relations." *International Studies Quarterly* 55: 503–520.

———. 2014. "The Body Doesn't Lie: A Somatic Approach to the Study of Emotions in World Politics." *International Theory* 6/3: 557–562.

McGlothlin, Erin. 2006. *Second Generation Holocaust Literature: Legacies of Survival and Perpetration*. Rochester, NY: Camden House.

Meagher, Robert Emmet, and Douglas Pryer (eds.). 2018. *War and Moral Injury: A Reader*. Eugene, OR: Cascade Books.

Meister, Robert. 2012. *After Evil: A Politics of Human Rights*. New York: Columbia University Press.

Minow, Martha. 1998. *Between Vengeance and Forgiveness: Facing History after Genocide and Mass Violence*. Boston: Beacon Press.

Moeller, Robert. 2001. *War Stories: The Search for a Usable Past in the Federal Republic of Germany*. Berkeley: University of California Press.

———. 2002. "Die Vertreibung aus dem Osten und westdeutsche Trauerarbeit." In *Das Vermächtnis annehmen: Kulturelle und biografische Zugänge zum Holocaust: Beiträge aus den USA und Deutschland*, eds. Brigitta Huhnke and Björn Krondorfer. Gießen: Psychosozial Verlag. Pp. 113–148.

Moeller, Susan. 1999. *Compassion Fatigue: How the Media Sell Disease, Famine, War and Death*. New York: Routledge.

Mohamed, Saira. 2015. "Of Monsters and Men: Perpetrator Trauma and Mass Atrocity." *Columbia Law Review* 115: 1157–1216.

Mojzes, Paul. 2009. "The Genocidal Twentieth Century in the Balkans." In *Confronting Genocide: Judaism, Christianity, Islam*, ed. Steven L. Jacobs. Lanham, MD: Lexington Books. Pp. 151–181.

Monroe, Kirsten. 2004. *The Heart of Compassion: Portraits of Moral Choice during the Holocaust*. Princeton, NJ: Princeton University Press.

Monterescu, Daniel, and Haim Hazan. 2018. *Twilight Nationalism: Politics of Existence at Life's End*. Stanford, CA: Stanford University Press.

Morris, Leslie. 2003. "Berlin Elegies: Absence, Postmemory, and Art after Auschwitz." In *Image and Remembrance: Representation and the Holocaust*, eds. Shelly Hornstein and Florence Jacobowitz. Bloomington: Indiana University Press. Pp. 288–303.

Müller-Hohagen, Jürgen. 1998. *Verleugnet, verdrängt, verschwiegen: Die seelischen Auswirkungen der Nazizeit*. Munich: Kösel.

Munch-Jurisic, Ditte Marie. 2018. "Perpetrator Disgust: A Morally Destructive Emotion." In *Emotions and Mass Atrocity: Philosophical and Theoretical Explorations*, eds. Thomas Brudholm and Johannes Lang. Cambridge, UK: Cambridge University Press. Pp. 142–161.

Münyas, Burcu. 2008. "Genocide in the Minds of Cambodian Youth: Transmitting (Hi)stories of Genocide to Second and Third Generations in Cambodia." *Journal of Genocide Studies* 10/3: 413–439.

Nadler, Arie. 2002. "Social-Psychological Analysis of Reconciliation: Instrumental and Socio-Emotional Routes to Reconciliation." In *Peace Education Worldwide: The Concept, Underlying Principles, the Research*. Mahwah, NJ: Erlbaum. Pp. 127–143.

Nathanson, Donald (ed.). 1987. *The Many Faces of Shame*. New York: Guilford Press.

Negev Coexistence Forum for Civil Equality. 2006. *The Indigenous Bedouins of the Naq-ab-Negev Desert in Israel*. Report submitted to the UN Permanent Forum on Indigenous Issues.

Neiman, Susan. 2019. *Learning from the Germans: Race and the Memory of Evil*. New York: Farrrar, Straus and Giroux.

Neumann, Wolfgang. 2002. "The Presence of the Past: Using Memory Work to Search for Psychological Traces of the Nazi Past in Contemporary Germans." *British Journal of Guidance & Counselling* 30/1: 5–16.

Niemann, Beate. 2008. *Mein guter Vater: Leben mit seiner Vergangenheit: Biografie meines Vaters als Täter*. Berlin: Metropol.

Nora, Pierre. 1996. *Realms of Memory*. New York: Columbia University Press.

Nur, Ofer Nordheimer. 2014. *Eros and Tragedy: Jewish Male Fantasies and the Masculine Revolution of Zionism*. Boston: Academic Studies Press.

Nussbaum, Martha. 2001. *Upheavals of Thought: The Intelligence of Emotions*. Cambridge, UK: Cambridge University Press.

———. 2013. *Political Emotions: Why Love Matters for Justice*. Cambridge, MA: Belknap Press of Harvard University Press.

Olick, Jeffrey. 2007. *The Politics of Regret: On Collective Memory and Historical Responsibility*. New York: Routledge.

Opher-Cohn, Liliane, Johannes Pfäfflin, Bernd Sonntag, Bernd Klose, and Peter Pogany-Wnendt. 1998. *Das Ende der Sprachlosigkeit? Auswirkung traumatischer Holocaust-Erfahrungen über mehrere Generationen*. Gießen: Psychosozial Verlag.

Ophir, Orna. 2015. "Looking Evil in the Eye/I: The Interminable Work of Forgiveness." In *Love and Forgiveness for a More Just World*, eds. Hent de Vries and Nils Schott. New York: Columbia University Press. Pp. 110–127.

Oren, Neta, and Daniel Bar-Tal. 2007. "The Detrimental Dynamics of Delegitimization in Intractable Conflicts: The Israeli-Palestinian Case." *International Journal of Intercultural Relations* 31: 111–126.

Pappe, Ilan. 2006. "The Bridging Narrative Concept." In *Israeli and Palestinian Narratives of Conflict: History's Double Helix*, ed. Robert Rotberg. Bloomington: Indiana University Press. Pp. 194–204.

Patterson, Monica Eileen. 2011. "Teaching Tolerance through Objects of Hatred: The Jim Crow Museum of Racist Memorabilia as 'Counter Museum.'" In *Curating Difficult Knowledge: Violent Pasts in Public Places*, eds. Erica Lerner, Cynthia Milton, and Monica Eileen Patterson. New York: Palgrave Macmillan. Pp. 55–71.

Pettigrew, Thomas. 1998. "Intergroup Contact Theory." *Annual Review of Psychology* 49: 65–85.

Pettigrew, Thomas, and Linda Tropp. 2000. "Does Intergroup Contact Reduce Prejudice? Recent Meta-Analytic Findings." In *Reducing Prejudice and Discrimination*, ed. Stuart Oskamp. Mahwah, NJ: Erlbaum. Pp. 93–114.

Pisano, Nirit G. 2015. "Ghosts in the Mirror: A Granddaughter of Holocaust Survivors Reflects the Faces of History." In *The Ethics of Remembering and the Consequences of Forgetting: Essays on Trauma, History, and Memory*, ed. Michael O'Loughlin. Lanham, MD: Rowman & Littlefield. Pp. 143–160.

Pitzele, Peter. 1998. *Scripture Windows: Toward a Practice of Bibliodrama*. Los Angeles: Alef Design Group.

Philpott, Daniel (ed.). 2006. *The Politics of Past Evil: Religion, Reconciliation, and the Dilemmas of Transitional Justice*. Notre Dame, IN: University of Notre Dame Press.

———. 2008. "Reconciliation: An Ethic for Responding to Evil in Global Politics." In *Confronting Evil in International Relations: Ethical Responses to Problems of Moral Agency*, ed. Renée Jeffrey. New York: Palgrave Macmillan. Pp. 115–149.

———. 2012. *Just and Unjust Peace: An Ethic of Political Reconciliation*. New York: Oxford University Press.

Pope, Stephen. 2014. "The Role of Forgiveness in Reconciliation and Restorative Justice: A Christian Theological Perspective." In *Restorative Justice, Reconciliation, and*

*Peacebuilding*, eds. Jennifer Llewellyn and Daniel Philpott. New York: Oxford University Press. Pp. 174–196.

Prager, Carol, and Trudy Govier (eds.). 2003. *Dilemmas of Reconciliation: Cases and Concepts*. Waterloo, ON: Wilfrid Laurier University Press.

Pyper, Jens Fabian (ed.). 2002. *Uns hat keiner gefragt: Positionen der dritten Generation zur Bedeutung des Holocaust*. Berlin/Wien: Philo.

Raczymow, Henri. 1994. "Memory Shot Through with Holes." *Yale French Studies* 85: 98–105.

Radstone, Susannah. 2001. "Social Bonds and Psychical Order: Testimonies." *Cultural Values* 5/1 (January): 59–78.

Reicher, Stephen. 1986. "Contact, Action and Racialization: Some British Evidence." In *Contact and Conflict in Intergroup Encounters*, eds. Miles Hewstone and Rupert Brown. Oxford: Basil Blackwell. Pp. 152–168.

Rieff, David. 2011. "The Persistence of Genocide." *Hoover Institution Policy Review* (February). (www.hoover.org/research/persistence-genocide; accessed May 28, 2019).

Roberts, Ulla. 1998. *Spuren der NS-Zeit im Leben der Kinder und Enkel: Drei Generationen im Gespräch*. Munich: Kösel.

Roht-Arriaza, Naomi, and Javier Mariezcurrena (eds.). 2006. *Transitional Justice in the Twenty-First Century: Beyond Truth versus Justice*. Cambridge, UK: Cambridge University Press.

Rosenberg, Marshall. 2005. *Getting Past the Pain between Us: Healing and Reconciliation without Compromise*. Encinitas, CA: Puddle Dancer Press.

Rosenthal, Gabriele (ed.). 1997. *Der Holocaust im Leben von drei Generationen: Familien von Überlebenden der Shoah und der Nazi-Täter*. Gießen: Psychosozial Verlag.

Rosoux, Valerie. 2008. "Reconciliation as a Peace-Building Process: Scope and Limits." In *The Sage Handbook of Conflict Resolution*, eds. Jacob Bercovitch, Victor Kremenyuk, and William Zartman. Los Angeles: Sage. Pp. 543–563.

Rotberg, Robert (ed.). 2006a. *Israeli and Palestinian Narratives of Conflict: History's Double Helix*. Bloomington: Indiana University Press.

———. 2006b. "Building Legitimacy through Narrative." In *Israeli and Palestinian Narratives of Conflict: History's Double Helix*, ed. Robert Rotberg. Bloomington: Indiana University Press. Pp. 1–18.

Rotberg, Robert, and Dennis Thompson (eds.). 2000. *Truth v. Justice: The Morality of Truth Commissions*. Princeton, NJ: Princeton University Press.

Rothberg, Michael. 2009. *Multidirectional Memory: Remembering the Holocaust in the Age of Decolonization*. Stanford, CA: Stanford University Press.

———. 2011. "From Gaza to Warsaw: Mapping Multidirectional Memory." *Criticism* 53/4 (Fall): 523–548.

Rubenstein, Richard. 1992. *After Auschwitz: History, Theology, and Contemporary Judaism* (2nd ed.). Baltimore: Johns Hopkins University Press.

Saguy, Tamar. 2019. "Introduction: When Groups Meet—Understanding How Power Dynamics Shape Intergroup Encounters." In *The Power of Dialogue between Israelis and Palestinians: Stories of Change from the School of Peace*, ed. Nava Sonnenschein and trans. Deb Reich. New Brunswick, NJ: Rutgers University Press. Pp. 1–14.

Said, Edward. 2003. *Freud and the Non-European*. London: Verso.

Saltzman, Lisa. 1999. *Anselm Kiefer and Art after Auschwitz*. New York: Cambridge University Press.

———. 2006. *Making Memory Matter: Strategies of Remembrance in Contemporary Art*. Chicago: University of Chicago Press.

Sanbar, Elias. 2001. "Out of Place, Out of Time." *Mediterranean Historical Review* 16/1: 87–94.

Santner, Eric. 1990. *Stranded Objects: Mourning, Memory, and Film in Postwar Germany*. Ithaca, NY: Cornell University Press.

Santorski, Jacek, and Co Agencja Wydawnicza. 2006. *Difficult Questions in Polish Jewish Dialogue: How Poles and Jews See Each Other*. Warszawa: Forum for Dialogue Among Nations.

Sasson-Levy, Orna. 2011. "Research on Gender and the Military in Israel: From a Gendered Organization to Inequality Regimes." *Israel Studies Review* 26/2: 73–98.

Sayigh, Rosemary. 2007. "Women's Nakba Stories: Between Being and Knowing." In *Nakba: Palestine, 1948, and the Claims of Memory*, eds. Lila Abu-Lughod and Ahmad Sa'di. New York: Columbia University Press. Pp. 135–158.

Scarry, Elaine. 1985. *The Body in Pain: The Making and Unmaking of the World*. New York: Oxford University Press.

Schlink, Bernhard. 2000. *Heimat als Utopie*. Frankfurt: Suhrkamp.

Schmetterling, Astrid. 2007. "Archival Obsessions: Arnold Dreyblatt's Memory Work." *Art Journal* (Winter): 71–83.

Schmidt, Wolf. 2000. "Peace Making by Storytelling." In *Bridging the Gap: Storytelling as a Way to Work through Political and Collective Hostilities*, ed. Dan Bar-On. Hamburg: Körber-Stiftung. Pp. 13–17.

Schneider, Christian. 1997. "Noch einmal 'Geschichte und Psychologie': Generationengeschichte als Modell psychohistorischer Forschung" *Mittelweg* 36/3: 45–56.

Schnitzer, Shira. 1998. "The Mistakes of the March: The March of the Living and the Limits of a Holocaust-Based Jewish Identity." *New Voices* (October): 20–36.

Schorsch, Jonathan. 2003. "Jewish Ghosts in Germany." *Jewish Social Studies* 9/3 (Spring–Summer): 139–169.

Schroeder, Doris, and Bob Brecher. 2003. "Transgenerational Obligations: Twenty-First Century Germany and the Holocaust." *Journal of Applied Philosophy* 20/1: 45–57.

Schwab, Gabriele. 2010. *Haunting Legacies: Violent Histories and Transgenerational Trauma*. New York: Columbia University Press.

Schwarz, Gudrun. 1997. *Eine Frau an seiner Seite: Ehefrauen in der "SS-Sippengemeinschaft."* Hamburg: Hamburger Edition.

Sciortino, Giuseppe. 2019. "Cultural Traumas." In *Handbook of Cultural Sociology*, eds. Laura Grindstaff, M. Lo Ming-Cheng, and John R. Hall. New York: Routledge. Pp. 135–143.

Segal, Elizabeth. 2018. *Social Empathy: The Art of Understanding Each Other*. New York: Columbia University Press.

Seltzer, Mark. 1997. "Wound Culture: Trauma in the Pathological Public Sphere." *October* 80 (Spring): 3–36.

Senfft, Alexandra. 2016. *Der lange Schatter der Täter: Nachkommen stellen sich ihrer NS-Familiengeschichte*. Munich: Piper.

Sensenig-Dabbous, Eugene. 2016. "The Musa Dagh History Hike: Truth-Telling, Dialogue and Thanatourism." In *The Armenian Genocide Legacy*, ed. Alexis Demirdjian. New York: Palgrave Macmillan. Pp. 229–242.

Shavit, Ari. 2013. *My Promised Land: The Triumph and Tragedy of Israel*. New York: Spiegel & Grau.

Shechter, Hava, and Gavriel Salomon. 2005. "Does Vicarious Experience of Suffering Affect Empathy for an Adversary? The Effects of Israelis' Visits to Auschwitz on Their Empathy for Palestinians." *Journal of Peace Education* 2/2 (September): 125–138.

Sheehi, Stephen. 2018. "Psychoanalysis under Occupation: Nonviolence and Dialogue Initiatives as a Psychic Extension of the Closure System." *Psychoanalysis and History* 20/3: 353–369.

Shnabel, Nurit, and Arie Nadler. 2010. "A Needs-Based Model of Reconciliation: Perpetrators Need Acceptance and Victims Need Empowerment to Reconcile." In *Prosocial Motives, Emotions, and Behavior: The Better Angels of Our Nature*, eds. Mario Mikulincer and Phillip R. Shaver. Washington, DC: American Psychological Association. Pp. 409–429.

Simon, Roger, Sharon Rosenberg, and Claudia Eppert (eds). 2000. *Between Hope and Despair: Pedagogy and the Remembrance of Historical Trauma*. Lanham, MD: Rowman & Littlefield.

Singer, Tania, and Claus Lamm. 2009. "The Social Neuroscience of Empathy." *The Year of Cognitive Neuroscience 2009: Annals of the New York Academy of Science* 1156: 81–96.

Smith, Brewster. 2004. "Realistic Empathy: A Key to Sensible International Relations." *Peace and Conflict: Journal of Peace Psychology* 10/4: 335–339.

Solomon, Zahava, Nathaniel Laor, and Alexander McFarlane. 2017. "Acute Posttraumatic Reactions in Soldiers and Civilians." In *Traumatic Stress: The Effects of Overwhelming Experience on Mind, Body, and Society,* eds. Bessel van der Kolk, Alexander McFarlane, and Lars Weisaeth. New York: Guilford Press. Pp. 102–114.

Sonnenschein, Nava. 2019. *The Power of Dialogue between Israelis and Palestinians: Stories of Change from the School of Peace.* Ed. and trans. Deb Reich. New Brunswick, NJ: Rutgers University Press.

Sontag, Susan. 2003. *Regarding the Pain of Others.* New York: Farrar, Straus and Giroux.

Spencer, Graham (ed.). 2011. *Forgiving and Remembering in Northern Ireland: Approaches to Conflict Resolution.* London: Continuum.

Sperling-Sinemus, Ursula. 2015. "Unglaubliche Lügen und unfassbare Wahrheiten—Wissen, um weiterzuleben." In *Beidseits von Auschwitz: Identitäten in Deutschland nach 1945,* eds. Nea Weissberg and Jürgen Müller-Hohagen. Berlin: Lichtig Verlag. Pp. 190–209.

Spitzer, Leo. 1999. "Back through the Future: Nostalgic Memory and Critical Memory in a Refuge from Nazism." In *Acts of Memory: Cultural Recall in the Present,* eds. Mieke Bal, Jonathan Crewe, and Leo Spitzer. Hanover, NH: University Press of New England. Pp. 87–104.

Staub, Ervin. 2006. "Reconciliation after Genocide, Mass Killing, or Intractable Conflict: Understanding the Roots of Violence, Psychological Recovery, and Steps toward a General Theory." *Political Psychology* 27/6: 867–894.

Staub, Ervin, and Daniel Bar-Tal. 2003. "Genocide, Mass Killing, and Intractable Conflict: Roots, Evolution, Prevention, and Reconciliation." In *Handbook of Political Psychology,* eds. David O. Sears, Leonie Huddy, and Robert Jervis. New York: Oxford University Press. Pp. 710–754.

Steinlauf, Michael. 1997. *Bondage to the Dead: Poland and the Memory of the Holocaust.* Syracuse, NY: Syracuse University Press.

Stern, Frank. 1992. *The Whitewashing of the Yellow Badge: Antisemitism and Philosemitism in Postwar Germany.* Trans. William Templer. Oxford: Oxford University Press.

Stier, Oren Baruch. 1995. "Lunch at Majdanek: The March of the Living as Contemporary Pilgrimage of Memory." *Jewish Folklore and Ethnology Review* 17/1–2: 57–66.

———. 2010. "Torah and Taboo: Containing Jewish Relics and Jewish Identity at the United States Holocaust Memorial Museum." *Numen* 57: 505–536.

Stiftung für die Rechte zukünftiger Generationen. 1999. *Was Bleibt von der Vergangenheit? Die junge Generation im Dialog über den Holocaust.* Berlin: Ch. Links.

Suleiman, Susan Rubin. 2006. *Crises of Memory and the Second World War.* Cambridge, MA: Harvard University Press.

Sztompka, Piotr. 2000. "Cultural Trauma: The Other Face of Social Change." *European Journal of Social Theory* 3/4: 449–466.

Tajfel, Henry (ed.). 1978. *Differentiation between Social Groups.* London: Academic Press.

Tajfel, Henri, and John Turner. 1979. "An Integrative Theory of Intergroup Conflict." In *The Social Psychology of Intergroup Relations,* eds. William Austin and Stephen Worchel. Monterey, CA: Brooks/Cole. Pp. 33–47.

Tangney, June Price, Jeff Stuewig, and Debra Mahek. 2007. "Moral Emotions and Moral Behavior." *Annual Review of Psychology* 58: 345–372.

Tavuchis, Nicholas. 1991. *Mea Culpa: A Sociology of Apology and Reconciliation.* Stanford, CA: Stanford University Press.

Teege, Jennifer. 2015. *My Grandfather Would Have Shot Me: A Black Woman Discovers Her Family's Nazi Past.* New York: The Experiment.

Teitel, Ruti. 2003. "Transitional Justice Genealogy." *Harvard Human Rights Journal* 16: 69–94.

Tint, Barbara. 2010. "Dialogue, Forgiveness, and Reconciliation." In *Forgiveness and Reconciliation: Psychological Pathways to Conflict Transformation and Peace Building,* eds. Ani Kalayjian and Raymond Paloutzian. New York: Springer. Pp. 269–285.

Titelman, Peter. 2008. "The Concept of the Triangle in Bowen Theory: An Overview." In *Triangles: Bowen Family Systems Theory Perspectives*, ed. Peter Titelman. New York: Haworth. Pp. 3–62.

Todorov, Tzvetan. 1996. "The Abuses of Memory." Trans. Mei Lin Chang. *Common Knowledge* 5/1: 6–26.

Touquet, Heleen, and Ana Milošević. 2018. "When Reconciliation Becomes the R-Word: Dealing with the Past in Former Yugoslavia." In *Reconciliation in Global Context: Why It Is Needed and How It Works*, ed. Björn Krondorfer. Albany, NY: SUNY Press. Pp. 179–198.

Treacher Kabesh, Amal. 2011. "On Being Haunted by the Present." *borderlands e-journal* 10/2: 1–21 (www.borderlands.net.au) accessed March 14, 2019.

Treber, Leoni. 2014. *Mythos Trümmerfrauen: Von der Trümmerbeseitigung in der Kriegs- und Nachkriegszeit und der Entstehung eines deutschen Erinnerungsortes*. Essen: Klartext-Verlag.

Truscott, Ross. 2015. "A South African Story of Disavowal: Toward a Genealogy of Post-Apartheid Empathy." In *The Ethics of Remembering and the Consequences of Forgetting: Essays on Trauma, History, and Memory*, eds. Michael O'Loughlin. Lanham, MD: Rowman & Littlefield. Pp. 229–248.

Tutu, Desmond. 1999. *No Future without Forgiveness*. New York: Doubleday.

Tzoreff, Yohanan. 2016. "Trust and Negotiations: Israel and the Palestinians, 2009–2015." In *The Role of Trust in Conflict Resolution: The Israeli-Palestinian Case and Beyond*, eds. Ilai Alon and Daniel Bar-Tal. Cham, Switzerland: Springer International. Pp. 169–195.

Ulanowicz, Anastasia. 2013. *Second-Generation Memory and Contemporary Children's Literature: Ghost Images*. London: Routledge.

Unruh, Trude (ed.). 1987. *Trümmerfrauen: Biografien einer betrogenen Generation*. Essen: Klartext-Verlag.

Van Alphen, Ernst. 1997. *Caught by History: Holocaust Effects in Contemporary Art, Literature, and Theory*. Stanford, CA: Stanford University Press.

Van der Kolk, Bessel, and Onno van der Hart. 1995. "The Intrusive Past: The Flexibility of Memory and the Engraving of Trauma." In *Trauma: Explorations in Memory*, ed. Cathy Caruth. Baltimore: Johns Hopkins University Press. Pp. 158–182.

Van der Kolk, Bessel, and Alexander McFarlane. 2007. "The Black Hole of Trauma." In *Traumatic Stress: The Effects of Overwhelming Experience on Mind, Body, and Society*, eds. Bessel van der Kolk, Alexander McFarlane, and Lars Weisaeth. New York: Guilford Press. Pp. 3–23.

Van Dijck, José. 2007. *Mediated Memories in the Digital Age*. Stanford, CA: Stanford University Press.

Van Kleef, Gerben A., et al. 2008. "Power, Distress, and Compassion: Turning a Blind Eye to the Suffering of Others." *Psychological Science* 19: 1315–1322.

Verwoerd, Wilhelm. 2003. "Toward a Response to Criticism of the South African Truth and Reconciliation Commission." In *Dilemmas of Reconciliation: Cases and Concepts*, eds. Carol Prager and Trudy Govier. Waterloo, ON: Wilfrid Laurier University Press. Pp. 245–278.

Verwoerd, Wilhelm, and Alistair Little. 2018. "Beyond a Dilemma of Apology: Transforming (Veteran) Resistance to Reconciliation in Northern Ireland and South Africa." In *Reconciliation in Global Context: Why It Is Needed and How It Works*, ed. Björn Krondorfer. Albany, NY: SUNY Press. Pp. 179–198.

Vetlesen, Arne Johan. 2005. *Evil and Human Agency: Understanding Collective Evildoing*. Cambridge, UK: Cambridge University Press.

Viviano, Frank. 2019. "Atrocities America Forgot." *New York Review of Books* (June 6): 50–51.

Volkan, Vamik. 2001. "Transgenerational Transmission and Chosen Trauma: An Aspect of Large-Group Identity." *Group Analysis* 34/1: 79–97.

———. 2013. *Enemies on the Couch: A Psychopolitical Journey through War and Peace*. Durham, NC: Pitchstone.

Von Kellenbach, Katharina, Björn Krondorfer, and Norbert Reck (eds.). 2001. *Von Gott reden im Land der Täter: Theologische Stimmen der dritten Generation seit der Shoah.* Darmstadt: Wissenschaftlicher Buchverlag.

Walker, Margaret Urban. 2006. *Moral Repair: Reconstructing Moral Relations after Wrongdoing.* Cambridge, UK: Cambridge University Press.

Weinrich, Harald. 2004. *Lethe: The Art and Critique of Forgetting.* Trans. Steven Rendall. Ithaca, NY: Cornell University Press.

Weissman, Gary. 2004. *Fantasies of Witnessing: Postwar Efforts to Experience the Holocaust.* Ithaca, NY: Cornell University Press.

Welzer, Harald. 2015. *Grandpa Wasn't a Nazi: The Holocaust in German Family Remembrance.* New York: American Jewish Committee.

Welzer, Harald, Sabine Moeller, and Karline Tschuggnall. 2002. *"Opa war kein Nazi": Nationalsozialismus und Holocaust im Familiengedächtnis.* Frankfurt: Fischer.

Whitebrook, Maureen. 2001. *Identity, Narrative, and Politics.* London: Routledge.

Wieviorka, Annette. 2006. *The Era of Witness.* Trans. Jared Stark. Ithaca, NY: Cornell University Press.

Wildfeuer, Armin. 2011. "Justice and Reconciliation." In *Participation and Reconciliation: Preconditions of Justice,* eds. Sami Adwan and Armin Wildfeuer. Opladen: Barbara Budrich. Pp. 119–132.

Wilke, Christiane. 2012. "Enter Ghost: Haunted Courts and Haunting Judgments in Transitional Justice." *Law Critique* 21: 73–92.

Williams, Nigel. 2015. "Anglo German Displacement and Diaspora in the Early Twentieth Century: An Intergenerational Haunting." In *The Ethics of Remembering and the Consequences of Forgetting: Essays on Trauma, History, and Memory,* ed. Michael O'Loughlin. Lanham, MD: Rowman & Littlefield. Pp. 125–142.

Wilson, Richard. 2001. *The Politics of Truth and Reconciliation in South Africa: Legitimizing the Post-Apartheid State.* Cambridge, UK: Cambridge University Press.

Winter, Jay. 2000. "The Generation of Memory: Reflections on the 'Memory Boom' in Contemporary Historical Studies." *Bulletin of the German Historical Institute* 27 (Fall): 69–92.

Wlodarski, Amy Lynn. 2015. *Musical Witness and Holocaust Representation.* Cambridge, UK: Cambridge University Press.

Wood, Amy Louise. 2009. *Lynching and Spectacle: Witnessing Racial Violence in America, 1890–1940.* Chapel Hill: The University of North Carolina Press.

Wood, David. 2016. *What Have We Done? Moral Injury of Our Longest Wars.* New York: Little, Brown and Company.

Wrochem, Oliver von (ed.). 2016. *Nationalsozialistische Täterschaften: Nachwirkungen in Gesellschaft und Familie.* Berlin: Metropol.

Wüstenberg, Ralf. 2003. *Die Politische Dimension der Versöhnung: Eine theologische Studie zum Umgang mit Schuld nach den Systemumbrüchen in Südafrika und Deutschland.* Gütersloh: Chr. Kaiser.

———. 2009. *The Political Dimension of Reconciliation: A Theological Analysis of Ways of Dealing with Guilt during the Transition to Democracy in South Africa and (East) Germany.* Trans. Randi Lundell. Grand Rapids, MI: Eerdmans.

Yalom, Irvin. 1995. *The Theory and Practice of Group Psychotherapy* (4th ed.). New York: Basic Books.

Yanay, Niza. 2013. *The Ideology of Hatred: The Psychic Power of Discourse.* New York: Fordham University Press.

Yerushalmi, Yosef Hayim. 1996. *Zakhor: Jewish History and Jewish Memory.* Seattle: University of Washington Press.

Young, Allan. 2002. "The Self-Traumatized Perpetrator as a 'Transient Mental Illness.'" *L'Evolution Psychiatrique* 67/4: 630–650.

Young, James. 2000. *At Memory's Edge: After-Images of the Holocaust in Contemporary Art and Architecture.* New Haven, CT: Yale University Press.

Zeitlin, Froma. 1998. "The Vicarious Witness: Belated Memory and Authorial Presence in Recent Holocaust Literature." *History & Memory* 10/2 (Fall): 5–42.

Zembylas, Michalinos. 2007. "The Politics of Trauma: Empathy, Reconciliation and Peace Education." *Journal of Peace Education* 4/2 (September): 207–224.

Zertal, Idith. 2005. *Israel's Holocaust and the Politics of Nationhood*. Trans. Chaya Glai. Cambridge, UK: Cambridge University Press.

# Index

www.ingramcontent.com/pod-product-compliance
Lightning Source LLC
Chambersburg PA
CBHW030642270326
41929CB00007B/175